LINCOLN'S
GETTYSBURG
ADDRESS

LINCOLN'S GETTYSBURG ADDRESS

Echoes of the
BIBLE
and Book *of*
COMMON
PRAYER

A. E. Elmore

SOUTHERN ILLINOIS UNIVERSITY PRESS

CARBONDALE

Southern Illinois University Press
www.siupress.com

20 19 18 17   4 3 2 1

Cover illustration: Lincoln's address at the dedication of the Gettysburg
National Cemetery, November 19, 1863. Library of Congress.

The Library of Congress has cataloged the hardcover edition as follows:

Elmore, A. E., 1938–
Lincoln's Gettysburg address : echoes of the Bible and Book of
Common Prayer / A. E. Elmore.
       p. cm.
Includes bibliographical references and index.
ISBN-13: 978-0-8093-2951-9 (cloth : alk. paper)
ISBN-10: 0-8093-2951-4 (cloth : alk. paper)
1. Lincoln, Abraham, 1809–1865. Gettysburg address—
Language. 2. Lincoln, Abraham, 1809–1865.—Oratory. 3. Bible.
English. Authorized—Language. 4. Episcopal Church. Book
of common prayer (1790)—Language. 5. Christianity and
politics—United States—History—19th century. 6. Political
culture—United States—History—19th century. I. Title.
E475.55.E466 2009
973.7092—dc22   2009005087

ISBN 978-0-8093-3560-2

In memory of Medgar Evers
1925–63

Brother, friend,
Best of men
In honored glory,
The unknown soldier

He gave his life
That others might have life
And have it more abundantly.

Contents

Preface

This book is dedicated to the least known of all the great heroes of the civil-rights movement, a man who gave his life for what Lincoln at Gettysburg called "a new birth of freedom." Medgar Evers, Mississippi field secretary of the National Association for the Advancement of Colored People, was shot in the back by white-supremacist Byron de la Beckwith shortly after midnight on June 12, 1963, during the one hundredth anniversary of the Emancipation Proclamation and the Gettysburg Address. He died in the narrow halls of a segregated hospital in one of the smallest, darkest hours of a new day.

The new birth for which Medgar Evers gave his life had been celebrated the year before his death when James Meredith, successfully represented in a titanic legal struggle by Evers and the NAACP, had ended more than a century of segregation at the University of Mississippi. The same new birth had been celebrated again just the day before Evers' death when two African American students, Vivian Malone and James Hood, had ended an even-longer history of segregation at the neighboring University of Alabama, where Governor George Wallace had made his famous but futile "stand in the schoolhouse door."

Only hours before Evers paid the price of his life for his faith in freedom, President John F. Kennedy went on national television to praise Alabama's students for ignoring "threats and defiant statements" and for keeping the peace. The unspoken reminder behind his words was the death and destruction that had rained down on Oxford, Mississippi, when, upon Meredith's entry into Ole Miss, Mississippi Governor Ross Barnett had roused an angry mob to arson and murder with threats and defiant statements. Kennedy's address on the evening of June 11 reminded the nation of the Emancipation Proclamation: "One hundred years have passed since Lincoln freed the slaves, yet their heirs, their grandsons, are not fully free." The president also reminded the nation of the Gettysburg Address and the document that Lincoln himself had echoed there, the Declaration of Independence: "Our nation was founded on the principle that all men are created equal." Because our nation's unequal treatment of black Americans represented "a moral issue . . . as old as the scriptures," Kennedy said he would ask Congress "to make a commitment it has not fully made in this century to the proposition that race has no place in American life or law." His chosen word "proposition" was taken straight from the Gettysburg Address.

After Evers' death and a stately burial in Arlington National Cemetery that was arranged by President Kennedy, Mrs. Myrlie Evers memorialized her beloved husband and father to their three children with a book called *For Us, the Living*. Her title was taken straight from the Gettysburg Address.

At the historic March on Washington just two months after Evers' death, Martin Luther King Jr. began one of the other greatest speeches in the history of humankind by invoking Lincoln: "Five score years ago, a great American, in whose symbolic shadow we stand today, signed the Emancipation Proclamation." At the heart of his speech, Dr. King continued to echo the Gettysburg Address: "I have a dream that one day this nation will rise up and live out the true meaning of its creed: 'We hold these truths to be self-evident: that all men are created equal.'"

During the two hundredth anniversary of the birth of Abraham Lincoln, Barack Obama of Illinois was sworn in as the first African American president in the nation's history. His inaugural address repeatedly echoed Lincoln's "new" from the "new birth of freedom" in the Gettysburg Address. Obama used the word no fewer than eleven times, including "a new age" and "a new life." Five times he invoked the name of God, more than any other president in history—even more than Lincoln, the first president to make that word a regular part of his presidential public addresses and proclamations. When President Obama invoked the "God-given promise that all are equal, all are free," anyone who remembered the Gettysburg Address would have remembered above all the "proposition that all men are created equal" from the opening sentence and the "under God . . . a new birth of freedom" from the closing.

Anyone who knew and remembered Medgar Evers would have heard his eloquent voice as well, for the physical, kinetic, and psychological resemblance between the civil-rights leader and the new president is remarkable. It appears in the soft-spoken words ribbed with determination, in the staccato movements of the arms, in the smiles both brief and patient, in the jaws no less friendly than firm. One of the great ironies of Obama's election was that Peggy Wallace Kennedy, the only daughter of former Alabama governors George and Lurleen Wallace, counted herself among his public supporters. The daughter's outspoken support for a black presidential candidate completed a remarkable turnaround for the first family of Alabama. Her public support for Obama in 2007 came forty-four years after George Wallace stood in the schoolhouse door and eleven years after her father, paralyzed by an attempted assassination, apologized to the two black students whose equality before the law he had done everything in his power as governor to deny. Wallace's example was never followed by former governor Barnett of Mississippi, who went to his grave still espousing the same racial prejudices and the same passion for inequality that had guided, or misguided, his entire public life.

This book owes a great debt to Harold Holzer, whose unequalled *Lincoln at Cooper Union* inspired the hope that another book about a single speech by Lincoln might be worth writing, and to the many-talented, infinitely patient Sylvia Frank Rodrigue, the editor at Southern Illinois University Press to whom Harold first introduced me. Sylvia has answered every question, solved every problem, and sailed around every questionable idea of mine with good sense and good humor. The entire SIU Press staff has been a great resource, particularly those editors most heavily and helpfully engaged with the text itself, Barb Martin, Wayne Larsen, and Mary Lou Kowaleski.

This book is perhaps unusual in that it grew out of the study of literature, not history. It was while teaching a course in American literature, before I had read a single one of the Lincoln studies cited hereafter, that I worked out my own "reading" of the Gettysburg Address in the long-familiar light of the King James Bible and the Book of Common Prayer. For those interested in a more comprehensive bibliography related to this greatest of all speeches, there is none better than Gabor Boritt's annotated "Bibliographical Note" in his inspiring and impressive study *The Gettysburg Gospel* (2006).

My oldest debt is to Flora Scott, who made her fifth-graders memorize the Gettysburg Address at a time when Lincoln ranked low on the list of popular subjects in the racially segregated public schools of Forest, Mississippi. Because of fearless Mrs. Scott, I have been carrying around the words of Lincoln in my head ever since I was ten, where they interacted with every Bible verse I ever read or memorized before or since. I have been blessed by many great teachers, of whom the following are but representative: Bertha (Miss Bernie) Bernhardt, English and Latin teacher at Forest High School; Charles Trawick Harrison (with Medgar Evers, one of the two greatest men I have ever known), Gilbert Gilchrist, and Monroe Kirk Spears at the University of the South (Sewanee); George Boyd and James Ferguson at Millsaps College; Guthrie Abbott at the University of Mississippi Law School; dissertation director and great friend Thomas Daniel Young at Vanderbilt University; and National Endowment for the Humanities seminar directors Larzer Ziff at the University of California–Berkeley, Stuart Tave at the University of Chicago, Jerry Ward at Tougaloo College, Morris Dickstein at the City University of New York, and William Ferris at the University of Mississippi, who would later serve as national director of the NEH.

Athens State University, where I have taught literature and law for over twenty years, has helped with my research in countless ways, including sabbaticals and travel. The greatest help has come from librarian Robert Burkhardt and his staff, including Barbara Grigsby Burks, Genne Johnston, Judy Stinnett, Tim Williams, Eugene Shockley, and the incomparably helpful Susan Herring. Thanks also to my dean in Arts and Sciences, historian Ronald Fritze, for helpful responses to the manuscript in progress and to John Kuhnle, my longtime friend from Vanderbilt days, who went through one of the last drafts making first-rate suggestions.

Thanks finally to the greatest blessings of my life, my sons, Charles and Jay, and their families, whose love and encouragement kept the low-burning candle in the long night from guttering into darkness.

LINCOLN'S
GETTYSBURG
ADDRESS

Prologue: Another Time, Another Place

At the beginning of the third century since the birth of Abraham Lincoln on February 12, 1809, all who love and admire this great-minded, good-hearted, and gifted man take comfort that more books have been written about him than about any other person in history except Jesus Christ and William Shakespeare. Despite the ever-swelling tide of books, however, the meanings of Lincoln's words often seem more lost in our day than in his own. This is especially true of the greatest of all his writings, the Gettysburg Address. The goal of the present study is to re-create the kind of reading of this great speech that Lincoln most plausibly intended and that his audience in 1863 most naturally applied to it—a reading calling for an opening statement before the evidence unfolds, a prologue presented in the hope of persuading a jury of twenty-first-century readers to cast off current preconceptions and take on those of another time and place.

We live in an age that has forgotten most of the bedrock assumptions of the age of Lincoln. One fundamental assumption was the key role of the Bible in Western thought and literature, a role it had been playing since 1440 when the newly invented printing press began to pour out an ever-increasing flood of Bibles in languages understood by ordinary people. Another fundamental assumption was even older, dating to the ancient Greeks and Romans. This was the great value assigned to the role of allusion and tradition in all the classical art forms such as literature, music, painting, and even acting. We have the misfortune to live in an age when "originality" of all kinds, no matter how ugly or outrageous, is all too often preferred to whatever is regarded as traditional or classical. In the age of Lincoln, a lack of novelty was the smallest of misdemeanors, far from the hanging offense it appears today, and was easily and immediately pardoned so long as more important goals were met. This is why, in his eulogy for two of the nation's founders who had drawn their last breath upon the same day—for Thomas Jefferson as the chief author of the Declaration of Independence and for John Adams as its leading advocate—Daniel Webster had declared in 1826:

> It has sometimes been said, as if it were a derogation from the merits of this
> paper, that it contains nothing new; that it only states grounds of proceeding, and

presses topics of argument, which had often been stated and pressed before. But it was not the object of the Declaration to produce any thing new. It was not to invent reasons for independence, but to state those which governed the Congress.[1]

What mattered to Webster, clearly, was not the *newness* of what was said but the *appropriateness* of it. Those of us who teach Shakespeare are sometimes taken aback by the attitude of students who devalue the world's greatest writer the moment they learn that no more than four of his thirty-seven plays from the first folio have plots of his own making: "In point of fact, Shakespeare invented very few incidents," says the renowned editor Hardin Craig. "Almost every episode in every play has somewhere a source or a suggestion."[2] Again we need to think, not of our current assumptions but those of earlier ages—to recall the assumptions that prevailed long before our contemporary world took on its blind devotion to whatever is seen as "original" and "modern."

Kenyon Cox, an artist writing on the cusp of this change in 1911 and remembered now, if at all, only as one of the early teachers of Georgia O'Keeffe, defined what he called "the Classic Spirit" in art:

> The Classic Spirit is the disinterested search for perfection; it is the love of clearness and reasonableness and self-control; it is, above all, the love of permanence and of continuity. It asks of a work of art, not that it shall be novel or effective, but that it shall be fine and noble. It seeks not merely to express disciplined emotion and individuality restrained by law. It strives for the essential rather than the accidental, the eternal rather than the momentary—loves impersonality more than personality, and feels more power in the orderly succession of the hours and the seasons than in the violence of earthquake or of storm. And it loves to steep itself in tradition. It would have each new work connect itself in the mind of him who sees it with all the noble and lovely works of the past, bringing them to his memory and making their beauty and charm a part of the beauty and charm of the work before him. It does not deny originality and individuality—they are as welcome as inevitable. It does not consider tradition as immutable or set rigid bounds to invention. But it desires that each new presentation of truth and beauty shall show us the old truth and the old beauty, seen only from a different angle and colored by a different medium. It wishes to add link by link to the chain of tradition, but it does not wish to break the chain.[3]

This is exactly the spirit that pervades the Gettysburg Address. That great, clear, impersonal address deals with the reasonable, the essential, and the eternal. It is steeped in the words and metaphors of the King James Bible and the Book of Common Prayer, interspersed with illuminating glances into other works such as the Declaration of Independence and the plays of Shakespeare. It consciously invokes these great works time and again. It shows their beautiful old truths in the rich, sad light of 1863. It transforms their lovely old language into something as close to classical perfection as any public speech has ever achieved. This is precisely the kind of transformation that makes Lincoln, like Shakespeare before him, truly original.

Just as Shakespeare did not create the ideas for most of his plots and scenes but the immortal language of them, just as Jefferson did not create most of the "topics of argument" or even most of the individual words but instead the organized clarity and force of the Declaration of Independence, so Lincoln, too, was a constant borrower who transformed whatever he took from his constant reading of other writers into strikingly new shapes and meanings. Take, for example, his best-remembered speech before the Gettysburg Address, the "House Divided" speech from 1858. Not only is the title itself borrowed from the Bible, but the very idea of applying it to America's internecine struggle between pro-slavery and antislavery principles originated not with Lincoln but with a prolific and eloquent abolitionist preacher whom he was reading on a regular basis. It originated with a man called to Lincoln's attention in the early 1850s by his law partner William Herndon. In his biography of Lincoln, Herndon fondly recalled those years and that preacher:

> I was in correspondence with Sumner, Greel[e]y, Phillips, and Garrison, and was thus thoroughly imbued with all the rancor drawn from such strong anti-slavery sources. I adhered to Lincoln, relying on the final outcome of his sense of justice and right. Every time a good speech on the great issue was made I sent for it. Hence you could find on my table the latest utterances of Giddings, Phillips, Sumner, Seward, and one whom I considered grander than all the others—Theodore Parker.[4]

In his July 2, 1854, "Sermon preached on the Dangers which Threaten the Rights of Man in America" (a sermon he published soon afterward), Theodore Parker had ringingly declared, "There can be no national welfare without national unity of action. This cannot take place unless there is national unity of idea in fundamentals. Without this a nation is 'a house divided against itself,' of course it cannot stand."[5]

Parker went on to say that "two distinct ideas—Freedom and Slavery"—define and divide this nation and must be resolved one way or the other. Either this nation will follow the "religious idea" of the Declaration of Independence with a "government of all, by all, and for all," a government that guarantees the natural rights promised by this document, a government in which "all are exactly equal in these rights, however unequal in their powers," or else it will "miserably perish" by following the teachings of the enslavers—"Mr. [John C.] Calhoun denied the self-evident truths of the Declaration of Independence; denied the natural, unalienable, and equal rights of man"[6]—and by spreading or returning the institution of slavery to the free states. Clearly, then, Lincoln borrowed his controlling metaphor not just from the Bible but more immediately from the Reverend

Parker. He borrowed it to express a crucial idea that the two men passionately agreed upon. Both men held to an expansive view of Christianity that led others to question whether Lincoln and Parker were orthodox Christians at all. Both men knew the Bible almost by heart, so that its language and metaphors would have been second nature to both. Lincoln knew exactly where he had found the inspiration for his phrase, and he knew that others, including Herndon, knew it, too. He shared his speech with a great many of his friends before he delivered it, inviting their responses, knowing very well that many other literate men interested in the slavery question would have been reading Parker's sermons and essays just as closely and as passionately as he.

What matters is that Lincoln turned the little seed he took from Parker into a greater work than his predecessor had ever produced or ever would produce. This is *not* plagiarism. Plagiarism tries to hide its source. This is literary allusion. Literary allusion honors and celebrates its source—or, in this case, its two sources. Virtually everyone who heard or read Lincoln's 1858 speech would have recognized his allusion to the words of Jesus as recorded in three different gospels, most clearly in Mark 3:25: "And if a house be divided against itself, that house cannot stand." At least *some* of Lincoln's listeners, Herndon among them, would have recognized Lincoln's debt to the Reverend Parker as well. All of Lincoln's works—and especially his greatest work, the Gettysburg Address—are filled with such allusions. Many of his allusions, as in the "House Divided" speech, echo more than one source. This is not a lack of originality, only a different *kind* of originality. Again and again it is clear that Lincoln's constant reusing and reshaping of the words of others forms the essence of his genius as a writer. Such echoing and reshaping was second nature to him, as natural and unbidden as his prodigious memory. He did not go in search of words so much as he opened the door and welcomed them in. But there were always more potential guests than places at his table, and he clearly knew how and why to pick and choose and when to close the door.

Lincoln always improved whatever words he welcomed into his speeches. Or to use a metaphor he might have chosen himself, he sharpened whatever ax he borrowed. His speech is far better written and far more compelling on all counts than Parker's. For Parker, the reference to a house divided is but one metaphor among many. Taken up for a moment, it is quickly dropped and never taken up again. For Lincoln, on the other hand, it forms the controlling metaphor of his entire speech. He sprinkles terms from house building throughout his speech—"machinery," "construction," "evidences of design," "scaffolding," "mould," "exactly fitted *niche*," "home production," and "home *producers*." At one point he carries his extended metaphor through an entire paragraph:

> We can not absolutely *know* that all these exact adaptations are the result of
> preconcert. But when we see a lot of framed timbers, different portions of which

we know have been gotten out at different times and places and by different work-men—Stephen [Douglas], Franklin [Pierce], Roger [Taney], and James [Buchanan], for instance—and when we see these timbers joined together, and see they exactly make the frame of a house or a mill, all the tenons and mortices exactly fitting, and all the lengths and proportions of the different pieces exactly adapted to their respective places, and not a piece too many or too few—not omitting even scaffold-ing—or, if a single piece be lacking we can see the place in the frame exactly fitted and prepared to yet bring such a piece in—in *such* a case, we find it impossible to not *believe* that Stephen and Franklin and Roger and James all understood one another from the beginning, and all worked upon a common *plan* or *draft* drawn up before the first lick was struck.[7]

Has any reputed conspiracy ever been so poetically described? Shortly before this passage, Lincoln had recalled Jesus' parable of the wise man who built his house upon a rock, safe from the floods and the winds, while the foolish man built his house upon sand: "And the rain descended, and the floods came, and the winds blew, and beat upon that house; and it fell: and great was the fall of it" (Matt. 7:27). Lincoln was clearly thinking of this verse when he wrote, "Under the Dred Scott decision, 'squatter sovereignty' squatted out of existence, tumbled down like temporary scaffolding—like the mould at the foundry served through one blast and fell back into loose sand—helped to carry an election, and then was kicked to the winds."[8] In poking fun at Douglas' "parental feeling"[9] for the idea of squatter sovereignty that the senator had sired and championed, Lincoln was clearly and cleverly playing with the idea of "house" in the sense of "household" or "family."

In the end, Lincoln's speech is far wiser than Parker's. Both men believed that America could not continue half slave and half free. Both men believed that freedom would in time prevail over slavery. Parker wrote, "Truth shall triumph, justice shall be the law! And if America fail, though she is one fortieth of God's family, and it is a great loss, there are other nations behind us; our truth shall not perish, even if we go down."[10] Parker invoked the biblical and apocalyptic word "perish" at least a dozen times in this one essay, just as Lincoln would invoke it so fittingly in his final phrase of the Gettysburg Address. But Parker believed that although the principle of freedom for which America stands would not perish, the United States itself *would*: "Now, I do not suppose it is possible for the Anglo-Saxons of America to remain as one nation for a great many years."[11] Because Americans "prefer local self-government," Parker declared, "I, therefore, do not look on the union of the States as a thing that is likely to last a great length of time, under any circumstances. I doubt if any part of the nation will desire it a hundred years hence."[12] For all his melancholy, Lincoln proved to be, of the two, much the more optimistic prophet about the survival of the nation itself:

I believe this government cannot endure, permanently half *slave* and half *free*.

I do not expect the Union to be *dissolved*—I do not expect the house to *fall*—but I *do* expect it will cease to be divided.[13]

In the end, Lincoln's prediction was the one that proved true. The Union was not dissolved; the house did not fall; the nation did not perish. And it is Lincoln's speech that has been remembered far longer than the more "original" speech of Theodore Parker, his immediate and demonstrable source.

Today we suffer the disadvantage of living in an age when the Bible, the Prayer Book, the Declaration of Independence, Shakespeare, and many other traditional literary treasures are no longer remembered the way they were in Lincoln's day. We live in an age when too often we read *about* the classics instead of reading them for ourselves, an age when reading the great touchstones of the past has fallen as far out of fashion as the iron-hooped skirts of the Civil War or Mr. Lincoln's stovepipe hat. Intellectual fads have replaced the King James Bible and Shakespeare with literary junk food. Memorizing passages from the Bible or *Hamlet* now seems passé if not absurd. If we don't know a thing, we assure ourselves that we can always look it up on the Internet. Professional educators of the Western world have ridiculed "rote memory" from our classrooms while every day in other parts of the world, ordinary people undertake to memorize entire books—the Koran is by far the most familiar example—and, day after day, succeed.

Even our theories of literature have dumbed down to justify the new reality. What more impressive justification can be found for our literary ignorance about primary texts and their sources than the polysyllabic pretentiousness of "postmodernist" theories such as "deconstructionism"? Here are giant squids of words formed from one-celled ideas, from viruses with no DNA of their own. Towering reputations at our greatest universities have been constructed on this worthless flotsam, while the world's greatest works have gone more and more unread and unexplored like abandoned shipwrecks.

The Gettysburg Address is a good place to stand and fight because it is one of the few classics that still is read, and not just by the millions who visit the Lincoln Memorial every year. In school and in the mainstream of ordinary life, it still sails serenely upon the ever-shrinking sea of our common knowledge. It is so brief that even the shortest attention span can absorb every word in a single sitting. It is so beautiful that even the dullest ear can hear its music. It is so significant that even the politically correct and condescending can sometimes stop calling Lincoln a "racist" long enough to admit that his little speech from the heart of the Civil War made a profound change in the way Americans framed their most fundamental political questions, especially that conflict-defining principle from the Declaration of Independence that "all men are created equal." History professor Mark M. Smith of the University of South Carolina recently declared of Lincoln's sympathy for black slaves in the *Chronicle Review*, an organ of the *Chronicle of Higher Education*: "The basis for this sympathy, of his humanitarian sentiment, was not a radical egalitarianism—*Lincoln shared in the arrogance of whiteness and racism*—but, rather, a more personal connection that he elaborated, through haptic metaphor, into a larger political concern concerning due return on labor" (emphasis added).[14] Can it not be *both* things, professor? Can it not be both principled and personal in the same body and the same brain? The simple truth is that Lincoln throughout his life *never* stopped believing with all his body, heart, mind, and soul in the "radical egalitarianism," the principled proposition at the heart of his Gettysburg Address that "all men are created equal." If Professor Smith is correct in this assertion heard again and again from so many other contemporary scholars that Lincoln "shared in the arrogance of whiteness and racism," the only inference to be drawn is that there is nothing to choose between Lincoln's racism and that of the slavery defenders such as John C. Calhoun, Jefferson Davis, and Alexander Stephens—or if there *is* anything to prefer in Lincoln's, it must be admitted and approved only through a professor's strange and magical words such as "haptic." Why do so many college professors today insist on warping the meaning of the word "racist" by applying it indiscriminately to slavery opposers and slavery defenders, people who held *opposite* beliefs about the good or evil of enslaving black people and about the truth or falsity of the idea that all human beings are created equal, who *knew* they held opposite beliefs, and who never for a moment pretended otherwise—at least not until after the slavery defenders had lost the Civil War and then did everything they could to throw sand over their own words and into the eyes of future generations? In Lincoln's day, the fundamental conflict was *always* between those who believed that all men are created equal and those who denied this in defense of black slavery.

In short, the current study goes beyond literary analysis to trace the moral and political meanings that Abraham Lincoln clearly intended to convey in his greatest speech. Even more than the Emancipation Proclamation that took effect the same year, the Gettysburg Address shifted the focus of the Civil War from an effort to save the Union to an effort to save not only the nation itself but also the *principles* for which it had been created in 1776. This nation, Lincoln reminded his audience, was founded on the fundamental assumption that "all men are created equal" and its inevitable corollary that the only legitimate rulers of equally created people are the people themselves. Thus, said Lincoln, the Union was fighting at Gettysburg to preserve representative government—"government of the people, by the people, for the people." In his speech at Gettysburg, as in countless speeches before, Lincoln was attacking slavery as this nation's greatest betrayal of our founding fathers' principle that all men are created equal. Without once mentioning the word "slavery" at Gettysburg, he was implicitly refuting the leaders of the South and their supporters in the North who defended slavery and who, in the same breath and the same philosophy, attacked or severely limited the principle of human equality. After the Civil War was over, the South and its defenders insisted that the only true cause of the Civil War had been states' rights threatened by an increasingly intrusive federal government symbolized by Lincoln. But *before* and *during* the Civil War, those who differed with Lincoln insisted that slavery was constitutionally, legally, and morally unimpeachable and was in fact God's plan for his people as revealed in His holy word, the Bible. This is a fundamental and recurrent theme in the dialogue of Lincoln's day that has been largely forgotten or ignored in our own. The Civil War was fought just as surely and just as passionately over the interpretation of the Bible and its derivatives such as the Book of Common Prayer as over the interpretation of the Declaration of Independence and the Constitution of the United States. Before the war, Jefferson Davis had declared in August 1849, "We rely on the Bible as authority for the establishment of slavery among men, and on the Constitution for its recognition throughout the United States." Throughout the war, as President of the Confederate States of America, he repeatedly referred to Southern rights, including the right to own slaves and to take them as property wherever their owners lawfully traveled, as "sacred," "just," and "holy." On October 3, 1864, he declared in Savannah, Georgia, "I believe that a just God looks upon our cause as holy, and that of our enemy as iniquitous," and "We are not engaged in a Quixotic fight for the rights of man; our struggle is for our inherited rights."[15] Thus the Civil War was fought, above all else, over the issue of slavery versus equality. It was fought over the Bible as interpreted by the Reverend Theodore Parker of Massachusetts versus the Bible as interpreted by the Reverend Frederick Ross of Alabama. It was fought over the Constitution as strictly construed by Jefferson Davis versus the Constitution as interpreted and amended in light of those "Quixotic" principles espousing the "rights of man" that were first enunciated for Americans in the Declaration of Independence and, almost a century later, immortally echoed in Abraham Lincoln's Gettysburg Address.

The Gettysburg Address is a national treasure. Yet in fundamental ways we have stopped trying to understand it in the light of those great works that Lincoln himself had loved and read and memorized. Nothing is more common in reading a scholarly work about Lincoln than to see it focusing on what the *author* knows best instead of on what Lincoln and his audience knew best. One would think from reading many of the celebrated and prize-winning books about the Gettysburg Address that Lincoln had come of age as a classical scholar at a great eastern university instead of as a self-educated farm boy from the South and Middle West who knew no language except English, who read more deeply than widely but who knew what he knew by heart—the King James Bible above all else. The purpose of the present study is to focus on what Lincoln knew best and most surely intended when he wrote the greatest speech in the history of the world.

The Forgotten Bible

Every scholar—every schoolchild—can recite that Lincoln grew up reading the King James Bible and echoed this great work in the greatest of his speeches, the Gettysburg Address. But scholars offer precious little chapter-and-verse evidence to document an idea that the whole nation, if not the whole world, takes for granted. For a time there was simply no need, because in Lincoln's own day the King James Bible was the book that most Americans, even the least educated, knew better than any other. Most Americans of his day, including Lincoln himself, could quote verse after verse and even whole chapters from memory and could recognize biblical allusions the moment they heard them. For example, sitting on the same platform with Lincoln at Gettysburg on November 19, 1863, was a young journalist named John Russell Young, who despite having no college education had already risen to become managing editor of the *Philadelphia Press*, owned by Lincoln's friend John Forney. In the sketch of his life that accompanies his 1904 book, *Men and Memories: Personal Reminiscences*, Young's attachment to his mother and her Bible is remembered in these words: "He recalled her teachings, and the memorizing of long chapters from the Bible, which he would recite to her."[1]

Historian George M. Marsden documents the unique place of the Bible at this time:

> The prestige of the Bible in the United States reached its apex in the mid-decades of the nineteenth century. Leaders as diverse as Nat Turner, Stonewall Jackson, and Abraham Lincoln seemed almost to speak naturally in biblical cadences. A radical like Turner or Ralph Waldo Emerson might regard himself as "a newborn bard of the Holy Ghost" [*Divinity School Address*]. Or others, such as Joseph Smith or Herman Melville, might produce their own versions of the biblical sagas. But more typical, even among many progressives, was an unquestioning reverence for the Bible. . . . there was no higher court of appeal.[2]

During Lincoln's own life, Thomas Babington Macaulay summed up the prevailing view of that time when in 1818 he called "the English Bible"—the King James Bible—"a book which, if everything else in our language should perish, would alone suffice to show the whole extent of its beauty and power."[3] Lincoln himself called it "the best gift God has given to man."[4] Theirs was an age of creativity, however, not of critical analysis. One struggles to find a single contemporary account or analysis of biblical allusions appearing in the writings of Emerson or Melville or even Hawthorne, whose stories overflow with biblical themes and language. This was a gap that would not be filled until the twentieth century. The same was true of the writings and speeches of Turner, Jackson, and Lincoln, except that in their cases, even twentieth-century scholars never filled the gap. In short, during Lincoln's lifetime, virtually everyone revered and echoed the King James Bible, but no one undertook to demonstrate its influence on particular works.

Thus, even though numerous readers fully recognized the astonishing beauty of the Gettysburg Address, no one bothered to point out its biblical allusions. Just after it was delivered, a Massachusetts newspaper called it "a perfect gem," and the *Philadelphia Press* called it an "immortal speech,"[5] neither offering one word about its language in biblical or literary terms. Likewise, without referring to the Bible at all, Emerson wrote of Lincoln in 1865, "His brief speech at Gettysburg will not easily be surpassed by words on any recorded occasion."[6] Those readers and reporters who analyzed the Gettysburg Address in any way focused entirely on political issues.

Many Democratic newspapers, for example, ridiculed its key assertion that the war was being fought to advance the ideal from the Declaration of Independence that all men are created equal, insisting instead that the only shared goal of the war was to preserve the union and the Constitution. Gabor Boritt has well stated what was almost certainly the typical reaction by listeners or readers at the time, "To many ears, the Gettysburg remarks may have appeared as poetry, to be enjoyed or ignored; not analyzed."[7] A nation at war had little need and practically no leisure for literary analysis.

Two-thirds of a century would pass before the Gettysburg Address produced anything approaching such an analysis. This was the Reverend William E. Barton's *Lincoln at Gettysburg*, published in 1930. Barton compared Lincoln's oratory to Saint Paul's and attributed his vocabulary to "his early reading of the Bible, *The Pilgrim's Progress, Robinson Crusoe* and a very few other good books."[8] But for whatever reason, this pioneer among close readers of the Gettysburg Address pointed out not one single biblical echo anywhere in the entire speech. The reason was certainly not any shortfall in Barton's own knowledge of the Bible. At a time when most churches required no degree from their ministers, this man who spent his entire adult life as a Congregational minister held degrees from both Berea College and Oberlin Theological Seminary. He finished his long career as a professor at Vanderbilt Theological School but still preached on Sundays at a local church. One of his sons later recalled Professor Barton's impressive knowledge of the Bible:

After breakfast came family prayers, each of us reading a verse in turn until the chapter was finished. Thus we read the Bible through many times, and when I was in high school and had begun my Greek, he took out his old Greek Testament and he and I read together, he helping me to stumble through.[9]

According to his son, Barton preached thousands of Bible-based sermons: "he loved to discover some obscure verse hidden in the Old Testament and proceed to build upon it from a fresh angle, startling his people into expectant interest."[10] He also wrote a two-volume work called *The Psalms and Their Story* and another series called *Bible Studies for Grown Folks*.[11] Nor was the reason for Barton's reticence connected to any belief that Lincoln was an "infidel," a charge from which Barton was in fact eager to exonerate his subject: "I knew, perhaps better than any biographer of Lincoln, just what kind of theology Lincoln heard preached in his boyhood, and if he revolted against it and was thought to have been an infidel, or even thought himself to have been one, I was in a fair position to judge of the extent and the quality of his supposed infidelity."[12]

There are two plausible reasons for Barton's silence about Lincoln's biblical allusions. First, the minister seems to have drawn a very sharp line between his roles as churchman and historian. When writing an earlier history called *The Soul of Abraham Lincoln*, Barton nowhere focused on Lincoln's knowledge or understanding of the Bible but always on the distinguishing points between his own history of the President and the histories of earlier writers such as Ward Lamon and William Herndon. On those rare occasions when Barton simply could not avoid touching upon the issue of Lincoln's relationship to the Bible, he chose to go no more deeply into it than his predecessors Herndon and Lamon had gone:

> We know the books he read—the Bible, *Pilgrim's Progress*, *Aesop's Fables*, *Robinson Crusoe*, and Weems' *Life of Washington*. It was a good collection, and he made the most of it. [Lincoln's stepmother] Sarah Bush Lincoln noted that while he did not like to work he liked to read, and she said, "I induced my husband to permit Abe to study" (Herndon, I, 36).
>
> John Hanks said of him, "He kept the Bible and *Aesop's Fables* always within reach, and read them over and over again."
>
> Sarah Bush did not claim that he showed any marked preference for the Bible. Lamon quotes her as saying, "He seemed to have a preference for the other books" (*Life*, pp. 34, 486). But he certainly read the Bible with diligence, as his whole literary style shows.[13]

It is precisely at this point that any reader would expect Barton to show the reader at least *one* connection between the Bible and Lincoln's literary style. But neither in this book nor in his *Lincoln at Gettysburg* published ten years later does he ever do so. It is as if Barton regarded his own biblical knowledge as something to be used only when writing or speaking as a minister and never when writing as a historian. Seeing himself as a newcomer in the field of history, Barton limited himself to the worn paths and clear footprints of previous historians, walking only in *their* tracks and hazarding none of his own.[14]

The second plausible explanation is that Professor Barton may wrongly have assumed that Lincoln's biblical allusions were, or would be, as obvious to the reading public of his day as they already were to his colleagues, his students, his family, and himself and may thus have hesitated to fill his book with what appeared to him to be already common knowledge. This could explain why he focused so exclusively on such sources as Daniel Webster and Theodore Parker. In short, Barton may simply have been unaware of what a huge decline in the public's knowledge of the Bible had occurred by the 1920s. Beginning in the late nineteenth century, the knowledge and influence of the King James had sunk into an ever-accelerating decline of which Barton may have been blissfully ignorant. Those who read the Bible every day of their lives are not always the best judges of biblical literacy among their fellow readers of the world.

In "The Demise of Biblical Civilization," Grant Wacker locates in the closing decades of the nineteenth century, beginning among the educated, an "erosion of confidence in the Bible" that by the 1890s "had become a gale of critical innovation."[15] This was but one of many reasons for a decline in the knowledge of the Bible among *all* classes in the twentieth century—especially knowledge of the King James Bible that over the years had come to seem, even to many believers, old-fashioned and hard to understand. By the time scholars in the 1940s, 1950s, and beyond created a wave of close and erudite readings of the Gettysburg Address that aspired to go beyond Barton's, public knowledge of the Bible had sunk to its all-time low since that magical moment when Protestantism and the printing press first gave birth to the translated Bible as the best-known and best-loved book of the Western world.

A 1993 article by Gustav Niebuhr in the *Washington Post* focuses on a recent survey by Barna Research Group showing that the King James Bible in particular had dramatically declined in familiarity throughout the twentieth century:

> Ever since colonial days, the King James Version of the Bible has been standard Scripture for American Protestants. Translated from the original Hebrew and Greek by scholars appointed by King James I of England, it was published in 1611, in the same decade the Pilgrims landed at Plymouth Rock.
>
> Its vocabulary is that of early modern English, similar to that used by William Shakespeare, in whose lifetime the King James Version appeared.
>
> But now, as the King James Version nears its 400th anniversary, is it beginning to lose its appeal—a casualty of a video-oriented generation that cannot understand words such as "thee" and "thou," "folly" and "farthing"?[16]

The survey showed that even among regular Bible readers, only those sixty-five years or older—many of whom have died since this article first appeared in 1993—still preferred the King James, while just one of every five readers under the age of twenty-seven was using it.

In the very next year, 1994, a survey conducted by George Gallup revealed that knowledge of the Bible drawn from any translation had fallen to unprecedented levels, according to an article by Karen R. Long of the Newhouse News Service:

> Gallup, whose company has tracked religious trends for 50 years, reports that basic Bible knowledge is at a record low.
>
> "The startling fact is Americans do not know what they believe or why," Gallup asserts. "We are drifting in this country. Biblical illiteracy presents not only a spiritual or religious problem in this nation but a cultural one as well."

Gallup's lament was reinforced by a former scholar at the Educational Testing Service.

> "Biblical literacy is not merely a matter of taste or a decline in cultural knowledge," said Winton H. Manning, formerly the senior scholar at the Educational Testing Service in Princeton, N.J. "Rather, the Bible has been the primary text by which the Western world has lived together and comprehended God, nature and mankind.
>
> "Now it has been largely lost because young people for 50 years or so . . . were not reared in the textual environment of the Bible. Young people today are not merely different, they are intellectually handicapped and they do not know it."[17]

All of this may help to explain why there has been so very little documentation by scholars during the late nineteenth, twentieth, or early twenty-first centuries of Lincoln's use of the Bible in the Gettysburg Address.

Even the homespun biographer Carl Sandburg sounded tentative and vague about Lincoln's knowledge of the Bible in his introduction to *Lincoln's Devotional*—a book of Bible verses owned by the President but not discovered and published until 1957:

> Among universal possessions of the American people are certain speeches and letters of Lincoln that are colored and in part drenched with biblical references and learning. Why did Lincoln say "Four score and seven" instead of the plain figure "eighty-seven" at the opening of his Gettysburg speech? Probably, it has been suggested, because in the Old Testament it reads most often "two score" instead of "forty," and "four score" instead of "eighty."[18]

In a book published just two years later about Lincoln's religious attitudes called *The Almost Chosen People*, William J. Wolf wrote of the Gettysburg Address,

"Some commentators have dismissed the religious implications of the address by pointing out that there are no biblical quotations in it and that the phrase 'under God' was an afterthought."[19] In his Pulitzer Prize–winning *Lincoln at Gettysburg* (1992), Garry Wills found so few biblical allusions in Lincoln's greatest speech that the Bible never even appears in the index to Wills' three-hundred-page book. One sentence in his book contains virtually everything Wills has to say on the subject: "The 'new birth of freedom' in the last sentence of the Address takes us back to the miraculous birth of the opening sentence; and behind this image, too, there is the biblical concept of people 'born again' (John 3:3–7)."[20] Wills, in fact, says more about the classical allusions of Gettysburg orator Edward Everett than about the biblical allusions of Lincoln. Yet Everett himself told Lincoln, "I should be glad, if I could flatter myself that I came as near to the central idea of the occasion, in two hours, as you did in two minutes."[21] Glenn LaFantasie's 1995 study of the Gettysburg Address in the *Journal of the Abraham Lincoln Society* cites the same John 3:3–7 as Wills, as well as "threescore years" and "fourscore years" from Psalm 90:10, but then adds, "Apart from these specific citations, however, it is difficult to pin down the sources of Lincoln's biblical language in the Gettysburg Address."[22] Allen Guelzo's 1999 book, *Abraham Lincoln: Redeemer President*, likewise nods to a couple of biblical allusions in the Gettysburg Address, most notably to the same 90th Psalm cited by LaFantasie, but then declares, unequivocally: "Even the structure of the Address owes more to the classical speeches he memorized out of the readers and orators he had borrowed in his youth, to Pericles' great ode on the Athenian dead, to Gorgias and Lysias, than to Moses or Paul."[23] Clearly, then, Everett and the living audience who listened to those two minutes from the President on November 19, 1863, were far more aware of the biblical allusions that formed Lincoln's "central idea" than were Sandburg, Wills, LaFantasie, Guelzo, and the whole vast choir of twentieth-century Lincoln scholars of whom this harmonious quartet appears to form a representative sample.

The twenty-first century has dawned upon a heightened interest in Lincoln's religious language. Recent studies have revealed few new insights into the *particulars* of Lincoln's use of the Bible in the Gettysburg Address but at least insist far more emphatically upon the *importance* of biblical allusion throughout the address. In an excellent study called *Lincoln's Sacred Effort* (2000), Lucas Morel has many enlightening things to say about Lincoln's religious views and the way they affected all his political speeches and decisions. Questioning the approach of Wills because he "highlights the influence of the Transcendentalists and 'rural cemetery' movement at the expense of elaborating the biblical elements of the Gettysburg Address," Morel promises to focus in his own work "on the biblical imagery and allusions of Lincoln's brief but poignant eulogy to the dead at Gettysburg."[24] The only shortcoming of Morel's approach is that he finds an overall "religious spirit" in the Address but, surprisingly in the light of his announced emphasis, a "lack of direct biblical references."[25] Joseph Fornieri likewise emphasizes, in *Abraham Lincoln's Political Faith* (2003), Lincoln's "evocative use of biblical language" in the Gettysburg Address, but he, too, falls short in his examples.

> The opening lines of the Gettysburg Address are perhaps the best example of Lincoln's evocative use of biblical rhetoric. The speech is utterly suffused with the style, cadence, and archetypes of the King James Bible. To commemorate the solemnity of the event, the opening "Four score and seven years" of the speech evoked the passage of time in the same manner as the King James Bible. For instance, it recalled the language of the Book of Esther 1:4 ("an hundred and fourscore days") and Psalm 90 ("The days of our years are three score years and ten"). Even the repetition of monosyllabic words paralleled the style of the King James Bible. The religious imagery of "dedicate," "consecrate," and "hallow" was used evocatively throughout the speech to reinforce the supreme sacrifice made by those who gave their lives for duty.[26]

Esther 1:4 is surely a less-apt source than Psalm 90, which Morel also cites, and the trio of "dedicate," "consecrate," and "hallow" traces more immediately to the Book of Common Prayer than to the King James Bible. But there is no doubt that Fornieri and Morel have faced Lincoln scholarship in the right direction with regard to the central role of the King James Bible in any interpretation of the Gettysburg Address that claims to reflect what Lincoln and his audience were thinking in November 1863.

Boritt in his 2006 book, *The Gettysburg Gospel: The Lincoln Speech That Nobody Knows*, also provides a wonderful historical context for Lincoln's great speech. Indeed, Boritt's own heroic survival of Nazi control of his country during World War II and later of Soviet control, particularly the suppression of the Hungarian uprising in 1956 when he and other dissidents came under Soviet fire, makes his context even richer and more moving. As for Lincoln's language, Boritt writes eloquently if all too briefly:

> [M]uch of what Lincoln said carried the rhythms of the Bible. This was the music of the ancient Hebrew and Greek turned into King James's English. This was the language he was raised on. "Four score and seven years ago." Psalm 90: "The days of our years are three score years and ten," one of the best-known sentences of the Book. "Brought forth" is not only the biblical way to announce a birth, including that of Mary's "first born son," but the phrase that describes the Israelites being "brought forth" from slavery in Egypt.
>
> Birth, sacrificial death, rebirth. A born-again nation. At a less than conscious level, Lincoln weaved together the biblical story and the American story: "Fathers." "Conceive." "Perish." "Consecrate." "Hallow." "Devotion." The devout in the cemetery heard Lincoln speak an intimately familiar beloved language. His

words pointing to rebirth went even deeper than the Christian message, if that was possible, reaching the primeval longing for a new birth that humankind has yearned for and celebrated with every spring since time immemorial.[27]

To question one small point of this—that Lincoln operated at a "less than conscious level"—is in no way to diminish the overall achievement of Boritt's impressive study. The enormous care that Lincoln took in writing, revising, and editing his own speeches and the precise reasons he gave for resisting even small changes by others create a powerful presumption against the notion that Lincoln was ever less than fully conscious in his literary effects. A perfect example of such care occurred when the young Republicans of New York were editing Lincoln's Cooper Union address for publication—a subject beautifully covered in Harold Holzer's *Lincoln at Cooper Union*, which like Boritt's is one of the finest books ever written about *any* aspect of Lincoln's life or career.[28] Even if one concedes for purposes of argument that Lincoln composed any of his best work at anything less than full consciousness, isn't it far more useful and rewarding to try to account for his *conscious* meanings, just as he himself tried to account for the conscious meanings and intentions of the founding fathers in his Cooper Union address, than to survey the unplatted suburbs of his unconscious, subconscious, or "less than conscious" mind?

Because we live in an age when presidents and other politicians routinely speak off the cuff or in the language of professional speechwriters and almost never compose for themselves the kind of carefully crafted speech that Lincoln always preferred to extemporaneous remarks, it is nearly impossible for many readers today to comprehend the conscious effort and enormous care that went into the composition of a Lincoln speech. The most famous address of his before the Gettysburg was the "House Divided" speech, remarked earlier, which was delivered before the Illinois Republican Convention in 1858. Here is the description that Herndon gave of Lincoln's painstaking preparation of this famous speech, which, as we have seen, features a biblical metaphor at its very heart:

This speech he wrote on stray envelopes and scraps of paper, as ideas suggested themselves, putting them into that miscellaneous and convenient receptacle, his hat. As the convention drew near he copied the whole on connected sheets, carefully revising every line and sentence, and fastened them together, for reference during the delivery of the speech, and for publication. The former precaution, however, was unnecessary, for he had studied and read over what he had written so long and carefully that he was able to deliver it without the least hesitation or difficulty. A few days before the convention, when he was at work on the speech, I remember that Jesse K. Dubois, who was Auditor of State, came into the office and, seeing Lincoln busily writing, inquired what he was doing or what he was writing. Lincoln answered gruffly, "It's something you may see or hear sometime, but I'll not let you see it now." I myself knew what he was writing, but having asked neither my opinion nor that of anyone else, I did not venture to offer any suggestions. After he had finished the final draft of the speech, he locked the office door, drew the curtain across the glass panel in the door, and read it to me. At the end of each paragraph he would halt and wait for my comments. I remember what I said after hearing the first paragraph, wherein occurs the celebrated figure of the house divided against itself: "It is true, but is it wise or politic to say so?" He responded: "That expression is a truth of all human experience, 'a house divided against itself cannot stand,' and 'he that runs may read.' The proposition also is true, and has been for six thousand years. I want to use some universally known figure expressed in simple language as universally well-known, that may strike to the minds of men in order to raise them up to the peril of the times. I do not believe I would be right in changing or omitting it. I would rather be defeated with this expression in the speech, and uphold and discuss it before the people, than be victorious without it."

Later Lincoln "invited a dozen or so of his friends over to the library of the State House, where he read and submitted it to them. After the reading he asked each man for his opinion."[29] It is hard to imagine any method of writing a speech that leaves less to chance and depends less upon the unconscious mind than Lincoln's characteristic method.

The fact that LaFantasie, Guelzo, Fornieri, Morel, and Boritt all cite Psalm 90 as a source for Lincoln's "Four score and seven years" raises another point that needs to be made early in this study. Each of these scholars makes the same point with the force of original discovery while crediting none of the others. Many other scholars have done the same thing. In his 2005 book, *The Eloquent President: A Portrait of Lincoln through his Words*, Ronald C. White Jr. focuses on Psalm 90 as the source of Lincoln's "Four score and seven" in the Gettysburg Address without mentioning any predecessors who had focused there before he did.[30] In *The Inspired Wisdom of Abraham Lincoln*, a 2008 book that focuses on Lincoln's faith and contains a section called "Bible References in the *Collected Works of Abraham Lincoln*," the only reference to the King James Bible that Philip L. Ostergard identifies from the Gettysburg Address is the "fourscore" of Psalm 90:10—he, too, citing no predecessor.[31] And there is nothing wrong with this. Each of these scholars almost certainly made the discovery for himself instead of learning it from someone else. It is probably impossible, and certainly pointless, to find the first scholar who ever put into print the perfectly obvious fact that Lincoln was echoing Psalm 90:10 in his opening words.

My own reading of the Gettysburg Address in biblical terms comes not from studying Lincoln scholarship but from reading and memorizing the King James Bible in the rural and small-town Baptist churches of my youth—churches that were still placing the same passionate emphasis upon the Bible as the source of all spiritual truth that they had placed in the days when Lincoln attended the same kind of Baptist churches as a boy. In like manner, I learned the Book of Common Prayer by attending the Episcopal Church in my adult years, just the way Lincoln first heard it since his wife was active in the Episcopal Church of Springfield for half of the years she lived in Springfield—the first eleven of the twenty-two years she spent there between 1839 and early 1861 when the Lincolns removed to Washington and the White House. In short, any connection that the present study may find between the words of the Gettysburg Address on the one hand and the words of the King James Bible or Book of Common Prayer on the other I found on my own by comparing the address with the documents in question. When I first worked out my own reading of the Gettysburg Address in biblical and liturgical terms for a course I taught for many years in American literature, I had read not a single one of the essays or books about Lincoln that are cited in this study. At first, the connections I saw and heard in teaching that course came quickly and easily—Psalm 90:10 in "Four score," Matthew's and Luke's accounts of the birth of Jesus in "conceived" and "brought forth," the Prayer Book in "dedicated" and in "consecrate," "dedicate," and "hallow," and a number of other allusions throughout the ten sentences of Lincoln's magnificent address that I had first memorized back in fifth grade. But after riding this first wave, I had to listen far more carefully for the quieter and more subtle references that my ears might have missed, all the while checking and double-checking the Bible and the Prayer Book to make sure that what I thought I was hearing was really there, just the way I remembered it. The last step was to consult biblical concordances in search of Scriptures that Lincoln might be alluding to but that I myself had forgotten or never learned.

Recent versions of the Bible and Prayer Book are worse than useless in a study of this kind. The most recent American Prayer Book (1979) is typified by the change of the perfectly simple and traditional, clear and melodic "Do this in remembrance of me" in the service of Holy Communion to "Do this for the remembrance of me." The latest version is wordy, unidiomatic, unclear, and un-musical—but, of course, *thoroughly modern.*

If one or more of the connections documented hereafter ever turns up in the writings of some predecessor uncited in these pages, I plead innocent of this person's influence but welcome his or her company. The more of us who see and hear Lincoln's allusions, the more quickly and confidently we may all expand our collective understanding of the sources of beauty and meaning in this greatest of all speeches. The words and meanings of any great poem, play, novel, or speech are social and shared, and the first of us to point out some jewel of a metaphor or an allusion is but a servant to the rest, with no rights of ownership attaching as a finder's fee. The play's the thing—or in this case the speech—and its glories belong to all who love and cherish it. Again, the goal of the present study is to hear the Gettysburg Address as it might have been heard in 1863 when the King James Bible was the common property of just about everyone, and the Prayer Book, although less *widely* known, was no less *well* known by those who knew it.

Lincoln's Knowledge of Bible and Prayer Book

Lincoln's most famous Bible now rests at Fisk University in Nashville, inscribed, "To Abraham Lincoln President of the United States The Friend of Universal Freedom From the Loyal Colored People of Baltimore, as a token of respect and Gratitude, Baltimore, 4th July 1864."[1] On September 7, Lincoln formally received this Bible at the White House, and the next day, a Washington newspaper recorded his acceptance speech that included this tribute: "In regard to this Great Book, I have but to say, it is the best gift God has given to man."[2] It is, of course, a King James Bible. Lincoln already owned other copies of the King James, including an Oxford edition given him by the mother of his friend Joshua Speed, for whom he had inscribed a photograph on October 3, 1861, "For Mrs. Lucy G. Speed, from whose pious hand I accepted the present of an Oxford Bible twenty years ago."[3] The stories are legion of Lincoln's intimate knowledge of the King James, long passages from which he could, and did, quote from memory. The incredible detail of his memory is illustrated by a story that happened in May 1864, just months before the Baltimore presentation.

> The secretaries [John] Nicolay and [John] Hay were amazed at one instance of Lincoln's familiarity with the Bible. In 1864 news had come of the Cleveland, Ohio, convention of a third party which nominated John C. Fremont for President. A friend drifted into the White House, gave Lincoln an account of the conversation, and said that instead of the many thousands expected there were present at no time more than 400 people. The President, struck by the number mentioned, reached for the Bible on his desk, searched a moment, then read the words: "And everyone that was in distress, and everyone that was in debt, and everyone that was discontented, gathered themselves unto him; and he became captain over them, and there were with him about four hundred men."[4]

What a perfect way for the witty but gentle Lincoln to deal with the troublesome Fremont, by having his Bible suggest that the four hundred attached to his renegade rival represented only the distressed, indebted, and discontented of this world! It took an uncanny knowledge of the Bible to find and fire such an arrow in the twinkling of an eye.

A friend from earlier days in Illinois, Frederick Iglehart, recalled that "Lincoln was a faithful student of the Bible" whose New Testament was "worn almost through with the rail-splitter's fingers. He once recited to me Christ's Sermon on the Mount without making a mistake. He said to me more than once that he considered Paul's sermon on Mars' Hill the ablest and most eloquent literary production ever spoken by mortal lip." Iglehart also recalled hearing Lincoln quote from memory, for an old dying woman whose will he had just made, a series of hymns, the entire 23rd Psalm, the first part of John 14, and "other quotations from the Scriptures."[5] Henry Champion Deming of Connecticut, who met Lincoln only after being elected to Congress in 1863, provided evidence that the president's devotion to the Bible continued to the end: "The books which he chiefly read, in his leisure hours were, the Bible, Shakespeare [and several humorous writers that included Robert Burns and Artemus Ward]. I frequently saw all these books in his hands, during a voyage of three days upon the Potomac, when the party consisted only of the President and his family, the Secretary of War and his aid[e] and myself."[6]

Lincoln's precise knowledge of the Bible informed all of his public speeches from the earliest days of his political career, as Allen Guelzo has observed:

> His speeches and public documents were littered with biblical allusions from the 1830s onwards, and he told John Langdon Kaine that "the Bible is the richest source of pertinent quotations." When one Presbyterian minister passed by a crowd where Lincoln was speaking, he good-naturedly hooted, "Where the great ones are, there will the people be." Lincoln instantly shot back, "Ho! *Parson* a little more Scriptural; 'Where the carces [carcass] is there will the eagles be gathered together'" (an allusion to Luke 17:37).[7]

Displaying the same precise memory for Scripture, Lincoln told an acquaintance named Abner Ellis that "he thought baptism by immersion was the true meaning of the word; for John baptized the Savior in the River Jordan because there was much water and they went down into it and came up out of it."[8] In this case, Lincoln was thinking precisely of two Bible passages (with emphasis added below). The first is from Mark 1:9–11:

> And it came to pass in those days, that Jesus came from Nazareth of Galilee, and was baptized of John in Jordan.
> And straightway *coming up out of the water*, he saw the heavens opened, and the Spirit like a dove descending upon him:
> And there came a voice from heaven saying, Thou art my beloved Son, in whom I am well pleased.

The second passage Lincoln was thinking of is John 3:22–23:

> After these things came Jesus and his disciples into the land of Judea; and there he tarried with them, and baptized.
>
> And John was also baptizing in Aenon, near to Salim, *because there was much water*: and they came, and were baptized.

Because we live in an age when books and the Internet are accessible to virtually everyone in this country and because modern educators have banished "mere memorization" from our schoolrooms, most Americans today have forsaken the fine old art of memorizing that flourished in the age of Lincoln. This is one more reason why so many scholars have so often overlooked this rich vein of precisely memorized language—much of it from his beloved King James Bible—that Lincoln carried around in his head and echoed in all of his speeches. Those who have never bothered to try to memorize long works routinely underestimate what an enormous amount of material can be learned and retained for long periods, a phenomenon that flourishes to this day in the world's less-literate societies even as it declines in the more literate, especially our own.

Once after Lincoln had recited a long passage from a humorous work and a visitor expressed surprise that he could commit so much material to memory, Lincoln replied, "If I like a thing, it just sticks after once reading it or hearing it."[9] This was quoted by the journalist Noah Brooks, Lincoln's friend, who devoted an entire section of his book *Washington in Lincoln's Time* to "Lincoln's Memory," commencing with this story:

> A notable meeting was held in the hall of the House of Representatives in January, 1865, when the United States Christian Commission held its anniversary exercises. Secretary Seward presided, and made a delightful address. As an example of Mr. Lincoln's wonderful power of memory, I noticed that a few days after that meeting in the Capitol he recalled an entire sentence of Mr. Seward's speech, and, so far as I could remember, without missing a word. This faculty was apparently exercised without the slightest effort on his part. He "couldn't help remembering," as he was accustomed to say.[10]

Brooks provided many other examples throughout his book of Lincoln's remarkably rapid and retentive memory. Such a memory was not merely extraordinary. It was phenomenal. It was photographic—not photographic like a Polaroid snapshot but photographic like a motion picture, for Lincoln always remembered more the *sound* of the words than their spellings. Brooks's many examples include a poem of over a hundred lines that Lincoln once quoted to an astonished man he had just met, telling the man as soon as he had completed the prodigious recitation, "'There! that poem was quoted by your grandfather Holmes in a speech which he made in the United States Senate in—' and he named the date and specified the occasion." Brooks continued, "Lincoln's power of memory was certainly very great; if he had been by any casualty deprived of his sight, his own memory would have supplied him with an ample and varied library."[11] Even in an age when memorizing was commonplace, Lincoln's ability was clearly exceptional—as prodigious as it was precise—and there was no book in the "varied library" of his mind that he knew so thoroughly and so intimately as the King James Bible. On another occasion, Lincoln described his mind in different terms. "My mind is like a piece of steel, very hard to scratch anything on it and almost impossible after you get it there to rub it out."[12] This is not in conflict with his observation that he remembered many things after just one reading or hearing. Memory alone could never have given him an understanding of the law or of Euclid's propositions. But once he had mastered those difficult matters, they were as permanently stored in his brain as a poem, a speech, or a chapter of the Bible.

Only one other religious book can remotely compare in literary influence to the King James Bible among English-speaking writers, and this is the Book of Common Prayer.[13] The Prayer Book includes such familiar rites as Baptism ("We yield thee hearty thanks, most merciful Father, that it hath pleased thee to regenerate *this infant*"—in the Episcopal Church, baptism typically means infant baptism, or christening, a practice rejected by Baptists and certain other fundamentalist denominations as unbiblical), Holy Communion ("We do not presume to come to this thy table, O merciful Lord"), the Solemnization of Matrimony ("Dearly beloved, we are gathered here"), and the Burial of the Dead ("We therefore commit his body to the ground; earth to earth, ashes to ashes, dust to dust"). Based in part on breviaries and missals from the Catholic Church but even more so on the Bible itself, the Book of Common Prayer was composed in 1549 by Archbishop Thomas Cranmer for the Church of England and later expanded by committees of churchmen. In 1789, the Prayer Book was revised by the Episcopal Church in America so as to eliminate all references to royalty before it was published for the congregations of the new nation in 1790. In particular, the American church replaced the prayer for the king with a prayer for the president. In 1799, "The Form of Consecration of a Church or Chapel"[14] was added—a service that Lincoln would specifically echo in his Gettysburg Address. His echoes of the Prayer Book are every bit as clear and insistent as his echoes of the King James Bible, just not quite so frequent.

When Lincoln met Mary Todd, she was living in Springfield with her beautiful older sister Elizabeth, wife of Ninian Edwards, prominent son of a former governor of Illinois. The Edwardses, who hosted the best and biggest soirees in town, attended Saint Paul's Episcopal Church in Springfield, and Mary regularly attended with them. This was why Lincoln walked to the home of the Episcopal priest Charles Dresser on November 3, 1842, and asked the Reverend Mr. Dresser over his breakfast table to perform Lincoln's marriage to Mary Todd, which was solemnized the next evening in the Edwards home. The very fact that Lincoln walked alone to make the request strongly suggests that he knew Dresser already, and the most plausible place to have met him would have been at Dresser's church while Lincoln was courting Mary. (Two years later, the Lincolns would buy their first home from Dresser.) Lincoln's best man, James Matheny, later wrote of the marriage: "Marriages in Springfield up to that time . . . had been rather commonplace affairs. Lincoln's was perhaps the first one ever performed with all the requirements of the Episcopal ceremony."[15] Like all other services and ceremonies of the Episcopal Church, this one was read straight from the Prayer Book, beginning with the familiar words, "Dearly beloved, we are gathered here in the sight of God, and in the face of this company, to join together this Man and this Woman in holy Matrimony." After the marriage, according to William J. Wolf in *The Almost Chosen People*, "Mary attended the Episcopal Church in Springfield and he accompanied her at times."[16]

Guelzo has discovered a fascinating and highly revealing 1894 interview in the *St. Louis Post-Dispatch*, given to a reporter by a black woman named Ruth Stanton, who had worked for the Lincolns in the 1840s. This interview provides a rare and in some ways unique account from a living contemporary of Mrs. Lincoln's active association with Saint Paul's Episcopal Church. Stanton said that she first worked in Springfield for the family of John Bradford, beginning in 1843. "Mrs. Lincoln belonged to the Episcopal Church, and so did the Bradfords." In time, "Mrs. Bradford sent me over to help Mrs. Lincoln every Saturday, for she had no servant and had to do her own house-work." In 1849, at fourteen, Stanton was sent by the Bradfords "to live with the Lincolns." Early that year, Lincoln returned from his two-year stint in the U.S. House of Representatives. In her late fifties at the interview, Stanton remembered Mrs. Lincoln vividly:

> Mrs. Lincoln was a very nice lady. She worked hard and was a good church member. Every Thursday the Sewing Society of the Episcopal Church would meet at Mrs. Lincoln's house and make clothes for the very poor people. She was very plain in her ways, and I remember that she used to go to church wearing a cheap calico dress and a sun-bonnet. She didn't have silk or satin dresses.

Ruth Stanton said that she worked for the Lincolns for "about a year."[17]

Stanton had known the Lincolns for about six years, since 1843, and had worked for them on Saturdays before coming to work for them full-time in 1849. The seven years she knew the Lincolns were the last seven of the eleven when Mrs. Lincoln was associated with the Episcopal Church. (There is no record that Mary was ever an official member by way of confirmation the way her sister Elizabeth was, but this would have not have prevented her active participation in the church.) We have the word of Emilie Todd Helm, a younger half-sister, that Mary attended the Episcopal Church from about 1839 until early 1850. Emilie is quoted in the biography of Mary Todd Lincoln that was written by Emilie's daughter, Katherine Helm, and published in 1928:

> Mary, although a dyed-in-the-wool Presbyterian at the time she came to Springfield [for a short visit in 1837, then to stay in 1839], as the guest of her sister Elizabeth, she, naturally, accompanied her hostess to church. Elizabeth, like Mary, had been brought up on the Shorter Catechism but had been confirmed in the Episcopal church at the time of her marriage to Ninian Edwards, who was an Episcopalian. Mary, having formed her church affiliations which were the same as those of her sister, continued to attend service in the Episcopal church until after the death of her little son, Edward Baker, February 20, 1850.[18]

Here is Wolf's account in *The Almost Chosen People* of the funeral for this son and the change it caused in the church affiliation and attendance of the Lincolns:

> Their second son Edward Baker died on February 1, 1850, just under the age of four, after an illness of fifty-two days. The grief-stricken parents, unable to locate the Episcopal clergyman who had married them and whose church they occasionally attended, turned to the Rev. James Smith of the First Presbyterian Church to conduct the funeral. A rugged Scotsman with a fine mind and an interesting fund of anecdotes, he was a helpful pastor to the bereaved parents. The Lincolns soon took a pew with an annual rental of fifty dollars and became regular attendants. Mrs. Lincoln became a member.[19]

During the two years that Lincoln served as a U.S. Congressman, 1847 to 1849, the Lincolns were usually in Washington or at Mary's father's home in Kentucky. But this does not affect the claim of her sister, supported by her housekeeper with regard to one long stretch of time, that whenever Mary Todd Lincoln was at home in Springfield up until the death of her son Eddie in 1850, she was in attendance at the Episcopal church. Indeed, during Lincoln's campaign for the U.S. Congress in 1843, says Keith Jennison, "The Democrats brought up everything they could think of against him, including many references to his being married to a 'high-toned Episcopalian.'"[20]

The only reference Lincoln ever seems to have made to any connection of his or Mary's with the Episcopal church appears in a letter to Martin S. Morris, dated March 26, 1843, concerning this very race for Congress against a number of opponents, including fellow lawyer Edward D. Baker after whom Lincoln's first son would later be named:

> There was, too, the strangest combination of church influence against me. Baker is a Campbellite, and therefore as I suppose, with few exceptions, got all that church. My wife has some relations in the Presbyterian churches and some with the Episcopalian churches, and therefore, wherever it would tell, I was set down as either

the one or the other, while it was everywhere contended that no Christian ought to go for me, because I belonged to no church, was suspected of being a deist, and had talked about fighting a duel.[21]

Thus we know that, according to his own word, Lincoln was by some "set down"—alleged or believed—to be an Episcopalian in 1843 during the very period when he and his wife were in some kind of attendance at the Episcopal Church in Springfield.

Lincoln always had, like a great novelist, a clear understanding of social class. He was a poor boy from the South who had moved to the North and made good without losing a dust mote of his common touch. He had married a girl who, after growing up on a Southern plantation, had moved north along with some of her sisters. The northern migration of the Todd females was motivated in part because their father had remarried after the death of their mother and had started a new family in Kentucky. Lincoln had been raised a Baptist, his wife a more socially prestigious Presbyterian. In America, and especially in the South, the Protestant denominations tended to arrange themselves into a predictable pecking order in the social scale, with Episcopalians at the top, then Presbyterians, then Methodists, and finally Baptists, who, as the likely most numerous group of all, were roughly on the same plane as everybody else, including the Campbellites. Mary's more socially successful sister Elizabeth was a convert to the Episcopal church, and Mary herself attended Elizabeth's church for over a decade.

However occasional Lincoln's attendance may have been at Saint Paul's Episcopal Church during the years that Mary attended there, *any* attendance would have put the Prayer Book in his hands. Once in those powerful hands, it would have been devoured as Lincoln devoured all books that caught his interest. John Hanks, a cousin who grew up with Lincoln, said, "He frequently read the Bible. He read *Robinson Crusoe*, Bunyan's *Pilgrim*['s] *Progress*. Lincoln devoured all the books he could get or lay hands on; he was a constant and voracious reader."[22] The Prayer Book authorized in 1789 was the one used in Lincoln's day. It sat in little holders behind each pew in the church that the Lincolns attended in Springfield and included all the additions that had been authorized after 1789, such as the Order for the Consecration of a Church or Chapel that was added in 1799. The various printings were identical except for small differences in punctuation and capitalization. The Prayer Book was a favorite gift from priests, parents, or fellow parishioners for special occasions such as weddings, christenings, confirmations, and birthdays. Either as gifts or by purchasing their own, many parishioners owned a personal copy. "To own a handsomely bound prayer-book and to occupy the family pew once a year was evidence enough of one's religious regularity" in the South where Mary Lincoln had grown up, according to William E. Dodd in *The Cotton Kingdom*.[23] Some of these personal copies were small enough to fit into a clutch or a coat pocket.

But even if Mary Lincoln never owned a Prayer Book and never took one home and even if Lincoln heard it only at his wedding and at occasional appearances in church, he certainly heard the Solemnization of Marriage and the Burial of the Dead. He certainly heard Morning Prayer and Holy Communion, the services read on Sunday mornings; at Morning Prayer, the Litany is added from time to time. Evening Prayer is another service he could have attended. Anyone present at any of these services was almost certain to read along, because all services from the Prayer Book consist of various responsive readings, one line spoken by the priest, the next by the congregation. Indeed, a correspondent for the *New York Herald* reported seeing Lincoln "read the service with the regular worshippers"[24] at Saint John's Episcopal Church on his first Sunday in Washington as president-elect. He could also have attended the Episcopal church in Springfield on special occasions when Holy Baptism and Confirmation provided the services of the day. The records of Saint Paul's show that Elizabeth Edwards was both baptized and confirmed on August 1, 1841, that three of her children were baptized on April 15, 1843, another on July 7, 1846, and the last-born on August 27, 1852, and that confirmations of two of these children occurred in 1855 and 1858. For whatever reason, Ninian Edwards was confirmed much later than Elizabeth—in 1858. Besides officiating at the Lincoln marriage, the Reverend Mr. Dresser performed the wedding of Mary and Elizabeth's sister Ann on October 25, 1846. His successor performed the wedding of one of the Edwards children in 1855.[25] Lincoln was living in Springfield when each of these services was performed and could have attended any or all of them except when out of town riding the court circuit.

According to Wayne C. Temple in *Abraham Lincoln: From Skeptic to Prophet*, on his very first trip out of Springfield as president-elect for a meeting in Chicago with Vice-President–elect Hannibal Hamlin, Lincoln attended an Episcopal church:

> When Sunday rolled around on the 25th [November 25, 1860], the God-fearing President-elect attended public worship services. On this particular occasion, he and Hannibal Hamlin accepted a cordial invitation to be the church guests of the Hon. Isaac Newton Arnold, a Congressman-elect and an old Republican friend of Lincoln's. Arnold escorted his distinguished charges to St. James' Episcopal Church on the corner of Cass and Huron, a new edifice erected in 1857 and staffed by the Rev. Dr. R. H. Clarkson as Rector. A local newspaper [the *Chicago Daily Journal*] announced on Saturday that divine services in the church would take place at 3:00 p.m. on Sunday.[26]

No available record indicates whether Dr. Clarkson read Morning Prayer, Evening Prayer, or Holy Communion at this midafternoon service, but he must have read one of these.

Three months later, on his first Sunday in Washington as president-elect, Lincoln attended another Episcopal church—Saint John's Episcopal near the

White House, the so-called Church of the Presidents. Arriving in the city in advance of his wife and sons after catching a night train from Philadelphia in a reluctant response to a reported assassination plot, Lincoln went with William H. Seward on the morning of February 24, 1861, to hear the celebrated Reverend Dr. Smith Pyne read either Morning Prayer or Holy Communion at an 11:00 service, the one where the reporter saw Lincoln reading along with the regular worshippers.[27]

By the time the two men went to church together, Seward had accepted Lincoln's offer to serve as secretary of state. No other contemporary would come close to matching the influence of Secretary Seward on Lincoln's presidential writings, from the Inaugural Address through all the proclamations that the two jointly issued from 1861 until Lincoln's death in 1865. These proclamations echo, often word for word, the language of the Book of Common Prayer that Seward knew virtually by heart from all his years of active participation in the Episcopal church. Seward's reliance on the lovely words of the Prayer Book could only have encouraged Lincoln to read the little book ever more attentively and thus to expose it more and more to his phenomenal memory. Secretary of the Treasury Salmon Chase and Secretary of the Navy Gideon Welles were also active members of the Episcopal church. In addition to these three Episcopalians in his cabinet, John Hay, Lincoln's assistant personal secretary, provides evidence in his personal diary that he was attending an Episcopal church near the White House around the time of the Gettysburg Address. Hay's entry for October 4, 1863, reads, "Went to the Episcopal church this morning, A. L. & I," referring to his brother Augustus Leonard and to a church that seems to have been already familiar. His November 26 entry, recorded just days after the Gettysburg Address, reads, "I heard a sermon from Dr. Hall in which he argued that our national troubles originated from a spirit of anarchy—that the affliction will not have been in vain if the war begets reverence for law."[28] Dr. Hall was almost certainly the Reverend Dr. Charles Hall of the Church of the Epiphany on G Street near Fourteenth Street, which is not quite as close to the White House as Saint John's but still within easy walking distance. Hay's omission of a first name suggests that he was already familiar with the rector and that the Church of the Epiphany was his church of choice at the time.

Lincoln heard Dr. Pyne, the Saint John's rector, conduct services on at least two other occasions. In the East Room of the White House on May 25, 1861, Pyne served as the lead minister at the funeral of Colonel E. Elmer Ellsworth, who had been shot dead by the proprietor of the Marshall House in Alexandria, Virginia, for tearing down a secessionist flag. Pyne read the service for the Burial of the Dead over the body of Colonel Ellsworth, a dear friend of Lincoln's. On December 10 of the same year, Lincoln and his wife attended the wedding of Captain Charles Griffin and Sarah "Sally" Sprigg, daughter of a former governor of Maryland.

There Dr. Pyne read the same service for the Solemnization of Marriage that the Lincolns had heard pronounced at their own marriage in Springfield many years before.[29] Nor was this the only Episcopal marriage that Lincoln attended in 1861. On May 16, while Mrs. Lincoln was visiting in New York, the president attended Trinity Episcopal Church, where Dr. Clement Butler performed the marriage of Miss M. G. Bradley to Lt. Lorenzo Thomas Jr., whose father, Thomas Sr., was serving as a Union general.[30]

Less than two months after Lincoln's first attendance at Saint John's with Seward, another Episcopal minister from the Washington area attracted attention in a very different way from the eloquent and entertaining Dr. Pyne. The *New York Tribune* reported on June 10, 1861: "In Christ Church, at Alexandria, today the Reverend Cornelius B. Walker, a Disunionist, preached a strong Secession sermon, significantly omitting the prayer for the President of the United States from the regular service." It was not long before the Reverend Walker departed Alexandria for a church in Henrico, Virginia, behind Confederate lines. But the priest's refusal to pray for the President of the United States in a suburb so close to Washington that its steeples and towers could be seen from the White House was an act of supreme defiance that would be repeated countless times by Episcopal priests throughout the war.

Early the next year, in another Episcopal church in Alexandria, a priest named Kensey Johns Stewart repeated the same defiant act on February 9, 1862, and was arrested for it. The *Washington National Intelligencer* was one of several newspapers to report the story, most of them misspelling the offender's name: "The Rev. Mr. Steward, the Episcopal Minister at Alexandria, who refuses to pray for the President, as is prescribed in the regular forms of his church, has been arrested for treason." After his arrest by a Union officer and a brief detainment, Stewart moved to Richmond and became a chaplain in the Confederate army. According to Edward Steers Jr., "In March of 1863, Stewart traveled to England where he spent a year putting together a special edition of the Episcopal Prayer Book for the Confederacy in conjunction with the Reverend Robert Gatewood, who later became head of the Confederate army's intelligence office."[31] This Confederate edition replaced the Prayer for the President of the United States with a Prayer for the President of the Confederate States. In *Come Retribution: The Confederate Secret Service and the Assassination of Abraham Lincoln*, William E. Tidwell provides evidence that Stewart may later have worked with John Wilkes Booth on a plot to kidnap Lincoln.[32]

Stewart's arrest by military authorities in Alexandria for refusing to say the prayer for the president became part of a familiar pattern that would continue throughout the war. As the Union Army reclaimed formerly Confederate cities and towns, similar incidents occurred in New Orleans, Louisiana, and Natchez, Mississippi, in 1862 and in Pine Bluff, Arkansas, and Portsmouth, Virginia, in

1863. The 1863 incidents occurred just two months before the Gettysburg Address. In this way, Lincoln was reminded again and again throughout the war of a prayer in the Book of Common Prayer that represented one of its most emotional and divisive issues. The issue became so inflamed that there came a time when Union newspapers treated as hard news the simple *reinstatement* of the old prayer in Southern churches. Thus on November 7, 1863, less than two weeks before Lincoln rose to speak at Gettysburg, John Forney's *Washington Chronicle* reported:

> On last Sunday regular Episcopal services were held in St. Paul's Church, Norfolk, Virginia, in which, of course, the President of the United States was prayed for. Two weeks previously a like service was held in Portsmouth, Virginia. These were the first occasions on which the prayer for the President of the United States had been used in the services in these cities since the passage of the secession ordinance.

The "of course" in the opening line is an index to how familiar the issue of the prayer for the president had become in a nation where Episcopalians made up but a tiny fraction of the total population.

A personal tragedy from the same month as Stewart's arrest provided Lincoln yet another link with the Episcopal church. On February 20, 1862, the Lincolns' ten-year-old son, Willie, the apple of every eye that knew him, died after weeks of suffering from what the local newspapers described as typhoid. Soon afterward, the Lincolns were visited in the White House and comforted by an Episcopal minister with a national reputation, Francis Vinton of Trinity Church in Manhattan. Among many distinctions, the Reverend Dr. Vinton was a leading authority on the Prayer Book and often preached on it. He would later end his long and distinguished career as a professor of ecclesiastical polity and canon law at General Seminary in New York. After visiting with the first family, Vinton sent the Lincolns copies of a number of his sermons, for which Mrs. Lincoln thanked him with a note written on White House stationery on April 13, 1862:

> Mrs Lincoln returns Rev Dr. Vinton's, interesting sermons, with her sincere thanks for his kind consideration.
> She asks his acceptance of a bouquet, and hopes the acquaintance so agreably [*sic*] commenced, may be renewed ere long.[33]

Personal tragedy was soon followed by public. Just two weeks after the death of Willie, another untimely death took Lincoln to Washington's Episcopal Church of the Epiphany, the church sometimes attended by John Hay. The first general to lay down his life for the Union was the young, handsome, hard-drinking Frederick Lander, almost as famous for his marriage to the enormously popular English actress Jean Margaret Davenport as for his heroic, gravity-defying ride down Talbott's Hill in the first land engagement of the war at Philippi, Virginia.

Lander was only forty years old when he died from a combination of wounds, disease, and alcohol. On March 6, 1862, Lincoln viewed the general's body at the home of Treasury Secretary Chase and then attended the young hero's funeral at the Church of the Epiphany, where Bishop Thomas Clark of Rhode Island recited that beautiful service from the Prayer Book called the Burial of the Dead.

The following year, during the very month when Lincoln first wrote and delivered the Gettysburg Address, two other events called his special attention to the Episcopal church. One was the wedding of Chase's bright and beautiful daughter Kate, who married Senator William Sprague of Rhode Island at her father's Washington home on November 10, 1863. There Lincoln heard Rhode Island Bishop Clark, the same bishop who had presided at General Lander's funeral, read the Form of Solemnization of Matrimony in what the *Washington Star* of November 11 called "the chaste, beautiful, and impressive language of the Episcopal faith." Just a week and a day before the Chase-Sprague wedding, the Lincolns had celebrated their own twenty-first anniversary of a marriage that had been conducted to the very same language.

The second event was a huge, front-page article on November 7 in the *Washington Chronicle*, owned and published by Lincoln's friend and supporter John Forney, a Pennsylvanian who also owned and edited the *Philadelphia Press* and worked a third job as Lincoln's hand-picked Secretary of the United States Senate. This article that ran to over thirty-three hundred words was a public letter from a group of Pennsylvania Episcopal priests strongly objecting to a pamphlet called *Bible View of Slavery*—a defense of slavery and secession composed by Episcopal Bishop John Henry Hopkins of Vermont, printed in New York, and distributed in their own state. An excellent summary of the Hopkins controversy appears in a pamphlet of November 12, 1863, written by Columbia College professor Henry Drisler and published by the Loyal Publication Society, a unionist group in New York City.

> The "Bible View of Slavery" is the title of an essay by Bishop Hopkins, of Vermont, reissued in a pamphlet of sixteen pages, by an association for the "Diffusion of Political Knowledge," in this city, to influence the recent election in Pennsylvania. Though professing only to bring forward the Biblical arguments in defence of slavery, it yet discusses political subjects, drawing an unfavorable picture of the immorality and crime of our free Northern States, as contrasted with the moral purity and primitive simplicity of the slave-holding Southern States. The value of its political teachings, with its bitter denunciation of the doctrines of the Declaration of Independence, filling four and a half of its sixteen pages, has been already passed upon by the people of Pennsylvania. Its attempt to press Holy Scripture into the cause of a system of tyranny almost unequalled in the history of our race, and founded on violence and robbery—a system which, frowned upon by the almost

universal reprobation of the Christian world, sets itself in defiant opposition to and raises its rebellious hand against the duly constituted authorities, has called forth the indignant protest of the noble Bishop of Pennsylvania, in whose diocese it was circulated.[34]

Drisler says in a note at the end of his own pamphlet that he has located a copy of Hopkins's 1861 pamphlet and can personally confirm that this includes a case for Southern secession that was silently cut from the Bishop's recent redaction for the people of Pennsylvania.

Seven Episcopal priests from Pennsylvania, speaking for many others in support of their own bishop, Alonzo Potter, who had objected to Hopkins' pamphlet before being counterattacked by his colleague, wrapped up their three-thousand-word letter in Forney's *Washington Chronicle* of November 7 with this eloquent conclusion:

It is the misfortune of some men that they never change. They learn nothing from the unfolding of Divine Providence. Not only the principles, but the policies of the past they hold sacred. But although they refuse to recognize the progress of mankind, they do often present aspects of character amazingly diverse. Far be it from me to allege that the Bishop of Vermont is of that cast-iron mould; but surely no man ever presented greater contrast of character than he when descending from the pulpit, where, with silvery voice and apostolic look, and benignant spirit, he has spoken of the law of Jesus, he enters into his study, and, with all the subtlety of a casuist, proceeds to defend out of the Bible a cruel system of bondage, in which human beings, sprinkled with the blood of Christ, are bought and sold, regardless of family ties, corrupted at will, beaten without measure or redress, at the hands of their fellow-Christians. They, who have known and honored and loved this golden-mouthed preacher, on witnessing, and being made to feel in their own pastoral spheres, this strange and cruel perversion of his noble powers, can but retort upon him his Virgilian phrase, "Quanto Mutatus subtilo," and protest against an attempt so "unworthy the servant of Jesus Christ," which they have always accounted him to be.

The protest does not impugn the Christian character of Bishop Hopkins, nor assert that he has consciously or with malice prepense committed an unworthy act. Christian men, in the infirmity of their carnal nature, do, from time to time, deeds over which angels weep, and sometimes, under a mental delusion, persist in them and justify them for a while without making shipwreck of faith and a good conscience. They who protested against the Bishop's missive as out of place in this diocese, and declared his attempts to advocate slavery as it exists in the cotton States to be, in their judgment, unworthy of any servant of Jesus Christ, expressed but their opinion of this individual act, not of the man from whom it proceeded, nor of the motive which prompted him to do it.

There can be no doubt that Forney had a copy of Hopkins' pamphlet before publishing this attack upon it, for even at his most partisan and pro-Lincoln, he was always a first-rate journalist. This means that Lincoln himself had access to the same pamphlet.

Before the two bishops had begun to attack one another's positions on slavery, Hopkins and Potter had both served as priests in Pennsylvania. In 1845, when Potter was made bishop of that diocese (an honor for which Hopkins was almost chosen), the bishop of Vermont had been invited to preach the sermon at Potter's consecration. In this sermon, Hopkins set forth his own conservative and hierarchical beliefs first in his choice of topic, *Episcopal Government*, and then in his citing of "our doctrine that the bishop is designed to govern," from which it follows, said Hopkins, that "those who disobey their bishop and separate from him, without just cause, are guilty of schism, which is one of the greatest crimes of which a [C]hristian can be guilty."[35]

Since the beginning of the 1850s, Hopkins had been writing books and pamphlets defending another kind of hierarchy—slavery—and the closely linked doctrine of the right of individual states to secede from the Union. His most recent work on that controversial issue, his 1861 *Bible View of Slavery* reissued in Pennsylvanian in 1863, had been paid for and distributed by the Copperhead Democrats of that state. Potter and the other priests who objected to that document knew that it was being circulated in the hope that it would help to elect a Democratic governor of that state in October 1863. Democrat George Woodward, a foe of conscription, was challenging Republican incumbent Andrew Curtin, a strong supporter of Lincoln's position on the war. Ten years later, in 1873, John Henry Hopkins Jr. would publish a biography of his father that fully acknowledged this political purpose behind the distribution of the pamphlet while denying that Bishop Hopkins harbored any such motive himself:

> A Churchman was the Democratic candidate for Governor of Pennsylvania in the October election, and the Churchmen among his prominent supporters were flooding the State with Bishop Hopkins's *Bible View of Slavery*. If—as was evident—*they* thought this to be a good electioneering document for their party—though never so intended by its author—it is no wonder that the Republicans looked at it in the same light exactly: and nothing could be thought of more likely to outweigh the prestige of a Bishop, than to enlist the services of another Bishop on the opposite side.[36]

Potter was the bishop whose prestige and whose protest against Bishop Hopkins' tract led to the article in Forney's newspaper just days before the Gettysburg Address.

In his *Bible View of Slavery*, Hopkins attacked a whole list of what he considered pernicious and wrong-headed ideas.

First on this list stand the propositions of the far-famed Declaration of Independence, "that all men are created equal; that they are endowed by their Creator
with certain unalienable rights; that among these are life, liberty, and the pursuit
of happiness." These statements are here called "self-evident truths." But with due
respect to the celebrated names which are appended to this document, I have never
been able to comprehend that they are "truths" at all.[37]

Later evidence will show that Hopkins took his contemptuous use of the word
"proposition" for those "truths" described as "self-evident" in the Declaration
of Independence directly from the writings of John C. Calhoun, the man from
whom Lincoln himself would borrow the word "proposition" to characterize this
crucial phrase from the Declaration that "all men are created equal." The difference, of course, is that Bishop Hopkins repeated Calhoun's word with the same
condescension and contempt as Calhoun himself, whereas in the Gettysburg
Address, Lincoln transformed the very same word into something extraordinarily
quiet, contemplative, and beautiful.

Clearly, then, Lincoln was exposed to the Episcopal Church and its Prayer
Book almost from the moment he met his future wife, and this exposure only
intensified once he became president, moved to Washington, and began to work
with Seward and other Episcopalians in his cabinet. In its 1828 edition, the Prayer
Book contains 364 pages, most of these devoted to hymns, to daily and seasonal
prayers, and to Bible passages that Lincoln would already have known. The most
interesting of those 364 pages are the 95 devoted to 18 services—an average of
about five pages per service, a bite-sized bit of reading easily chewed and swal-
lowed during a boring sermon—and the 15 pages of the Catechism and Articles
of Religion that appear alongside these services. It would have been the most
natural thing in the world for Lincoln the voracious reader to have read these
most interesting pages during idle moments in services, as for example when
rows were slowly emptying for members to take communion at the church altar.
Certainly Lincoln would have become familiar with the titles of services just
from opening or browsing the Prayer Book, services that he could have returned
to as the need arose. We shall see just how familiar Lincoln came in time to be
with phrases that he would precisely echo in the Gettysburg Address. A number
of these phrases from the Prayer Book appear nowhere at all in the King James
Bible. However and whenever he learned the words and cadences of the Book of
Common Prayer, for the first or final time, Lincoln was always predisposed to
learn whatever he learned for the long haul.

Although my own approach to Lincoln's use of the Prayer Book is very different
from that of previous scholars and was formed before I had any knowledge of them,
the two I have discovered who ever saw any connection between Lincoln's writings
and the Prayer Book ought to be noted in the interest of full disclosure and accor-
dance of full credit. The first to find the Prayer Book a possible influence on some of

Lincoln's writing—though, oddly enough, not on the Gettysburg Address—ended by questioning more than affirming the Prayer Book, at least as a *fully conscious* influence. This was Daniel Kilham Dodge, who in 1924 wrote a pocket-sized book called *Abraham Lincoln: Master of Words*. Dodge located the influence of the Prayer Book, such as it was, only in Lincoln's presidential proclamations:

> The two literary influences that appear in the proclamations are the Bible and the Book of Common Prayer. As we have already seen, the first influence is not new but appears at all periods of Lincoln's writings, private as well as public. The second seems to be confined wholly to this one class of writings, belonging to the presidential period.

After rejecting the possibility that Secretary of State Seward, an active Episcopalian, may have influenced the language of these proclamations—a rejection that later and unimpeachable evidence will clearly prove wrong—Dodge staggered toward an uncertain conclusion, assuming yet another "less than conscious" Lincoln whose memory was not even ordinary, much less photographic:

> It is not at all unlikely that Lincoln often failed to realize that he was using the words of the Prayer Book when apparently quoting from it. The phrases had probably lodged themselves in his memory during some church service, to be drawn upon later at the proper time. It is easy, too, to exaggerate the extent of an apparent literary influence and to refer to it features that really proceed from other sources. The habit, for example, of using words in pairs, which the proclamations show in common with the Prayer Book, may have been suggested by the formal language of the law.

The examples provided by Dodge so that "the reader may decide for himself" include a proclamation from August 12, 1861, for a national day of fasting, which begins, "And whereas it is fit and becoming in all people, at all times, to acknowledge and revere the supreme government of God."[38]

A more recent scholar than Professor Dodge, Philip B. Kunhardt Jr., has revisited the same issue in *A New Birth of Freedom: Lincoln at Gettysburg* (1983) and come to a more positive conclusion about the possible influence of the Prayer Book on Lincoln. All punctuation, italics, and the parenthetical "italics added" are Kunhardt's own:

> Here was his inclination, during his presidency, to couple words, a style of repetition straight out of the Prayer Book. "To *confess* and *deplore*" was a good example (italics added). "To pray with all *fervency* and *contrition*" . . . "remembrance of our own *faults* and *crimes*" . . . "by the *labors* and *sufferings* of our fathers." In his recent establishment of a Thanksgiving Day, Lincoln had used the same technique: "to *set apart* and *observe*." . . . "a day of *Thanksgiving* and *Praise*." Today [the day

of the Gettysburg Address] he echoed the style and strength of the Prayer Book again: "*so conceived* and *so dedicated*"; "*fitting* and *proper*"; "*little note* nor *long remember.*"[39]

Both scholars confine the possible echoes largely—in Kunhardt's case, exclusively—to these doubled phrases. Unlike Kunhardt, Dodge was never able to make up his mind whether Lincoln was even echoing the Prayer Book in the first place and if he *was*, whether he was echoing it in full consciousness of his source.

No default position is more favored by scholars in the arts and humanities than that of the "unconscious writer" who somehow manages to reflect the culture of his time but is declared non compos mentis when it comes to consciously and precisely echoing a particular work of literature, even when there is no reason to doubt that the writer knew the work in question perfectly well and even when the internal parallels appear far too precise to be accounted for by mere chance. Long past the days of Professor Dodge, this predisposition has been reinforced by those "postmodernist" and "deconstructionist" theories that proclaim authorial intentions and textual meanings to be indeterminable or unknowable. In "Remember the Reader" from the *Chronicle Review* of December 19, 2008, Rita Felski rightly questions the contemporary theory that all texts are "fundamentally unknowable"[40] but omits the logical argument that if the theory is true, then the theory itself, being a text, is fundamentally unknowable. Consider that if all texts are fundamentally unknowable, it follows that what a text *seems* to say has no greater claim to truth or legitimacy than what that text seems *not* to say. Thus, "all texts are fundamentally knowable" is a perfectly legitimate interpretation of "all texts are fundamentally unknowable." In short, the theory undermines or negates itself. These silly, self-negating, and often self-serving theories—self-serving because their inventors fashion and hold the only keys that allow even partial escape from the gulags they themselves erect in the first place—would have amused the tough-minded Lincoln. His whole career as lawyer and political leader rested on the axiom that writers of wills and writers of constitutions have knowable intentions and that their documents have determinable meanings. Legal cases of many kinds, from the interpretation of wills and contracts to the interpretation of the United States Constitution, hinge on the reality of these very things, and so, too, do political issues, sometimes of the most critical kind. It was, after all, Lincoln's Cooper Union Address revealing the views and intentions of the founding fathers with regard to slavery that had largely determined the outcome of the most important election in American history—a remarkable sequence of events remarkably well covered in Harold Holzer's *Lincoln at Cooper Union: The Speech That Made Abraham Lincoln President.*

No one, not even the most radical deconstructionist, has questioned that Lincoln knew the King James Bible. The King James provides even more of the allusive power packed into the Gettysburg Address than the Prayer Book. The entire address, from beginning to end, is built around the central metaphor that Christians perceive throughout the Bible. This is the metaphor of birth, death, and rebirth. This metaphor is a commonplace that all Christians agree upon, even when disagreeing intramurally about virtually everything else. Certainly Lincoln's audience at Gettysburg on November 19, 1863, would have found his birth-death-rebirth metaphor as familiar as any comparison he could possibly have chosen. As it happens, even to readers today who know little or nothing about the Bible, Lincoln is such a clear and forceful writer that he makes the basic meaning of the metaphor perfectly clear with the words "conceived," "brought forth," "gave their lives," and "new birth."

But the words *behind* those words—particularly the words of the King James Bible that he so precisely and so beautifully echoed—have an enormous bearing upon the range and depth of Lincoln's meanings. No writer ever loved literary allusion more than Lincoln, if one may judge from how often and how effectively he used it. Lincoln never seemed to aim at originality for its own sake. He desired always to echo and refashion the language of the past so as to reshape the way that his audience would see the present moment and envision the long future. What Lincoln did in echoing the Bible in the Gettysburg Address is no more plagiarism than his echoing of Theodore Parker in his "House Divided" speech. What he achieved was a supremely inspired example of literary allusion—the intentional echoing of familiar works that is practiced by all great writers in all ages. Lincoln knew that the central metaphor and meaning of Christianity are the birth, death, and resurrection of Jesus Christ, who, in the eyes of most of Lincoln's listeners, has atoned for the sins of the world and provided for the salvation of fallen humankind through grace. Lincoln also knew that by identifying the United States with the Messiah, he could present this nation as the chosen vessel for free and representative government. He knew that free and representative government was threatened with an untimely death but could now, on this consecrated battlefield, be reborn and reaffirmed in its most sacred principles, including that central principle so outrageous to so many of his political enemies in his own day—"that all men are created equal."

The present study is unconcerned with the question of whether Lincoln was ever a fully believing Christian except to note what is abundantly clear about so many issues surrounding this great man—that his own words on any subject dear to his own heart shed far more light than anyone else's before or since. In a handbill posted to the voters of his district in 1846 when he stood as a successful candidate for Congress, he declared, "That I am not a member of any Christian Church, is true; but I have never denied the truth of the Scriptures."[41] In his reply to the African American citizens of Baltimore who presented their Bible to him in September of 1864, he said, "All the good the Saviour gave to the world was communicated through this book. But for it we could not know right from wrong. All things most desirable for man's welfare, here and hereafter, are to be found portrayed in it."[42] In 1865, after Lincoln's death, Congressman Henry C. Deming recorded the words that Lincoln had shared with him on an unspecified occasion sometime between 1863, when Deming first met the president, and Lincoln's death on April 15, 1865: "When any church will inscribe over its altar, as its sole qualification for membership, the Savior's condensed statement of the substance of both law and gospel, 'Thou shalt love the Lord thy God with all thy heart, and with all thy soul, and with all thy mind, and thy neighbor as thyself,' that church will I join with all my heart and all my soul."[43] The present study focuses on the question of how Lincoln selected and reshaped the language that was most familiar to him and his audience on November 19, 1863, as a way of advancing the sacred principles of human freedom, human equality, and representative government in words that were as powerful and enduring as they were beautiful.

Birth and Rebirth

The Gettysburg Address

Fourscore and seven years ago our fathers brought forth upon this continent a new nation, conceived in liberty and dedicated to the proposition that all men are created equal. Now we are engaged in a great civil war, testing whether that nation, or any nation so conceived and so dedicated, can long endure. We are met on a great battle-field of that war. We are met to dedicate a portion of it as the final resting-place of those who here gave their lives that that nation might live. It is altogether fitting and proper that we should do this. But, in a larger sense, we cannot dedicate, we cannot consecrate, we cannot hallow this ground. The brave men, living and dead, who struggled here have consecrated it far above our poor power to add or detract. The world will little note nor long remember what we say here; but it can never forget what they did here. It is for us, the living, rather to be dedicated here to the unfinished work that they have thus far so nobly carried on. It is rather for us to be here dedicated to the great task remaining before us; that from these honored dead we take increased devotion to that cause for which they here gave the last full measure of devotion; that we here highly resolve that these dead shall not have died in vain; that the nation shall, under God, have a new birth of freedom; and that Governments of the people, by the people, and for the people, shall not perish from the earth.

—Abraham Lincoln, delivery text as written down by
Joseph Ignatius Gilbert of the Associated Press just after the speech[1]

The metaphor of birth and rebirth is the unifying and overarching metaphor of the Gettysburg Address. It dominates the best-known and best-loved sentences in the entire address—the first and the last—and influences all the smaller metaphors in between, like a supergiant star controlling the motions of all the less-powerful stars within its range. Just as Lincoln's final sentence will envision "a new birth of freedom" and a newly rededicated nation blessed with the kind of government that "shall not perish from this earth," so his first sentence invokes the birth of a "new nation" in the metaphor of a newborn child. In that great opening sentence, the birth of this nation is specifically linked to the birth of Jesus Christ as described in the lovely, familiar words of the Gospel of Matthew 1:18–25:

> Now the birth of Jesus Christ was on this wise: When as his mother Mary was espoused to Joseph, before they came together, she was found with child of the Holy Ghost.
>
> Then Joseph her husband, being a just man, and not willing to make her a public example, was minded to put her away privily.
>
> But while he thought on these things, behold, the angel of the Lord appeared unto him in a dream, saying, Joseph, thou son of David, fear not to take unto thee Mary thy wife: for that which is conceived in her is of the Holy Ghost.
>
> And she shall bring forth a son, and thou shalt call his name JESUS: for he shall save his people from their sins.
>
> Now all this was done, that it might be fulfilled which was spoken of the Lord by the prophet, saying,
>
> Behold, a virgin shall be with child, and shall bring forth a son, and they shall call his name Emmanuel, which being interpreted is, God with us.
>
> Then Joseph being raised from sleep did as the angel of the Lord had bidden him, and took unto him his wife:
>
> And knew her not till she had brought forth her newborn son: and he called his name JESUS.

The key words Lincoln echoed from the Bible are Matthew's "conceived" and "brought forth," themselves echoing the Old Testament words of the prophet Isaiah: "Behold, a virgin shall conceive, and bear a son, and shall call his name Immanuel" (7:14), "And I will bring forth a seed out of Jacob" (65:9). In an age when most of his listeners would have known the King James Bible almost as well as he, the meaning of Lincoln's opening sentence could not have been clearer that day in late November 1863—that the United States has been "conceived" and "brought forth" as the savior of liberty, equality, and representative government for the entire world.

The same two verbs appear in Saint Luke's equally familiar description of the birth of Jesus when the angel of the Lord tells Mary: "And, behold, thou shalt conceive in thy womb, and bring forth a son, and shalt call his name JESUS" (1:31). But the Gospel of Luke adds homelier details than those found in the Gospel of Matthew: "And she brought forth her firstborn son, and wrapped him in swaddling clothes, and laid him in a manger; because there was no room for them in the inn" (2:7). Luke's words have the additional felicity of associating the birth of Jesus with the poor and lowly of this earth. The book of Isaiah, that most Messianic of all the Old Testament prophecies, overflows with the idea that the Messiah will appear first as a common and suffering man: "He is despised and rejected of men; a man of sorrows, and acquainted with grief" (53:3). Jesus himself, born in a stable to humble people, said again and again in the New Testament that the least of this earth may rise to become the greatest: "The stone which the builders rejected, the same is become the head of the corner" (Matt. 21:42). "So the last shall be first, and the first last" (Matt. 20:16). If a baby whose crib was nothing but a manger in a stable could become the savior of the world, is it unimaginable that a man born in a log cabin could become President of the United States or that a whole class of people born as slaves could become free or that a nation torn by civil war could restore itself and, at least in the preservation of its rare and precious form of government, never perish from the earth?

There can be no doubt that Lincoln, throughout his years in the White House, specifically connected the birth of Jesus with the birth of the United States. Between April 15, 1861, and April 11, 1865, a period covering almost exactly forty-eight months, the president issued exactly forty-eight official proclamations, an average of one a month. All except one—a sort of bookkeeping proclamation of April 23, 1863, that cancelled Lincoln's signature on a contract because the U.S. seal had been omitted—conclude with the same dating system that is illustrated by the very first, a Proclamation Calling Militia and Convening Congress: "In Witness Whereof I have hereunto set my hand, and caused the Seal of the United States to be affixed. Done at the City of Washington this fifteenth day of April in the year of our Lord One thousand, Eight hundred and Sixty-one, and of the Independence of the United States the Eighty-fifth. Abraham Lincoln."[2] In addition, the same system of dual dating appeared on a frequently reused Draft Order from June of 1863 that was *not* labeled a proclamation, an order that Lincoln signed many times.[3]

The president's unusual choice of a subject for the biblical verb "brought forth" is "our fathers." The usual subject for this common verb in the Bible and Shakespeare and everywhere else is the *mother* of the child. Mothers "bring forth." Fathers "beget." One mother after another brings forth a child in the Bible. Luke uses the very same word in his account of the birth of John the Baptist, the only child of Mary's sister Elisabeth. "Now Elisabeth's full time came that she should be delivered; and she brought forth a son" (Luke 1:57), just a short while before Mary "brought forth her firstborn son" (Luke 2:7). In the very first appearance of "brought forth" in the entire Bible, the earth appears metaphorically as a mother: "Let the earth bring forth the living creature" (Gen. 1:24). In the prophetic book of Isaiah, God's chosen nation of Zion appears in the same metaphor: "as soon as Zion travailed, she brought forth her children" (66:8). In Lincoln's favorite Shakespearean play, Macbeth counsels Lady Macbeth, "Bring forth men children only" (1.7.72).[4] Lincoln's use of "fathers" as the subject of "brought forth" is, therefore, most unusual and perhaps even unique in the literature of the English language. This is a clear and shining example of how Lincoln, even when highly traditional in his choice of words, is able to use these traditional words in strikingly original ways.

And yet Lincoln's association was not formed from thin air. There *is* a biblical connection between "our fathers" and "brought forth." With Lincoln's incredibly detailed knowledge of scripture, he would certainly have known that elsewhere in the King James Bible, the phrase "bring forth" is used in the sense of "to save" or "to deliver." It appears with precisely this meaning in 1 Samuel 12:8, where Moses and Aaron are remembered for delivering the fathers of the children of Israel out of Egypt and into the Promised Land: "When Jacob was come into Egypt, and your fathers cried unto the Lord, then the Lord sent Moses and Aaron, which brought forth your fathers out of Egypt, and made them dwell in this place." What makes Lincoln's use of the phrase so striking and unusual is that he *combines* the two meanings, the meaning of birth and the meaning of delivery. And this combination fits perfectly with the story of the birth of Jesus.

On the literal level, Lincoln's "our fathers" refers to the founding fathers of our own nation who wrote and signed the Declaration of Independence. But the phrase works equally well in terms of Lincoln's underlying biblical metaphor, which is the birth of the Messiah. The New Testament makes clear that Jesus had two fathers, one earthly and one heavenly. When he was twelve years old, his parents took him to Jerusalem for Passover. As Mary and Joseph left for home, Jesus remained in the temple talking with the "doctors" (Luke 2:46) until his parents missed him on the road and returned to Jerusalem.

> And when they saw him, they were amazed: and his mother said unto him, Son, why hast thou dealt with us? behold, thy father and I have sought thee sorrowing.
> And he said unto them, How is it that ye sought me? wist ye not that I must be about my Father's business? (Luke 2:48–49)

Here Mary refers to Joseph as "thy father." Yet when Jesus refers to "my Father's business," he is clearly referring to his *heavenly* Father. Each of these fathers has in some sense "brought forth" Jesus. His heavenly Father decreed that Mary should become pregnant by the Holy Spirit and bring forth the Son of God. His earthly father, Joseph, helped Mary in every way he could with her pregnancy and birth after learning that she had not been unfaithful to him with another man. The Bible suggests that until after the birth of Jesus, Mary and Joseph were alone in a stable behind the inn in Bethlehem, so that Joseph was the only person who could have delivered the baby. After that, he became the child's protector as well. His first act of protection was to take mother and son into Egypt in order to escape the decree of King Herod ordering the death of all newborn males throughout Judea. In short, Jesus was "brought forth" by his plural fathers just as this nation was brought forth by ours.

Even to those who cannot or will not see these biblical allusions, Lincoln's reference to the birth of this nation is perfectly clear from "conceived" and "brought forth." The *New York World*, a Democratic newspaper, poked sarcasm at the president's "obstetric analogies"[5] while saying nothing of his biblical allusions. But to anyone then or now with an open mind and a thimbleful of biblical knowledge, Lincoln's opening sentence of the Gettysburg Address specifically invokes the birth of Jesus Christ as recorded in the King James Bible. This invocation is reinforced at every turn. One of Lincoln's greatest gifts as a writer was his ability to construct sentences that rise with what seems like inevitability toward their most emphatic and important words and phrases. Thus in his magnificent opening sentence, the verb forms "brought forth," "conceived," and "dedicated" are positioned so that they receive an irresistible emphasis from the reading or speaking voice. It is simply impossible to pronounce that opening sentence without feeling one's voice rise and strengthen to italicize these key and vital words. The same is true when the voice arrives at that famous ringing phrase from the Declaration of Independence that closes the sentence—a phrase underscoring the idea of birth with the word "created" and ending with the most emphasized word of all, "equal." But there is one surprising phrase that receives a rhetorical emphasis for reasons that are not so obvious. This is the little phrase "new nation" in the very heart of the sentence. The word "new" is so small and unobtrusive, the word "nation" is so familiar, and the two are joined so skillfully and gracefully by alliteration that one must ask *why* Lincoln gave this little pair such a conspicuous location and so much unavoidable emphasis. The answer to this question will perhaps reveal as much about Lincoln's style as his more obvious reliance on the patently biblical words "conceived" and "brought forth." Before looking at the answer, it is important to insist and underscore that Lincoln had choices. Instead of "nation," he could have chosen "country," with exactly the same denotative meaning, exactly the same number of syllables for the same rhythm, exactly the same alliterative tie to a word right next to it ("conceived"), plus the additional attraction of echoing the highly popular anthem of "America" that Americans had been singing since 1831, its first verse famously beginning with "My country, 'tis of thee" and its last verse famously beginning with "Our fathers' God, to thee, Author of liberty."

But the choice of "a new nation" better supports Lincoln's central metaphor of a newborn child and a new birth. Lincoln did not have to be a Latin scholar to suspect or surmise that the word "nation" shares the same etymological base as "natal," "native," and "nativity"—a base clearly connected with the idea of birth. The very first appearance of nation in the King James Bible undergirds this connection: "Now the Lord had said unto Abram, Get thee out of thy country, and from thy kindred, and from thy father's house, unto a land that I will shew thee. And I will make of thee a great nation" (Gen. 12:1–2). Abram, whose name

44

God changes in Genesis 17:5 to Abraham, meaning "father of many nations," is led by the Lord to leave his own "country," a geographical term that means the land lying *contra*—against or opposite—some other land, in order to form a new "nation" made up of his own "seed" (Gen. 12:7), meaning his own descendants or his own family. The word *new* can only reinforce this connection. Later in the address, Lincoln will exploit the connection even more explicitly by declaring that "this nation shall have a new birth of freedom." The birth of this nation in the opening sentence refers to its legal and physical creation in 1776, whereas the "new birth" of the closing sentence is clearly a spiritual event that is prophesied and hoped for but has not come to pass. As for the "new" of "new nation" and "new birth," this is a word as spiritually large as it is physically small, appearing time and again in the Bible as one of the key words and symbols of Christianity. To believing Christians, Jesus is the author of the "new covenant" (Heb. 8:8, 8:13, 13:24), the savior who died to make what the Book of Common Prayer calls a "new birth" possible for a "new creature" (Gal. 6:15). Jesus recited to his disciples at the Last Supper the famous words that would be forever repeated in the ritual of the Lord's Supper: "For this is my blood of the new testament, which is shed for many for the remission of sins" (Matt. 26:28). In the heart of Lincoln's first sentence appears the word "new," and in the heart of his second, the word "test-ing." One of the meanings of "testing" is "the making of a will" or testament.[6] Both "new" and "testing" receive unusual emphasis because of their locations and Lincoln's poetical rhythms. The overwhelming majority of Lincoln's audi-ence would have read the Old and New Testaments of the King James Bible all their lives and would have shared in countless communion services where the wine forever symbolizes Jesus's "blood of the new testament." Such an audience would have been primed to hear "testament" and "new testament" at the slightest suggestion, and Lincoln's suggestion was more than slight. The biblical promise "Behold, I make all things new" (Rev, 21:5) is a promise that awaiting all believers after their new birth is a "new Jerusalem" (Rev. 3:12, 21:2) or "a new heaven and a new earth" (Rev. 21:1). Thus the opening of the Gettysburg Address specifically associates the "new nation" of the United States with Mary's newborn son, with the "new testament" he has given to all heirs and believers in his resurrection and eternally commended to them in his communion service, and with "a new heaven and a new earth" that they shall one day inherit.

The combining of "new" and "nation" into a single phrase never occurs in the King James Bible, not one time, but it *does* famously occur in another source that Lincoln knew equally well—Shakespeare's *Henry VIII*. Just weeks before deliv-ering the Gettysburg Address, Lincoln wrote to a Shakespearean actor named James Hackett: "Some of Shakespeare's plays I have never read; while others I have gone over perhaps as frequently as any unprofessional reader. Among the latter are Lear, Richard Third, Henry Eighth, Hamlet, and especially Macbeth."[7]

Henry VIII is, then, one of only five Shakespearean plays identified by Lincoln himself as among those he read the most and, therefore, knew the best. The phrase "new nations" appears in a stirring vision that Shakespeare places in the mouth of Thomas Cranmer, Archbishop of Canterbury and father of the Prayer Book, in the final scene of this play. Cranmer speaks stirringly of a golden age that will bless the whole world because of a child whom the archbishop is baptizing and christening in this very scene. This child is the future Queen Elizabeth, daughter of Henry VIII and Anne Boleyn. Cranmer prophesies in lines 34 to 56 of this final, defining scene that although Elizabeth herself will die a virgin without heirs, her ashes will, phoenix-like, raise up a great successor who will carry on her golden age and create "new nations":

> In her days every man shall eat in safety,
> Under his own vine, what he plants; and sing
> The merry songs of peace to all his neighbours:
> God shall be truly known: and those about her
> From her shall read the perfect ways of honour,
> And by those claim their greatness, not by blood.
> Nor shall this peace sleep with her: but as when
> The bird of wonder dies, the maiden phoenix,
> Her ashes new create another heir,
> As great in admiration as herself;
> So shall she leave her blessedness to one,
> When heaven shall call her from this cloud of darkness,
> Who from the sacred ashes of her honour
> Shall star-like rise, as great in fame as she was,
> And so stand fix'd: peace, plenty, love, truth, terror,
> That were the servants to this chosen infant,
> Shall then be his, and like a vine grow to him:
> Wherever the bright sun of heaven shall shine,
> His honour and the greatness of his name
> Shall be, and make new nations: he shall flourish,
> And, like a mountain cedar, reach his branches
> To all the plains about him: our children's children
> Shall see this and bless heaven.

Lincoln would instantly have seen that the most famous "new nation" created by Elizabeth's rising star of a successor, James I of the King James Bible, was the United States of America. Of the thirteen colonies from which the United States was formed, the two oldest—Virginia and Massachusetts, from which other colonies were later cut and formed—were established during James I's prosperous and memorable reign and later became birthplaces of the first six

American presidents. The first English settlement to survive in the new world was at Jamestown, Virginia, in 1607, honoring in its very name the two monarchs saluted and celebrated at the close of Shakespeare's *Henry VIII*.

There can be no doubt that Lincoln had applied his prodigious memory to the plays, scenes, and lines of Shakespeare as surely as he had to the books, chapters, and verses of the King James Bible. John T. Stuart, who knew Lincoln long and well, told Herndon after Lincoln's death: "Lincoln used to Carry around in the Circuit Court tramp with him say from 1846—to 1855. Euclid's Geometry—Shakespear: he could well repeat much of Shakespear." Another longtime friend, William G. Green, made the same point to Herndon: "By the by Shakespear—Burns & Byron were his favorite books. He nearly knew Shakespear by heart."[8]

But if "brought forth" and "conceived" are instant reminders of biblical accounts of the birth of Jesus, and "new nation" a more subtle biblical reference to Christian birth and rebirth, what is "dedicated"? The word appears many times in the King James Bible, but not one appearance relates to the birth of Jesus. Lincoln's literary source for this key word was not the Bible but the Book of Common Prayer. In a service called the Public Baptism of Infants, "dedicated" makes a resonant and memorable appearance that is perfectly appropriate on all counts. During this service, also known as christening, three godparents stand with the newborn child at the baptismal font. On behalf of the child, these three renounce "the devil and all his works" and declare their belief in "the Articles of the Christian faith." After they have done so, the priest holding the infant beside them declares that this child is here and now "dedicated" to God and to Christian principles: "Grant that whosoever is here dedicated to thee by our office and ministry, may also be endued with heavenly virtues, and everlastingly rewarded, through thy mercy, O blessed Lord God, who dost live and govern all things, world without end. *Amen.*" The *Oxford English Dictionary* cites this very sentence from Archbishop Cranmer's Prayer Book that first appeared in the mid-1500s as only the second use of the verb "dedicate" in the history of the English language. (Just a few years before Cranmer issued the Prayer Book, the verb was either coined or first recorded by another priest in the service of King Henry VIII, William Palsgrave, who tutored the king's children and in 1530 wrote, "I dedycate a church."[9]) Thus in Lincoln's opening metaphor, this nation was "conceived," then born or "brought forth," and finally "dedicated" in a service of baptism or christening. This nation was officially named—in Lincoln's metaphor, christened at its baptism—"The United States of America" by the document that made us a nation, the Declaration of Independence. Just as the service of baptism announces the "Articles of the Christian faith" as the principles to which the child is "dedicated," so the Declaration of Independence announces *its* principles as "self-evident truths." Chief among these and first to be named is that "all men are created equal."

47

At the time of Jesus, there was of course no infant baptism where children were officially named. When he was "about thirty years of age" (Luke 3:23) and at the very beginning of his ministry, Jesus was baptized by his cousin John the Baptist. But as a baby, Jesus underwent the ceremonial dedications appropriate for a Jewish male. The first of these—circumcision—has much in common with christening. "And when eight days were accomplished for the circumcising of the child, his name was called JESUS" (Luke 2:21). Just as Christian children are named at their baptism a few days after birth, so Jewish males at the time of Jesus were named at their circumcision a few days after birth. Another example is the circumcision of John the Baptist, who at the same age of eight days was given his father's name of Zacharias and then, at the insistence of his mother, "called John" instead (Luke 1:60). A second ceremony involving the baby Jesus was his visit to the temple some forty days after his birth—the waiting period prescribed by the Torah before the mother was purified after the birth of a male child. During this visit, a prophet named Simeon and a prophetess named Anna singled out Jesus to his parents and to the public as a child whose life was already dedicated to the Lord. Simeon called Jesus both "the Lord's Christ" (Luke 2:26) and "a light to lighten the Gentiles, and the glory of thy people Israel" (Luke 2:32). Anna, who was a "widow of about fourscore and four years" (Luke 2:37), "gave thanks likewise unto the Lord, and spake of him to all that looked for redemption in Jerusalem" (Luke 2:38). For all these reasons, the word "dedicated" resonates on many levels in the opening sentence of the Gettysburg Address. Just as the Messiah was conceived, brought forth, and then named and dedicated in certain ceremonies memorialized in the Bible, so the United States of America was conceived, brought forth, and then named and dedicated in the famous Declaration of Independence.

As always, Lincoln's use of words is precise. His words and context always point precisely to his sources. Thus, in his magnificent opening sentence, he uses "dedicated" from the Prayer Book to complete the metaphor of the conception-birth-baptism of this nation. The words "conceived" and "brought forth" are straight from the Bible, the word "dedicated" straight from the Prayer Book. Lincoln later echoes the full phrase from the service of baptism, "here dedicated," in his last and longest sentence of the Gettysburg Address. There it appears with yet another phrase precisely associated with baptism in the Prayer Book—"new birth." It may surprise those who know the Bible only in generalities that "new birth" appears *nowhere* in the King James Bible. Yet it makes two familiar appearances in the Prayer Book—familiar, that is, to all who learn their Catechism and Articles of Religion from this book. In the Catechism, baptism is explained as a sign and symbol of the candidate's spiritual death and rebirth: "A death unto sin, and a new birth unto righteousness; for, being by nature born in sin, and the children of wrath, we are hereby made the children of grace." The Articles

48

of Religion to which the godparents pledge their Christian faith as surrogates for the baptized child also include the identical phrase "new birth": "Baptism is not only a sign of profession, and mark of difference, whereby Christian men are discerned from others that be not christened; but it is also a sign of regeneration, or new birth."

In short, echoing two Gospels from the Bible plus the language of baptism from the Prayer Book, Lincoln precisely invokes two Christian metaphors in his magnificent opening sentence—conception-birth-baptism and birth-death-rebirth. The first metaphor necessarily implies the second, because the symbolic meaning of baptism to any Christian *is* birth, death, and rebirth. The believer, born in original sin, symbolically dies to his or her sin in the cleansing water, then rises to newness of life or rebirth. As Romans 6:4 puts it, "Therefore we are buried with him by baptism into death: that like as Christ was raised up from the dead by the glory of the Father, even so we also should walk in newness of life." Thus Lincoln's metaphor of birth, death, and rebirth binds together the entire Gettysburg Address, and nowhere is the metaphor more clearly stated than in the first sentence and the last. Appropriately, Lincoln's opening sentence focuses mainly upon birth and his closing sentence mainly upon rebirth or "new birth," as it is called in both the Catechism and the Articles of Religion. The two opening and the two closing sentences of the Gettysburg Address all contain the word "dedicated," and all are clearly constructed around the metaphor of birth, baptism, and rebirth.

Those who question whether the word "dedicated" was so closely tied to baptism that Lincoln would have consciously connected the two need only consult a service from the Book of Common Prayer called the Consecration of a Church or Chapel. This service was added to the American Prayer Book in 1799 and printed thereafter in all editions. The service uses "dedicated" as its key word, taken straight from the Public Baptism of Infants, for describing what happens in the sacrament of baptism. One whole section in the Consecration of a Church or Chapel is devoted to describing six sacraments, services, or events that would, in the natural course of things, be celebrated later in the newly consecrated house of worship. These six are baptism, confirmation, communion, preaching, matrimony, and thanksgiving. Here is the paragraph from the Consecration describing baptism, with emphasis added:

> REGARD, O Lord, the supplications of thy servants, and grant that whosoever shall be *dedicated* to thee in this house by baptism, may be sanctified by the Holy Ghost, delivered from thy wrath and eternal death, and received as a living member of Christ's Church, and may ever remain in the number of thy faithful children.

The word "dedicated" never appears in connection with the other five church events prayed for in the same service. In the Prayer Books of Lincoln's day, this

Consecration of a Church or Chapel and the earlier Public Baptism of Infants form two of the eighteen church services. Read in conjunction with one another, these two services provide the strongest internal evidence that "dedicated" was the single word most closely and traditionally associated with the service and sacrament of baptism.

Lincoln's metaphor of birth and christening for the creation of this nation by the Declaration of Independence was so natural in the context of his day that no one should be surprised to learn he was not even the first to use it. Lincoln's predisposition in all his speeches was to stitch and quilt them from words and ideas that were commonplace. The same metaphor had already been employed by Lincoln's polar opposite in all things political—John C. Calhoun. Lincoln and Calhoun differed in the fundamental principles of their political philosophies, even though both men had, for radically different reasons, opposed the Mexican War when Calhoun was a senator and Lincoln a representative in the Thirtieth Congress. What the two men had in common was that both were passionate, retentive readers and precise writers intent on saying whatever they had to say with clarity and conviction. In his last years, Calhoun attended the Episcopal Church in South Carolina even though he never formally joined it. Like Lincoln, he never joined *any* church or denomination. In his "Discourse on the Constitution and Government," composed in late 1849 and early 1850 during the last difficult months of his life and included in the collected *Works* that his friend, protégé, and editor Richard K. Cralle published in the early 1850s, Calhoun recorded these memorable words about his country:

> It dates its origin with the Declaration of Independence. That act is styled,—"The Unanimous Declaration of the thirteen United States of America." And here again, that there be no doubt how these States would stand to each other in the new condition in which they were about to be placed, it concluded by declaring,—"that these United Colonies are, and of right ought to be, free and independent States;" "and that, as free and independent States, they have full power to levy war, conclude peace, contract alliances, and to do all other acts and things which independent States may of right do." The "United States" is, then, the baptismal name of these States,—received at their birth;—by which they have ever since continued to call themselves; by which they have characterized their constitution, government and laws;—and by which they are known to the rest of the world.[10]

Whether Lincoln's opening metaphor was an echo of Calhoun's or simply a parallel to it, he was most certainly echoing Calhoun when he chose the most controversial word in his opening sentence and indeed in his entire address, the word "proposition." Chapter 8 details how this key and controversial word traces in a clear straight line to the great archangel of the Southern doctrines of nullification and secession.

Lincoln closes his address with the same metaphor with which he opens it—birth, baptism, and rebirth. But the baptism at the close of the Gettysburg Address is different from the baptism at the opening. The first baptism is for a newborn baby, a nation born on July 4, 1776. This first baptism or christening is invoked in the two opening sentences. The baptism invoked in the two closing sentences is for the same nation that has now grown up. Indeed, by November 19, 1863, this nation is showing signs of aging and wear that come with being four score and seven years of age and "engaged in a great civil war." According to one of the most famous and familiar passages in the King James Bible, Psalm 90:10, "The days of our years are threescore years and ten; and if by reason of strength they be fourscore years, yet is their strength labour and sorrow; for it is soon cut off, and we fly away." In Lincoln's extended metaphor, the "strength" of the United States by November 1863 has turned into "labour and sorrow," and the question has become whether our aging, wounded, and divided nation "can long endure." The baptism Lincoln invokes at the end of his immortal address is not by water but by fire. This baptism is just as biblical as baptism by water. It is a baptism first described by John the Baptist in the Gospel of Mark.

Baptizing multitudes of believers in the river Jordan, John one day announced another kind of baptism that would come from another person "mightier than I" (Mark 1:7): "I indeed have baptized you with water: but he shall baptize you with the Holy Ghost" (Mark 1:8). Later, when this person—Jesus—actually comes to be baptized, John announces that here at last is the man who holds the new power to baptize with the Holy Ghost. In the following quotation, emphasis has been added to the key word:

> And John bare record, saying, I saw the Spirit descending from heaven like a dove, and it abode upon him.
>
> And I knew him not: but he that sent me to baptize with water, the same said unto me, Upon whom thou shalt see the Spirit descending, and *remaining* on him, the same is he which baptizeth with the Holy Ghost.
>
> And I saw, and bare record that this is the Son of God. (John 1:32–34)

Earlier chapters in the present book have shown what a close reader of the Bible Lincoln always was and how he once focused his close reading specifically on the way that John baptized believers in the river Jordan. In the passage just quoted, Lincoln could not possibly have overlooked the word "remaining" in its one and only appearance in the entire New Testament of the King James Bible. In the Old Testament of the same Bible, the same word makes just over a dozen appearances. The first of these contributes dramatically to the weight and significance of its solitary New Testament appearance.

When the children of Israel travel from Egypt to the Promised Land, they stop or move according to the Lord's command. A cloud by day and a fire by night cover the tabernacle bearing the sacred ark of the Israelites: "So it was alway: the cloud covered it by day, and the appearance of fire by night" (Num. 9:16). Whenever the cloud lifted from the tabernacle, whether by day or by night, the children of Israel moved. Whenever it returned, they stopped. It is during this journey to the Promised Land, in Num. 9:22–23, that the word "remaining" appears for the very first time in the King James Bible, with emphasis added below:

> Or whether it were two days, or a month, or a year, that the cloud tarried upon the tabernacle, *remaining* thereon, the children of Israel abode in their tents, and journeyed not: but when it was taken up, they journeyed.
>
> At the commandment of the Lord they rested in the tents, and at the commandment of the Lord they journeyed.

To Christians, it is the Spirit of God—the Holy Spirit also known as the Third Person of the Trinity—that is "remaining" both in this Old Testament passage and in the New Testament passage where Jesus is baptized. The cloud or spirit *remaining* upon the tabernacle to direct the journey of the Israelites into the Promised Land is the same spirit *remaining* upon Jesus at his baptism in the one and only appearance of this crucial word in the New Testament. When Lincoln invokes "the great task *remaining* before us" in his magnificent closing sentence of the Gettysburg Address, he is clearly recalling both the biblical account of the Promised Land and the biblical account of the baptism of Jesus.

The Book of Common Prayer frequently uses the word "remain" with the same meaning and associations it has in the Bible. Six of the eighteen services in the Prayer Book, including Holy Communion and the Consecration of a Church or Chapel, have a closing blessing that focuses on the vibrant biblical word "remain": "The peace of God, which passeth all understanding, keep your hearts and minds in the knowledge and love of God, and of his Son, Jesus Christ our Lord: And the blessing of God Almighty, the Father, the Son, and the Holy Ghost, be amongst you, and remain with you always. *Amen.*" The same word was clearly a natural choice for Lincoln. He had used it with perfect appropriateness in the most beautiful speech he ever delivered that was not written out in advance, his farewell address at Springfield on February 11, 1861: "Trusting in Him, who can go with me, and remain with you and be every where for good, let us confidently hope that all will yet be well."[11]

Lincoln's "resting-place" for the Union dead originates in the same Old Testament story of the Israelites' journey to the Promised Land. The very first "resting place" in the King James Bible appears in connection with this story. The Israelites journey a symbolic three days from Mount Sinai to find their first "resting place": "And they departed from the mount of the Lord three days' journey: and the ark of the covenant of the Lord went before them in the three days' journey, to search out a resting place" (Num. 10:33). The same phrase appears in Isaiah's prophecy of the Promised Land of the Messiah: "And my people shall dwell in a peaceable habitation, and in sure dwellings, and in quiet resting places" (Isa. 32:18). For Christians, the ultimate resting place is the Promised Land of heaven: "Now therefore arise, O Lord God, into thy resting place . . . and let thy saints rejoice in goodness" (2 Chron. 6:41). Archbishop Cranmer used the very same phrasing to translate Psalm 132:8 for the Prayer Book: "Arise, O Lord, into thy resting-place." A similar phrase, "they may rest from their labours," appears in a vision of heaven in Revelation 14:13 and again in the Burial of the Dead.

The word "final" that modifies "resting-place" in the fourth sentence of the Gettysburg Address contrasts in fascinating ways with its synonym "last" in the tenth sentence. The English language abounds with more synonyms for common objects and ideas than any other language in the history of the world. This is because it is two languages merged into one by the Norman Conquest of England in 1066. This conquest grafted the French language onto the English, although the process would take about a century to complete, producing around 1150 what we now call Middle English. "Final" derives from French, and "last" from Anglo-Saxon, or Old English. Of any two synonyms, the native-English word is almost always the more common. Thus, in the King James Bible, "last" appears no fewer than eighty-one times as an adjective or a noun, whereas "final" never appears at all. "Final" also never appears in Shakespeare or *The Pilgrim's Progress*. The adverb form of "finally" makes only six appearances in the King James, one in *The Pilgrim's Progress*, and one in Shakespeare—in "finally and lastly" from a comical speech by a character in *The Merry Wives of Windsor* (1.1.130–31) who gets laughs with fancy words and redundant phrases. Not one of the six appearances in the Bible is closely associated with death. Once again it is the Prayer Book that features a word, or some form of it, in the very sense that Lincoln uses it in the Gettysburg Address and with the same associations. In the same baptismal service that made "dedicated" so familiar to Episcopalians, the word "finally" makes a stirring appearance near the end of the service. The minister offers a prayer over the newly baptized infant (italics in original; boldface added): "And humbly we beseech thee to grant, that *he*, being dead unto sin, may live unto righteousness, and being buried with Christ in his death, may crucify the old man, and utterly abolish the whole body of sin; and that, as *he is* made *partaker* of the death of thy Son, *he* may also be *partaker* of his resurrection; so that, **finally**, with the residue of thy holy Church, *he* may be *an inheritor* of thine everlasting kingdom, through Christ our Lord. *Amen.*" A very similar use of "finally" appears in the closing of the prayer for the president from the service of Morning Prayer, a prayer to which Lincoln had every reason to pay the very closest attention: "O Lord, our heavenly Father, the high and mighty Ruler of the universe, who dost from thy throne behold all the dwellers upon earth, most heartily we beseech thee with thy favour to behold and bless thy servant, the President of the United

States, and all others in authority; and so replenish them with the grace of thy Holy Spirit, that they may always incline to thy will, and walk in thy way. Endue them plenteously with heavenly gifts; grant them in health and prosperity long to live; and **finally**, after this life, to attain everlasting joy and felicity; through Jesus Christ our Lord. *Amen.*" In both prayers, "finally" is clearly associated with the end of this life and the beginning of the next.

The terms "Holy Spirit" and "Holy Ghost" are interchangeable throughout the King James Bible. Jesus first promised his gift of the Holy Spirit to his disciples when he departed this earth. Just before his ascension into heaven, he told them he would send the "Spirit of truth" as their comforter.

> And I will pray the Father, and he shall give you another Comforter, that he may abide with you for ever;
>
> Even the Spirit of truth; whom the world cannot receive, because it seeth him not, neither knoweth him: but ye know him; for he dwelleth with you, and shall be in you.
>
> I will not leave you comfortless: I will come to you. (John 14:16–18)

Both the prophecy of John and the prophecy of Jesus were fulfilled at Pentecost:

> And when the day of Pentecost was fully come, they were all with one accord in one place.
>
> And suddenly there came a sound from heaven as of a rushing mighty wind, and it filled all the house where they were sitting.
>
> And there appeared unto them cloven tongues like as of fire, and it sat upon each of them.
>
> And they were all filled with the Holy Ghost, and began to speak with other tongues, as the Spirit gave them utterance. (Acts 2:1–4)

Because the Holy Ghost appeared at Pentecost in "cloven tongues like as of fire," this second baptism is also known as the baptism of fire. The *Oxford English Dictionary* defines "baptism of fire" as "the grace of the Holy Spirit imparted through baptism." Thus the baptisms of water and fire, although very different experiences, were intimately and indissolubly associated from the moment that John baptized Jesus in the river Jordan and have remained so ever since.

This association has been reinforced over the centuries in numerous ways. For example, the church in England—first Catholic, then Anglican—promoted a conscious connection for hundreds of years between the baptism of water and the baptism of fire. On Pentecost Sunday, which falls seven Sundays after Easter, the English church traditionally performed most of its baptisms, especially of older candidates whom the Prayer Book calls "Those of Riper Years." Because of this tradition, Pentecost was transformed into White Sunday, or Whitsunday, named for the white garments traditionally worn by baptismal candidates. It is no surprise that even in the Prayer Book of Lincoln's day, there was a special Communion preface to be read only during Whitsuntide.

> THROUGH Jesus Christ our Lord, according to whose most true promise, the Holy Ghost came down as at this time from heaven, with a sudden great sound, as it had been a mighty wind, in the likeness of fiery tongues, lighting upon the apostles, to teach them, and to lead them to all truth, giving them both the gift of divers languages, and also boldness with fervent zeal constantly to preach the gospel unto all nations, whereby we have been brought out of darkness and error, into the clear light and true knowledge of thee, and of thy Son Jesus Christ.

What could be a more perfect closing for Lincoln's great speech than a reference to the second baptism—the baptism of spirit and fire? After all, the spirit and fire of civil war still raged across the nation at the very moment Lincoln was uttering his magnificent closing words. His words called for a second baptism, a second dedication of this great nation. This rededication would be everlasting. In the summer of 1776, the first baptism by water had brought a new name to a "new nation" that had been "conceived in liberty" and then dedicated to the sacred proposition that all men are created equal. Lincoln clearly hoped and believed that the second baptism by spirit and fire would bring forth a "new birth of freedom" upon this consecrated battlefield of Gettysburg in the dying autumn of 1863. The first baptism had given the world the proposition that all men are created equal. The second baptism, Lincoln hoped, would give the world "a new birth of freedom" that would not only end "a great civil war" but preserve forever upon this earth America's form of democratic, representative government—"government of the people, by the people, for the people." Perhaps he dreamed as well of another gift that was given at Pentecost, the ability of people speaking different "tongues" to understand and communicate with one another, as North and South had long ago lost the ability to do.

The famous Psalm 90 invoked by Lincoln in his two opening words, "Four score," reappears in the Prayer Book. It appears in Archbishop Cranmer's very similar translation in the service called the Burial of the Dead, among the Psalms to be quoted after the minister's opening words. Lincoln would have known, too, of an "eighty and seven years" in the King James: "And Methuselah lived an hundred eighty and seven years, and begat Lamech. . . . And all the days of Methuselah were nine hundred sixty and nine years: and he died" (Gen. 5:25, 27). But only the earlier phrase from Psalm 90 would have been altogether fitting and proper, for by 1863 the United States had endured for a little longer than the Biblical lifespan of a representative human being (not a massively long-lived Methuselah) and was now in the "fourscore" part of life that is "labour and sorrow" and "soon . . . passeth away." The whole question facing Lincoln was whether this fourscore-and-seven-year-old nation "can long endure." It is clear that Lincoln always chose words for their sound as surely as for their sense, and the beautiful assonance that appears in "four," "score," and "ago"—soon to be repeated yet again in the "forth" of "brought forth" and then later in the address in "so nobly"—could never have occurred with "eighty and seven years ago."

Lincoln's assonance is so rich and repetitive that it becomes a sort of internal rime. This was always a prominent feature in his writing, as in "*loth* to *close*" from the ending of his First Inaugural Address. Lincoln's spelling, as illustrated by "loth" for "loath," "four score" for "fourscore," "previlege" for "privilege" in other writings, and his frequent "it's" for the possessive pronoun, is as hit-or-miss as one would expect from someone who, as he himself once said, "never went to school more than six months in my life."[12] The man who habitually read books out loud and who remembered word for word remarkably long passages that were spoken in his presence had an aural memory, retaining the order and sounds of words but not always their correct spellings.

The exact phrase "fourscore and seven" also appears in the King James Bible. This appearance would have been only a secondary consideration or reinforcement, but it occurs in a context that clearly supports Lincoln's metaphors and message. It occurs in an accounting of the twelve tribes of Israel in the days before Solomon's temple was built. The tribesmen of Issachar, fifth son of Jacob (Jacob was also known as Israel), "were valiant men of might, reckoned in all by their genealogies fourscore and seven thousand" (1 Chron. 7:5). It was the reuniting of a free Israel—divided into two kingdoms both before and after the unifying reigns of David and Solomon—that was the great dream of Isaiah and other prophets who envisioned a reunifying king or Messiah: "they shall be no more two nations, neither shall they be divided into two kingdoms any more at all" (Ezek. 37:22). After the reigns of David and Solomon, the restoration of the temple, Solomon's temple, had become the enduring symbol of this reunion. Jesus, whose twelve disciples echoed the twelve tribes of Israel, identified himself as the Messiah when he promised, "Destroy this temple, and in three days I will raise it up" (John 2:19). What could have been more appropriate for Lincoln's purposes than the reunion of the tribes of his own divided nation under one "temple"—one government, one capital, one shared political faith?

The phrase "our fathers" recalls the most famous prayer in Christendom, "Our Father which art in heaven, Hallowed be thy name" (Matt. 6:9, repeated many times in the Prayer Book with "who" instead of "which"). The word "hallow" will soon follow in Lincoln's Address. But the plural form, "our fathers," resonates even more precisely. In addition to the connection with Jesus and his two fathers, it also recalls God's saving of his Old Testament chosen people, the Israelites: "For thou didst separate them from among all the people of the earth, to be thine inheritance, as thou spakest by the hand of Moses thy servant, when thou broughtest our fathers out of Egypt, O Lord God" (1 Kings 8:53). Saint Peter links "our fathers" not only with the ancient Israelites but also with God the Father whose Son is Jesus Christ: "The God of Abraham, and of Isaac, and of Jacob, the God of our fathers, hath glorified his son Jesus" (Acts 3:13). Lincoln had used this very phrase "the God of our fathers" in his brief and moving farewell address at Springfield on February 11, 1861: "Let us all pray that the God of our fathers may not forsake us now."[13] In a Fourth of July 1858 sermon that Lincoln had almost certainly read before he wrote the Gettysburg Address, Theodore Parker began with this headnote: "'We hold these truths to be self-evident, that all men are created equal; that they are endowed by their Creator with certain inalienable rights; that among these are life, liberty, and the pursuit of happiness.'—What our fathers said in their Declaration."[14] In both his farewell address to the U.S. Senate in January 1861 and his inaugural address as Provisional President of the Confederate States of America the following month, Jefferson Davis had invoked "the God of our fathers" in defense of Bible-supported, Constitution-supported slavery.[15] The fact that Lincoln and Stephen A. Douglas, in their famous debates before huge crowds, had spoken again and again of the founders of this nation as "our fathers" is but another indication of how natural and how widespread the use of biblical language—and especially "our fathers"—had become by the middle years of the nineteenth century.

One of the most resonant phrases in the opening sentence, "conceived in liberty," points just as clearly to Lincoln's major political source, the Declaration of Independence, as it does to the King James Bible, specifically recalling the Declaration's famous "life, liberty, and the pursuit of happiness." Lincoln's phrase is also a perfect predicate and preparation for the phrase "new birth of freedom" in the final sentence. The word "freedom" never appears in the Declaration but makes a memorable appearance in the Constitution in the first of the ten amendments now known as the Bill of Rights. Lincoln follows the order of history by using "liberty" in his opening sentence and "freedom" in his closing. Lincoln loved and honored both documents but always preferred the Declaration of Independence to the Constitution. He once famously declared, "I have never had a feeling politically that did not spring from the sentiments embodied in the Declaration of Independence."[16] John Locke's theory of an inborn, inalienable right to liberty is at the very heart of Thomas Jefferson's Declaration of Independence. In turn, Locke's theory owes much to the Christian doctrine—the theological centerpiece of the Bible-translating, Bible-quoting reformers—that the old testament based on law has been superceded by a new testament based on grace and that this new testament of grace provides perfect liberty to anyone who believes in Jesus Christ as the Messiah. Indeed, some of the earliest appearances of "liberty" in the English language are bound up with the meaning of "Freedom from the bondage of sin, or of the law."[17] This meaning is illustrated by the reformer John Wyclif's 1382 quotation, "Forsoth where is the spirit of God, there is liberte." Wyclif was here translating a passage in 2 Corinthians where the law of the old testament is regarded as a snare in comparison to the liberty that comes from living in the spirit of Jesus Christ. To quote from the later King James translation, the truth that frees the Christian believer appears not in "tables of stone" (2 Cor. 3:3) like those of the Ten Commandments or in the "veil" represented by "the reading of the old testament; which veil is done away in Christ" (2 Cor. 3:14). For the old testament is based on the law, whereas the new testament is based on the liberty that flows from the grace and love of Jesus Christ: "For the law was given by Moses, but grace and truth came by Jesus Christ" (John 1:17). In a book Lincoln had indisputably read, *The Pilgrim's Progress*, Evangelist teaches Christian that Legality is the son of the bondwoman Mount Sinai (the mountain where Moses received the Ten Commandments in tables or tablets of stone): "Now if she with her children are in bondage, how canst thou expect by them to be made free? This *Legality* therefore is not able to set thee free from thy Burden."[18] In exactly the same way, the Declaration of Independence signaled to Lincoln a fundamental and, he hoped, permanent shift from the narrow, class-infected legalism of European monarchy to a new order "conceived in liberty," in equality, and in free and representative government.

It is almost impossible to overstate the importance of the translated English Bible, especially the Wyclif, the Tyndale, the Geneva, and the King James in the development of modern democratic institutions, first in England and then in America. A wonderful and enlightening book on the subject is by Benson Bobrick, *Wide as the Waters: The Story of the English Bible and the Revolution It Inspired* (2001), which builds to this stirring conclusion:

> When Jefferson wrote that "all men are created equal," he was speaking from within an inherited culture that accepted the right of every man to consider all matters according to his own reason and conscience. And that right implied equality. It was (or was regarded as) a sacred right, and that is part of what resounds in the sentence "We hold these truths to be sacred and undeniable," which was Jefferson's original turn of phrase.[19]

One wonders if Jefferson might have been spared some of the tarring and feathering he has endured for centuries from the right wing of all political parties, especially since John C. Calhoun started stirring the pot, if only the poor man had never replaced "sacred and undeniable" with "self-evident"!

Even as Lincoln's "conceived in liberty" echoes Matthew and Luke, it also represents an intriguing play on words that may tie the birth of America to the birth of Jesus Christ in quite a different way. The libertine side of "liberty" has spun off such phrases as "liberty-wife," meaning "mistress," in the old Child ballad, "Young Johnstone," and Daniel Defoe's "The poor man had taken liberty with a wench" in *Robinson Crusoe*. When Laertes warns Ophelia against sexual indulgence before marriage, she in turn warns her brother against the hypocrisy of being a "puff'd and reckless libertine" himself (*Hamlet* 1.3.49). Shakespeare conjoins "Lust and liberty" in *Timon of Athens* (4.1.25). The Bible specifically warns against letting liberty degenerate into lust: "use not liberty for an occasion to the flesh" (Gal. 5:13), least of all to those "works of the flesh" that include "adultery" and "fornication" (Gal. 5:19–20). In his famous Psalm 51, King David, the most celebrated ancestor of Jesus, repents of his libertine adultery with Bathsheba (even though it eventually produced his greatest son, Solomon) by remembering his own life, his own conception and birth, in terms of original sin: "I was shapen in iniquity; and in sin did my mother conceive me" (51:5). "Conceived in liberty" thus suggests the very opposite of "conceived in wedlock." In the Gospel of Matthew, Joseph believes that Mary has conceived illegitimately by another man until the angel of the Lord tells him, "that which is conceived in her is of the Holy Ghost" (1:20) By the same token, King George IV and all his ministers and minions regarded the birth of the United States as completely illegitimate from conception to christening, and indeed forever after.

Even that almost invisible phrase "upon this continent" contributes to the same idea. It was upon this virgin continent as our mother that our fathers conceived and later brought forth this nation. It was at the First Continental Congress in 1774 that "our fathers" and "this continent" first conceived, producing a declaration of personal rights, including life, liberty, property, and assembly. It was at the Second Continental Congress on July 4, 1776, that our fathers actually "brought forth" this nation by adopting Thomas Jefferson's Declaration of Independence. Although the country was not fully delivered from danger until many years later by the victorious Continental Army at Yorktown in 1783, we celebrate the birth and christening of our nation from the July 4 signing, which gave us both our baptismal name and the fundamental principles to which we were "dedicated" at our christening. That Lincoln perfectly understood this early history of our nation is obvious from his First Inaugural, written nearly three years before the Gettysburg Address:

> The Union is much older than the Constitution. It was formed in fact, by the Articles of Association in 1774. It was matured and continued by the Declaration of Independence in 1776.[20]

In the clearer, simpler metaphor he chose for the Gettysburg Address, Lincoln turned "formed" into "conceived" and "matured and continued" into "brought forth." Note too that the word "continent" has yet another meaning that associates it with the story of the birth of Jesus. The word can mean "chaste," which is exactly what the angel tells Joseph that Mary has been. Although "continent" never appears in the King James Bible, its negative forms "incontinent" (2 Tim. 3:3) and "incontinency" (1 Cor. 7:5) are both there.

Today we have lost the old idea of associating the United States of America with the continent from which it was formed, but from the Declaration of Independence to the Gettysburg Address, this idea was a commonplace, as in Continental Congress, Continental Army, and Continental dollar. In a book written by an Episcopal rector that Lincoln and just about every other American had read—Mason Weems' famously patriotic if often apocryphal *Life of Washington*—the Parson waxes poetic about our "greatest Continent" while ridiculing the idea that so accomplished a man as our first president must have been born a European. "*So great a man could never have been born in America!*—Why that's the very *prince of reasons* why he should have been born here!"

> By the same rule, where shall we look for Washington, the greatest among men, but in *America*? That greatest Continent, which, rising from beneath the frozen pole, stretches far and wide to the south, running almost "*whole the length of this vast terrene,*" and sustaining on her ample sides the roaring shock of half the watery globe. And equal to its size, is the furniture of this vast continent, where the Almighty has reared his cloud-capt mountains, and spread his sea-like lakes, and poured his mighty rivers, and hurled down his thundering cataracts in a style of the *sublime*, so far superior to any thing of the kind in other continents, that we may fairly conclude that great men and great deeds are designed for America.[21]

In Lincoln's metaphor, Weems' "greatest Continent" with "her ample sides" is mother to a "new nation" conceived in 1774, born and christened the United States of America in 1776. Clearly, the mother of this country seemed as titanic as "our fathers," as remarkable for her size and strength as for her breathtaking beauty.

Lincoln's phrase "upon this continent" also recalls a famous Old Testament as well as a famous New Testament phrase. The Old Testament phrase is "long upon the land" and appears in the fifth of the Ten Commandments: "Honour thy father and thy mother: that thy days may be long upon the land which the Lord thy God giveth thee" (Exod. 20:12). One of Lincoln's arguments in the Gettysburg Address is that this nation may "long endure" and indeed may never "perish from the earth" *if*—and only if—we honor the first principles of our founding fathers. The New Testament phrase echoed by "upon this continent" is "upon this rock." The name of Peter, one of the twelve disciples, literally means "rock," and Jesus plays upon Peter's name in a famous passage that opens with the question, "Whom do men say that I the Son of man am?" (Matt. 16:13).

> And Simon Peter answered and said, Thou art the Christ, the Son of the living God.
> And Jesus answered and said unto him, Blessed art thou, Simon Barjona: for flesh and blood hath not revealed it unto thee, but my Father which is in heaven.
> And I say also unto thee, That thou art Peter, and upon this rock I will build my church; and the gates of hell shall not prevail against it. (Matt. 16:16–18)

Here Jesus reveals to his followers for the first time that he is the Messiah. His transfiguration will soon come, followed by his passion, death, and resurrection. In what the *Collected Works of Abraham Lincoln* calls the "final text" of the Gettysburg Address because it was the last copy Lincoln is known to have written out in his own hand, the preposition "upon" is shortened to "on."[22] But on February 4, 1864, earlier in that very same month when he would mail out a text to American historian George Bancroft that Lincoln would soon recopy into the "final text," the President wrote Edward Everett, "I send herewith the manuscript of my remarks at Gettysburg."[23] This manuscript, now known as the Edward Everett copy, was sent to Everett to sell at a Sanitary Fair in New York. It retains the word "upon" that Lincoln actually spoke at Gettysburg.[24] In summary, the switch from the longer, more allusive "upon" to the shorter, simpler "on" was a late, solitary, and perhaps uncertain call for Lincoln, because he did it two different ways in the same short month of February 1864 and, in all of the previous drafts or copies he ever made had used "upon." He made the change for only one recipient, Bancroft, and there is no evidence that it was made after Lincoln's usual consultation with other readers and advisers. Whether Lincoln ever fully made up his mind, we shall never know. Had he lived longer into a peacetime, he would almost certainly have been asked to make additional copies of the Gettysburg Address, and then we should have had a more definitive answer about "upon" versus "on." The King James itself provides a parallel to Lincoln's late and lonely shift. When the Fifth Commandment from the Old Testament is repeated in the New Testament, "upon" shrinks to "on": "Honour thy father and mother; which is the first commandment with promise; That it may be well with thee, and thou mayest live long on the earth" (Eph. 6:2–3). In both cases—the King James Bible and the Gettysburg Address—the first choice seems, in literary terms, decidedly the better.

It is by now abundantly clear that the phrase "dedicated to the proposition that all men are created equal" echoes not only the Declaration of Independence but also the rite of Holy Baptism: "Grant that whosoever is here dedicated to thee by our office and ministry, may also be endued with heavenly virtues, and everlastingly rewarded, through thy mercy, O blessed Lord God, who dost live, and govern all things, world without end. *Amen.*" Whenever Lincoln adopted a ritual word or phrase, he never failed to repeat it. Thus he repeated the word "dedicated" from the first sentence in the very next sentence. Then he repeated it again in each of his closing sentences, the ninth and the tenth. In the ninth, he used the variation "dedicated here," which better suited the rhythm of that sentence. In the tenth and final sentence, he used the exact phrase from the baptismal ceremony, "here dedicated." Throughout the Gettysburg Address, Lincoln was clearly attracted not just to the Prayer Book's "dedicated" but also to the modifier "here" that precedes "dedicated." The adverb "here" appears in no fewer than eight different verb phrases that form a leitmotif throughout the address—"here gave," "struggled here," "say here," "did here," "dedicated here," "fought here," "here dedicated," and "here highly resolve." Until the "final text," there were *nine* phrases containing "here." As for the idea itself—the dedicatory idea that all men are created equal—this derives as just as clearly and insistently from the New Testament as from the Declaration of Independence. Acts 10:34 declares that "God is no respecter of persons." Colossians 3:11 confirms the equality of all believers in Christ: "there is neither Greek nor Jew, circumcision nor uncircumcision, Barbarian, Scythian, bond nor free: but Christ is all, and in all."

In his opening sentence, Lincoln begins with birth—"brought forth"—and then flashes back to conception. In the second sentence, he flashes back even further with the words "engaged" and "testing." In terms of the Christmas story, Mary and Joseph were already engaged by the time Mary was found to be with child. But as soon as Joseph learned of her condition, their engagement was immediately and dramatically tested. Joseph was "minded to put her away privily"—that is, to end the engagement quietly and privately. One of the questions racking America at the time of secession was how to conceptualize the relationship between the seceding states and the Union. Was this a marriage being ended by a sudden desertion and the removal of jointly owned property without a proper and lawful divorce? Was it something less than a marriage, a sort of engagement or mere voluntary alliance, that could be abandoned at any time, as Calhoun and other apologists for the South had been insisting for years? Or was it a relationship even *more* binding than a marriage, as Lincoln had insisted in his First Inaugural?

> Physically speaking, we cannot separate. We cannot remove our respective sections from each another, nor build an impassable wall between them. A husband and wife may be divorced, and go out of the presence, and beyond the reach of each other; but the different parts of our country cannot do this.[25]

What legal remedies remained after one section of the country had seceded? From the moment Lincoln made clear that he rejected the idea of any divorce or division and was determined to keep the Union together at all costs, the national "testing" of a civil war became the inevitable consequence. Now in the first sentence of the Gettysburg Address, the dominant metaphor is that of birth and christening, but there is also an inevitable hint of the *parents* of the child that is "conceived" and "brought forth." What kind of relationship did those parents have? In the opening four sentences, the metaphor of birth is constantly juxtaposed with the metaphor of marriage. Were Mary and Joseph even married when Jesus was born? Like their relationship, the union of the Northern and Southern states into the United States of America by the Declaration of Independence in 1776 had by 1863 turned into an ambiguous and ill-defined kind of relationship with a highly uncertain and very likely tragic outcome.

The Gospels of Matthew and Luke make clear that Joseph, despite the agony of believing his betrothed has been unfaithful to him and despite his temptation to "put her away privily," chooses *not* to destroy his union with Mary. The shifting and uncertain nature of their relationship during their difficult time forms a remarkable parallel to the relationship between the two warring sides during the Civil War. Without delving into what Lincoln once called the "the long complicated statements of Christian doctrine,"[26] anyone can see from the Bible alone that Joseph and Mary were in a hard-to-define relationship between the time they were first "espoused" (Luke 1:27) and the time that he finally "knew her" (Matt. 1:25) after the birth of her first child and thus completed their marriage on every count. That a marriage is not legally complete until physically consummated is a feature of marriage law throughout the world and the history of mankind. Before that consummation, were the couple merely engaged, as "espoused wife" seems to suggest in Luke 2:5, or already lawfully married, as the unqualified words "husband" and "wife" seem to suggest in Matthew 1:19–20? Or were they engaged in such a way, as some have asserted, that under Jewish law, their being engaged was exactly the same as being married? We shall see that it is not the answer to the question that is important here, but the *question itself.*

Why? Because this is the same question that was being asked by everyone about the relationship between the Union and the seceded states during the Civil War, including the very moment when Lincoln delivered his Gettysburg Address. The Confederate states argued that the union of the states had never been anything but voluntary and conditional and therefore had never produced anything so binding and permanent as a marriage—or else, if a marriage *had* occurred, then the Southern states had immediately qualified for a divorce once the North had violated the terms of the marital contract by threatening the South's Constitutional right to own slaves. (Lincoln's election in November 1860 was the announced cause of this threat.) But if a divorce was in order, what was required to complete it? The South maintained that no negotiations or formalities were necessary at all and that it could, unilaterally and at any time, do with the Union what Joseph was minded to do with Mary—"put her away privily." Southerners believed that the North should either unprotestingly accept the South's secession, as President James Buchanan so obligingly did at first, or else grant what today would be called a no-fault divorce. One problem with this view was the property settlement. Did the seceded states own, for example, the federal forts within their borders? It was South Carolina's laying claim to Fort Sumter that in fact ignited the war. Southerners believed that the South was free either to go her own way or to negotiate with the North for a more favorable remarriage that would more fully guarantee her slaveholding rights. This would turn out to be precisely the position taken by many of the supporters of General George McClellan when he ran as the presidential nominee of the Democratic Party in the election of

1864. How easy it is to forget now how many Northerners during the Civil War were perfectly willing to give up the Union in preference to fighting for it and how many others were perfectly willing not only to maintain but to strengthen slavery as the price of union!

Whether viewed as a mere engagement now broken or a marriage now ended or a marriage merely threatened, the relationship of the two warring sections was clearly in a desperate state when Lincoln composed his Gettysburg Address. Clearly, he himself looked forward to some kind of reaffirmation of the old marriage vows that had, in his view, been sworn to in the Declaration of Independence and reaffirmed once already in the Constitution. Just as a rebirth does not negate the original birth, so a reunion of a separated couple does not negate their original marriage. Lincoln's hope and dream—his vision—was that a successful resolution of the war would silence all the questions about the legitimacy and permanency of the original marriage.

Once again, Lincoln was not the inventor of his metaphor of choice, was not the first, that is, to picture the union of North and South as a marriage. A notable predecessor was Bishop John Henry Hopkins in a lecture delivered in 1851 and published soon afterward as a widely circulated little book. In both lecture and book, Hopkins had prefaced his argument that slavery is biblically approved with an extended metaphor:

> The North and the South should always be considered as wedded together, before heaven and earth, in the glorious Covenant of the Constitution. We have taken each other, in that solemn compact, "for better, for worse, till death do us part."[27]

When Hopkins wrote this, he was hoping that Southerners would, voluntarily and with compensation, emancipate all slaves and return them to their African homeland. In this they would be following the "position of those Southern patriots, who, like Jefferson, denounced the institution of slavery" and who affirmed the "far-famed doctrine of the Declaration of Independence" as "the fundamental principle of our government."[28] In just a few years, Hopkins would reverse himself completely on these positions, arguing that the South had every right to end the marriage by secession, that African slaves were actually much better off under their Southern masters than back in their African ancestral homeland, and that the Declaration of Independence, far from being "fundamental," was nothing but the series of false "propositions" John C. Calhoun had always represented it to be.

All of this is prologue to the opening phrase of Lincoln's third sentence, "We are met." This phrase is highly reminiscent of the familiar words that open the best-known, best-loved service in the Prayer Book, the Solemnization of Marriage: "Dearly beloved, we are gathered." This service has been so widely adopted for marriages by couples of all faiths that virtually everyone now knows its ritualized language, and this was true in Lincoln's day as well. The implication of

Lincoln's ritualized words "We are met" is that the marriage vows uniting this nation were in some way being reaffirmed or renewed even as the sacred ground on which he stood at Gettysburg was being consecrated. "We are met" is remarkably close to "we are gathered" in both structure and meaning. In an early draft, Lincoln had repeated the ritualistic "We are met" from the third sentence in his fourth sentence. Later he changed the "We are met" of the fourth to "We have come." Far from reducing the tie to the wedding ceremony, this change only *strengthened* it, because the marriage ceremony proclaims, in back-to-back sentences, "we are gathered" and "these two persons come now to be joined." In short, in his final version, Lincoln duplicates the form and meaning of "we are gathered" with "We are met" and then duplicates the main verb of "come now to be joined" with "We have come to dedicate."

The conclusion of the fourth sentence in praise of the Union dead, "who here gave their lives that that nation might live," is a clear echo of the central story of Christianity: "Greater love hath no man than this," Jesus taught in John 15:13, "that a man lay down his life for his friends." Jesus laid down his own life not just for his friends but for all mankind: "I am the good shepherd . . . and I lay down my life for the sheep" (John 10:14–15). As these passages demonstrate, the term of choice for a sacrificial death in the King James Bible is not "give" but "lay down." Only once in the entire King James does any form of the word "give" use any form of the word "life" as its object, but this passage is memorable indeed. It occurs in Mark 10:45, where Jesus says of himself, "For even the Son of man came not to be ministered unto, but to minister, and to give his life a ransom for many." Out of his sacrificial death came new life—new birth—for all believers. Thus the Union dead who "gave their lives" are clearly linked in their sacrificial deaths with the sacrificial death of the Christ who "gave his life." In an even more familiar passage to most Christians, John 3:16, the word "gave" makes perhaps its most memorable appearance in the entire Bible: "For God so loved the world, that he gave his only begotten Son, that whosoever believeth in him should not perish, but have everlasting life." This verse has been a part of the service for Holy Communion ever since Cranmer's first version in 1559 and is perhaps the best-known of all verses to Protestant Christians.

To summarize the four opening sentences of the Gettysburg Address, Lincoln has used the birth of Jesus and the relationship of Mary and Joseph as a metaphor for the birth and "testing" of this nation. At the same time, he has taken us through the stages of the nation's history, from its birth and conception to its testing by civil war and finally to its dreams and hopes of reunion or remarriage. The tact and skill of Lincoln make the biblical metaphor and the political history work seamlessly together. One reason for his success is that he avoids simple chronological order. He speaks of birth before he speaks of conception. This exactly reflects the order of the Gospel of Matthew, which begins its account of Mary, Joseph, and Jesus with "Now the birth of Jesus was on this wise" (1:18). Only later in this verse are we told that "Mary was espoused to Joseph." Still later, in the very same verse, we are told of the immaculate conception—"she was found with child of the Holy Ghost." Later still, in yet another verse, we are told how testing her pregnancy was for Joseph, who was "not willing to make her a public example" (1:19). It took an angel to end the conflict within Joseph: "Joseph, thou son of David, fear not to take unto thee Mary thy wife: for that which is conceived in her is of the Holy Ghost" (1:20). It bears repeating that Joseph did not fully take Mary as his wife, did not complete their marriage by consummating it, until *after* the birth of Jesus: "And knew her not till she had brought forth her firstborn son" (1:25). That is, the full marriage would only follow the conception, the testing, and the bringing forth.

By giving his account in an intentionally out-of-order fashion, Lincoln is able to find significant connections between two stories that could never be made perfectly congruent. What matters is that both stories tell of birth and the promise of rebirth, of a marriage that for a long time remains ill-defined and somehow incomplete, and of repeated threats of disaster and death. Even after the great opening event in both stories—a birth that would change the whole world—many profound questions remained to be answered. The most profound question remaining for Lincoln and his listeners on November 19, 1863, was whether the Civil War would end for better or for worse. Would it end in a glorious reunion or remarriage reaffirming and renewing the principles of the original union as stated in the Declaration of Independence or in something far, far worse—in either a tragic remarriage where slavery and the "rights" of slaveholders were ingloriously reaffirmed or in an agony of disunion, death, and mourning?

The genius of Lincoln appears in the words that he chose to frame all these underlying questions. He chose words that could suggest, with equal force and precision, love on the one hand, war on the other, or marriage on the one hand, death and burial on the other. In the second sentence, for example, the word "engaged" invokes the matrimonial as clearly as the martial. One engages a true love as surely as one engages an enemy. What a perfect word for describing a house divided by civil war! The verb "met" in the third sentence has exactly the same double meaning. It is hard to say which phrase is more familiar—"We have met the enemy" or "I have met the love of my life." The word "portion" in the fourth sentence also has a double meaning recalling both marriage and death. One meaning of "portion" is a dowry: "the portion and sinew of her fortune, her marriage-dowry," as Shakespeare writes in *Measure for Measure* (3.1.230–31). The second meaning of "portion" is that part of an estate passing to an heir from the maker of a will or from a person dying intestate. This meaning appears in a question asked by two children in Genesis 31:14: "Is there yet any portion or inheritance for us in our father's house?"

The word "field" that follows "portion" is associated with both war and love, with death and renewal, with the battlefield and the consecrated field. Lincoln lived before the phrase "playing the field," but he certainly understood Shakespeare's scene where Petruchio "conquers" his delightful bride, Katharina, in *The Taming of the Shrew*, causing Hortensia to proclaim, "the field is won" (4.5.23). Jesus himself is repeatedly associated with the word "field," from the "shepherds abiding in the field" (Luke 2:8) at his birth to the "field of Golgotha and dead men's skulls" where, in the language of Shakespeare's *Richard II*, Jesus died (4.1.144). The thirty pieces of silver Judas took for betraying Jesus to his death were used to buy a "potter's field, to bury strangers in" (Matt. 27:7).

The final word in the Gettysburg Address that clearly combines marriage and death is the word "cause" from "that cause for which they gave the last full measure of devotion." The marriage ceremony in the Prayer Book uses as its Gospel reading a declaration by Jesus: "For this cause shall a man leave father and mother, and shall cleave to his wife: and they twain shall be one flesh" (Matt. 19:5). Later Saint Paul transformed these very words of Jesus into an allegory of Christ as the bridegroom and the church as his bride in Ephesians 5.31–32:

> For this cause shall a man leave his father and mother, and shall be joined unto his wife, and they two shall be one flesh.
> This is a great mystery: but I speak concerning Christ and the church.

The word "cause" is just as powerfully associated with the *death* of Jesus Christ. The Roman governor Pontius Pilate asks Jesus at his trial if he has ever claimed to be the king of the Jews, to which Jesus answers, "Thou sayest that I am a king. To this end was I born, and for this cause came I into the world, that I should bear witness unto the truth" (John 18:37). Pilate sentences him to death but only after making a famous declaration, "I have found no cause of death in him" (Luke 23:22), which is repeated in the Prayer Book among the Bible readings appointed for the holy week of Easter. Once again, Lincoln has used the words of the Bible and the Prayer Book to associate the Union dead with the sacrificial death of Jesus. At the same time, he has associated the marriage of North and South with the sacred marriage of Christ and church.

Both verbs in Lincoln's second and third sentences are in passive voice—"*are* engaged" and "*are* met." The same passive voice appears in the opening line of the marriage ceremony, "Dearly beloved, we are gathered," echoing Matthew 18:20: "For where two or three are gathered together in my name, there am I in the midst of them." This famous verse also appears in *Lincoln's Devotional*.[29] Why did Lincoln choose "met" instead of "gathered"? In terms of both meaning and biblical resonance, there is little to choose between them. Faced with a choice between words very close in meaning and allusive power, Lincoln always seemed to prefer the shorter and simpler. The simpler "are met" appears but once in the Bible, in the Psalms that Lincoln so dearly loved: "Mercy and truth are met together" (85:10). Perhaps because of this, Lincoln had chosen the phrase many years before, in 1842, to praise "the mightiest name on earth": "This is the one hundred and tenth anniversary of the birth-day of Washington. We are met to celebrate this day."[30] One advantage of "met" over "gathered" is that "met" works better with Lincoln's "come." Forms of both "met" and "come" make memorable appearances is the story of two brothers at war, Jacob and Esau. Lincoln will powerfully invoke this story of civil war elsewhere in the Gettysburg Address. The two words appear in "my brother meeteth" (Gen. 32:17) and "Esau came, and with him four hundred men" (Gen. 33:1). But perhaps the most compelling reason Lincoln preferred "met" is simply the sound of it. He was able to construct a very simple, very effective sentence in "We are met on a great battle-field of that war." The words "met," "great," and "that" all end in *t*, and "field" ends in a *d*, which is a voiced *t*. The *t* also accentuates the key word in the sentence, which is "battle." The other unifying sounds in the sentence—the opening and closing *w* sound and the *r* sound of "are," "great," and "war"—work to soften and make more musical the drum-like tattoo of the *t*.

Just like "are met," the word "engaged" makes only one appearance in the entire King James Bible, but how it resonates! Jeremiah in the Old Testament alternates between prophecies of the Babylonian captivity and of the ultimate salvation of God's people, the Israelites. In one of his visions of deliverance, Jeremiah sees the Israelites as regaining their self-governance, with the Lord inspiring a governor to approach His presence who otherwise would never have found the courage to engage his fearful human heart and "to approach unto me":

> Their children shall be as aforetime, and their congregation shall be established before me, and I will punish all that oppress them.
>
> And their nobles shall be of themselves, and their governor shall proceed from the midst of them; and I will cause him to draw near, and he shall approach unto me: for who is this that engaged his heart to approach unto me? saith the Lord.
>
> And ye shall be my people, and I will be your God. (30:20–22)

What would have made this passage so fascinating to Lincoln is that Jeremiah associates God's punishment of the Israelites specifically with the denial of liberty to their own brothers and neighbors:

> Therefore thus saith the Lord; Ye have not hearkened unto me, in proclaiming liberty, every one to his brother, and every man to his neighbour: behold, I proclaim a liberty for you, saith the Lord, to the sword, to the pestilence, and to the famine; and I will make you to be removed into all the kingdoms of the earth. (34:17)

In short, the Israelites were losing their liberty, their self-government, according to the prophet Jeremiah, precisely because they would not free their own slaves!

By invoking the marriage ceremony, Lincoln calls into play all the phrases that call for the kind of unending unity he so passionately desired for the union of the states—"so long as ye both shall live," "till death us do part," and "Those whom God hath joined together, let no man put asunder." Nor does marriage end at the grave, according to the Prayer Book. In addition to its familiar appearance near the beginning of the marriage service, the word "come" appears memorably at the closing:

> GOD the Father, God the Son, God the Holy Ghost, bless, preserve, and keep you: the Lord mercifully with his favour look upon you, and fill you with all spiritual benediction and grace, that ye may so live together in this life, that, in the life to come, ye may have life everlasting. *Amen.*

The idea of this closing is that the couple being married will be together not just in this life but in "the life to come," where they will share "life everlasting." In the same way, Lincoln's "come" in the Gettysburg Address introduces "a final resting place" for those who lived together and died together that our nation "might live." In the Bible, "resting place" makes five honorific appearances, most lyrically of all in Isaiah's vision of a paradise for God's chosen people—"my people shall dwell in a peaceable habitation, and in sure dwellings, and in quiet resting places" (Isa. 32:18). The Union soldiers who "here gave their lives" to save the Union and its principles have thus followed in the footsteps of the Messiah, whose bride is the church and its believers. The Messiah came to earth "to give his life a ransom for many" (Matt. 20:28), who because of him "should not perish, but have everlasting life" (John 3:16). Lincoln half-prays, half-prophesies that this "married" Union and the kind of government it stands for "shall not perish from the earth," which is the closest thing to "life everlasting" that anything mortal can aspire to.

The same small but significant "come" makes appearances in the Burial of the Dead as eloquent as those in the Solemnization of Marriage. Indeed, it appears no fewer than eight times in this solemn and beautiful service, where it invokes the Savior's "second coming in glorious majesty to judge the world." It also quotes the comforting words that the Savior will speak at this second coming: "Come, ye blessed children of my Father, receive the kingdom prepared for you from the beginning of the world." In short, throughout the Gettysburg Address, the words and phrases of love and war, of marriage and funeral, are lyrically and indivisibly intertwined.

Marriage and funeral are two of the great ceremonies of life. One of the most common of Freudian slips is to confuse these two words—to say "marriage" or "funeral" when one means to say the other. The traditional distinction between comedy and tragedy is that comedy ends with a falling in love or marriage and tragedy with a death or funeral. There is almost no humor in Dante's greatest work, and yet he named it *Il Commedia—The Comedy* that his admirers later elevated to *The Divine Comedy*—because it ends happily in Paradise with a series of marriages that Dante finally and fully comes to understand against the backdrop of divine grace. These are the marriages of Adam and Eve, of Saint Francis and Patience, and, above all, of Christ and his Bride the Church. The question for Lincoln and for his audience was what kind of outcome this nation and its principles would have in the end. Would the Union complete her marriage and strengthen her vows, or would it end up dead and divided? This was the great question left unanswered at the end of the Gettysburg Address. But there is a definite upbeat in Lincoln's invitation to a national resolve that "government of the people, by the people, for the people shall not perish from the earth." Lincoln suggested that even if this nation dies, her principles and form of government will not. This is precisely the view of Lincoln's great source Theodore Parker, who in his "house divided" sermon from 1854 had said: "And, if America fail, though she is one fortieth of God's family, and it is a great loss, there are other nations behind us; our truth shall not perish, even if we go down."[31]

The final word of the second sentence, "endure," is one of the most evocative in the entire address. It is another in a series of words recalling the story of the saving of God's chosen people in the Old testament and the story of the Messiah who comes to save the whole world in the New. Its very first appearance in the entire King James Bible comes in the story of Jacob and Esau, precisely at the point where the two brothers depart from one another in peace. Jacob gives his brother a gift and a blessing in recompense for the birthright and the blessing he has stolen from Esau in earlier days. Jacob says he will leave first: "I will lead on softly, according as the cattle that goeth before me and the children be able to *endure*" (Gen. 33:14; emphasis added here and hereafter). The second appearance is equally resonant, referring to the exodus of the Israelites from Egypt to the Promised Land. Moses has been told that he will be given laws for his people to follow so that his burdensome responsibilities as judge will be reduced and the long, hard journey to Canaan expedited: "If thou shalt do this thing, and God command thee so, then thou shalt be able to *endure*, and all this people shall also go to their place in peace" (Exod. 18:23). But the book of the Bible that contains by far the largest number of appearances of the word "endure" is Psalms, a book that Lincoln dearly loved and often quoted. It is the only book where the word "long" is joined with the word "endure." This occurs in Psalm 72, called "A Psalm for Solomon." The Psalmist exalts the great and wise king Solomon who will bring glory and peace to his nation. In verses 4 through 7, emphasis has been added to both of the key words:

> He shall judge the poor of the people, he shall save the children of the needy, and shall break in pieces the oppressor.
> They shall fear thee as *long* as the sun and moon *endure*, throughout all generations.

He shall come down like rain upon the mown grass: as showers that water the earth.

In his days shall the righteous flourish; and abundance of peace so *long* as the moon *endureth.*

The climactic verse of the chapter also includes the key words: "His name shall *endure* for ever: his name shall be continued as *long* as the sun: and men shall be blessed in him: all nations shall call him blessed" (72:17). Not surprisingly, Christians would later see Solomon as a type of Christ and apply all these exalted words to the Messiah.

The assertion that "the mercy of God endureth for ever" appears an astonishing twenty-six times in the lovely, litany-like Psalm 136, in which the pattern is always to conclude with these very words. Verses 10 through 16 from this famous chapter recall specifically the journey of the Israelites out of Egypt to the Promised Land;

To him that smote Egypt in their firstborn: for his mercy endureth forever:

And brought out Israel from among them: for his mercy endureth forever:

With a strong hand and with a stretched out arm: for his mercy endureth forever.

To him which divided the Red sea into parts: for his mercy endureth forever:

And made Israel to pass through the midst of it: for his mercy endureth forever:

To him which led his people through the wilderness: for his mercy endureth forever.

In the New Testament, Jesus says to his disciples: "And ye shall be hated of all men for my name's sake: but he that endureth to the end shall be saved" (Matt. 10:22). In the gospel of John, "perish" and "endure" appear together in one verse for the only time in the Bible, with emphasis added here and hereafter: "Labour not for the meat which *perisheth*," says Jesus, "but for that meat which *endureth* unto everlasting life" (John 6:27). The loveliest appearance of all is in Paul's letter to the Hebrews: "Looking unto Jesus the author and finisher of our faith; who for the joy that was set before him *endured* the cross, despising the shame, and is set down at the right hand of the throne of God" (12:2). The word is equally busy and beloved in the Book of Common Prayer, making seventy-five different appearances that include most of the verses just quoted. It was the possible failure of the United States to endure as a union that represented "death" to Lincoln in his metaphor of birth-death-rebirth that dominates the Gettysburg Address. At the same time, the sacrificial death of the Union soldiers at Gettysburg is his inspiration for believing in a "new birth of freedom" that will cause this nation to "long endure" and perhaps never "perish from the earth." The promise of reunion symbolized by the Union victory at Gettysburg represents the hope of rebirth, the promise that this nation and the free government for which it stands will endure—perhaps "under God" forever.

Those who would find Lincoln's use of such a word as "endure" a mere accident or some vague and unconscious response to the culture of his time should never forget how much of the Bible he carried not just in his head but on the very tip of his tongue. They should also keep in mind the options that any good writer has enjoyed for centuries. After 1150, the appearance or behavior of a monarch could be either "kingly" (English) or "royal" (French)—and by the time of Chaucer in the late 1300s, could also be "regal" by borrowing from the scholarly language of Latin, a process that would greatly accelerate in the Renaissance, which followed Chaucer's death by less than a century. A "lawyer" (English) or "attorney" (French) would prepare a last "will" (English) and "testament" (French) for either a native-English or Norman-English client. Thus, a nation might "last" (English) or "endure" (French) or "survive" (also French but not entering the English language until 1473).[32] The word "survive" apparently smelled too much of the inkhorn for William Tyndale in the 1520s, if indeed he knew the word at all, for when he translated his New Testament in 1525, he consistently used the older word "endure" and never the word "survive." When Tyndale translated a few books of the Old Testament in the 1530s, he again used only "endure" and never "survive." Tyndale's translation would serve as the major source for all later translations up to and including the King James translation of 1611. A rigorous word count by Ronald Mansbridge of the Tyndale Society, using a representative sample of Bible chapters, concluded that more than 81 percent of the words in the King James come from Tyndale—including, of course, "endure."[33]

Obviously the rhythm of Lincoln's sentence, which calls for a two-syllable word, would have immediately ruled out "last" as an option. But why did Lincoln not choose "survive"? By 1863 the word had become just as familiar and just as widely understood as "endure." This is very clear from the speech of Edward Everett delivered on the same day and from the same platform as Lincoln's address. Everett's approximately fourteen thousand words include both "endure" *and* "survive." But "survive" was the word he clearly favored, for it appears at least five times in some form compared to a single appearance for "endure." The single appearance of "endure" occurs early on, in the phrase, "whether this august republican Union . . . should perish or endure."[34] Notice how the first part of Everett's construction centers on the high-sounding, Latin-borrowed "august," which, like "survive," never appears in the King James at all, while his second part—"perish or endure"—is altogether biblical or King Jamesian. This undigested mix of styles is a major reason why Everett's words did not long endure while Lincoln's simple and familiar words echoing the most beloved of books became famous overnight and have remained so ever since. Lincoln also had a model for a much more eloquent use of "survive" in Daniel Webster's eulogy for Jefferson and John Adams, wherein Webster had imagined Adams as saying before the Declaration of Independence, "Sink or swim, live or die, survive or perish, I give my hand and my heart to this vote."[35] But Lincoln himself chose "endure" because it is, like most of his beautifully chosen words, a simple, old-fashioned, defining word of the King James Bible in which "survive" never appears at all.

Thus the assertion that Lincoln's language is biblical or King Jamesian means that it relies very heavily, and indeed almost entirely, on words that appear in the King James Bible. Most of the words used by Lincoln in the Gettysburg Address that do not appear in the identical form or with the exact same meaning in the King James—"brave," "continent," "devotion," "fitting," "nobly," "resolve," and "testing"—*do* appear there in some other form and *sound* just as biblical as the others. This is also true of the phrases "new birth" and "under God." Neither phrase appears anywhere in the Bible, but the individual words appear many times in their own right. The only three words in the Gettysburg Address that appear *nowhere* in the King James in any form whatsoever are "proposition," the "civil" of "civil war," and "detract." About "proposition," the most controversial word in the entire address, there is much to say later. The word "civil," although unbiblical, appears in the Prayer Book in the title of that very prayer that was to cause Lincoln and the Union so much grief during the Civil War and was called "*A Prayer for the President of the United States, and all in civil Authority.*" Of course Lincoln also chose the term "civil war" to stand down the notion proposed by both Southerners and Copperheads that this was a war fought between independent and sovereign states—a "war between the states." As for the word "detract," it entered the English language only in the 1500s, the same century when its synonym "subtract" also entered, with neither word making it into the King James.

The King James Bible is remarkable for the simplicity of its diction, getting by on barely eight thousand frequently repeated words, as compared to over thirty thousand words in the writings of William Shakespeare, who was still writing when the King James was translated in 1611.[36] Garry Wills is right to challenge the long-standing myth that Lincoln's language can be accounted for as "Saxon" or "Anglo-Saxon": "Some have claimed, simplistically, that Lincoln achieved a 'down-to-earth' style by using short Anglo-Saxon words rather than long Latin ones in the Address. Such people cannot have read the Address with care."[37] In the so-called Final Text, there are 272 words, counting as two words the hyphenated form, "battle-field" Although 212 of these 272 are Anglo-Saxon, this is misleading. According to *The Story of English*, "Computer analysis of the language has shown that the 100 most common words in English are all of Anglo-Saxon origin."[38] Lincoln's habitual simplicity required him to use again and again a great many of these most common words, words like "a," "and," "are," "but," "here," "of," "the," "that," and "we." Setting these little building blocks aside, I count 104 words remaining in the Gettysburg Address, of which 60 are Latinate. This percentage still makes Lincoln somewhat more Anglo-Saxon in his word choice that most of his peers, because there are more words in the English language derived either from Latin *or* from the Latin-based French language than from Old English—also known as Anglo-Saxon—which was the original base from which the whole language slowly grew. But what gives Lincoln's language its distinctive flavor is *not* that it is a bit more Anglo-Saxon than the norm but that is so overwhelmingly biblical, with 269 of its 272 words appearing in some form in the King James.

By comparison, Everett's address, as it appeared in published form in 1864, runs to fifty-four pages and about fourteen thousand words. A careful count of his words and phrases that clearly and directly echo the King James Bible turns up an average of perhaps one word or phrase *every two pages*, whereas Lincoln's address can hardly go two *words* without a clear-cut biblical allusion. Everett had graduated from the Harvard Divinity School and certainly knew the Bible and the Prayer Book. Although he echoes both of these, he does so only intermittently and with no discernible pattern of any kind. His biblical and liturgical echoes never rise to the level of a clear and sustained metaphor. His most extended and most clear-cut reference to the Book of Common Prayer, if anything from such a diffuse and orotund writer can ever be called clear-cut, is his direct quotation of "sedition, privy conspiracy, and rebellion." It is worth noting how different Everett and Lincoln sound when they echo any literary work—how different, for example, Everett's agonizingly slow and roundabout reference to the Prayer Book sounds from Lincoln's precise, seamless, unselfconscious, and lightning-like allusions to both Bible and Prayer Book:

> Not content with the sanctions of human justice, of all the crimes against the law of the land it is singled out for the denunciations of religion. The litanies of every church in Christendom whose ritual embraces that office, as far as I am aware, from the metropolitan cathedrals of Europe to the humblest missionary chapel in the islands of the sea, concur with the Church of England in imploring the Sovereign of the Universe, by the most awful adjurations which the heart of man can conceive or his tongue utter, to deliver us from "sedition, privy conspiracy, and rebellion." And reason good; for while a rebellion against tyranny,—a rebellion designed, after prostrating arbitrary power, to establish free government on the basis of justice and truth,—is an enterprise on which good men and angels may look with complacency, an unprovoked rebellion of ambitious men against a beneficent government, for the purpose—the avowed purpose—of establishing, extending, and perpetuating any form of injustice and wrong, is an imitation on earth of that first foul revolt of "the Infernal Serpent," against which the Supreme Majesty of heaven sent forth the armed myriads of his angels, and clothed the right arm of his Son with the three-bolted thunders of omnipotence.[39]

Everett is quoting from the Litany in the Prayer Book, more particularly from these lines:

> From all sedition, privy conspiracy, and rebellion; from all false doctrine, heresy, and schism; from hardness of heart, and contempt of thy Word and Commandment.
> *Good Lord, deliver us.*

What one hears from Everett throughout the long passage above is a jumble of sources and styles. It is hard to find a phrase anywhere in this long paragraph, including "the heart of man can conceive, or his tongue utter," that in whole or significant part precisely echoes a verse from the Bible. By the same token, one has to fight through a forest of untrimmed trees and underbrush to understand that the speaker is even quoting from the Prayer Book. What he seems to be saying at first is that *all* church services all over the world contain words denouncing "sedition, privy conspiracy, and rebellion." Even when one finally locates the actual source of these words in the Litany that appears in both the Prayer Book of the Church of England and the Prayer Book of the Episcopal Church of America, one cannot help seeing that Everett has stripped the words too bare to retain any of the rhythm of the source from which he has drawn them. At the end of his long, tortuous paragraph, he has cast his three-part phrase about sedition, privy conspiracy, and rebellion into the fiery organ tones of John Milton's *Paradise Lost*, there to burn and roar with the infernal serpent and its three-bolted thunders. Lincoln's music is as clear and simple as David's harp. Everett's is a cacophony of clashing instruments and styles.

Regardless of what each is saying, Lincoln always *sounds* better than Everett. Lincoln uses far fewer metaphors and is far more faithful to those he chooses. The music of his diction elevates the familiar and the simple to the level of great poetry. As his first sentence uses the long *o* for its assonance or internal rime, so his second sentence uses the long *a* for the same effect: "Now we are en*ga*ged in a *great* civil war, testing whether that *na*tion, or any *na*tion so conceived and so dedi*ca*ted, can long endure." This sort of thing goes on throughout the speech. In addition to a rhythm remarkably close to that of poetry is the constant drumbeat of artful repetition. Every single one of the ten sentences in the address contains at least one appearance of the first-person-plural pronoun—"we," "us," "our." Supplemented by two appearances of "us" and one of "our," "we" alone appears ten times. This is more than any other word and indeed any other homograph except "that," which appears thirteen times but as two different words: eight times as a subordinate conjunction and five times as a demonstrative adjective. The "we-us-our" drumbeat is an unmistakable echo of the services and prayers in the Book of Common Prayer: "Our Father . . . forgive us" (Lord's Prayer), "We receive this Child" (Baptism), "we are gathered" (Marriage), "we may be preserved in body and soul" (Confirmation), "we may be gathered unto our fathers" (Visitation of the Sick), and "we . . . commit his body to the ground; earth to earth" (Burial of the Dead). Of course "we" is also an unmistakable echo of "We hold these truths to be self-evident: that all men are created equal . . ." from the Declaration of Independence and "We the people of the United States, in order to form a more perfect union" from the preamble to the Constitution.

Lincoln's metaphor of birth and rebirth is built, as we have seen, around two kinds of baptism. The first is of a newborn nation being baptized by water as an infant. The last is of an aging America caught up in "a new birth of freedom" and a baptism of fire. There is nothing difficult or exotic about this extended metaphor to anyone who is as familiar with the King James Bible as were both Lincoln and his audience at Gettysburg. But because we today have lost their intimate familiarity with the work that served as his chief and continual source and reference, there is no choice but to work our way through the Gettysburg Address one word, one phrase, one verse at a time.

Implicit in the story of the birth of Jesus is its happy outcome. Implicit in the death of Jesus is the even happier outcome for his believers. From birth comes rebirth. From death comes life. Birth and rebirth—birth and resurrection—this is the sustained metaphor that ties together the Gettysburg Address from beginning to end. Even when Lincoln also invokes the rituals of marriage and burial, he does so within this overarching context of birth and new birth. Throughout his address, Lincoln never once loses sight of the central idea that a nation born, baptized, and dedicated in 1776 as a kind of messiah among the nations of the earth has gathered its people to be rededicated and reborn upon a great battlefield of a great civil war in 1863. Reborn and rededicated on this solemn and ceremonial occasion, this nation will—it is to be hoped—be reunited happily in marriage in God's good time. It will be a marriage in which the tragic issue of slavery that separated North from South in the first place will be forever ended by reaffirming the same guiding principle to which the nation was first dedicated by the founding fathers on July 4, 1776—the sacred and immortal principle that "all men are created equal."

Fitting and Proper

The phrase "fitting and proper" in the fifth sentence—the final sentence of the first half or first act of the Gettysburg Address—grew directly, and demonstrably, from "meet and right" in the Book of Common Prayer's service of Holy Communion. All four adjectives mean the same thing. Lincoln and Seward began by stealing "meet and right" straight from Holy Communion and placing the phrase straight into their Proclamation of Thanksgiving issued on July 15, 1863, just days after the two great victories at Vicksburg and Gettysburg. Reminding all Americans of these two great victories and the great sacrifices this nation had paid for them, the president and his secretary of state declared, "It is meet and right to recognize and confess the presence of the Almighty Father and the power of His Hand equally in these triumphs and in these sorrows."[1] This proclamation contains many other words taken straight from the same service—"Almighty God," "vouchsafe," and "supplications and prayers." In Holy Communion, "Almighty God" appears four times, and "vouchsafe" and "prayers and supplications" three times apiece. Like "meet and right," all these are obviously ritualized words or phrases. Lincoln and his photographic memory would surely have recognized that the Bible was *not* the source for all three. "Vouchsafe," for example, appears nowhere in the King James, nor does "meet and right." Did the president recognize Seward's source as the Prayer Book he had read, recited, and listened to so many times in church? Did Seward share his source with the president, either on his own initiative or in response to Lincoln's curiosity? A "no" to either question seems unlikely, a "no" to both, simply beyond belief.

The most ritualized phrase in all of Holy Communion is "meet and right." But an even more compelling reason for its appearance in the Lincoln-Seward Proclamation of Thanksgiving is that this ritualized phrase appears in the communion service specifically in connection with the idea of thanksgiving:

Priest. Let us give thanks unto our Lord God.
Answer. It is meet and right so to do.

The same words "meet" and "right" are then repeated by the presiding priest and once again in connection with the giving of thanks:

> IT is very meet, right, and our bounden duty, that we should, at all times, give thanks unto thee, O Lord, Almighty, everlasting God.

Seward must have been proud and pleased that he had found a phrase for the Thanksgiving proclamation that had been associated for three hundred years and more with giving thanks to the Lord. It is hard to imagine that he would *not* have shared this pleasure with Lincoln, because both men were so passionate about words and ideas. Clearly the final sentence quoted above is the paradigm for Lincoln's "It is altogether fitting and proper that we should do this."

In their very next proclamation issued less than three months later, the October 3 proclamation of the general thanksgiving that our nation still follows to this day on the last Thursday of every November, the president and his secretary selected another phrase that means essentially the same thing as "meet and right." They chose "fit and proper." The changing of the phrase may have been occasioned by nothing more than a need for some variety in the many proclamations they issued together. Their very first proclamation, issued back on April 15, 1861, had used "I . . . have thought fit" and "I deem it proper."[2] The October proclamation now combined these very words in one phrase:

> No human counsel hath devised nor hath any mortal hand worked out these great things. They are the gracious gifts of the Most High God, who, while dealing with us in anger for our sins, hath nevertheless remembered mercy. It has seemed to me fit and proper that they should be solemnly, reverently and gratefully acknowledged as with one heart and one voice by the whole American People. I do therefore invite my fellow citizens in every part of the United States, and also those who are at sea and those who are sojourning in foreign lands, to set apart and observe the last Thursday of November next, as a day of Thanksgiving and Praise to our beneficent Father who dwelleth in the Heavens.[3]

The reference to "those who are at sea" and the overflow of "and" in the closing sentence of this proclamation directly recall the Prayer Book's Forms of Prayer to be Used at Sea, especially this closing prayer of thanksgiving: "And, we beseech thee, give us grace to improve this great mercy to thy glory, the advancement of thy gospel, the honour of our country, and, as much as in us lieth, to the good of all mankind. And, we beseech thee, give us a sense of this great mercy, as may engage us to a true thankfulness." When someone expressed a desire to sell the original of this October proclamation as a benefit for soldiers, John Nicolay's response on April 1, 1864, shows that the proclamation had been "written by Seward and is in his handwriting."[4] Even without Nicolay's definitive evidence, a careful reader would have questioned some of these words as having come from Lincoln or at least from Lincoln alone, for the President was never in the habit of using—except in direct quotations—totally archaic words such as "hath" and "dwelleth."

But Lincoln was also never in the habit of issuing official pronouncements without his personal approval. More than any other president in history, he worried a great deal about the effect of his public speeches and pronouncements. Gideon Welles, who served with fellow Episcopalian Seward in both Lincoln's and Andrew Johnson's cabinets, published a book in 1869 countering the claims of Charles Francis Adams that Seward deserved more credit than Lincoln himself for what had been said and done during Lincoln's time in office. One of Welles' main points related specifically to Seward's writing things for Lincoln: "Mr. Seward held a ready and prolific pen, and had a mind fertile in expedients, but his judgment and conclusions were not so always so sound and reliable as to pass without revision and Executive emendations and approval."[5] The fact that the October proclamation has more uses of "I," "me," or "my" than the one from July suggests that Lincoln may have been more personally involved in its drafting. It would have been the most natural thing in the world for Lincoln to have shared with his secretary of state what he wanted or needed in an upcoming proclamation. No president was ever more aware of the importance of words and their effect on public morale. Certainly "fit and proper" is simpler and clearer than "meet and right" and much more in keeping with Lincoln's own predispositions and habitual preferences in his choice of words.

The word "meet" in the Prayer Book's sense of "suitable" or "appropriate" had become archaic to many people by 1863, particularly in spoken English. Even in the King James Bible, only 25 of the 132 appearances of "meet" convey the meaning of "suitable" or "appropriate." Of these 25, one had been so misunderstood a century or more before Lincoln that a new word was created, almost comically, from the misunderstanding. The word "helpmeet" came into being from a failure to understand the phrase "help meet" from the King James. Here is how the *OED* explains the word "helpmeet": "A compound absurdly formed by taking the two words "help meet" in Gen. ii. 18, 20 ('an help meet for him,' i.e. a help . . . suitable for him) as one word."[6]

From his earliest days, Lincoln had a passion for clarity in everything he said or wrote. He made this point to a minister named John Gulliver, who had praised him for clarity after Lincoln's speech at Norwich, Connecticut, in early 1860:

> I remember how, when a mere child, I used to get irritated when any body talked to me in a way I could not understand. I don't think I ever got angry at anything else in my life. But that always disturbed my temper and has ever since. I can remember going to my little bedroom, after hearing the neighbors talk of an evening with my father, and spending no small part of the night walking up and down, and trying to make out what was the exact meaning of some of their, to me, dark sayings. I could not sleep, though I often tried to, when I got on such a hunt after

an idea, until I had caught it; and when I thought I had got it, I was not satisfied until I had repeated it over and over, until I had put it in language plain enough, as I thought, for any boy I knew to comprehend. This was a kind of passion with me, and it has stuck by me, for I am never easy now, when I am handling a thought, till I have bounded it north, and bounded it south, and bounded it east, and bounded it west. Perhaps that accounts for the characteristic you observe in my speeches, though I never put the two things together before.[7]

Lincoln's old law partner and biographer William Herndon—always a skeptical man, especially of ministers, and sometimes too much so—pointed out a raft of alleged inaccuracies in this account and thus impugned the whole account. It remained for Harold Holzer in his recent and masterful book on the Cooper Union Address to vindicate the fundamental truth of it by demonstrating that Gulliver had sent the account to Lincoln himself for any objections from the president before the article was ever published. In Holzer's words, "The reverend, whom Herndon acknowledged to be 'a gentleman and a true Christian,' would certainly not have allowed the piece to appear in print had the president objected."[8] It would have been perfectly in character for Lincoln to have suggested to Seward something clearer, simpler, more straightforward than "meet and right" for the proclamation declaring a permanent Thanksgiving. Even if Seward on his own came up with "fit and proper," he would surely have known that it sounded more like the president for whom he was writing than the Prayer Book's "meet and right."

For "fit" and "proper" were words that Lincoln had used before and was clearly comfortable with. Riding the train to Washington for his first inauguration, the newly elected president had made a number of speeches along the way, all of them largely impromptu and therefore an index to the range of words that sprang most naturally to his lips. On the steps of the capitol at Columbus, Ohio, he said, "If any of the other candidates had been elected, I think it would have been altogether becoming and proper for all to have joined in showing honor, quite as well to the office, and the country, as to the man."[9] Later along the way, at Buffalo, New York, he used the word "fit": "Your worthy Mayor has thought fit to express the hope that I may be able to relieve the country from its present—or I should say, its threatened difficulties. I am sure I bring a heart true to the work."[10] In Albany, New York, he used "altogether befitting"[11] when replying to the governor and "fitting" alone when addressing the legislature: "now I think it were more fitting that I should close these hasty remarks."[12] In New York City, he used "fitting" once again:

I do suppose that while the political drama being enacted in this country at this time is rapidly shifting in its scenes, forbidding an anticipation with any degree of certainty to-day what we shall see to-morrow, that it was peculiarly fitting that

I should see it all up to the last minute before I should take ground, that I might be disposed by the shifting of the scenes afterward again to shift.[13]

In the same speech, the president-elect used "proper" as well, saying that since the election he had been avoiding public speaking, believing "that was the proper course for me to take."[14] Then he repeated the same word: "I have kept silence for the reason that I supposed it was peculiarly proper that I should do so until the time came when, according to the customs of the country, I should speak officially."[15] In Wilmington, Delaware, he was "flattered by the encomiums you have seen fit to bestow upon me."[16] Clearly, then, "fit," "fitting," and "proper" all came naturally to Lincoln. He liked all forms of the word "fit." Years before Gettysburg, in an unpublished fragment, he had reflected on the Declaration of Independence and its claim that "all men are created equal" in these memorable and biblical words, "The assertion of that *principle*, at *that time*, was *the* word, *'fitly spoken'* which has proven an 'apple of gold' to us."[17] Here, Lincoln was clearly echoing the beautiful words of Proverbs 25:11: "A word fitly spoken is like apples of gold in pictures of silver." It seems very likely, then, that "fit and proper" in the October 3 Thanksgiving Proclamation bears the personal stamp of Abraham Lincoln.

An old misconception that the secretary of state wrote or collaborated with Lincoln on the Gettysburg Address has long since been laid to rest in the scholars' field, the proof provided by Seward himself. The clearest statement of the truth appears in John M. Taylor's biography *William Henry Seward: Lincoln's Right Hand*: "The next day, one of those who had just heard Lincoln asked Seward if he had had any hand in the president's speech. Seward replied that nobody but Abraham Lincoln could have made that address."[18] At the same time, it is true that Lincoln often turned to Seward for verbal suggestions and opinions in cases where he himself was determined to have the last word. The most famous example had occurred when Lincoln was composing his First Inaugural Address, and Seward had suggested this paragraph to use at the end:

I close. We are not and must not be aliens or enemies but fellow countrymen and brethren. Although passion has strained our bonds of affection too hardly, they must not, I am sure they will not, be broken. The mystic chords which proceeding from so many battle fields and so many patriot graves pass through all the hearts and all the hearths in this broad continent of ours will yet again harmonize in their ancient music when breathed upon by the guardian angel of the nation.[19]

Lincoln transformed this into something even better—much better:

I am loth to close. We are not enemies, but friends. We must not be enemies. Though passion may have strained, it must not break our bonds of affection. The mystic chords of memory, stretching from every battle-field, and patriot grave, to every living heart and hearthstone, all over this broad land, will yet swell the chorus of the Union, when again touched, as surely they will be, by the better angels of our nature.[20]

Seward was himself echoing James Madison from "The Federalist No. 14," who, in turn, was echoing in places the Consecration of a Church from the Book of Common Prayer:

> Hearken not to the voice which petulantly tells you that the form of government recommended for your adoption is a novelty in the political world; that it has never yet had a place in the theories of the wildest projectors; that it rashly attempts what it is impossible to accomplish. No, my countrymen, shut your ears against this unhallowed language. Shut your hearts against the poison which it conveys; the kindred blood which flows in the veins of American citizens, the mingled blood which they have shed in defense of their sacred rights, consecrate their Union and excite horror at the idea of their becoming aliens, rivals, enemies.[21]

Anyone with an eye or an ear can perceive that Lincoln's words are both clearer and lovelier than Seward's or Madison's. Indeed, as literature, they are in a class by themselves. Even if Seward was the first to write or suggest "fit and proper" for the October 3 Thanksgiving Proclamation, these were clearly words that Lincoln had used before and would use even more brilliantly in the Gettysburg Address, where he would transform "fit and proper" into the more melodious "fitting and proper."

Thus Lincoln, with some degree of assistance from Seward, moved from the Prayer Book's "meet and right" in July to "fit and proper" in October. Then he and he alone came up with "altogether fitting and proper" for the November Gettysburg Address. Tracing the process by which he arrived at such a poetical final choice may seem wearisome to those who regard words as nothing more than units for carrying meaning the way electrical impulses carry messages in computers. But for word lovers who know how painstakingly difficult great writing can be, nothing is more pleasurable and instructive than to watch a genius tracking and finding the best possible word from an almost infinite range of possibilities. Obviously, one influence on Lincoln's choice was the Book of Common Prayer with which Seward the Episcopal churchwarden was so intimately familiar. If one individual reintroduced Lincoln to the Book of Common Prayer during his White House years, causing him to look at it more closely than he ever had before, Seward is surely the one because he was so active in his church and because the president and his secretary of state worked so closely and so often together. Reading Seward's proclamations, an always word-conscious and word-loving president could hardly have suspended his curiosity about words that sounded so much like the Bible and at the same time so different, too. In this case as in so many others, Lincoln never stopped at simple borrowing but always sharpened and improved whatever phrase he borrowed.

Edward Everett, who gave an advance copy of his own speech to Lincoln so that the two would not say the same things, chose the phrase "just and proper" for his own indirect echo of the Prayer Book, using "just and proper" three times in three consecutive sentences.[22] Now "just" is a very common word in the King James Bible. It appears in numerous compound phrases—from "a just man and perfect" in Genesis 6:9 to "a good man, and a just" in Luke 23:50 to "just and equal" in Colossians 4:1. But in addition to avoiding any duplication of Everett, Lincoln was unlikely for his own personal reasons to choose the word "just" over the word "fit" or "fitting." The word "just" can also mean "righteous" in the sense of an eye for an eye, and Lincoln was always more predisposed to mercy than to unvarnished justice. Like Everett's "just," the "fit" of the October proclamation appears throughout the King James Bible—from "fit for the battle" in 1 Chronicles 12:8 to "fit for the kingdom of God" in Luke 9:62. But as compared to "fit," "fitting" in the Gettysburg Address is an enormous improvement. For one thing, "fitting" has the same number of syllables as its companion word, "proper," and this makes for a more harmonious sound. As for "proper," the second half of the phrase, it not only appears in the October Thanksgiving proclamation but is also the adjective form of the noun "propriety" that Lincoln had used in the oldest surviving draft of the Gettysburg Address: "This we may, in all propriety do."[23] The rhythm of "fitting and proper" is a clear improvement over "fit and proper," and the overall effect is much more poetical and musical. We have seen that Lincoln had included both "fitting" and "proper" in his speeches on the way to the White House without ever joining the two into a single phrase. Clearly, when he put them together at last for his Gettysburg Address, this was *his* phrase. Lincoln was so pleased with "fitting and proper" that he used it again in his Second Inaugural Address,[24] the second-greatest speech of his life.

Equally clearly, the original mold for Lincoln's sentence was the Communion service in the Prayer Book, "It is meet and right so to do," and, more especially, "It is very meet, right, and our bounden duty, that we should, at all times, and in all places, give thanks unto thee, O Lord, Almighty, everlasting God." Both sentences provide powerful internal evidence that Lincoln knew this service and used it as the structural base for his fifth sentence. In the second of these back-to-back sentences from the Prayer Book, appears the very same kind of construction that occurs in Lincoln's sentence: "It is" + two synonyms of approbation and approval + "that we should" + verb + object. That phrase-by-phrase echoing is indicative of a fully intentional literary allusion. It is a perfect example of how Lincoln took something from a ritual that was far less widely known than the Bible and transformed it into something much clearer to the average person. He kept the sound and rhythm of the Prayer Book's ritual, and even its structure, but substituted his own simple and down-to-earth phrase "fitting and proper" for the more archaic "meet and right."

The next step in Lincoln's transformation of his fifth sentence into poetry was his adding the word "altogether." He added it as the first part of the silver frame that would surround "fitting and proper." Once the rich, rousing, King Jamesian "altogether" had replaced the Prayer Book's gray little adverb "very," the whole frame began to sparkle. Those who recall Lincoln's magnificent Second Inaugural Address will recall his later but equally wonderful use of "altogether."

> Fondly do we hope—fervently do we pray—that this mighty scourge of war may speedily pass away. Yet, if God wills that it continue, until all the wealth piled by the bond-man's two hundred and fifty years of unrequited toil shall be sunk, and until every drop of blood drawn with the lash, shall be paid by another drawn with the sword, as was said three thousand years ago, so still it must be said "the judgments of the Lord, are true and righteous altogether."[25]

In the Second Inaugural, "altogether" is associated with a God of righteousness. But even there it does not come across as a cold word. In most of its biblical appearances, it is very warm indeed, as in that warm and familiar description from the Song of Solomon where the lover—allegorized into the Messiah by later Christians—is described as "altogether lovely" (5:16). The word strongly suggests the social strength and warmth of "all together." When one hears, "It is altogether fitting and proper that we should do this," one almost feels that "we"—the "we" that appears in some form in every sentence of the Gettysburg Address—are now reciting the words together "all together" like a congregation reciting a ritual. The warmth of "altogether" is underscored by two virtually identical passages from the Book of Numbers: "I took thee to curse mine enemies, and, behold, thou hast blessed them altogether" (23:11), and "I called thee to curse mine enemies, and, behold, thou hast altogether blessed them these three times" (24:10). The second part—the closing part—of the silver frame that Lincoln placed around "fitting and proper" is the Prayer Book ending "that we should" followed by verb and object. The verb and object in the Prayer Book is "give praise" to God. The verb and object in the Gettysburg Address are "do this"—that is, dedicate this ground to God. Thus the little eleven-word sentence that Lincoln fashioned for the heart of his Gettysburg Address—the shortest sentence in the whole address—became in its final form, especially in its "altogether fitting and proper," an apt and beautiful blend of the King James Bible and the Book of Common Prayer. Yet there can be no doubt that every word in Lincoln's fifth sentence would have been recognizable and understandable in its own right to even the least-educated person in his audience.

The service of Holy Communion that provided Lincoln his model for the fifth sentence relies on the very same symbolism as the service of Baptism. The

Catechism declares that communion and Baptism are the only two sacraments essential to salvation:

> *Question.* HOW many sacraments hath Christ ordained in his Church?
>
> *Ans.* Two only, as generally necessary to salvation; that is to say, Baptism, and the Supper of the Lord.

The Catechism goes on to explain why Christ ordained the Lord's Supper.

> *Quest.* Why was the sacrament of the Lord's Supper ordained?
>
> *Ans.* For the continual remembrance of the sacrifice of the death of Christ, and of the benefits which we receive thereby.
>
> *Quest.* What is the outward part or sign of the Lord's Supper?
>
> *Ans.* Bread and wine, which the Lord hath commanded to be received.
>
> *Quest.* What is the inward part or thing signified?
>
> *Ans.* The body and blood of Christ, which are spiritually taken and received by the faithful in the Lord's Supper.
>
> *Quest.* What are the benefits whereof we are partakers thereby?
>
> *Ans.* The strengthening and refreshing of our souls by the body and blood of Christ, as our bodies are by the bread and wine.

The communion service itself describes what this "strengthening" means when it says that Christ "did humble himself, even to the death upon the cross, for us miserable sinners, who lay in darkness and the shadow of death; that he might make us the children of God, and exalt us to everlasting life." Thus the bread and wine symbolize both Christ's death and the "benefits" of that death—resurrection, rebirth, everlasting life. By the end of Lincoln's fifth sentence, which closes out the first half or first "act" of his address, his audience has heard language specifically and irresistibly connected with the two very sacraments, baptism and communion, that are "generally necessary" to salvation. Both of those sacraments symbolize death and rebirth in both the Bible and the Book of Common Prayer. What could be more apt and beautiful—what, indeed, more fitting and proper?

Lincoln used great patience and care to put special emphasis on his "fitting and proper" sentence. This is the fifth and final sentence in the first act or movement of the Gettysburg Address. Every other sentence in the Gettysburg Address is tied to a predecessor by at least one key word that in most cases is a memorable echo of the King James Bible. For example, the biblical "conceived" and the liturgical "dedicated" from the first sentence are repeated in the same form and the same order in the second sentence. It bears repeating that the word "dedicated" from the first two sentences later reappears with exactly the same suggestion of baptism in the last two sentences, the ninth and tenth. Another word from the first sentence that reappears in the second is "nation." The word "war" from the second sentence is repeated in the third. Who, having heard them once, can ever forget the immortal words of Isaiah 2:4, "and they shall beat their swords into plowshares, and their spears into pruninghooks: nation shall not lift up sword against nation, neither shall they learn war any more"? The word "great" appears in both the second and third sentences of the Gettysburg Address and in a similar kind of prepositional phrase: "in a great civil war," "on a great battle-field of that war." In turn, "battle-field of that war" from the third sentence is echoed by "portion of that field" in the fourth sentence, which is another of the never-ending biblical echoes. It is an echo of both "portion of the field" in a description of a burial place from 2 Kings 9:25 and "portion" in the sense of a rightful inheritance from Psalm 16:5, "The Lord is the portion of mine inheritance." Without tracing through every sentence these sentence-to-sentence echoes and links, another kind of echo appears when the "new nation" of the opening sentence is echoed in the "new birth" of the closing. Now what is so striking about the fifth sentence, "It is altogether fitting and proper that we should do this," is that the unexpected *absence* of an echo from earlier sentences is what makes this sentence stand out. This highly conspicuous and unusual sentence wraps up Lincoln's stately introduction of five sentences and marks them off from his rousing conclusion of five. It concludes the first act or movement of the address and prepares us for the second. The only echoed words in this short sentence in the very heart of Lincoln's speech are tiny ones such as "it," "that," and the omnipresent "we." Precisely because the fifth sentence contains so little repetition and none involving major words, the reader is compelled to pronounce the entire sentence very slowly and to make a full stop before the next sentence whose opening words signal a major shift in thought—"But, in a larger sense." With these opening words, the shift from introduction to conclusion is complete. How brilliantly has Lincoln slowed down the music with his fifth sentence and allowed the curtain to fall! The second act of the Gettysburg Address is now ready to begin, the curtain ready to rise once more.

Consecrate—Dedicate—Hallow

The second act of the Gettysburg Address opens with the sixth sentence and the words "But, in a larger sense." The two acts are equal in number of sentences, with five each. But in terms of words, the second is much longer. This makes sense, because the first act is introduction, and the second is conclusion. The first act says, "We are here today to celebrate the birth and rebirth of a nation dedicated to the principle of equality by consecrating this cemetery, and it is altogether appropriate that we should do so." The second act says, "But we cannot consecrate with words alone what these heroic dead have consecrated with their great deeds but can only renew our dedication to the cause for which they died, in the hope that this nation, and the representative government for which it stands, will be reborn and rededicated for all time." In the sixth sentence, which is the opening sentence of the second act, Lincoln focuses on three words, three transitive active verbs—the famous trinity of "dedicate," "consecrate," "hallow." He introduces each of these sonorous and impressive words with the small, familiar words, "we can not." His nearly perfect iambic rhythm forces the reading voice to emphasize the three largest and most crucial words in the sentence—"dedicate," "consecrate," "hallow." Did Lincoln draw this trinity of lovely words from the poet's eye of pure inspiration or, as we have seen him do so often, from that small and familiar store of literary sources he knew so well and loved so dearly?

The first thing to note is the presence of ritual, because all three words, despite small differences in connotation, mean essentially the same thing, just as "fitting" and "proper" do. We have seen that English has three words for a great many common objects or ideas because of the unique history of the language. After William the Conqueror's French had fully grafted on to King Harold's English around 1150, the blended language called Middle English also borrowed words directly from Latin, the ultimate source of French. "Hallow" is the oldest of this trio, dating back to Old English. "Consecrate" was introduced into the English language, according to the *OED*, by Chaucer in the "Monk's Tale" from his *Canterbury Tales* in 1386. Chaucer almost certainly took his "consecrat" from the Latin Vulgate Bible but may have been influenced as well by similar forms in French, a language in which he was also fluent, having translated *Le Roman de la rose* into English. "Dedicate" was one of the many thousands of words borrowed or adapted directly from Latin during the Renaissance that began less than a hundred years after Chaucer's death in 1400. According to the *OED*, the first appearance of "dedicate" as an English verb was in 1533.[1] Even though all three of Lincoln's words appear in the King James Bible, they never appear together in one sentence or one verse or even one chapter.

It was not the Bible but the Book of Common Prayer that provided Lincoln's precise and immediate source. The fact that all three words appear together in one rousing sentence from a service in the Prayer Book suggests beyond a reasonable doubt that this service was Lincoln's precise source for "dedicate," "consecrate," and "hallow." This service is called the Form of Consecration of a Church or Chapel. It is a perfect source indeed for a ceremony that David Wills, the organizer of the Gettysburg ceremonies, always referred to as a "consecration."

The key sentence is found within a prayer that is to be read aloud by the bishop in attendance. Because certain words in the Prayer Book already appear in italics, the three key words are boldfaced below.

Then the Bishop, kneeling, shall say the following
Prayer.
O ETERNAL GOD, mighty in power, and of majesty incomprehensible, whom the heaven of heavens cannot contain, much less the walls of temples made with hands, and who yet hast been graciously pleased to promise thy especial presence wherever two or three of thy faithful servants shall assemble in thy name to offer up their praises and supplications unto thee; vouchsafe, O Lord, to be present with us, who are here gathered together, with all humility and readiness of heart, to **consecrate** this place to the honour of thy great name, separating it henceforth from all **unhallowed**, ordinary and common uses, and **dedicating** it to thy service, for reading thy holy Word, for celebrating thy holy sacraments, for offering to thy glorious Majesty the sacrifices of prayer and thanksgiving, for blessing thy people in thy name, and for all other holy offices. Accept, O Lord, this service at our hands, and bless it with such success as may tend most to thy glory, and the furtherance of our happiness, both temporal and spiritual, through Jesus Christ our blessed Lord and Saviour. *Amen.*

Note how the three words appear in three successive phrases and how each phrase manages to highlight each of the three key words: "consecrate this place"—"from all unhallowed"—"dedicating it to thy service." Lincoln would underscore the same three words even more dramatically by putting all three into the same present tense, placing each verb into a ritual phrase beginning "we can not," and then in the three final known copies that he prepared in early 1864 for donation or publication (the Everett, the Bancroft, and the Bancroft recopied into what is now called the Bliss copy or final text), visually highlighting each verb phrase with an emphatic, finger-pointing dash: "But, in a larger sense, we can not dedicate—we can not consecrate—we can not hallow—this ground." It is also the verb tense that distinguishes Lincoln's baptismal "dedicated" in the first, second, ninth, and tenth sentences from "dedicate" in the fourth and sixth. The two different forms and tenses spring demonstrably from two different services.

The bishop's prayer at the consecration of a church is preceded by a statement that he, as the presiding official at the consecration, is directed to make to the congregation. This is a statement that includes not just "unhallowed" but also "devotion" and its adjective and adverb forms, "devout" and "devoutly," which are boldfaced below. "Devotion" will soon appear, of course, in Lincoln's "last full measure of devotion."

> DEARLY beloved in the Lord, forasmuch as **devout** and holy men . . . have erected houses for the public worship of God, and separated them from all unhallowed, worldly, and common uses, in order to fill men's minds with greater reverence for his glorious Majesty, and affect their hearts with more **devotion** and humility in his service . . . let us not doubt but that he will also favourably approve our godly purpose of setting apart this place in solemn manner, for the performance of the several offices of religious worship, and let us faithfully and **devoutly** beg his blessing on this our undertaking.

The word "devotion" appears yet again in a statement immediately following the prayer, a statement made while the standing bishop is "turning his face towards the Congregation." This statement has the form of a prayer without the usual kneeling or sitting:

> Grant, we beseech thee, blessed Lord, that whosoever shall draw near to thee in this place, to give thee thanks for the benefits which they have received at thy hands, to set forth thy most worthy praise, to confess their sins unto thee, and to ask such things as are requisite and necessary as well for the body as for the soul, may do it with such steadiness of faith, and with such seriousness, affection, and **devotion** of mind, that thou mayest accept their bounden duty and service, and vouchsafe to give whatever in thy infinite wisdom thou shalt see to be most expedient for them.

After this statement, the Bishop, now sitting, says: "BLESSED be thy Name, O Lord, that it hath pleased to put it into the hearts of thy servants to appropriate and **devote** this house to thy honour and worship." Remember that the word "devotion" never appears in the King James. Yet here is some form of it appearing five different times in a service of barely four pages in the Prayer Book—strikingly persuasive evidence that Lincoln took "devotion" from the Book of Common

Prayer. In the King James, the nearest approach to "devotion" is "devotions," making its one and only appearance in Paul's sermon on Mars' Hill that Lincoln considered the greatest speech ever:

> Then Paul stood in the midst of Mars' hill, and said, Ye men of Athens, I perceive that in all things ye are too superstitious.
>
> For as I passed by, and beheld your devotions, I found an altar with this inscription, TO THE UNKNOWN GOD. Whom therefore ye ignorantly worship, him declare I unto you. (Acts 17:22–23)

Here "devotions" clearly means something different from what Lincoln intended in his "last full measure of devotion." Tyndale translated the King James "devotions" as "the maner how ye worship youre goddes," a translation adopted by the Cranmer and the Geneva Bible.[2] Any reader of the King James can see at once that the word "devotions" in this passage does *not* mean what the Prayer Book and Lincoln mean by "devotion," which is religious fervor. In short, the internal evidence is overwhelming that Lincoln, who had a perfect memory for words and phrases he read or heard, drew four key words in the Gettysburg Address from the Order for the Consecration of a Church or Chapel in the Prayer Book—"consecrate," "dedicate," and "hallow" from one rousing prayer and "devotion" from the bishop's statements to the congregation that bracket and surround this prayer.

We have said that one good reason Lincoln might have turned to this service for consecrating a church was the language that David Wills had used in his invitation:

> Gettysburg Nov. 2 1863
> To His Excellency,
>   A. Lincoln,
>   President of the United States,
>   Sir,
>   The Several States having Soldiers in the Army
> of the Potomac, who were killed at the Battle of Gettysburg, or have
> since died at the various hospitals which were established in the
> vicinity, have procured grounds on a prominent part of the Battle
> Field for a Cemetery, and are having the dead removed to them and
> properly buried.
>   These Grounds will be Consecrated and set apart to this Sacred
> purpose, by appropriate Ceremonies, on Thursday, the 19th instant,—
>   Hon Edward Everett will deliver the Oration.
>   I am authorized by the Governors of the different States to invite
> you to be present; and participate in these Ceremonies, which will
> doubtless be very imposing and solemnly impressive.

It is the desire that, after the Oration, you, as Chief Executive of the Nation, formally set apart these grounds to their Sacred use by a few appropriate remarks.

It will be a source of great gratification to the many widows and orphans that have been made almost friendless by the Great Battle here, to have you here personally; and it will kindle anew in the breasts of the Comrades of these brave dead, who are now in the tented field or nobly meeting the foe in the front, a confidence that those who sleep in death on the Battle Field are not forgotten by those highest in Authority; and they will feel that, should their fate be the same, their remains will not be uncared for.

We hope you will be able to be present to perform this last solemn act to the Soldiers dead on this Battle Field.

I am with great

Respect, Your Excellency's

Obedient Servant,

David Wills

Agent for

A. G. Curtin Gov. of Penna.

and acting for all the States[3]

Wills' invitation to a ceremony where "These Grounds will be Consecrated and Set apart to this Sacred purpose" was a reprise of the same language he had used in inviting Edward Everett on September 23: "This burial-ground will be consecrated to this sacred and holy purpose."[4] From the start, David Wills had planned a ceremony of *consecration* but, as an active Presbyterian himself, he is unlikely to have intended any reference at all to the Consecration of a Church or Chapel from the Episcopal Prayer Book.

Wills reinforced his point in both letters by adding the word "sacred." He did the same thing in letters to others besides Lincoln and Everett. His October 30, 1863, letter to Ward Lamon, U.S. marshal for the District of Columbia, was reprinted on the second page of the Washington newspaper *The Daily National Intelligencer* on November 9, just ten days before the ceremony:

> SIR: The several loyal States having soldiers dead on the battle-field of Gettysburg have united in arrangements for the removal and proper burial of the remains of these fallen heroes in a cemetery on the battle-field. The grounds will be consecrated and set apart to the sacred purpose by appropriate and imposing ceremonies on Thursday, the 19th day of November next.

Lamon was a personal friend of Lincoln, who had made him marshal. Lamon's November 4 response to Wills, reprinted on the same page of the newspaper, contains over a half dozen of the same words or phrases, italicized hereafter, that would later appear in Lincoln's address: "I regard it no less a solemn duty than a pleasure to those who enjoy the protection of a *Government* under which all *civil* and religious *liberty* are secured to unite in *consecrating* a National Cemetery as a sacred *resting-place* for our country's heroes who fell at Gettysburg," Lamon began, before invoking "the *brave men* who lost their *lives* . . . in defense of our country" and "those who *so nobly* fell battling for *freedom*." But even if Lincoln was influenced by a word here or there from Lamon, it was never a word that stemmed from Lamon alone but always from some more significant source as well.

Wills also used the word "dedicatory" to describe the ceremony—or at least the president's part of it. On page 1 of its November 13 issue, Forney's *Washington Daily Chronicle* printed the entire program in Wills' own words:

> The procession will proceed to the Cemetery grounds, when a prayer will be offered up by Rev. T. H. Stockton, chaplain of the United States House of Representatives, and the oration delivered by Hon. Edward Everett; after this, a dirge, selected for the occasion, by Professor Longfellow, will be sung by a choir.
>
> This will be followed by dedicatory remarks by the President of the United States, setting apart the grounds for the sacred use for which it has been prepared.

Wills' use of "consecration" to describe the whole ceremony and his use of "dedicatory remarks" to describe the president's part in it were both retained in the title of a book published by Everett in Boston in January of 1864—*Address of Hon. Edward Everett at the Consecration of the National Cemetery at Gettysburg, 19th November, 1863, with the Dedicatory Speech of President Lincoln*. It is hardly surprising, however, that this distinction between two words so similar in meaning was not observed by all who covered the event. For example, the special correspondent for the *New York Times*, in his eyewitness account of all the events of November 19, 1863, began his article: "The ceremonies attending the dedication of the National Cemetery commenced this morning."[5] One of the headlines above his article reads, "Dedication of the National Cemetery at Gettysburgh."[6] The word "dedication" is just as much a religious term as "consecration." Its root meaning, according to the *OED*, is "a setting apart and devoting to the Deity or to a sacred purpose with solemn rites."[7] This explains why "dedicated" appears as a key word in the Public Baptism of Infants in the Prayer Book, where the child is dedicated to God and to sacred principles.

Lincoln managed, of course, to include both "consecrate" and "dedicate" in his address and to add "hallow" as well, using all three terms essentially as synonyms. At the same time, he respected their connotational and metrical differences when he changed "The brave men, living and dead, who struggled here, have *hallowed* it far above our poor power to add or detract" to "*consecrated* it." Note that Wills, the immediate source for "consecrate" and "dedicate," never used "hallow." Lincoln's source for the three words as a unit, as a trinity, was clearly the Prayer Book. What would have been more natural for the president to have recalled, after reading the words of Wills, than the service in the Prayer Book called the Order of Consecration of a Church or Chapel, where all three words appear together in a single sentence? Everett, a graduate of Harvard Divinity School, almost certainly consulted the same service, for he used "consecrate" in his fifth paragraph and "unhallowed" in his tenth, "unhallowed" being the very form of the word that appears in the Prayer Book. However, he never used "dedicate" at all, in any form, in any paragraph—not once in fourteen thousand words. It is typical of the differences between the two speakers that Lincoln is consistently clear-cut and point-to-point in his borrowings from any source, whereas Everett is always vague and hit-or-miss. In short, it was perfectly in character for Lincoln to have turned to a specific Prayer Book source for the three words meaning "to consecrate" and to have made his use of that source as clear as if he had left a note behind.

But the question remains why Lincoln, invited to help consecrate a *cemetery* as sacred ground, found it appropriate to echo a service for consecrating a *church*? In other words, why did he associate consecrating a cemetery with consecrating a church? The answer is that from time immemorial, cemeteries have been part of churchyards. When Lincoln had been asked to contribute an account of his life for a campaign biography back in 1860, his response had been brief: "It can all be condensed into a single sentence, and that sentence you will find in Gray's Elegy, 'The short and simple annals of the poor.'"[8] Lincoln was referring to one of his all-time favorite poems, Thomas Gray's "Elegy Written in a Country Churchyard." The cemetery of Gray's poem is clearly part of the church grounds, for the poet refers to the "churchway path" (1.114) over which the dead body is borne to the grave from the church in which the first part of the service is conducted. Gray's "unhonored dead" (1.93) from this poem that Lincoln loved so much would be recalled, with an appropriate twist, in the "honored dead" of the Gettysburg Address. The connection between Gray's poem and the Gettysburg ceremony seems even more poignant when one recalls how death had robbed all the young men buried in the newly consecrated cemetery at Gettysburg of any chance to reach their full potential in life and had robbed some of them, their bodies mangled in death, of even their personal identity. Gray's poem celebrates those whose names are unknown to the great world outside the country cemetery where their bodies lie—"some mute, inglorious Milton" (1.59)—the same situation that obtained with so many nameless young men among the Union dead who were cut down in the prime of their unfulfilled promise.[9]

One of the most remarkable features of the sentence "But, in a larger sense, we can not dedicate—we can not consecrate—we can not hallow—this ground" is that it comes very close to being perfect iambic meter. Lincoln made a habit all his life of reading out loud and very slowly. This habit was very useful for developing his sense of rhythm—or enhancing the sense of rhythm he was born with. He especially loved to read the plays of Shakespeare out loud and was commended more than once as a fine reader and actor by those who heard him. For example, F. B. Carpenter, who spent six months in the White House painting the signing of the Emancipation Proclamation that now hangs in the Capitol, recounted how the president, from memory, had quoted to him and a visitor from New York named Samuel Sinclair certain long and stirring passages from *Hamlet* and *Richard III*. Lincoln explained to the two men how these passages were sometimes "misapprehended" by actors and then demonstrated with both his remarks and his recitations exactly how he thought they should be understood and acted out. His opening speech from *Hamlet* was delivered, says Carpenter, "with a feeling and appreciation unsurpassed by anything I ever witnessed upon the stage."[10] Then Lincoln turned to one of King Richard III's soliloquies. First he explained why the "sophomoric" way that most actors interpret it is wrong and why an interpretation based on "the most intense bitterness and satire" is the right way. Then he proved his point by performing the scene "with a degree of force and power that made it seem like a new creation to me."[11]

> I could not refrain from laying down my palette and brushes, and applauding heartily, upon his conclusion, saying at the same time, half in earnest, that I was not sure but that he had made a mistake in the choice of a profession, considerably, as may be imagined, to his amusement. Mr. Sinclair has since repeatedly said to me that he has never heard these choice passages of Shakespeare rendered with more effect by the most famous of modern actors.[12]

All of the lines that Lincoln recited were in blank verse—unrimed iambic pentameter. No one can immerse himself in Shakespeare the way Lincoln did without absorbing those intoxicating iambic rhythms. In his younger days Lincoln had tried writing poems, complete with rime and a meter that was almost always iambic. Although none of these productions ever rose to the level of his best prose, they joined with his constant reading and recitation of Shakespeare to shape his magnificent prose into musical rhythms. Lincoln is among the most poetical and musical of prose writers, as can be seen by looking closely at the rhythms within the sentence beginning "But, in a larger sense."

This sentence is a series of iambic feet. The first foot of Lincoln's line, "But in," is reversed, like the first foot of a great many of Shakespeare's iambic lines, especially in his sonnets. This means that the accent falls on the first syllable instead of the second. (Even when this happens, however, the sensitive reader still hears a sort of ghost accent on the second syllable as well, so that one can choose to say "But *in*" almost as easily as one says "*But* in.") Only this reversed

CONSECRATE—DEDICATE—HALLOW

foot at the beginning and one extra unaccented syllable that is bracketed below
keep Lincoln's sentence from being perfectly iambic:

/ _ _ / _ / _ / _ / _ /
But in a larger sense, we can not dedicate—

_ / _ / _ / _ / _ / _ /
we can not consecrate—we can not hallow—[this] ground.

Nor is the iambic pattern peculiar to this one sentence. The iambs assert themselves periodically throughout the entire address, beginning with the opening
words:

/ / _ / _ / _ / _ / / _ / _ / _ /
Four score and seven years ago our fathers brought forth upon this continent

The opening of the eighth sentence is even more regular than that of the first
or the sixth:

_ / _ / _ / _ / _ / _ / _ /
The world will little note, nor long remember, what we say

The pattern is never clearer, never more insistent than in the closing words:

/ _ / _ / _ / _ / _ / _ / _ / _ /
. . . of the people, by the people, for the people, shall not perish from the earth.

Lincoln's editing of the speech into its final published form gave even greater
emphasis to the iambic beat when he moved the phrase "under God" from after
"shall" to before "shall."

The irony is that Lincoln's lack of a formal education may help to account for
his highly poetical prose, because what he does with rhythm is a violation of con-
ventional wisdom. Books on composition have advised for two hundred years and
more that prose should avoid those elements peculiar to poetry—meter and rime.
The following advice comes straight from those countless articles and textbooks
used over the last couple of centuries in English and American schools to teach
composition to students. Writing in the *Contemporary Review* in April 1885, just
two decades after the death of Lincoln, Robert Louis Stevenson summarized what
had been the prevailing view for Lincoln's age and long before: "Prose must be
rhythmical, and it may be as much so as you will; but it must not be metrical. It may
be anything, but it must not be verse."[13] The idea that meter will not serve in English
prose appears in David Irving's *Elements of English Composition* from 1803:

> The doctrine of the Greek and Roman critics has induced some to imagine, that our
> prose writings may be regulated by spondees and trochees, iambuses and paeons,

and other metrical feet. But, to refute the notion, nothing farther is necessary than its being applied to practice.[14]

Irving's advice also included a rationale for writers to rely on long words:

> Long words are commonly more agreeable to the ear than monosyllables. They please by the succession of sounds which they present: and accordingly the most musical language possess them in the greatest abundance.[15]

In the Gettysburg Address, only "proposition" and "altogether" have as many as ten letters. Only "dedicated" and "consecrated" join them as words of four syllables. Lincoln's average word is a scant four letters long. Over 200 of his 272 words are just one syllable long. Over 250 are no longer than two syllables. I can find no contemporary of Lincoln, literary or political, who used so many small words in a major work. Other composition books of Lincoln's day frowned on all forms of redundancy and repetition. For example, Alexander Jamieson's *Grammar of Rhetoric and Polite Literature, Comprehending the Principles of Language and Style, the Elements of Taste and Criticism; with Rules for the Study of Composition and Eloquence* pontificated in 1826:

> As sentences should be cleared of *redundant words*, so also of *redundant members*. As every word ought to present a *new idea*, so every member ought to contain a *new thought*. Opposed to this, stands the fault with which we sometimes meet, of the last member of a period [sentence] being nothing else than the echo of the former, or the repetition of it in different form.[16]

William F. Barton, writing many years later, criticized Lincoln on precisely this ground.

> Lincoln would have thought well not to say "a great civil war" and "a great battle-field." One use of that adjective, he might have thought sufficient.
> If Lincoln had reviewed his speech more deliberately he might have become convinced that it was unfortunate to use the word "that" as many as thirteen times.

Barton added: "A critic would probably say that it would have been better rhetorically if the word 'devotion' had not been repeated in the sentence which contains it twice."[17]

Clearly, then, Lincoln's constant repetitions of words such as "that" and "we," his redundancies built into "fitting and proper" and into "consecrate," "dedicate," "hallow," and "devotion" and his constant repetition of the idea of birth, death, and rebirth throughout his speech violated almost every academic norm of his day. The Gettysburg Address uses and reuses the same short and simple words over and over but includes just enough long words to create variety. We have already seen how masterful Lincoln is in his use of vowel repetition called assonance.

He is equally accomplished at the use of alliteration, or the repetition of initial consonant sounds: "Four . . . forth," "score . . . seven," "continent . . . conceived . . . created," "new nation," "portion . . . place. . . . proper," "dedicate . . . dead . . . detract," "poor power," "little note nor long," "unfinished . . . fought . . . far," "devotion . . . devotion . . . dead . . . died," "that these," "that this," "not . . . nation . . . not," and "people . . . people . . . people . . . perish." The final alliteration of the three "people" and "perish" suggests that Lincoln intended for these words to receive a greater emphasis than the little prepositions "of," "by," and "for." From beginning to end, he relies on every conceivable kind of repetition—of individual sounds, of individual words, of entire phrases. He even uses outright rime in his final sentence with "birth" and "earth," as he would use it in his Second Inaugural in yet another iambic sentence: "Fondly do we hope—fervently do we pray—that this mighty scourge of war may speedily pass away."

The essence of Lincoln's style is a poetic simplicity that has no fear of regularity, repetition, rime, or meter. Just as Lincoln relies on only one sustained metaphor of birth-death-rebirth throughout his speech, so he relies on only a few simple and familiar words, ritualistically repeated. This helps to produce an air of conviction that is impossible to achieve through those elegant and complicated figures of speech of the kind that Edward Everett was so wrongly celebrated for using. After Everett's death in 1864, Lincoln privately remarked to Noah Brooks, "Now, do you know, I think Edward Everett was much overrated. He hasn't left any enduring monument."[18] What Lincoln said about the simple eloquence of Henry Clay in his eulogy for that statesman could just as well have been said about his own:

> Mr. Clay's eloquence did not consist, as many fine specimens of eloquence [do], of types and figures—of antithesis and elegant arrangement of words and sentences; but rather of that deeply earnest and impassioned tone, and manner, which can proceed only from great sincerity and a thorough conviction, in the speaker of the justice and importance of his cause.[19]

The "dedicate"-"consecrate"-"hallow" sentence is a perfect example of such simple eloquence.

Earlier in this study we saw that the four appearances of "dedicated," as distinguished from the two appearances of "dedicate," clearly echo the service of Holy Baptism. We have now observed that the two appearances of "dedicate" echo with equal clarity the service for the Consecration of a Church or Chapel. The six total appearances of "dedicate" in both tenses outstrip all other words in the address except "that," we," "the," and "here." Again, it is easy to distinguish between the clear, consistent, and focused way that Lincoln uses the language of allusion and the hodgepodge way that Everett does. It is typical of Everett's writing that his words "consecrate" and "unhallowed" are separated by several pages and that he never uses any form of the word "dedicate." Just as Lincoln's writing is always focused and concentrated, always revealing its sources in a clear, consecutive, and consistent manner, Everett's always seems vague, disconnected, and arbitrarily strung together. In this instance, Everett omits the third word of the very triad he seems to be echoing. But in most cases, Everett's writing is based on addition and complexity, Lincoln's on subtraction and simplicity. Everett is a painter piling up effects until he goes too far, just as Carpenter went too far in his painting of Lincoln signing the Emancipation Proclamation, the artist's final draft falling short of his first. Lincoln, on the other hand, is like a sculptor cutting away stone until nothing but essence remains.

Lincoln's key metaphor throughout the Gettysburg Address is birth, rebirth, and baptism. Holy Baptism appears behind only Holy Communion among the special services of the Prayer Book, both of these coming just after the regular services of Morning Prayer and Evening Prayer. The special services also include marriage and burial. It is appropriate that baptism appears ahead of marriage and burial, because the first act in the ministry of Jesus was his baptism in the river Jordan by his cousin John. The baptism of later followers, usually in their infancy, would represent the death and resurrection of their Savior. This idea is clearly stated both in the Bible and in the three baptismal services of the Prayer Book—Public Baptism of Infants, Private Baptism of Infants, and Baptism of Those of Riper Years. Indeed the Prayer Book often *quotes* the Bible. All three baptisms contain, near their end, this key sentence, "as he died and rose again for us, so should we, who are baptized, die from sin, and rise again unto righteousness." The "rise again" of this sentence is a direct echo of the Bible, of Matthew 20:18–19, where Jesus foretells his own death and resurrection:

> Behold, we go up to Jerusalem: and the Son of man shall be betrayed unto the chief priests and unto the scribes, and they shall condemn him to death,
> And shall deliver him to the Gentiles to mock, and to scourge, and to crucify him: and the third day he shall rise again.

The baptismal services also use the phrases "born again" and "born anew." "Born again" comes straight from the last sentence of John 3:3, which is quoted word for word in the Prayer Book, "Except a man be born again, he cannot see the kingdom of God." "Born anew," on the other hand, is a phrase that flowed *only* from the graceful pen of Archbishop Cranmer. Lincoln would choose as his direct echo of the rebirth symbolized by baptism neither of these phrases but a third phrase altogether—"new birth." It bears repeating that "new birth" appears nowhere in the King James Bible and, like "born anew," it appears *only* in the Prayer Book, for it, too, flowed from Cranmer's prolific and poetical pen. The phrase "new birth" first appeared in the archbishop's Forty-Nine Articles of 1553 and made its way into both the Articles of Religion and the Catechism that were added to the Prayer Book. In the American Prayer Book of Lincoln's day, the Catechism, which immediately follows the three services of Baptism, contains the very same phrase in this passage:

> Question. How many parts are there in a Sacrament?
> Answer. Two; the outward visible sign, and the inward spiritual grace.
> Question. What is the outward visible sign or form in Baptism?
> Answer. Water; wherein the person is baptized, *In the name of the Father, and of the Son, and of the Holy Ghost.*
> Question. What is the inward and spiritual grace?
> Answer. A death unto sin, and a new birth unto righteousness; for, being by nature born in sin, and the children of wrath, we are hereby made the children of grace.

In the Prayer Book of 1828, the Articles of Religion immediately follow the Psalter and come just before the various consecrations, including the Consecration of a Church or Chapel.

Long before 1828, the church had condensed Cranmer's Forty-Two Articles to Thirty-Nine, of which the twenty-seventh, called *Of Baptism*, appears this way in the Prayer Book:

> Baptism is not only a sign of profession, and mark of difference, whereby Christian men are discerned from others that be not christened; but it is also a sign of regeneration, or new birth, whereby, as by an instrument, they that receive Baptism rightly are grafted into the Church: the promises of the forgiveness of sin, and of our adoption to be the sons of God by the Holy Ghost, are visibly signed and sealed: faith is confirmed, and grace increased by virtue of prayer unto God.

Thus the phrase "new birth" from the Catechism and the Articles of Religion joins "here dedicated" and "devotion" as three clear markers that Lincoln sometimes used words or phrases from the Book of Common Prayer that appear *nowhere* in that same form in the King James Bible.

Even "in a larger sense," the little phrase that introduces the trinity of "consecrate," "dedicate," and "hallow" and has been altogether ignored by most scholars, rewards inspection. Who can hear this phrase without recalling the Gettysburg Address? This tells us that the words are unique to Lincoln or at least untypical of other writers. Very much like the earlier "fathers brought forth," this phrase works against the reader's expectations and forms the very opposite of a cliché. The cliché would have been "deeper sense" or "higher sense," invoking the usual metaphor of vertical size. In its place, Lincoln gives us a metaphor suggestive of horizontal size—suggestive of earth as opposed to high mountain or deepest ocean. Why did he choose the word "larger"? In the first place, the word fits perfectly with the epic, larger-than-life scale of "our fathers," "on this continent," "great civil war," "great battle-field," and "altogether fitting and proper," without overworking the more boldfaced "great." In the second place, "in a larger sense" fits perfectly with the phrase "conceived in liberty" because "free" or "at liberty" is one of the traditional meanings of "large." Shakespeare loved the phrase "at large," using it no fewer than twenty times among the sixty-odd appearances of "large" in his plays. In the third place, the word "large" makes extraordinarily apt and powerful appearances in the King James Bible. By far the most apt in the Old Testament are those describing the Promised Land of the Lord's chosen people: "And I am come down to deliver them out of the hand of the Egyptians, and to bring them up out of that land unto a good land and a *large*, unto a land flowing with milk and honey" (Exod. 3:8, emphasis added). Judges 18:20 calls this Promised Land "a *large* land" that "God hath given," and Nehemiah 9:35 calls it a "*large* and fat land." Equally apt appearances of "large" in the New Testament describe the upper room where Jesus will share with his disciples his "blood of the new testament" (Mark 14:24, Luke 22:20). For their last supper together, Jesus sends his disciples to find "a *large* upper room furnished" (Luke 22:12) or "a *large* upper room furnished and prepared" (Mark 14:15). Lincoln's "in a larger sense" thus forms another of those unexpected, easily overlooked phrases with a biblical illusion clearly shining inside of it. These are the phrases that make the Gettysburg Address so unique. Once again, by using simple if sometimes surprising words from the King James, Lincoln has connected this new nation to the deliverance of the Old Testament fathers out of Egypt and to the birth, death, and resurrection of the New Testament Messiah.

There are, it is clear, two very different kinds of literary allusion represented by Lincoln's use of his two favorite sources, and he is equally adept at both. Lincoln's allusions to the King James Bible rested on the reasonable assumption that his audience would in most cases recognize his source. He knew that not everyone would recognize every one of his biblical allusions but that most people would recognize most of them. The person who recognized few or none would clearly have been the exception. This kind of confident literary allusion is ancient and universal. When Jesus taught his disciples the Lord's Prayer that closes with, "For thine is the kingdom, and the power, and the glory" (Matt. 6:13), he would certainly have known and certainly expected his disciples to know that he was echoing 1 Chronicles 29:11: "Thine, O Lord, is the greatness, and the power, and the glory . . . thine is the kingdom, O Lord." Jesus's dying words upon the cross, "My God, my God, why hast thou forsaken me?" (Matt. 27:46), are taken word for word from Psalm 22:1. Lincoln could make the same confident assumption about *his* audience. On the other hand, any allusions that Lincoln made to the Prayer Book were founded on a different kind of assumption and therefore represent a different kind of literary allusion. In Lincoln's day as in our own, Episcopalians made up only a small percentage of the American population. It was to be expected that most of Lincoln's listeners would recognize few or none of his allusions to the Prayer Book. Any person who *did* recognize most of them—Seward, for example, or Everett, or members of the Confederate leadership who might have stolen a peek at his famous speech—would clearly have been the exception. Why, then, did Lincoln use them at all? After all, he was a speaker who always preferred clarity and simplicity to everything else and tried to communicate with every person in his audience. He was a man who made a point of never talking above his audience, or down to it. There are at least two good answers to this question.

First, the language of the Prayer Book would have conveyed a sense of ritual even to those who had never heard its words. Anyone hearing "It is altogether fitting and proper that we should do this" recognizes that this is the language of ritual. The first time one joins in the pledge of allegiance to the flag as a child, one has yet to commit the words to memory. Indeed, one may not even know what they mean as they fall like a foreign language upon a youthful ear. But every child is aware of being in the presence of some kind of shared social experience based on a sequence of words recited in a particular way—in the presence, that is, of some form of ritual. This childhood experience is repeated throughout one's life when joining a club or fraternal organization, going to court for the first time, or attending an unfamiliar place of worship. Ritual is part of the universal human experience, and all human beings seem predisposed to respond to it in some hard-to-explain but oddly positive way, especially when the ritual occurs on some important and emotionally charged occasion.

The second reason is that the language of the Prayer Book consists, for the most part, of either a direct repeating or a beautiful reconfiguring of scriptural passages. The Reverend Dr. Francis B. Vinton, the rector of Trinity Church in New York who comforted the Lincolns after the terrible, untimely death of their son Willie in 1862, suggested in one of his sermons, "*The principles* of our Prayer-Book are those of Holy Scripture. Nine-tenths of all that is contained therein is in the very words of the Bible."[20] For example, the typical listener at Gettysburg who knew the Bible well but had never attended an Episcopal service could have, and almost certainly would have, recognized "dedicate," "consecrate," and "hallow" as the language of the King James Bible. It is true that the words never appear together in one sentence in the King James the way they do in the Prayer Book. However, these three words *do* cluster in one *book* of the Old Testament, the book of 2 Chronicles. There they cluster around one of the most important events in the entire history of Judaism as recounted in the Old Testament—the building of the temple for the worship of the Lord during the reign of Solomon and its consecrating, dedicating, and hallowing not only for Solomon's reign but also for the reigns of all the kings to come. "And king Solomon . . . and all the people *dedicated* the house of God" (7:5, emphasis added in these citations).

"Solomon *hallowed* the middle of the court that was before the house of the Lord." (7:7). Just as "dedicated" and "hallowed" are juxtaposed in chapter 7, so "consecrated" and "dedicated" are juxtaposed in chapter 31: "the tithe of holy things which were *consecrated* unto the Lord" (31:6), "the offerings and the tithes and the *dedicated* things" (31:12). A few chapters later, "hallowed" makes its last appearance in the very last chapter of 2 Chronicles: "the house of the Lord which he had *hallowed* in Jerusalem" (36:14). When the writers of the Order for the Consecration of a Church or Chapel in the Prayer Book looked back through the Bible for appropriate language to be used by the bishop for consecrating a Christian church, what would have seemed more appropriate than this biblical language that had been used to consecrate, dedicate, and hallow the temple of the Lord in the Old Testament?

The second and perhaps more intriguing reason for Lincoln to have used the language of the Prayer Book is that it was known and used far more in the Confederacy than in the Union, at least by the highest leadership and the most influential citizens. In the South, the Episcopal Church was especially strong among those slave-owning, slavery-defending aristocrats who constituted most of the civilian and the military leadership. Lincoln chose to use the language of the enemy for reasons that will be addressed more fully later.

Lincoln was such a clear writer that he could take an idea implicit in a literary allusion and still make it understandable even to a listener who had never read the literary source and had no way of recognizing the allusion. One can see this happening throughout the nearly 150 years since the Gettysburg Address. A very clear and powerful writer who had met and talked with Lincoln, Harriet Beecher Stowe, reviewed the President's career in a book she published in 1868 called *Men of Our Times*:

> Sooth to say, our own politicians were somewhat shocked with his state-papers at first. Why not let us make them a little more conventional, and file them to a classified pattern? "No," was his reply, "I shall write them myself. *The people will understand them.*" "But this or that form of expression is not elegant, not classical." "*The people will understand it,*" has been his invariable reply.

No one has ever improved upon Stowe's summary of Lincoln's style: "His rejection of what is called fine writing was as deliberate as Saint Paul's, and for the same reason—because he felt that he was speaking on a subject which must be made clear to the lowest intellect, though it should fail to captivate the highest."[21] Stowe's analysis perfectly explains why his greatest speech of all, the Gettysburg Address, has been deeply admired and publicly honored even by those who are ignorant of every literary device ever recommended. Any reasonably intelligent listener can understand that in Lincoln's opening sentence, he is describing the conception and birth of this nation. Anyone who can understand even that much is unlikely to have any problem with the word "dedicated." All over the world one can witness the ceremonies of dedicating a newborn child in some ritual, dedicating that child to God and often to some principle as well. It happened with Jesus and with John the Baptist in ancient Judea, as we have seen, and it happened in various ways in Lincoln's America.

In short, one of the beauties of the Gettysburg Address is that it exists, like all great literature, on more than one level. Each reader or listener may take from it according to the individual's own knowledge and ability, just as one takes from Shakespeare in the same measure. Of course the language of the Gettysburg Address will sound richer and lovelier to those who can hear at least some of its literary allusions, just as a symphony by Mozart will sound lovelier and richer to those who can hear the great composer's musical allusions to the Haydn he so often honored. Ironically, in our own day, it is often the *least* educated of the world—the least formally educated at any rate—who can still hear and enjoy Lincoln's echoes of the King James Bible, a work read today mostly by the poorest and least-educated congregations. In his own day, the King James Bible put Lincoln in touch with virtually everyone in the audience—even with the editors of the *New York World*, who intentionally ignored the biblical allusions they did not wish to give him credit for. But then as now, his allusions to the Book of Common Prayer worked for a different reason—simply because each allusion fits the context so perfectly on its own, without regard to that work or to any other.

O Brave New Words

When an art critic named P. G. Hamerton complained that James McNeill
Whistler's *Symphony in White No. III* was "not precisely a symphony in
white" because this painting of two women in white on a white sofa contains
other colors as well, the prickly artist fired back a famous arrow that included
the barbed dots below:

> *Bon Dieu!* did this wise person expect white hair and chalked faces? And does
> he then, in his astounding consequence, believe that a symphony in F contains no
> other note, but shall be a continued repetition of F, F, F? . . . Fool![1]

By the same token, Lincoln is not *always* echoing the Bible or the Book of Common Prayer in the Gettysburg Address, not always advancing the metaphor of
birth and rebirth with every word. Every writer—every artist—has to mediate
among competing demands. From time to time, beginning with "proposition"
in the opening sentence, Lincoln drew certain words from other sources. When
there was no biblical or liturgical choice that suited his context, he did exactly
what Whistler did with colors. He chose whatever word seemed most natural and
appropriate. Lincoln's four closing sentences contain some of the most resonant of
all his biblical allusions in the address. But they also contain an unusual number
of words with origins *other* than the Bible or the Prayer Book. One of these is the
word "brave" in the seventh sentence.

The oldest meaning of "brave" in English is "courageous," dating from Caxton in 1485. But by 1568, according to the *OED*, "brave" had taken on a second
meaning of "finely dressed," "splendid" or "handsome."[2] This was to be the only
meaning that made its way into the King James Bible: "In that day the Lord will
take away the bravery of their tinkling ornaments about their feet, and their
cauls, and their round tires like the moon" (Isa. 3:18). In its second meaning, the
word appears famously in *The Tempest* by Shakespeare, which was performed just
about the time the King James Bible first appeared in 1611: "O brave new world, /
That has such people in it!" (5.1.183–84). In the eighteenth century and even into

the nineteenth when Lincoln was first learning to read, "brave" in the sense of "splendid" seems to have become more common in all forms of literature than "brave" in the sense of "courageous." But the times they were a-changing.

One big reason for the change, at least on the American side of the Atlantic, was the immediate and enduring popularity of Francis Scott Key's "Star-Spangled Banner." Composed after an all-night naval battle Key had personally witnessed during the War of 1812, this rousing poem was set to the tune of a popular English drinking song called "Anacreon's Ode" and soon became the song of first choice for all patriotic occasions in the new country, especially on the Fourth of July. Thus "the land of the free and the home of the brave" was just as familiar to Lincoln growing up as it is to anyone growing up in America today. After Key's death, the song appeared in a book of 1857 called *Poems of the Late Francis Scott Key*. The poems for this book had been collected by the author's brother-in-law Chief Justice Roger Taney, who in the very same year—such is the irony of history—wrote the wretched Dred Scott decision. The preface to Key's poems announced that the Chief Justice was informing most Americans for the first time of the circumstances surrounding the composition of Key's most famous poem of all:

> After several years of respectful solicitation, to those possessing the manuscript, permission to publish it has been obtained, together with a narrative, from the accurate pen of Chief Justice Taney, brother-in-law of Mr. Key, of the circumstances originating and attending, the composition of the national ballad, entitled, "The Star Spangled Banner." As probably few of those who read and admire, that thrilling effusion, are acquainted with its history, and as it is desirable to fix the same, in a more enduring form than the memory of private friendship, it is believed that it will be eminently satisfactory, that an opportunity has now been presented for giving it to the press.[3]

One of the eighteenth-century English poets who likely influenced Key's use of "brave" in the sense of "courageous" was William Collins. We know from F. B. Carpenter's *Inner Life of Abraham Lincoln* that in 1864 when the president was visiting the cemetery next to the Soldiers Home in Washington to which he and his family often retreated, Lincoln quoted from memory, for a group of weeping companions, a stanza by Collins that begins, "How sleep the brave, who sink to rest, / By all their country's wishes blest."[4] Lincoln was not alone in admiring these words. General Winfield Scott quoted the same couplet when sending his regrets to David Wills, organizer of the Gettysburg consecration, for being unable, "on account of infirmities," to attend the Gettysburg consecration. Scott's letter of regrets was published in Everett's 1864 book that included all the invitees' letters, speeches, and contributions:

Having long lived with and participated in the hardships and
dangers of our soldiers, I can never fail to honor
"the brave, who sink to rest,
By all their country's wishes blest."[5]

Another eighteenth-century poet who used "brave" just the way Collins did, and just as Key later would, was William Cowper. The most adulatory poem in all of Key's volume of poems is called "To Cowper." One of Cowper's most rousing poems, "On the Loss of the Royal George" (1782), focuses on the word "brave" in the sense of "courageous":

Toll for the brave—
The brave! that are no more:
All sunk beneath the wave,
Fast by their native shore.

An even more celebrated poem by Cowper was *The Task* (1785), which includes lines that could have served as Lincoln's epitaph:

A brave man knows no malice, but at once
Forgets in peace the injuries of war,
And gives his direst foe a friend's embrace.

Cowper, an outspoken opponent of slavery, fought all his life to free himself from the same melancholy that burdened Lincoln but that kept neither man from becoming a prolific writer. *The Task*—which itself must surely have influenced another of Lincoln's word choices in "the great task remaining before us"—contains passionate and eloquent attacks on slavery, especially in "Book Two." In her biography of Mary Todd Lincoln, Katherine Helm quoted a recollection from Mary's half-sister Emilie Todd Helm of seeing Lincoln once reading with rapt attention an antislavery poem by Cowper.[6] In summary, the word "brave" meaning "courageous" made its most famous appearance before the Gettysburg Address in the song that later became America's national anthem, whose author may well have taken it from his own favorite poet, Cowper. By 1863, the use of "brave" in this sense had become so commonplace that Wills employed it in his invitations to both Everett and Lincoln.

Lincoln never strayed long, however, from the language of Bible and Prayer Book. After the "brave men" so reminiscent of Collins, Cowper, and Key, he returned immediately to his more traditional sources with the phrase "living and dead." Romans 14:9 features these very words but in reverse order: "For to this end Christ both died, and rose, and revived, that he might be Lord both of the dead and living." By far the most familiar passage in the King James where the words "living" and "dead" are closely allied and in the order Lincoln employed appears in the familiar story where King Solomon has to choose between two mothers, each of whom, after the death of the infant son of one of the women, lays claim to the survivor. "And the other woman said, Nay; but the living is my son, and the dead is thy son. And this said, No; but the dead is thy son, and the living is my son" (1 Kings 3:22). Even those who know little else about the Bible have heard this story about Solomon's gift of the child to the true mother. He gave it to the mother who simply could not bear to see the living child separated by the sword and who was willing to make any sacrifice to save the life of the child, whether it was hers or not, even as the other mother was crying out coldly, "Let it be neither mine nor thine, but divide it" (1 Kings 3:26). Solomon saw that the true mother, the only true mother, was the one who put the life of the child above any selfish desires. This story was a perfect metaphor for the Civil War. The rebellious South, like the unfit mother, had cried out for secession even though this meant dismemberment and death for a national unity that had been brought forth, christened, and dedicated by the Declaration of Independence. The Union soldiers at Gettysburg had laid down their lives to keep this nation alive and altogether whole. The implication of Lincoln's allusion to the Solomon story is that both the love of the true mother and the wisdom of the wisest judge in the Bible lent their moral support to the survival of the living union of the United States of America.

The nearest approach to "living and dead" in the New Testament is a lovely and familiar sequence in John 11:25–26 containing "life," "dead," "live," and "die" in this very order and made all the more familiar and impressive by appearing as the opening words in the magnificent Order for the Burial of the Dead in the Prayer Book:

> I AM the Resurrection and the Life, saith the Lord; he that believeth in me, though he were dead, yet shall he live: and whosover liveth and believeth in me shall never die.

Appearing also in this same Burial of the Dead, which Lincoln had heard intoned at the funeral service for General Lander in March of 1862, are the words "fourscore," "brought forth," "ground," "earth," "come," "second coming," and "rest from their labours."

In another highly revealing, highly resonant choice of words, Lincoln echoes the word "struggled." This word makes but a single, unforgettable appearance in the King James Bible, an appearance as apt as it is powerful. No other word chosen by Lincoln reveals a more perfect union between the Gettysburg Address and the most beloved of all English Bibles. The single appearance of "struggled" in the King James occurs in connection with two brothers who "struggled together" from the womb, formed two nations, waged war upon one another, came close to killing one other, and then laid down all the arms of war to embrace and make peace forevermore. The Gettysburg Address offers no finer example of Lincoln's ability to find the absolutely perfect word for every context.

> And Isaac entreated the Lord for his wife, because she was barren: and the Lord was entreated of him, and Rebekah his wife conceived.
>
> And the children struggled together within her; and she said, If it be so, why am I thus? And she went to enquire of the Lord.
>
> And the Lord said unto her, Two nations are in thy womb, and two manner of people shall be separated from thy bowels; and the one people shall be stronger than the other people; and the elder shall serve the younger.
>
> And when her days to be delivered were fulfilled, behold, there were twins in her womb.
>
> And the first came out red, all over like an hairy garment; and they called his name Esau.
>
> And after that came his brother out, and his hand took hold on Esau's heel; and his name was called Jacob: and Isaac was threescore years old when she bare them. (Gen. 25:21–26)

This story is just as appropriate to Lincoln's purposes as the story of Solomon's wisdom in saving a child. For one thing, it is a story that anticipates the Matthew and Luke accounts of the birth of Jesus by invoking the key word "conceived" in connection with a child, Jacob, whose birth will forever change the course of history. Jacob will become the founder of a nation, Israel, with his twelve sons as the founders of the twelve tribes. From him, in a direct line of descent, will come Jesus the Messiah, born of the house of David in Bethlehem of Judea. As God prophesies in Isaiah, "I will bring forth a seed out of Jacob" (65:9). Thus "conceived," "brought forth," "nation," and "struggled" are all associated with Jacob, who, born as the second twin, took the birthright belonging to Esau, his older brother. Just as Jacob will grow up to become the father of God's chosen nation, Israel, so Esau will become the father of neighboring Edom. At one point, the two brothers met each other with all the trappings of war, when Esau came with four hundred men and Jacob in terror prayed to the Lord, "Deliver me, I pray thee, from the hand of my brother, from the hand of Esau: for I fear him, lest he will come and smite me, and the mother with the children" (Gen. 32:11). Instead, the warring brothers' meeting ended in peace: "And Esau ran to meet him, and embraced him, and fell on his neck, and kissed him: and they wept" (33:4)—exactly the outcome that Lincoln dreamed would happen after the Civil War between the Northern and Southern brothers of the United States. For all these reasons, Lincoln's powerful allusion to Jacob and Esau and the warring kingdoms of these two brothers was the perfect biblical metaphor for the American Civil War. It is also well worth noting that when John Locke defined "birthright" in the first of his *Two Treatises of Government*, he did so by focusing on the story of Jacob and Esau.[7]

There is even a sense in which the South can be seen as the Esau or older brother of the story, since Virginia was the oldest of the English colonies formed upon the new continent of America. The leaders of Virginia passionately asserted that their birthright to independence had been stolen by the younger Northern states when the election of Abraham Lincoln challenged the spread of slavery and when Lincoln's own decisive actions to protect the Union challenged the doctrine of secession. Virginia itself would become a symbol of disunion and brother-against-brother when its northwestern end split off in 1861 to remain a loyal part of the Union and was admitted as the new state of West Virginia on June 20, 1863, just days before the Battle of Gettysburg.

Lincoln's "consecrated it far above our poor power" specifically and eloquently echoes Paul's letter to the Ephesians, where he describes Jesus Christ as "Far above all principality, and power, and might, and dominion, and every name that is named, not only in this world, but also in that which is to come" (1:21). Likewise, "our poor power to add or detract" recalls a whole series of biblical verses. The first, which comes directly from the mouth of Jesus, focuses on the inability of human beings to change or add to whatever is already fixed by God: "Which of you by taking thought can add one cubit unto his stature?" (Matt. 6:27). The rest are commandments that warn the reader against adding to or subtracting from the consecrated word of God, as though Lincoln views the soldiers of Gettysburg as saints or prophets and their deeds as holy scripture that must never be altered by addition or subtraction. "Ye shall not add unto the word which I command you, neither shall ye diminish ought from it," says Deuteronomy 4:2. The Book of Revelations likewise issues a similar warning: "If any man shall add unto these things, God shall add unto him the plagues that are written in this book: And if any man shall take away from the words of the book of this prophecy, God shall take away his part out of the book of life" (22:18–19). The Preacher in Ecclesiastes asserts that God's *works* are just as fixed and unchangeable as his *words*: "I know that, whatsover God doeth, it shall be for ever: nothing can be put to it, nor any thing taken from it" (3:14).

It bears repeating, however, that the Bible never uses the specific word "detract." It uses "diminish" or "take away" for the same idea. Had Lincoln valued biblical allusion and nothing else, he would have chosen either "our poor power to add or diminish" or "our poor power to add or take away." That he chose neither option makes clear that he was choosing among a *number* of motives and purposes. The biblical "diminish" would have been the weakest of all the plausible choices available to him. Although it echoes the *d* sound from "add" just as "detract" does, it is otherwise an unemphatic word that would have destroyed Lincoln's poetical rhythms. The biblical "take away" sounds better than "diminish," but it, too, disrupts the rhythm and would have closed the sentence with an unemphatic adverb. Except for being nonbiblical, the word "detract" is a perfect choice on all counts. With "add," it forms a pair of closely related mathematical terms. And yet Lincoln's pair sounds less *exclusively* mathematical than "add or subtract," a phrase he had invoked in a speech on his way to Washington in early 1861, when he said of certain remarks he had previously made, "I have seen no occasion since to add to them or subtract from them."[8] The phrase "add or detract" has the same rhythm as "add or subtract" but *means* more because "detract" implies much more than mathematics. It even *sounds* better because the closing sound of "add" is repeated in the opening sound of "detract." Indeed, the *t* sound at the end of "detract" is the same consonant sound as *d* except for being voiceless. Unlike "diminish," "detract" ends on an accented syllable, which makes the sentence end on a natural upbeat. "Detract" is as clear and simple as its sister-word "subtract" and yet sounds much, much better and resonates far more.

According to the *OED*, "detract" entered the English language in 1509 in a quotation that paired it with the synonym "takinge away": "Some time addynge, somtyme detractinge and takinge away such thinges as semeth me necessary and superflue." The noun form of "detraction" entered soon after in 1528 in the quotation, "we saw the additions, detractions, and corrections." The word "subtract" entered the language in the opposite order. The noun form of "subtraction" entered in 1400, the verb "subtract" in 1548. Once the verb "subtract" was invented, it began almost at once to replace "detract" as the word of choice in the study and discipline of mathematics.[9] In language, however, rejection often spurs new growth in a new direction. "Subtract" remained mathematical to its core and still is to this day, while "detract" took on the additional meaning of "disparage." Shakespeare reflects this new meaning when a character says of the uncouth Caliban in *The Tempest*, "His forward voice now is to speak well of friend; his backward voice is to utter foul speeches and to detract" (2.2.95–97). But Shakespeare's most famous use of the word with its new meaning comes in Falstaff's celebrated "catechism" to Prince Hal on death and honor in *Henry IV, Part One* (5.1.129–44), where the comic knight's use of "detraction" clearly means "disparagement."

> *Fal.* I would 'twere bed-time, Hal, and all well.
> *Hal.* Why, thou owest God a death.
> *Fal.* 'Tis not due yet; I would be loath to pay him before his day. What need
>   I be so forward with him that calls not on me? Well, 'tis no matter; hon-
>   our pricks me on. Yea, but how if honour prick me off when I come on?
>   how then? Can honour set to a leg? no: or an arm: no: or take away the
>   grief of a wound? no. Honour hath no skill in surgery, then? no. What is
>   honour? a word. What is in that word honour? what is that honour? air. A
>   trim reckoning! Who hath it? he that died o' Wednesday. Doth he feel it?

> no. Doth he hear it? no. 'Tis insensible, then? Yea, to the dead. But will
> it not live with the living? no. Why? detraction will not suffer [allow] it.
> Therefore I'll none of it. Honour is a mere scutcheon [badge]: and so ends
> my catechism.

Lincoln knew that certain Americans, particularly the rebels of the South, were all too ready to heap detraction upon whatever the Union army had achieved at Gettysburg. But he also knew that the honor and glory of "what they did here" was now fixed beyond the power of detracting men to alter a powerful and perhaps immortal historical truth.

Lincoln had yet another source for "add or detract" that was much nearer in time and place than Shakespeare. It is a source that even the cautious Robert Bray affirms. Bray's article in the Summer 2007 *Journal of the Abraham Lincoln Association*, "What Lincoln Read," gives high marks to the likelihood that Lincoln had read at least volumes 4, 7, 8, and 9 of Thomas Jefferson's *Works* published in 1853–54. Bray gives an "A+" to the likelihood that Lincoln had read the seventh volume, *Correspondence*.[10] In a letter to John Adams written from Paris on September 4, 1785, as the two were negotiating a treaty with the nations of the Barbary pirates who had long preyed on American shipping and kidnapped hostages for ransom, Jefferson wrote these words at the very start of his letter:

> On receipt of your favors of August the 8th and 23rd, I conferred with Mr.
> Barclay on the measures necessary to be taken, to set our treaty with the pirati-
> cal States into motion, through his agency. Supposing that we should begin with
> the Emperor of Morocco, a letter to the Emperor and instructions to Mr. Barclay,
> seemed necessary. I have therefore sketched such outlines for these, as appear to me
> to be proper. You will be so good as to detract, add to, or alter them as you please,
> to return such as you approve under your signature, to which I will add mine.[11]

If Lincoln with his phenomenal memory summoned up "add" and "detract" from a letter written by one of his political heroes, this would surprise no one. But it underscores another point about the echoing of previous writers—namely, that not all references to literary predecessors qualify as literary allusion. When Lincoln alluded to Jefferson's "all men are created equal" in the opening sentence, he had every reason to expect that his audience would immediately recognize his source. By the same token, he would *never* have expected a general audience to recognize a 1785 letter from Jefferson to Adams as a source for "add or detract." The first is an example of literary allusion, telling us not only about the workings of Lincoln's mind but also about the meanings of his speech. The second is something different and much less important. Literary allusion rests on a reasonable expectation that the audience will recognize the echo. Lincoln's use of Jefferson's letter tells us *only* about Lincoln's mind—about his personal admiration for the source. It tells us nothing about the meanings of his speech to the *audience* who heard it in late November of 1863 or read it soon afterward.

The little word "poor" that modifies "power to add or detract" proves to be a surprisingly robust example of literary allusion. The word abounds in the King James Bible, very often in association with Jesus: "Blessed are the poor in spirit: for theirs is the kingdom of heaven" (Matt. 5:3). "For ye know the grace of our Lord Jesus Christ that, though he was rich, yet for your sakes he became poor, that ye through his poverty might be rich" (2 Cor. 8:9). But none of the biblical references to "poor" notably enriches or underscores the meaning of Lincoln's use of the word in the context of his seventh sentence. In that context, it was another of Lincoln's great loves—the works of Shakespeare—which proved more influential than the Bible. Shakespeare has a whole series of famous phrases associating the word "poor" with death and oblivion, as in "Alas, poor Yorick! I knew him, Horatio" (*Hamlet* 5.1.202) and "Alas, poor Romeo! he is already dead" (*Romeo and Juliet* 2.4.13). The most resonant of all these phrases rolls like thunder and lightning out of Lincoln's favorite play by Shakespeare, *Macbeth*:

> Life's but a walking shadow, a poor player
> That struts and frets his hour upon the stage
> And then is heard no more: it is a tale
> Told by an idiot, full of sound and fury,
> Signifying nothing. (5.5.24–28)

The evidence that Lincoln associated the word "poor" with the idea of death and oblivion—the oblivion that occurs to both teller and tale, to speaker and to spoken word—appears even before the Gettysburg Address. Speaking of slavery during the seventh and final debate with Douglas, Lincoln had declared, "That is the issue that will continue in this country when these poor tongues of Judge Douglas and myself shall be silent."[12]

Lincoln's eighth sentence, beginning "The world will little note," is of particular interest because it has the fewest *obvious* biblical and liturgical allusions of any of the ten. In this limited sense, it may be his most "original" of all, wonderfully clear and spare, wonderfully Lincolnian in its simplicity. In its reliance on the *t, w,* and *r* sounds, it is remarkably like sentence three, "We are met on a great battle-field of that war," which is also very simple. But Lincoln's biblical allusions in the eighth sentence are no less apt or powerful for being less obvious than some of his others. One of its loveliest phrases, "little note nor long remember," subtly recalls a very beautiful passage from John (16:16–21). This passage is particularly appropriate because it prophesies the death of Christ, the death that will remove him for a painful and uncertain period of time from those on earth who have loved him most, just as the Union dead who gave their lives at Gettysburg have now been removed for a time from their own loved ones upon this earth.

A little while, and ye shall not see me: and again, a little while, and ye shall see me, because I go to the Father.

Then said some of his disciples among themselves, What is this that he saith unto us, A little while, and ye shall not see me: and again, a little while, and ye shall see me: and, Because I go to the Father?

They said therefore, What is this that he saith, A little while? we cannot tell what he saith.

Now Jesus knew that they were desirous to ask him, and said unto them, Do ye enquire among yourselves of that I said, A little while, and ye shall not see me: and again, a little while, and ye shall see me?

Verily, verily, I say unto you, That ye shall weep and lament, but the world shall rejoice: and ye shall be sorrowful, but your sorrow shall be turned into joy.

A woman when she is in travail hath sorrow, because her hour is come: but as soon as she is delivered of the child, she remembereth no more the anguish, for joy that a man is born into the world.

Just as a woman "remembereth no more" the pain of birth in the joy of beholding her newborn child, so you, too—Jesus tells his disciples—will no longer remember the pain of our separation once we meet again. Lincoln's similar thought is that the world "will little note nor long remember what we say here" and will only remember "what they did here" upon this battlefield of pain and death, especially after all the swords of war have been beaten into plowshares, and our nation has finally and joyfully reunited. All that will be remembered then is the glory of the brave men who died to save their country for "a new birth of freedom." It has often been remarked that Lincoln was wrong in his prophecy, that the world has not only remembered what he said but will never stop remembering. But is the president's praise for the Union dead any less lovely or noble because his prophecy was too modest to include the words of his own great speech?

Even more biblical allusions appear when Lincoln's negative constructions are turned into positive. The positive or opposite of "little note" is "notable," which takes any student of the King James Bible straight to that chapter in the Book of Acts where Pentecost is described. This chapter famously describes how the baptism of the Holy Ghost came down upon the apostles in "cloven tongues like as of fire" (2:3). It is precisely this baptism of fire that Lincoln invokes in his two closing sentences when he asks this war-torn nation to undergo a new dedication, a new baptism, a new birth. At Pentecost, Peter preached a sermon abounding in the words of the Old Testament and approaching Paul's eloquence at Mars' Hill: "your young men shall see visions, and your old men shall dream dreams" (Acts 2:17), "And on my servants and on my handmaidens I will pour out in those days of my Spirit; and they shall prophesy" (2:18). Before God again pours out his Spirit in this way, "The sun shall be turned into darkness, and the moon into blood, before that *great and notable* day of the Lord come" (2:20, emphasis added). The positive or opposite of "nor long remember" is the constantly repeated "remembrance" of the Lord's Supper in words appearing first in Luke 22:19–20 and later in the Prayer Book:

> And he took bread, and gave thanks, and brake it, and gave unto them, saying, This is my body which is given for you: this do in remembrance of me.
> Likewise also the cup after supper, saying, This cup is the new testament in my blood, which is shed for you.

In short, when Lincoln spoke to listeners steeped in the language of the King James of what "the world will little note nor long remember," what would have been more natural to recall than two crucial events associated with the Savior that appear in the Bible as "great and notable" and "in remembrance of me"?

Lincoln's last two sentences, the ninth and tenth, begin with the same ritualistic "It is" that opens the fifth sentence about which we have had so much to say already—"It is altogether fitting and proper that we should do this." The two closing sentences begin in similar fashion: "It is for us, the living, rather, to be dedicated here," and "It is rather for us to be here dedicated." The fifth sentence, as seen earlier, echoes the language of Holy Communion, while these last two sentences echo the language of Holy Baptism in their key word, "dedicated," a word already examined here at great length in relation to the sacrament and ritual of baptism. How appropriate that all three sentences beginning with "It is" echo one or the other of those two great sacraments considered by the Prayer Book to be essential to salvation—baptism and communion—and that both sacraments clearly embody Lincoln's sustained metaphor of birth, death, and rebirth!

We have seen that whenever one hears the language of the Prayer Book, one almost always hears in the background some language from the Bible. Those who hear one of the two sources hear an aria, a solo; those who hear both hear a duet. Even that simple phrase from the Prayer Book, "It is meet and right so to do," which Lincoln slowly transformed into "It is altogether fitting and proper that we should do this," first took shape in the Bible. When Cranmer came up with this melodious phrase for his first Prayer Book published in 1549, he was echoing Tyndale's 1534 translation of Moses' response to the Egyptian pharaoh who had ordered him to perform a religious ceremony in a way that violated conscience: "it is not mete so to do" (Exod. 8:26). Tyndale's statement would later be taken verbatim into the King James Version.

There is another "it is" construction in the Bible that almost certainly influenced Lincoln's three sentences that begin this way, most especially the last two. This "it is" appears in one of the most famous chapters of the Bible, Romans 8. This famous chapter has long been favored by congregations like those of Lincoln's father, Thomas, who march to the somber drumbeat of the doctrine of predestination. One doctrine that Lincoln never rejected from his father's church was a belief in some form of predestination. Note that the two closing sentences of the Gettysburg Address employ a language not only of exhortation—"that we here highly resolve"—but also of resignation and acceptance: "to *be* dedicated here," "to *be* here dedicated." As it happens, the eighth chapter of Romans presents a surprisingly cheerful form of predestination. It is much more in harmony with Hamlet's "There's a divinity that shapes our ends, / Rough-hew them how we will" (5.2:10–11) than with that theology of hopelessness that drove George Eliot's Silas Marner into long dark years of gloom and seclusion. Lincoln's own version of predestination always sounded more like Hamlet's than Marner's. He never lost faith that things would turn out all right in the end if we human beings, having done our very best, leave the rest to God's will and grace. Romans 8 celebrates predestination as the ultimate liberation for those who love the Lord.

Keying on a metaphor drawn from slavery and emancipation—the freeing of all believers from "the bondage of corruption" that is then transformed "into the glorious liberty of the children of God" (8:21)—Saint Paul turns in the closing verses of the celebrated eighth chapter of Romans to a vision in which predestination works only good to those who love the Lord (8:28–39):

> And we know that all things work together for good to them that love God, to them who are the called according to his purpose.
>
> For whom he did foreknow, he also did predestinate to be conformed to the image of his Son, that he might be the firstborn among many brethren.
>
> Moreover whom he did predestinate, them he also called: and whom he called, them he also justified: and whom he justified, them he also glorified.
>
> What shall we then say to these things? If God be for us, who can be against us?
>
> He that spared not his own Son, but delivered him up for us all, how shall he not with him also freely give us all things?
>
> Who shall lay anything to the charge of God's elect? It is God that justifieth.
>
> Who is he that condemneth? It is Christ that died, yea rather, that is risen again, who is even at the right hand of God, who also maketh intercession for us.
>
> Who shall separate us from the love of Christ? shall tribulation, or distress, or persecution, or famine, or nakedness, or peril, or sword?
>
> As it is written, For thy sake we are killed all the day long; we are accounted as sheep for the slaughter.
>
> Nay, in all these things we are more than conquerors through him that loved us.
>
> For I am persuaded, that neither death, nor life, nor angels, nor principalities, nor powers, nor things present, nor things to come,
>
> Nor height, nor depth, nor any other creature, shall be able to separate us from the love of God, which is in Christ Jesus our Lord.

Any reader can see that the sentence beginning "It is Christ that died, yea rather" and ending "maketh intercession for us" includes all five of the words that open

Lincoln's last sentence—"It is rather for us," five words that have already appeared in his next-to-last sentence. This does not quite rise to the precise, every-hair-in-place kind of allusion that has been the hallmark of so many previous examples. But Lincoln's memory was so prodigious, his ear so finely attuned to words, his knowledge of the Bible so precise, the context of Romans 8 so rich, and the connection between the "risen again" Messiah and a nation rising to a "new birth" so appropriate that the difference between the fit of this allusion and of other biblical allusions in the Gettysburg Address is only a matter of degree. Eight separate verses from this very same eighth chapter of Romans appear in *Lincoln's Devotional*,[13] where no other chapter in the Bible is so richly represented. Furthermore, the appropriateness of Romans 8 to the Christian idea that death is simply a step into rebirth, resurrection, and eternal life was independently confirmed in 1892 when the Episcopal Church, while revising the Prayer Book of Lincoln's day, decided to add most of the verses of this chapter—fourteen through thirty-nine—to the service for the Burial of the Dead, where they are read at every Episcopal funeral to this day.

The "unfinished work" of Lincoln's ninth sentence is another phrase rich with biblical allusions. Although "unfinished" never appears in the King James, over half of the thirty appearances of "finished" in the Old Testament refer to finishing one or the other of the two most sacred objects of the Israelites—the tabernacle and the temple. In the New Testament, Jesus says to his Father just before his crucifixion, "I have finished the work which thou gavest me to do" (John 17:4). His last words upon the cross are "It is finished" (John 19:30). Called "the author and finisher of our faith" (Heb. 12:2), Jesus declares in another passage that his "meat"—his moral sustenance during his mission upon this earth—is to finish his Father's work:

> Jesus saith unto them, My meat is to do the will of him that sent me, and to finish his work.
>
> Say not ye, There are yet four months, and then cometh harvest? behold, I say unto you, Lift up your eyes and look on the fields; for they are white already to harvest. (John 4:34–35)

Once again, Lincoln has specifically associated this nation with the Messiah, whose task is to finish the work on earth required by his Father. For those who share the same easy knowledge of the Bible as Lincoln and his listeners, the lesson of the "unfinished work which they who fought here have thus far so nobly advanced" is that *now* is the time to finish that work, now in late 1863 when this nation can and must rededicate itself to the task of gathering the fields that are "white already to harvest" by winning the war and by affirming the principle that all men are created equal with a daring and definitive end to two and a half centuries of slavery. As always, we can see Lincoln's biblical knowledge reflected in his joining of words, as when he joins "unfinished" with "work" instead of with "task." Finally, Lincoln's allusions to the biblical "finished" take yet another turn when in his ninth sentence he puts the word "unfinished" and the word "fought" together almost cheek by jowl and thereby calls to mind one of the most poetical passages ever composed by Saint Paul or anyone else: "I have fought a good fight, I have finished my course, I have kept the faith" (2 Tim. 4:7).

We have seen again and again that even Lincoln's smallest phrases, routinely ignored by scholars, often yield up surprising and significant information like tiny clues at a crime scene. One such phrase is "thus far" from "thus far so nobly carried on," later revised to "thus far so nobly advanced." "Thus far" is not only a very old phrase in English but a more dignified choice than "so far" or any other synonym. For such a familiar phrase, Lincoln was by no means limited to any one particular source. But there is much to learn about the mind of this great writer from looking closely at even his most common phrases. For one thing, this one may not be as common as it first looks. Only twice does it appear in the King James Bible, and neither text is memorable. It appears frequently, however, in Shakespeare. It appears at least twenty times in thirteen different plays, including six times in *Henry VIII* alone, a play that appeared on the short list of those that Lincoln said he read most often. In terms of relevancy to the Gettysburg Address, the most apt appearance is almost certainly the one in *Cymbeline*. Cymbeline is a Briton who has lived his youth in Rome where he was knighted by Augustus Caesar. Now, having risen to the throne of Britain, he feels compelled to fight against the fatherland and emperor with whom he will, surprisingly, reunite in the end. Lucius, a Roman, is departing the country and castle of Cymbeline in a scene that opens dramatically with the king's line, "Thus far; and so farewell" (3.5.1). This scene is suffused with a sense of impending civil war when "noble Lucius," as Cymbeline calls him in line 12, answers the king in lines 2–5: "Thanks, royal sir. / My emperor hath wrote, I must from hence. And am right sorry to report that I must report ye / My master's enemy."

Another intriguing possible source is Thomas Paine, a writer everyone agrees that Lincoln had read, including even the ever-cautious Robert Bray. In his *Dissertation on First Principles of Government* (1795), Paine says many wise things that Lincoln would affirm in the Gettysburg Address. One is: "A nation, though continually existing, is continually in a state of renewal and succession. It is never stationary. Every day produces new births." Lincoln's extended metaphor is, of course, birth and renewal. A second is: "There never yet was any truth or principle so irresistibly obvious that all men believed it at once." This was the very reason that Lincoln preferred "proposition" to "self-evident truth." In this same *First Principles*, Paine also sums up his objections to England's or France's—or any other nation's—lack of a written constitution, with emphases that are Paine's own: "All these things have followed from the want of a constitution; for it is the nature and intention of a constitution to *prevent governing by party*, by establishing a common principle that shall limit and control the power and impulse of party, and that says to all parties, *thus far shalt thou go and no further*."[14] Paine despised organized religion but believed in both God and an afterlife. He knew the King James Bible as well as any Christian minister and certainly knew that his last italicized phrase was a tribute to the book of Job where God speaks out of the whirlwind, saying that He alone controls the universe and the lives of men: "Where wast thou when I laid the foundations of the earth?" (Job 38:4). "And said, Hitherto shalt thou come, but no further" (Job 38:11). With these literary antecedents in mind, one can read Lincoln's "thus far so nobly advanced" in two ways. It is "thus far" because of what remains for Americans to do in late 1863—that is, to "highly resolve" to end "a great civil war" with "a new birth of freedom." But it is also "thus far" because of what remains for *God* to do in the working out of His sometimes inscrutable but always providential will.

Lincoln's change from "nobly carried on" to "nobly advanced" was made, according to his private secretary John Nicolay, just a few days after Gettysburg, when Wills requested a copy of the address, and the president worked through it with his two secretaries. Both the "carried on" that Lincoln spoke at Gettysburg and the "advanced" he substituted for it in consultation with his secretaries are associated with the Israelites' exodus from Egypt into the Promised Land. The children of Israel ask Moses in Exodus 14:11, "wherefore hast thou dealt thus with us, to carry us forth out of Egypt?" A dramatic foreshadowing of this great exodus occurs when Jacob instructs his son Joseph, then a powerful prince in Egypt: "But I will lie with my fathers, and thou shalt carry me out of Egypt, and bury me in their buryingplace" (Gen. 47:30). Jacob's wish is honored: "For his sons carried him into the land of Canaan, and buried him" (Gen. 50:13). Lincoln's "advanced" is just as biblical as "carried" and works even better in terms of the exodus from Egypt into the Promised Land of Canaan: "And Samuel said unto the people, It is the Lord that *advanced* Moses and Aaron, and that *brought your fathers* up out of the land of Egypt" (1 Sam. 12:6, emphasis added). "Advanced" also works well for reasons unconnected with the Bible. Like "engaged" and "met," it has both a military and a romantic meaning. The two meanings often intertwine, as when Shakespeare writes in *The Merry Wives of Windsor*, "against all checks, rebukes and manners / I must advance the colours of my love / And not retire" (3.4.84–86). Fenton, the handsome young hero who makes this boast, refuses to retire from his amorous advances until he has taken his colors and his cause all the way to a marriage with the heroine. We still speak of a suitor's "advances." Finally, "advanced" works well because it is regularly associated with progress of the most honorable and noble kind in a way that the homelier "carried on" rarely if ever attains to.

Of the key words in Lincoln's ninth sentence, the word "nobly" is the only one that rings no bell from the King James Bible. Just like "poor," however, "nobly" appears in abundance and with precisely the right meaning in Shakespeare. There are numerous examples in all the plays. Perhaps the most apt, even combining "so" with "nobly," comes from the closing scene of *Cymbeline* in a description of the Posthumous whom Cymbeline has banished but now welcomes home as the hero of the civil war: "The forlorn soldier, that so nobly fought" (5.5.405). Cowper also wrote a very stirring passage containing the phrase "bled nobly." Many others who hated slavery and longed to see its demise shared Lincoln's love for Cowper. In the very speech from which Lincoln borrowed the metaphor for his "house divided" speech, Theodore Parker quotes an antislavery passage from *The Task* that he says was learned from his mother "when I was a little boy, and sat in her lap."[15] Cowper devotes most of book 5 of *The Task* to the question of what makes human beings politically and spiritually free. In one of his most memorable passages, he reserves his highest praise, not for those who have died for their country but for those who have died defending the "shrine of Truth":

> Patriots have toil'd, and in their country's cause
> Bled nobly, and their deeds, as they deserve,
> Received proud recompense. We give in charge
> Their names to the sweet lyre. The historic muse,
> Proud of the treasure, marches with it down
> To latest times; and Sculpture, in her turn,
> Gives bond in stone and ever-during brass
> To guard them, and to immortalize her trust:
> But fairer wreaths are due, though never paid,
> To those who, posted at the shrine of Truth,
> Have fallen in her defence. (5.705–15)

Anyone who remembered these lines could confirm that their president at Gettysburg had honored the Union dead for giving their lives not just to save a country but also to serve truth and to set men free. They had died, said Lincoln, defending the most sacred truth of all from the document that first named and baptized and dedicated us a nation—the truth "that all men are created equal."

The "great task remaining before us" from the tenth and final sentence recalls several biblical passages. First, the word "task" recalls the Egyptian bondage from which God had "brought forth" His chosen people before guiding them safely home to the Promised Land. The word "task" in the King James Bible appears *only* in the Book of Exodus and *only* in regard to the Egyptian bondage that led to the Israelites' great escape and their exodus into Canaan. This was surely part of the reason that Cowper chose the word as the title of his greatest poem.

Every biblical appearance of "task," "tasks," or "taskmasters" comes exclusively from the story of the "task in making brick" (Exod. 5:14) when the straw necessary to the task is withheld from the captive Jews by the pharaoh's taskmasters. "And the taskmasters hasted them, saying, Fulfil your works, your daily tasks, as when there was straw" (Exod. 5:13). The abuse of the Israelites by the pharaoh's taskmasters for failing at this unreasonable task triggered the Jewish exodus into the Promised Land. Many centuries later, this exodus would become the most familiar and beloved metaphor in the spirituals composed by American slaves. "Go down, Moses" is the perfect example, urging God to "let my people go." God had promised to free His chosen people the Israelites from their bondage, and He did. Could He not, sang the slaves of America in their haunting, exhilarating spirituals, free His other people, too? Second, "the great task remaining before us" specifically recalls the baptism of spirit and fire promised by John at the baptism of Jesus in the river Jordan. Remember that at his baptism, the Spirit of the Lord is seen "remaining" upon Jesus as the Messiah or Son of God (John 1:33). Finally, the "before us" of the "great task remaining before us" is also biblical. In his dealings with Pharaoh, Moses is constantly "before Pharaoh" (Ex. 4:21, 7:9, 9:10, 9:13, 11:10) or "before the Lord" (Ex. 6:12, 6:30, 16:9, 16:33, 27:21, 28:12, 28:29, and so on), and the Lord is constantly leading the Israelites from Egypt into the Promised Land, "before them by day in a pillar of a cloud . . . and by night in a pillar of fire . . . before the people" (Ex. 13:21–22). This is the same cloud that is seen "remaining" upon the tabernacle in Numbers 9:22. The specific phrase "before us" appears twice in the New Testament, in "the hope set before us" (Heb. 6:18) and in "the race that is set before us" by "Jesus the author and finisher of our faith" (Heb. 12:1–2), upon whom the Spirit of the Lord is seen "remaining" at his baptism.

Lincoln's phrase "the last full measure" is another magnificent example of his ability to transform a highly traditional, perfectly familiar phrase into something stunningly unique. Under its main entry for "measure," the *OED* devotes a paragraph to "*full, good, short* etc. *measure*" and illustrates "full measure" with a quotation from 1706: "What's wanting in his Guns is made up in his Cups, which are sure to have full measure."[16] The phrase occurs in Shakespeare as well, and something very like it in the King James Bible: "Fill ye up then the measure of your fathers" (Matt. 23:32). But no writer in the English language, it appears, had ever thought of placing the word "last" before "full measure," as Lincoln did in November 1863. The word "last" is full of biblical associations—the Last Supper, the last days, the "last trump" of the Last Judgment when "the trumpet shall sound, and the dead shall be raised incorruptible" (1 Cor. 15:52). The added word "last" slows down the whole phrase and makes it extraordinarily dignified, reflective, lyrical, and exalted. The phrase becomes almost as suggestive of music as of mere quantity, with "last," "full," and "measure" all suggesting music. The reader is reminded of all the other words in the address that can also suggest it, particularly "score" and "note." The other words include "seven" (the seventh or "leading" note), "proposition" (a name for the subject in a fugue), "equal," "final," "resting," "long," and "resolve" (to change from discord into harmony). Indeed, once the music box is opened, it is difficult to separate *many* of Lincoln's terms from some kind of connection with music.

Another phrase from the tenth sentence, "that these dead shall not have died in vain," echoes a favorite phrase from throughout the King James—"in vain" accounts for no fewer than 54 of the 111 appearances of "vain" in the Bible—and most specifically of all echoes Saint Paul's "if righteousness come by the law, then Christ is dead in vain" (Gal. 2:21). This famous verse from Galatians means that righteousness comes not from the Old Testament law but from the New Testament grace that Christ has provided by shedding his "blood of the new testament" (Matt. 26:28, Mark 14:24) upon a cross of death. Once again, the deaths of the brave men who struggled at Gettysburg are specifically associated with the sacrificial death of Jesus Christ, who brought salvation to mankind just as these men have brought salvation to their nation. By means of biblical allusion endlessly repeated and reinforced, Lincoln makes the very same association between Jesus Christ and the Union dead that Julia Ward Howe had already made in 1861 in her *Battle Hymn of the Republic*—that stirring poem first published in *Harper's Magazine*, set to the tune of *John Brown's Body*, and adopted by virtual acclamation as the song of the Union Army: "As He died to make men holy, let us die to make men free."[17]

As always, Lincoln's biblical allusions never rule out secular allusions as well. Gabor Boritt persuasively associates Lincoln's "shall not have died in vain" with a phrase attributed to General George Washington in Parson Weems' popular biography. Boritt writes:

> "We here highly resolve that these dead shall not have died in vain—" the crowd again interrupted with applause as Lincoln conjured up an image and words that had been hidden inside of so many since their childhood. "Their fall was not in vain," said the very popular Parson Weems's George Washington when he visited the graves of his soldiers.[18]

It is not just possible but entirely plausible that Lincoln intended both allusions for his little phrase. The reference to Washington fits perfectly with Lincoln's belief that the "honored dead" from the Civil War would inspire the rebirth of the nation for whom they had laid down their lives.

The capstone for all these associations is the phrase "under God" in Lincoln's tenth and final sentence. Would Lincoln have come up with such a capstone, such a key phrase, only as "an afterthought"? Fortunately, scholars have begun to rethink the old assumption that Lincoln inserted this phrase only as he was speaking. It is a question that deserves to be considered with deliberation and care, as it will be in the next chapter.

One of the most hotly debated questions in Lincoln scholarship is the origin of Lincoln's phrase "government of the people, by the people, for the people." In his *Life of Lincoln*, law partner William Herndon recalled what he believed was Lincoln's source. Herndon said that upon returning home after a trip to Boston in the spring of 1858,

> I brought with me additional sermons and lectures by Theodore Parker, who was warm in his commendation of Lincoln. One of these was a lecture on "The Effect of Slavery on the American People," which was delivered in the Music Hall in Boston, and which I gave to Lincoln, who read and returned it. He liked especially the following expression, which he marked with a pencil, and which he in substance afterwards used in his Gettysburg address: "Democracy is direct self-government, over all the people, for all the people, by all the people."[19]

The earnest but erratic Herndon, who suffered equally from alcoholism and too much belief in his own rightness about things, is a troublesome but important source for those seeking the truth about any aspect of Lincoln's life and work. Herndon is right too often to be ignored and wrong too often to be embraced. In this instance, he seems to be referring to Parker's *Additional Speeches, Addresses, and Occasional Sermons*, a copy of which is indeed found among the books Herndon owned. However, "The Effect of Slavery on the American People" appears nowhere in that volume. Indeed, "The Effect of Slavery" had not appeared in print *at all* by the time Herndon returned from Boston.

It is another address from *Additional Speeches*, an 1852 address called "Some Account of My Ministry," that was almost certainly Lincoln's actual source for the famous phrase. In it, Parker declared, "I have great faith in America; in the American idea; in the ideal of our government,—a government of all the people, by all the people, for all the people."[20] Even in this address, Parker was simply repeating a phrase he had used in an even-earlier speech called "Slave Power in America," delivered before the New England Anti-Slavery Convention in Boston on May 29, 1850, but not included in *Additional Speeches*:

> Now, there are two opposite and conflicting principles recognized in the political action of America: at this moment they contend for the mastery, each striving to destroy the other.
>
> There is what I call the American idea. I so name it, because it seems to me to lie at the basis of all our truly original, distinctive, and American institutions. It is itself a complex idea, composed of three subordinate and simple ideas, namely: The idea that all men have unalienable rights; that in respect thereof, all men are created equal; and that government is to be established and sustained for the pur-

pose of giving every man an opportunity for the enjoyment and development of all these unalienable rights. This idea demands, as the proximate organization thereof, a democracy, that is, a government of all the people, by all the people, for all the people; of course, a government after the principles of eternal justice, the unchanging law of God; for shortness' sake, I will call it the idea of freedom.

In this earlier speech, Parker had gone on to argue that the opposite of a democracy is "an aristocracy, that is, a government of all the people by a part of the people—the masters; against a part of the people—the slaves; a government contrary to the principles of eternal justice, contrary to the unchanging law of God."[21] Parker would add an anticlimactic "and" to his tripartite phrase when he repeated it in "Some Thoughts on the Progress of America," delivered before another anti-slavery convention on May 31, 1854:

> America was settled by two very different classes of men, one animated by moral or religious motives, coming to realize an idea; the other animated by only commercial ideas, pushing forth to make a fortune or to escape from gaol. Some men brought religion, others only ambition; the consequence is, two antagonistic ideas, with institutions which correspond, antagonistic institutions.
>
> First there is the Democratic idea: that all men are endowed by their Creator with certain natural rights; that these rights are alienable only by the possessor thereof; that they are equal in all men; that government is to organize these natural, unalienable, and equal rights into institutions designed for the good of the governed; and therefore government is to be of all the people, by all the people, and for all the people.[22]

It seems overwhelmingly likely indeed that one or more of these speeches was the major source for Lincoln's "of the people, by the people, for the people."

But Parker had his *own* source for this phrase, having adapted it from the most celebrated of all nineteenth-century orators, Daniel Webster. Allen Guelzo is one of a number of scholars who argue for Webster as Lincoln's major source for "of the people, by the people, for the people." Guelzo writes, "Even in its final cadence (which was a direct echo of Daniel Webster's crushing 'Reply' to [Senator Robert Y.] Hayne in 1830, that the United States was not a mere assembly of state legislatures but 'the people's government, made for the people, made by the people, and answerable to the people'), the address had the thumbprint of 'an old Henry Clay Whig.'"[23] This is yet another example where the right answer is not *either* but *both*. In this case, even the erratic William E. Barton gets the answer right: "Lincoln, wherever he may originally have been impressed by these words or their equivalent, gained his familiarity that led to their use through his reading both of Daniel Webster and of Theodore Parker."[24] In support of Barton's position, we need only recall that Parker was Webster's greatest admirer until the famed Massachusetts senator's shocking support for the Fugitive Slave Law of 1850 thoroughly disenchanted the younger man. Parker knew the words of Webster probably better than anyone else in the world. The longest and perhaps most passionate speech Parker ever made was his eulogy for Webster, overflowing with equal parts of admiration and disappointment.

What Parker borrowed from Webster becomes clear if we look at more than just the single sentence that Guelzo has quoted from Webster's reply to Hayne in late January of 1830. Hayne was a senator from South Carolina. Two years later, he would give up his seat to John C. Calhoun after Calhoun resigned the vice-presidency under pressure from President Andrew Jackson and others. (Jackson detested Calhoun because of his notorious nullification doctrine, which brought the state of South Carolina close to secession and prompted Old Hickory to write Martin Van Buren that Calhoun's "best former friends say . . . he ought to be hung."[25]) Sen. Hayne was a faithful disciple and mouthpiece for Calhoun's gospel that state sovereignty was anterior to and superior to federal sovereignty and provided the one and only forum for expressing the ultimate sovereignty of the people. Thus, each state may decide for itself whether to obey a particular federal law, depending on whether the federal government has acted within its constitutionally limited powers in passing that law. This radical doctrine, called nullification, held that states may unilaterally ignore or disobey any federal law of any kind whenever they believed it to be unjustified and unconstitutional. Webster replied to Hayne on the floor of the Senate:

> This leads us to enquire into the origin of this government and the source of its power. Whose agent is it? Is it the creature of the State legislatures, or the creature of the people? If the government of the United States be the agent of the State governments, then they may control it, provided they can agree in the manner of controlling it; if it be the agent of the people, then the people alone can control it, restrain it, modify or reform it. It is observable enough that the doctrine for which the honorable gentleman contends leads him to the necessity of maintaining not only that this general government is the creature of the States, but that it is the creature of each of the States severally, so that each may assert the power for itself of determining whether it acts within the limits of its authority. It is the servant of four-and-twenty masters, of different wills and different purposes, and yet bound to obey all. This absurdity (for it seems no less) arises from a misconception as to the origin of this government and its true character. It is, sir, the people's Constitution, the people's government, made for the people, made by the people, and answerable to the people. The people of the United States have declared that this Constitution shall be the supreme law. We must either admit the proposition or dispute their authority. The states are unquestionably sovereign, as far as their sovereignty is not affected by this supreme law. But the State legislatures, as political bodies,

however sovereign, are yet not sovereign over the people. So far as the people have given power to the central government, so far the grant is unquestionably good, and the government holds of the people, and not of the State governments. We are all agents of the same supreme power, the people.[26]

When this fuller context is laid out, it is immediately clear that all three phrases that Parker borrowed and adapted in speech after speech come straight from Webster's reply to Hayne—"of the people" (which appears three times in the passage cited above but not once in the snippet quoted by Guelzo), "by the people," and "for the people."

Parker's contribution was to place all three phrases consecutively into one sentence. However, by inserting the word "all" to produce "of all the people, by all the people, for all the people," he diluted the force of what otherwise would have been a dramatic and enormous improvement. Lincoln knew Webster's reply to Hayne as surely as he knew any speech by Parker. Herndon himself says that in preparing the First Inaugural Address, Lincoln "afterward called for Webster's reply to Hayne, a speech which he read at New Salem, and which he always regarded as the finest specimen of oratory."[27] How can there be any reasonable doubt, with the evidence all before us, that Lincoln knew and used *both* Webster *and* Parker as sources?

In order to make a different point, let us return for a moment to the phrase from Parker's 1858 speech that Herndon wrongly identified as a direct source for the Gettysburg Address. Parker's phrase in that speech betrays the verbal fingerprint of John C. Calhoun, the political enemy most often cited by both Parker and Lincoln. Notice the close resemblance between Parker's "over all the people, for all the people, by all the people" and the following passage from Calhoun's *Discourse on Government*, which first appeared in print in 1851. Writing about the federal Constitution, Calhoun had declared: "It remains now to show, *by whom*, it was ordained and established; *for whom*, it was ordained and established; *for what*, it was ordained and established, and *over whom*, it was ordained and established."[28] The italics are Calhoun's own. He goes on to repeat and discuss each of these phrases, still clad in their italic jackets. Almost certainly, Parker in his 1858 speech was consciously echoing not just Webster but Calhoun. Like Lincoln himself, the Reverend Mr. Parker often used the language of the enemy to make war *against* the enemy.

In short, Lincoln's "of the people, by the people, for the people" is a phrase directly descended from Parker's speeches from the 1850s and ultimately descended from Webster's speech of 1830. Like Parker, who was a minister (albeit a very liberal one), Lincoln exhibits a powerful predilection for three-part phrases of this kind. Both the Bible and the Prayer Book are full of such trinities. Matthew 28:19 reads, "Go ye therefore, and teach all nations, baptizing them in the name of the Father, and of the Son, and of the Holy Ghost." The highly familiar triad "in the name of the Father, and of the Son, and of the Holy Ghost" is repeated throughout the Prayer Book.

Lincoln's "of the people, by the people, for the people," directly recalling both Webster and Parker and perhaps also stealing one of Lincoln's many sidelong glances at Calhoun, is an improvement on the writing of all of these men. Lincoln had almost certainly read all the speeches in question—Webster's 1830 reply to Hayne, Parker's 1850 and 1854 speeches, Parker's 1858 speech, and even the work by Calhoun, first published in 1851, which Parker is playing with in the 1858 speech. Lincoln's phrase is a monument for the ages. He built it in much the same way as when he echoed and improved Seward and Madison in his First Inaugural Address. The difference between Webster or Parker on the one hand—or Madison and Seward for that matter—and Lincoln on the other is the difference between good writing and great writing. As he always did, he demonstrated a better ear than his predecessors, greatly improving upon all of them with his perfectly simple and beautiful "of the people, by the people, for the people." In comparing Lincoln's words and phrases with his sources, one is often reminded of Mark Twain's observation, "The difference between the *almost*-right word & the *right* word is really a large matter—it's the difference between the lightning bug and the lightning."[29] Lincoln's disposition was always to use old words and old phrases in surprisingly new ways, making the old seem refreshingly new. It is doubtful that any writer ever did this better.

One of Lincoln's most fascinating and revealing word choices is his use of "liberty" in the first sentence and "freedom" in the last. At the beginning of the address, he associates the nation's conception, birth, and baptismal christening with "liberty." Then he associates the nation's "new birth" and baptism by fire at the end of the speech with "freedom." Why did Lincoln depart from his usual practice of selecting one word and simply repeating it and instead employ two synonyms in two different contexts? There are at least two good reasons. First, Lincoln was a poet and understood fully that the sound of a word can be just as important as the sense of it. "Conceived in liberty" is poetry. "Conceived in freedom" is not. "A new birth of freedom" is poetry. "A new birth of liberty" is not. Second, "liberty" is more appropriate than "freedom" for the first sentence of the Gettysburg Address because in that sentence the conception, birth, and baptism of this nation are specifically associated with the Declaration of Independence. The word "liberty" makes its unforgettable appearance in the Declaration of Independence in the glorious phrase "life, liberty, and the pursuit of happiness." "Freedom" is absent from the Declaration but appears famously in the Bill of Rights to the Constitution. What "new birth of freedom" weighed more on Lincoln's mind in 1863 than his desire to end the centuries-old curse of slavery? His Emancipation Proclamation was already starting to end it, but he knew that it would take a constitutional amendment to finish this great task. No one knew better than Lincoln that the very First Amendment to the Constitution, introduced by James Madison, had featured "freedom" among its immortal words: "Congress shall make no law respecting an establishment of religion, or prohibiting the free exercise thereof, or abridging the freedom of speech, or of the press, or of the right of the people peaceably to assemble, and to petition the government for a redress of grievances." Two of the greatest blessings of the "new birth of freedom" prophesied by Lincoln in the Gettysburg Address were the Thirteenth Amendment, which he lived to see passed by Congress, and the Fourteenth, which he helped to inspire, first with his life and his teachings and finally with his death.

One of the fascinating things about the French-named "liberty" and the Saxon-named "freedom" is that they have survived as nearly identical twins for almost a thousand years of the English language. Anyone who has looked up the two words in a good dictionary can only be stunned at how close in meaning these two words have remained for so many centuries. Most synonyms share the fate of siblings who grow more and more apart and less and less alike with age. As close as "consecrate," "dedicate," and "hallow" are to one another in meaning, try substituting either "dedicated" or "hallowed" for "consecrated" in Lincoln's "have consecrated it far above our poor power to add or detract" to see just how quickly and dramatically even small differences in meaning or sound spoil the whole effect. "Dedicate" fits the rhythm but not the meaning. "Hallowed" fits neither. One of the reasons that "liberty" and "freedom" have stayed so close in meaning is that their original base meaning has never changed. This base meaning is *freedom from slavery*. What a perfect foundation for Lincoln's message! What a perfect reminder that liberty and freedom are incompatible with slavery, that in giving freedom to the slave, we give it to all people, and that when we take it from some, we risk losing it for all! The King James Bible is a clear reminder of the base or original meaning behind both words. Acts 22:28 says, "And the chief captain answered, With a great sum obtained I this freedom. And Paul said, But I was free born." Fearful of Paul's free-born Roman citizenship, the captain hurried him to Felix the governor, who, also in fear, "commanded a centurion to keep Paul, and to let him have liberty" (Acts 24:23). Three different times in the climactic third act of *Julius Caesar*, Shakespeare treats "liberty" and "freedom" as identical twins in meaning: "Liberty! Freedom! Tyranny is dead!" shouts Cinna when Caesar's kingly ambitions are struck down (3.1.78). "Liberty, freedom, and enfranchisement!" adds Cassius (3.1.81). "Let's all cry, 'Peace, freedom, and liberty!'" (3.1.110), concludes Brutus (3.1.110). Brutus then defends the conspiracy by asking the people, "Had you rather Caesar were living and die all slaves, than that Caesar were dead, to live all free men?" (3.2.25–26). Brutus underscores the idea that liberty and freedom are the opposite of slavery when he adds, "Who is here so base that would be a bondman?" (3.2.31–32) When Brutus takes his own life at the end, another character tells a slave that now the great Roman is "Free from the bondage that you are in" (5.5.54).

The last two phrases of the Gettysburg Address—"shall not perish" and "from the earth"—are phrases perfectly chosen from the King James Bible to underscore and conclude Lincoln's metaphor of the United States as the messiah of the world. The first phrase recalls that most famous of all verses, at least to Protestant Christians, John 3:16: "for God so loved the world, that he gave his only begotten son, that whoever believeth in him should not perish, but have everlasting life." The moment that Lincoln's audience heard him say, "shall not perish," everyone who knew the Bible would have thought, *"but have everlasting life."* It would have been an irresistible completion of this most familiar of all biblical allusions. At the same time, however, everyone would have known that no *nation* can be everlasting, since the earth itself is not: "Of old hast thou laid the foundation of the earth: and the heavens are the work of thy hands. They shall perish, but thou shalt endure" (Ps. 102:25–26). Only God himself and whatever God chooses to save can endure forever. Jeremiah 10:11 says of the false gods who never created this world in the first place, "The gods that have not made the heavens and the earth *shall perish from the earth*" (emphasis added). Again echoing Jeremiah, Lincoln clearly implies that the equality and democracy promised in this nation's Declaration of Independence are *not* false gods doomed to perish from the earth. Instead, says Lincoln, this nation and its oldest, dearest principles—above all, the two crowning principles that "all men are created equal" and that the only true government is "of the people"—*shall not perish from the earth.* Lasting as long as the earth lasts is the closest that any human institution can come to eternal life this side of heaven.

Whether he is using words from the Bible, the Prayer Book, Shakespeare, Cowper, Key, or the Declaration of Independence, Lincoln is always echoing. At the same time, he is always transforming whatever he has borrowed into something uniquely his own that sounds altogether fresh and new. This may be the most astonishing achievement of the Gettysburg Address—that into such an amazingly short work, Lincoln could pour so much of what he had read and absorbed throughout a lifetime of reading and reflection—and still end with such a stunningly original masterpiece.

"Under God"—Aforethought or Afterthought?

A longstanding belief among many historians holds that Lincoln spontaneously added the words "under God" in the very act of delivering his Gettysburg Address—as what William J. Wolf has called an "afterthought."[1] This belief arises from the fact that neither of the two surviving manuscripts that now compete for the honor of having been Lincoln's delivery copy includes "under God." In his *Gettysburg Gospel*, Gabor Boritt makes a compelling case that the Hay copy, not the Nicolay, was Lincoln's delivery copy—if either was.[2] The Nicolay copy contains a sentence "This we may, in all propriety do," which underwent a major transformation into "It is altogether fitting and proper that we should do this," the words that appear in both the Hay copy and the transcribed newspaper accounts. The Nicolay copy completely omits one of the last two sentences. Clearly, then, if Lincoln read from either of these two nominees, Boritt is right that it must have been the Hay. The problem is more complicated, however, because Lincoln *could* have read from a copy that included "under God" but has since been lost to us. Boritt does not think this is what happened, but many other scholars do.

The surviving evidence overwhelmingly supports the proposition that Lincoln's delivery copy *did* include the words "under God" and was therefore neither the Nicolay nor the Hay. The only evidence to the contrary is purely negative. The negative evidence is the simple fact that no one has located a manuscript in Lincoln's hand that both predates the address and includes the words in question. Those who can never convict for murder without a body, no matter how overwhelming the evidence that the accused is guilty as charged, may close their eyes and ears in advance. For everyone else, the evidence follows.

In 1930, the last year of his life, William E. Barton published his book called *Lincoln at Gettysburg*. It was the last in a series of books written about Lincoln by this Congregational minister who had been born in Lincoln's Illinois in 1861. As the first scholar to present an account of what had been said and done at Gettysburg that was based upon the testimony of a large number of eyewitnesses, Barton interviewed many of these eyewitnesses himself and collected written accounts from others. A widely traveled man, he served as pastor of

Shawmut Church in Boston (where he knew Julia Ward Howe) and as pastor of the First Congregational Church in Oak Park, Illinois, before becoming a professor of religion at Vanderbilt University in Nashville, Tennessee. Apart from contemporary newspaper accounts, Barton may be our richest single source of information—albeit a troublesome and uneven one—about what happened that day. He was also a passionate, intelligent collector of Lincoln books and texts. In Boston, Barton personally knew both Edward Everett Hale and Hale's brother Charles, a reporter for the *Boston Advertiser*. Charles Hale was present at Gettysburg with "notebook and pencil in hand" and, according to Barton, "was positive that he caught every word. He took down what he declared was the exact language of Lincoln's address, and his declaration is as good as the oath of a court stenographer."[3] There is no reason to doubt Professor Barton's contention that Hale provides a highly reliable source for what Lincoln actually said that day. And there is absolutely no doubt that the Hale text includes the words, "that the nation shall, under God, have a new birth of freedom."

But did the same words appear in Lincoln's delivery copy? They did. We know this because the Associated Press reporter Joseph Ignatius Gilbert left behind his own account of what was said and done that day. Barton himself quotes Gilbert's account—in part—in his *Lincoln at Gettysburg* before distorting and mischaracterizing it. Gilbert's account was first given to the National Shorthand Reporters' Association in Cleveland, Ohio, in August 1917. In those days, it was not at all uncommon for newspaper reporters to take training in shorthand, and Gilbert was one of those who did. At the Cleveland meeting, he told his audience that he had originally planned to take down Lincoln's speech in shorthand, just as he had earlier transcribed the "full text" of Everett's much-longer oration. But Gilbert said he was so caught up in what Lincoln was saying that he stopped transcribing: "Fascinated by his intense earnestness and depth of feeling, I unconsciously stopped taking notes and looked up at him just as he glanced from his manuscript with a far away look in his eyes as if appealing from the few thousands before him to the invisible audience of countless millions whom his words were to reach."[4] This could have created a major problem for any reporter. However, Gilbert continued, "Before the dedication ceremonies closed the President's manuscript was copied, with his permission; and as the press report was made from a copy no transcript from shorthand notes was necessary."[5] No one has ever put forth any good reason to question this account from an experienced and reliable reporter. Barton himself fully accepted Gilbert's claim, saying that the AP reporter "had Lincoln's manuscript and copied from that."[6] The AP's own *AP History* confirms Gilbert's account in its summary of the year 1863: "As President Abraham Lincoln delivers his address dedicating the cemetery at Gettysburg, Pennsylvania on November 19, AP stringer Joseph Ignatius Gilbert takes down his words in shorthand. Afterwards, Gilbert borrows Lincoln's handwritten text, copies it word for word in longhand, and uses that as the basis for his AP story, which was published in numerous newspapers, including the New York Times, New York Tribune, New York Herald, and Brooklyn Daily Eagle [unitalicized in original]."[7] Did the AP version of Lincoln's address used by all those newspapers include "under God"? It most certainly did, and in the very place those words appear in the Hale transcription: "that the Nation shall under God have a new birth of freedom." The differences are trivial—for example, that Hale set off the words "under God" with commas whereas Gilbert did not.

Douglas L. Wilson was the first scholar to demonstrate in his masterful study called *Lincoln's Sword: The Presidency and the Power of Words* (2006) what he correctly describes as "the virtual identity between the 266-word text Gilbert copied from Lincoln's delivery manuscript and what was taken down from his spoken words by Charles Hale."[8] Wilson proves his point by reprinting both the Gilbert and the Hale texts, which are also reprinted in the appendix to the present study. Wilson adds in a footnote that Gilbert's account of writing down the exact words from Lincoln's delivery text was independently confirmed by another reliable reporter at Gettysburg that day—John Russell Young. Both Gilbert and Young worked for Lincoln's close friend John W. Forney, who while serving as Secretary of the Senate was also the owner and editor of both the *Philadelphia Press* and the *Washington Chronicle*. In his 1901 memoir called *Men and Memories*, Young wrote, "John W. Forney was my first master, and I served him for some years in the early days of the *Press*."[9] Young also said that "Lincoln had no more strenuous friend than John Forney."[10] As for himself, "I saw a great deal of Lincoln from time to time during the war. For a time I was the private secretary of John W. Forney, who as secretary of the Senate and owner of the Administration newspaper, The [*Washington*] *Chronicle*, was near the President."[11] Gilbert was almost as close to John Forney as Young was. In a part of his address to the Shorthand Association never cited by Barton, Gilbert recalled of those days, "Being connected with 'The Philadelphia Press' and 'The Washington Chronicle,' the administration newspapers published by Col. Forney, then Secretary of the U.S. Senate, I was occasionally at Washington in the dark days when disasters at the front, threats of foreign intervention, popular discontent, quarrels in the Cabinet and importunities of office seekers made life burdensome for the despondent, almost despairing, occupant of the White House."[12] As Barton pointed out in his 1930 study, Forney himself was also present at Gettysburg: "Colonel John W. Forney, a veteran newspaper man and a hard drinker, having drunk heavily all day, was called out by a serenade that Hay and others arranged for his benefit. Forney rebuked his hearers for giving him more hearty cheers than they had given the President."[13] Thus, with their close connection to Forney and his pro-Lincoln Washington and Philadelphia newspapers, both Gilbert and Young had easy access to the president.

In his *Men and Memories*, Young says of the Gettysburg Address, "It was my duty to report the speech on behalf of the Philadelphia *Press*, to sit at the side of Lincoln as he pronounced the immortal words, and write them down in shorthand as they came from his lips." Young describes how physically close he sat to the President on that historic occasion: "I sat within a few feet, on the second bench of the press people." (Gilbert, representing the AP, had an even better position on the platform.) As the President rose to speak, Young recalled, "I took up the pencil and began to take him in shorthand. . . . To my surprise, almost it seemed before Mr. Lincoln had begun to speak, he turned and sat down. Surely these five or six lines of shorthand were not all. Hurriedly bending over the aisle I asked if that was all. 'Yes, for the present,' he answered." Like Gilbert, however, Young never had to use his shorthand notes because, as he himself attests, "I did not write the report which appeared in the *Press*, as the manuscript had been given to the Associated Press, and the transcription of my notes was unnecessary."[14] On that day, the Associated Press was one man—Young's colleague Joseph Gilbert.

Why have so many scholars overlooked or ignored this rock-solid evidence that Lincoln's delivery copy was copied word for word by Gilbert just after it was delivered and that this copy included the words "under God"? Why have so many scholars, with so little evidence of any kind, championed either the Nicolay or the Hay copy as Lincoln's delivery text when *neither* could possibly have been the text if Gilbert told the truth, because neither text includes "under God"? Again, Wilson provides the likely answer. It is almost certainly because scholars have uncritically accepted Barton's totally unfounded belief—prompted by the loose ends he found no other way to tie together—that Gilbert's AP version of the speech was "made up hastily, partly from his own notes and partly from Lincoln's manuscript."[15] Wilson was the first scholar to point out that Barton's assertion on this point is unsupported by *any* evidence at all. Barton either ignored or misread the very words of Gilbert that he himself had collected and quoted. Gilbert had told the shorthand association unequivocally that he had made "no transcript" of his shorthand notes of Lincoln's speech and that everything he wrote down that day regarding the president's words came from Lincoln's own manuscript. Never once did he say that he had combined his notes with the words he copied from Lincoln. What this means is that unless Gilbert and Young were both liars, we *have* the delivery text and have *always* had it. We have it in Gilbert's word-for-word copy of the manuscript from which Lincoln read at Gettysburg. Because this copy includes the words "under God," we may be certain that they appeared in the delivery copy.

Why Lincoln's delivery copy vanished soon after he read it at Gettysburg and has never turned up since is totally irrelevant to the issue of the reliability of Gilbert and Young, even though it will surely remain among the most interesting unanswered questions in all of Lincoln scholarship. All that matters for our purposes is that Gilbert transcribed the delivery manuscript word for word. He did so while Lincoln was still on the platform. Is it possible that the president, tired and perhaps already beginning to suffer from the varioloid infection that would soon put him into a sick bed, left the platform without his manuscript in hand? If so, he would have left it with a reporter who was representing both the Associated Press and his trusted friend John Forney. Even if the president left his manuscript *unintentionally* on the platform, he would have had the reassuring knowledge that his speech had just been copied verbatim for an entire journalistic network. Following a suggestion by Garry Wills, Wilson argues for a still more plausible possibility—that after returning to Washington, Lincoln "may have authorized sending his delivery copy to [Gettysburg organizer David] Wills without realizing that his only remaining text was the incomplete Nicolay copy."[16] Both Garry Wills and Wilson believe that David Wills may then have sent the delivery copy to Edward Everett to use in his book, published in 1864, which reprinted all the speeches, prayers, and events of the Gettysburg consecration and included the words "under God." Again, the central point is that Lincoln's missing delivery text, while an interesting issue, is not a *determinative* one.

Barton's confusion on this whole question almost certainly traced to a magazine article that John Nicolay wrote for *The Century Magazine* in 1894, entitled "Lincoln's Gettysburg Address." Writing almost thirty years after Lincoln's death, Nicolay assumed that the president's reading copy at Gettysburg had been the manuscript now known as the first draft or Nicolay copy, the first page of which was written in Lincoln's hand on letterhead Executive Mansion stationery. Because this copy does not contain "under God" while Gilbert's AP copy *does*, Barton's assumption that Gilbert *must* have relied on more than the president's reading copy becomes perfectly understandable. One false assumption has simply created another. The truth is that neither Nicolay nor Lincoln's other secretary, John Hay, stayed close to the president at Gettysburg. They knew next to nothing about how he had written his speech and nothing at all about which version he had read from. Describing his time at the Gettysburg dedication, Young wrote later, "I am afraid I pestered Hay on the subject for an advance sight of the manuscript, were there one; but Hay, ever generous and helpful, as I remember, either knew no more than I or would not tell me."[17] The truth is that Hay knew no more than Young about Lincoln's manuscript, and Nicolay little more than either.

What the two secretaries *did* know was that a few days after delivering the Address, the president, responding to a letter from David Wills, decided to have a look at more than one copy, as Nicolay explains in his 1894 *Century* article: "By his direction, therefore, his secretaries made copies of the Associated Press report as it was printed in several prominent newspapers. Comparing these with his original draft, and with his own fresh recollection of the form in which he delivered it, he made a new autograph copy—a careful and deliberate revision—which has become the standard and authentic text."[18] By this time, whether because he had lost it or sent it already to Wills or someone else, Lincoln no longer had the actual delivery copy—the one from which Gilbert had copied his AP text. Not realizing this, Nicolay wrongly assumed that the first draft, the one written partly on Executive Mansion stationery, had also been Lincoln's delivery copy. The *Century* article shows us that Lincoln regarded the Associated Press copy of his address as the most authoritative of all the newspaper accounts. This in itself helps to confirm Gilbert's testimony of having copied Lincoln's delivery manuscript. With the delivery manuscript no longer available, it would make sense that Lincoln looked back to the AP text precisely because he expected it to be an exact copy of his delivery text, apart from whatever mistakes had been introduced by telegraph operators or newspaper editors. Without his delivery text in hand, it would make perfect sense that Lincoln decided to consult whatever he could lay his hands on, including what Nicolay calls "his original draft," now known as the Nicolay copy. It is this copy that Nicolay reproduced in facsimile in the 1894 *Century Magazine*, wrongly assuming it to have been Lincoln's delivery copy at the Gettysburg ceremony.

In short, the red herring in all of this is Nicolay's assumption that this original draft—and it *was* the original draft or the nearest thing to it that survived—was also Lincoln's delivery text on the platform at Gettysburg. Another red herring introduced by Nicolay himself is his contention that the Revised Autograph Copy assembled that day in Lincoln's office was identical to the copy mailed to George Bancroft about three months later, the copy that Nicolay says "has properly become the standard text." Nicolay offers no evidence for this claim, which raises all sorts of questions and problems:

> In addition to that from Mr. Wills, other requests soon came to him for autograph copies. The number he made, and for what friends, cannot now be confidently stated, though it was probably half a dozen or more, all written by him with painstaking care to correspond word for word with his revision. If in any respect they differed from one another, it was due to accident and against his intention.[19]

Everyone seems to agree that changing the article "the" to "a" before "final resting-place," moving the phrase "under God" from after "shall" to before shall," and changing "the unfinished work that they have thus far so nobly carried on" into "the unfinished work which they who fought here have thus far so nobly advanced" are all improvements.

But the problem Nicolay never addresses is that the copy Lincoln prepared for Edward Everett in February of 1864 and the copy he sent later in the same short month to George Bancroft *differ*. The difference is in the first sentence: "Four score and seven years ago our fathers brought forth upon this continent, a new nation, conceived in Liberty, and dedicated to the proposition that all men are created equal." The earlier copy sent to Everett retains the preposition "upon" that Lincoln had used at Gettysburg, whereas the Bancroft copy substitutes "on" for "upon." In addition, when Lincoln recopied the Bancroft copy a few days later into what is now called the Bliss copy or Final Text, he omitted the word "here" between the words "they" and "gave" in the last sentence, where, in the Everett Text, he writes of "that cause for which they here gave the last full measure of devotion." One presumes that this was intentional, and, indeed, most literary scholars regard the omission as a small improvement. But by the same token, the change from "upon" to "on" seems a small step backward. If Nicolay was right in recollecting that what he called "the standard text" and we today call the Bliss Copy or Final Text was first drawn up just a few days after the Gettysburg consecration, then something is obviously askew. Why would Lincoln have used "upon" at Gettysburg, then switched to "on" a few days later in the presence of his secretaries, then switched back to "upon" for the Everett copy he sent out early in February of 1864, and then returned once again to "on" for the Bancroft copy sent out later in that same short month? The only explanation for such differences that Nicolay himself allows for is that they were "due to accident." But why would Lincoln be consistent with most of his other changes and yet go back and forth between "upon" and "on"? Can this mean that the flaw lies somewhere in Nicolay's recollection?

Other problems have easier answers. In his *Century* article, Nicolay assumed that because the word "poor" appears before "power" in the Nicolay copy but not in the AP copy, which Lincoln and his secretaries had before them during the rewriting, then the "word 'poor' [was] omitted" during delivery.[20] Professor Wilson clears up this problem by showing that "the AP dispatch first printed in the major New York newspapers, which eventually found its way into the *Collected Works* and Lincoln scholarship generally, contains three errors that did not originate with Gilbert."[21] These errors introduced by others may well have contributed to Barton's misapprehension that Gilbert had relied on his shorthand notes and not just on Lincoln's delivery copy. Wilson demonstrates that "poor" did in fact appear in Gilbert's AP text after all. In short, Lincoln's reading copy at Gettysburg was *not* the Nicolay copy but a copy that Lincoln no longer had in his possession a few days after the event. It was the very absence of this copy that caused him to check his marvelous memory against the AP accounts and other sources before reconstructing his speech and adding a sprinkling of changes. Just *when* he made these changes, however, is by no means clear. Because of the continued absence of Lincoln's delivery copy and because of the many faulty assumptions and unanswered questions in Nicolay's 1894 article that in turn had such a pernicious influence on Barton's view of the testimony of AP writer Joseph Ignatius Gilbert, our knowledge of exactly when and in what order Lincoln made changes to the Gettysburg Address *after* Gettysburg remains shrouded in many uncertainties.

The evidence about what Lincoln read *at* Gettysburg, however, is much clearer. The evidence comes down to this: first, Gilbert copied Lincoln's reading text for the Associated Press on the day of delivery; second, Gilbert's AP copy, freed from errors inserted into it later by others, is essentially identical with Charles Hale's shorthand version made while Lincoln spoke; and, third, both of these authoritative documents include the words "under God." It follows, then, that Lincoln could *not* have added these words as he was delivering his address upon the platform at Gettysburg. Nevertheless, the *belief* that he added them, stemming from Nicolay's 1894 article, reinforced by Barton's 1930 book, and repeated by numerous scholars since, has taken on a life of its own. It has become an article of faith that lives on in defiance of the overwhelming evidence to the contrary. It is like a cat with many lives, leaping up with renewed vigor every time its throat is cut. Let us see if a hypothetical stake in the hypothetical heart of this hypothetical cat might keep it in its crypt.

Assume, strictly for purposes of argument, that uncertainty remains as to whether Gilbert actually and accurately transcribed Lincoln's delivery text. Starting with this purely hypothetical assumption, which flatly contradicts all the facts and evidence just witnessed, let us frame this question, "Is it plausible, as so many scholars have assumed, that on that platform at Gettysburg Lincoln added the words, 'under God,' during the very moment when he was uttering the words before them?" In short, is this famous phrase a mere afterthought or spontaneous declaration, as opposed to something that Lincoln had carefully thought through before using? Does it suffer from the fate of most spontaneous declarations by failing to fit perfectly with the rest of the speech? This is a crucial question because if the phrase is just as appropriate to Lincoln's metaphors and meanings as any other, just as *perfect* as any other, then the exact moment of its birth matters infinitely less than the health of the baby. In short, the ultimate *hypothetical* question is not whether "under God" was in the reading copy, which is a *factual* question. The ultimate hypothetical question is whether, under the totality of the circumstances, "under God" is more plausibly seen as a carefully considered and fully assimilated choice or as a spontaneous declaration. In short, is it aforethought or afterthought?

The first thing to observe is that "under God" does indeed fit perfectly with everything else in the speech. It has none of the common defects associated with spontaneous or extemporaneous remarks. No one had a more acute appreciation of those defects than Abraham Lincoln, which is precisely why he always tried to avoid making extemporaneous speeches, especially on important occasions. Asked to make one the night before his Gettysburg Address, Lincoln felt duty-bound to disappoint the insistent crowd:

The inference is a very fair one that you would hear me for a little while at least, were I to commence to make a speech. I do not appear before you for the purpose of doing so, and for several substantial reasons. The most substantial of these is that I have no speech to make. [Laughter.] In my position it is somewhat important that I should not say any foolish things.

A VOICE—If you can help it.

MR. LINCOLN—It very often happens that the only way to help it is to say nothing at all. [Laughter.][22]

And yet, historians, despite acknowledging the president's extreme reluctance to make extemporaneous remarks at any time or place, have nevertheless allowed "under God" to slide unchecked and almost unnoticed into the category of spontaneous interjection.

Barton himself is an early example. Despite his belief that "Lincoln spoke little in public, and what he said he wrote out carefully," Barton also declared, "An interesting question relates to the words 'under God.'" Finding them nowhere in what he mistakenly believed was the delivery copy, he concluded, "My own belief is that Lincoln interpolated them under the deep feeling of the occasion."[23] In *Lincoln the President*, published in 1945, J. G. Randall was equally contradictory: "For such an address to have been hastily prepared, or for the President to have trusted to the moment, would have been altogether contrary to Lincoln's habit."[24] But then, a mere two pages later as he turns to consider "under God," Randall abruptly and unaccountably changes his tune: "The speech as prepared had not included these words, but the newspaper reports as well as all of Lincoln's later revisions, contain them; they were added by Lincoln as he spoke."[25] This clearly assumes the very spontaneity that Randall has just denied. Benjamin P. Thomas in his 1952 *Abraham Lincoln* agrees: "The words 'under God' do not appear in either the first or second draft of Lincoln's address. They came to him while he spoke."[26] There is no doubt that this misperception still has currency. In *The Eloquent President* of 2005, Ronald C. White Jr. asks rhetorically if Lincoln added the words "on the spot," says this would have been "uncharacteristic," but then, with no more explanation for his shift than his predecessors give for theirs, abruptly embraces the theory that the words were indeed "inserted" as an "interjection."[27] In *The Gettysburg Gospel* of 2006, Boritt imagines that Lincoln "added 'under God' to his remarks at Gettysburg" in "the moment's inspiration," pausing to add them "a little awkwardly."[28]

Is it not far more plausible and far more in keeping with everything we know about Lincoln's mind and manner that he would have made a deliberate and careful decision to add this phrase well *before* he spoke? This is the very conclusion that John Nicolay arrived at in his *Century* article in 1894. Mistakenly believing that Lincoln's delivery text had nowhere included "under God," Nicolay treated this phrase as one of several that he believed Lincoln had added on the day of delivery but only after many hours of "silent thought":

> The phrase, "Shall have a new birth of freedom," was changed as follows: "Shall, under God, have a new birth of freedom," a change which added dignity and solemnity.
>
> The above changes show that Lincoln did not read his address, but that he delivered it from the fullness and conciseness of thought and memory, rounding it out to nearly its final rhetorical completeness. The changes may have been prompted by the oratorical impulse of the moment; but it is more likely that in the interval of four hours occupied by coming to the grounds, and the delivery of Mr. Everett's oration, he fashioned the phrases anew in his silent thought, and had them ready for use when he rose to speak.[29]

How reasonable, how plausible! Clearly, then, even if "under God" never appeared in his delivery copy, the president had far more time that day to come up with two little words than he probably had to devote to any other two words in his entire speech. He had over four hours with essentially nothing to do. Except for waving, nodding, and applauding, what else could he do that day except *think*? He had already read an advance copy of Everett's speech in its entirety and did not need to hear every syllable of the old orator's two-hour speech. Why do so many scholars believe that after keeping his mind blank and idle for all that time, Lincoln suddenly gave birth to a perfect phrase, like Athena springing perfectly wise and beautiful from the brain of Zeus? The circumstantial evidence is simply overwhelming that no matter what the precise moment may have been when "under God" made its way into the Gettysburg Address, it did *not* arrive ad libitum and at the last moment on the wings of a sudden emotion. Nicolay, who knew Lincoln very well indeed, recognized just how implausible and unlikely this would have been.

Remember the time frame. "The line of march was taken up at 10 o'clock," the *New York Times* reported next day, "and the procession marched through the principal streets to the Cemetery, where the military formed in line and saluted the President. At 11½ the head of the procession arrived at the main stand."[30] Barton's account, based on the recollection of eyewitnesses, is very similar:

> The procession was to have started at ten o'clock. At that hour, Mr. Lincoln, dressed in black and wearing a tall hat and white gauntlets, emerged from the home of Mr. Wills and mounted a waiting horse. The crowd pressed in upon him and he was compelled to hold an informal reception on horse-back. It was eleven o'clock before the procession got under way.

At the cemetery, says Barton, Everett arrived a half hour late. For all these reasons, "The exercises began at noon, an hour late."[31] There was music and a prayer before Everett spoke, then more music before Lincoln spoke. Everyone agrees that Everett spoke for almost precisely two hours. It was therefore well past 2:00 when Lincoln rose to speak. Between four and five hours had elapsed since he had walked out of the Wills house where he did his last known writing on the speech. Lincoln spent at least part of his time platform going over his own speech, as Barton learned from accounts of eyewitnesses: "He took his manuscript from his pocket, adjusted his spectacles, and during the closing portion of Everett's oration, refreshed his memory as to the content of his own speech."[32] Thus, even making the factually unfounded assumption that "under God" was added on stage, this would obviously have been a far more reasonable and plausible time for making the final decision to add the phrase than when Lincoln was actually addressing the great throng. In short, considered either factually or hypothetically, Lincoln's famous phrase was never an afterthought.

What makes "under God" a fascinating problem of a very different kind is that it appears nowhere in Lincoln's usual sources. It appears nowhere in the King James Bible. Of course, the word "God" appears hundreds of times and is preceded by many different prepositions but never by "under." It appears nowhere in the Book of Common Prayer—apart from the preface to the American Prayer Book, about which more will be said. It appears nowhere in the works of Shakespeare. Yet, it sounds *very* familiar to an audience today because President Dwight D. Eisenhower added it to the Pledge of Allegiance in 1954, and ever since, millions of American schoolchildren have recited it while saluting the flag in school. Most Americans alive today have recited this pledge more times than they can remember, starting in their most impressionable years.

It is worth considering alternative prepositions or other words that Lincoln might have placed before "God," such as "with God," "before God," "through God," "by God," "following God," "relying on God," "believing in God," or "with the help of God." Considering what is wrong with these alternatives underscores the absolute perfection of Lincoln's choice and increases to near-certainty the already overwhelming likelihood that "under God" was *not* spontaneous. This phrase works in every way, on every level. It is astonishingly clear and simple. The two words sound beautiful and natural together. There is no other phrase Lincoln could have borrowed or chosen for "under God" that comes anywhere close to succeeding in all the ways that his chosen words succeed.

What is even more surprising is that "God" itself—that simplest of words for the Deity—had been so shockingly rare in *all* major speeches of *all* fifteen presidents before Abraham Lincoln. Thirteen of those fifteen presidents had delivered at least one inaugural address. Because John Tyler and Millard Fillmore had replaced presidents who died in office, they, of course, never delivered one. All thirteen presidents who delivered at least one inaugural had invoked the Deity at least once. Five presidents—George Washington, Thomas Jefferson, James

Madison, James Monroe, and Andrew Jackson—had been elected to two terms. Thus a total of eighteen inaugural addresses had been delivered before Lincoln gave his first. It so happened that neither Washington nor Madison had made mention of a higher power in their second inaugurals, so that a grand total of sixteen inaugural addresses had appeared with one or more names for the Deity before Lincoln took his oath of office in 1861. What is truly shocking is that only twice in those sixteen addresses had *any* president ever referred to the Deity by the name of "God." We know, too, that Lincoln knew this. Harold Holzer points out in his *Lincoln President Elect* that while preparing his own first inaugural, Lincoln checked out a library book containing all the previous inaugural addresses:

> For the inaugural, his inquiries began early. On November 13, just a week after his election, . . . Lincoln had borrowed from the Illinois State Library, located one flight below his Capitol office suite, a copy of Edwin Williams's indispensable two-volume 1848 reference work, the *Statesman's Manual*. Formally titled *Presidents' Messages, Inaugural, Annual, and Special, from 1789 to 1846*, it contained the full texts of the key utterances of all of Lincoln's predecessors.

"These old texts," Holzer adds, "provided both inspiration and ammunition."[33]

In his first inaugural, Washington called upon the "Almighty Being," an example that was followed by a long chain of imitators. Adams invoked "that Being who is supreme over all." Jefferson remembered "the Being in whose hands we are" in his second inaugural. Madison in his first inaugural called on that "Almighty Being whose power regulates the destiny of nations." It seems clear that from the beginning, presidents were reading their predecessors before writing their own inaugurals. Monroe started a new chain by echoing the "overruling Providence" of Jefferson's first inaugural with a "gracious Providence" in his own first inaugural. John Quincy Adams followed suit with "overruling Providence." Jackson in his first inaugural followed the new choice but used a lower-case form of it in "that Power whose providence mercifully protected our national infancy." Then in his second inaugural, Jackson revived Washington's "Almighty Being." This set off yet another chain of "Being." For Martin Van Buren, it was "Divine Being." For William Henry Harrison, it was "that good Being who has blessed us." For James Knox Polk, it was the "Divine Being who has watched over and protected our beloved country from its infancy." Then Zachary Taylor returned to "Providence" with his "Divine Providence," which was almost certainly the literary inspiration for the next two presidents to continue the same key word. Franklin Pierce chose "beneficent Providence." James Buchanan chose "Divine Providence." Thus the two leading contenders for the name of the Deity among American presidents before Lincoln's first inaugural were "Being" with eight citations and "Providence" with seven. For whatever reason, these two most favored words never once appeared together in the same address, most presidents having made but one reference to the Deity in any given speech and typically no more than two.

In his second inaugural, Monroe chose "Almighty God" over the usual terms, thus becoming the first and only president among the founding fathers to use "God" in *any* inaugural address. "Almighty God" is a phrase from the Bible that also opens many prayers in the Book of Common Prayer. It opens three prayers in the service of Holy Communion as well as a prayer of General Thanksgiving that appears in Morning Prayer, Evening Prayer, and the Litany. It is worth recalling that Monroe was one of four Virginia Episcopalians among the first five presidents. The only other president besides Monroe who ever used the word "God" in any inaugural address before Lincoln's two terms was Buchanan, a Pennsylvania Presbyterian who in 1857 had used both "Divine Providence" and "God of our fathers." "God of our Fathers" was not only a favorite phrase of political speakers in the 1850s but would later form the inspiration for a hymn of that name composed for the centennial of the Declaration of Independence. Thus *only two presidents*—Monroe and Buchanan—had ever used "God" in any inaugural address before Lincoln, both in highly ritualized phrases. What is even more astonishing is that one of these two, Buchanan, was the *only* president before Lincoln who had ever used the word "God" in any State of the Union address. On December 3, 1860, after the secession of South Carolina and the threatened secession of her sister states, Buchanan had declared in his final State of the Union: "As sovereign States, they, and they alone, are responsible before God and the world for the slavery existing among them."[34] Abraham Lincoln would become the first president in history to make "God" a regular part of his major addresses. He would make the word a part of almost *all* of them.

He did not, however, make it a part of his very first. In his first inaugural on March 4, 1861, Lincoln followed the example of the overwhelming majority of his predecessors by avoiding the word "God" altogether. He sounded closest to Washington when he settled instead on "Heaven" and the "Almighty Ruler of nations." In his own first inaugural, Washington had used both "Heaven" and "that Almighty Being who rules over the Universe." Clearly, the imitation of Washington—that sincerest form of flattery—was always appealing to Lincoln. In terms of presidential precedent for Lincoln's choice of the unobtrusive but melodious "under" in the Gettysburg Address, Washington again holds the best claim. In his fourth State of the Union address, in the final year of his first term, President Washington had implored the citizens of America "to strengthen and confirm their attachment to that Constitution of Government upon which, under Divine Providence, materially depend their union, their safety, and their happiness."[35]

Note that "under God" is *not* a traditional or ritual phrase like "Almighty God" or "God of our fathers." One sentence very near the end of Lincoln's first inaugural would prove prophetic of the more personal language he would soon begin to use for the Deity in all of his major speeches and proclamations. This sentence reads: "Intelligence, patriotism, Christianity, and a firm reliance on Him, who has never yet forsaken this favored land, are still competent to adjust, in the best way, all our present difficulty."[36] The very next month after his first inaugural, Lincoln began to use "God" and "our Lord" in his public speeches and proclamations. Once he began, he used them far more than often than any other president before him and, indeed, far more often than any president *since*. On April 22, 1864, Lincoln signed the law that first put the motto "In God We Trust" on U.S. currency. This motto had been devised by Secretary of the Treasury Salmon Chase, an Episcopalian and boyhood student of his father's brother, the Right Reverend Philander Chase, first Episcopal bishop of Ohio and later first bishop of Illinois. Secretary Chase almost certainly took the phrase from the final stanza of "The Star Spangled Banner." We know that Chase had memorized the essence of this stanza because he had quoted it from memory—the slight misquotations prove that he was not copying it—in an eloquent letter of 1841 that had castigated recent mob violence in Cincinnati, Ohio, first against Jews and then against blacks, and had predicted better days ahead for those who love liberty:

> In a little while multitudes will come out of their hiding place and join the advancing host of Liberty. As the prospect of victory brightens voices, as of many waters, will swell the chorus:
> "And conquer we must
> For our cause it is just
> And let this be our motto 'In God is our Trust'!"[37]

All four of Lincoln's State of the Union addresses, as well as his message to Congress in special session on July 4, 1861, invoke the name of "God." All of his many proclamations calling for fasting or thanksgiving invoke "God," and with the single exception noted earlier, every one of the forty-eight proclamations he ever issued, beginning with the Proclamation Calling Militia and Convening Congress on April 19, 1861, closed with the same ritualized formula noted earlier: "Done at the City of Washington, this fifteenth day of April, in the year of our Lord one thousand eight hundred and sixty-one, and of the Independence of the United States the eighty-fifth."[38] It bears repeating that these proclamations, issued one a month on average throughout Lincoln's four years and a few days in the White House, show how inseparably linked in his own mind were the birth of Jesus Christ and the birth of this nation.

The presence of "under God" in the preface to the Book of Common Prayer does not, of course, make it a ritual phrase or even a familiar one. Lincoln would never have expected any significant part of his audience to have read any preface, even one to the Bible or the Prayer Book. But he himself had a compelling motive to read the Prayer Book preface, and, therefore, we should not too quickly dismiss this little two-page essay at the beginning of all the Prayer Books in Lincoln's day as a possible influence on his choice of the phrase. As we have seen before and will see again more fully in later chapters, the "Prayer for the President of the United States and all in civil Authority" formed a vexing problem for Lincoln and his administration from the very start of the Civil War. The reason for this was that Southern Episcopalians and their sympathizers flatly refused to recite this prayer and sometimes added insult to injury by reciting instead a prayer for the president of the *Confederate* States. The preface, which took up but two pages in every single Book of Common Prayer published in America between 1789 and 1863, always followed the title page and the table of contents. It was there to explain how and why the American Prayer Book differed from the Anglican Prayer Book. In the second of nine paragraphs—most consisting of a single sentence like this one—appears the phrase "under God."

> The *Church of England*, to which the Protestant Episcopal Church in these States is indebted, under God, for her first foundation, and a long continuance of nursing care and protection, hath, in the Preface of her Book of Common Prayer, laid it down as a rule, that "The particular forms of divine worship, and the rites and ceremonies appointed to be used therein, being things in their own nature indifferent and alterable, and so acknowledged, it is but reasonable that, upon weighty and important considerations, according to the various exigencies of times and occasions, such changes and alterations should be made therein, as to those who are in places of authority should, from time to time, seem either necessary or expedient."

The change of a prayer for the King of England into a prayer for the president of the United States was the single most important reason for revising the Anglican into the American Prayer Book. As the preface goes on to say, "The attention of the Church was, in the first place, drawn to those alterations in the Liturgy, which became necessary in the prayers for our civil rulers, in consequence of the Revolution."

Lincoln could reasonably have expected that "under God" might recall, at least to a few politically astute listeners, President Washington's "under Divine Providence." He could also have reasonably expected that "under God" might recall to even more listeners that poetical and beautiful "under heaven" that graces the book of Ecclesiastes: "And I gave my heart to seek and search out by wisdom all things that are done under heaven" (1:13). An even more celebrated passage from the third chapter of Ecclesiastes contains essentially the same poetical phrase.

> To every thing there is a season, and a time to every purpose under the heaven:
> A time to be born, and a time to die; a time to plant, and a time to pluck up that which is planted;

. . .

A time to love, and a time to hate; a time of war, and a time of peace. (3:1–2, 8)

The New Testament applies the same lovely phrase "under heaven" to Jesus Christ himself: "for there is none other name under heaven given among men, whereby we must be saved" (Acts 4:12). Even more to the point, there is a famous passage that connects the word "nation" specifically to "under heaven." The passage appears as part of the famous description of Pentecost, which supplied Lincoln with his rousing closing metaphor in the Gettysburg Address. This is the metaphor of the second baptism, the baptism of the Holy Spirit in tongues of fire. Remember that the entire description of Pentecost (Acts 2:1–11) is quoted in the Book of Common Prayer, to be read throughout the season of Pentecost or Whitsuntide. Here is the passage on which we are currently concentrating.

> And they were all filled with the Holy Ghost, and began to speak with other tongues, as the Spirit gave them utterance.
> And there were dwelling at Jerusalem Jews, devout men, out of every nation under heaven. (Acts 2:4–5)

At Pentecost, these men "out of every nation under heaven" were able to hear and understand in their own language "the wonderful works of God" (Acts 2:11). With such a perfect literary antecedent in the Bible and the Prayer Book for "under heaven," why did Lincoln choose "under God" instead?

The answer is that Lincoln's ultimate test for any word or phrase was clarity. The phrase "under heaven" would have been ambiguous and unclear because it has, unavoidably, two different meanings. First, "heaven" can mean the home of God. The Lord's Prayer that Jesus taught to his disciples begins, "Our Father which art in heaven" (Matt. 6:9, Luke 11:2). Second, by an obvious association, it means God himself. "Father, I have sinned against heaven"—against God—says the prodigal son to his earthly father in the parable that Jesus told in Luke 15:21. Had Lincoln written "this nation, under heaven," the meaning of "under God" would have been drowned out by the meaning of "under God's home" or "in this mortal world." To the biblically aware, however, Lincoln could still have recalled with his "nation under God" the "nation under heaven" of Acts 2:5 that gets repeated in the service for Whitsuntide in the Prayer Book.

Is this, then, a case where Lincoln had no specific, clear-cut literary source for "under God" itself? No doubt there are those who would think better of him if it *were*. But again and again we have seen that Lincoln always preferred the borrowed ax to the brand-new. This case is no different. There was indeed a plausible source known and loved by Lincoln, who used the phrase "under God" and used it more than once. That source was George Washington. It was not, however, *President* George Washington, whose only use of the word "God" in any public speech or proclamation appears to have been the "Almighty God" of his October

3, 1789, proclamation making the last Thursday in November a day of national thanksgiving.[39] It was *General* George Washington. The general's most resonant use of "under God" came in his public orders on the very day he first received a copy of the Declaration of Independence! On July 9, 1776, as commander of the Continental Army, he issued this general order: "The several brigades are to be drawn up this evening on their respective parades at six o'clock, when the Declaration of Congress, showing the grounds and reasons of this measure, is to be read with an audible voice. The General hopes this important event will serve as a fresh incentive to every officer, and soldier, to act with Fidelity and Courage, as knowing that now the peace and safety of his Country depends (under God) solely on the success of our arms."[40] One week earlier, on July 2, expecting the Declaration to be approved any day in Philadelphia, Washington had issued similar words to his troops as part of another general order: "The time is now near at hand which must probably determine, whether Americans are to be, Freemen, or Slaves. . . . The fate of unborn millions will now depend, under God, on the Courage and Conduct of this army."[41] It seems not just plausible but probable that Lincoln the voracious reader had somewhere come across Washington's "under God." Interestingly, Parson Weems never quotes any of Washington's uses of "under God" but offers the phrase himself in a rapturous description of the death of Washington: "Sons and daughters of Columbia, gather yourselves together around the bed of your expiring father—around the last bed of him to whom under God you and your children owe many of the best blessings of this life."[42] Professor Barton makes the startling suggestion that Washington may have taken the phrase from Weems instead of the other way around. "It is notable that the expression 'under God' was not unfamiliar to Washington himself, and we can but wonder if he, as well as Lincoln, got it from Parson Weems."[43] Throughout all of his work, Barton careens between solid scholarship and occasional brilliant insights on the one hand and outrageous claims of this sort on the other. While it is at least possible that Lincoln took the phrase from Weems, to suggest that *Washington* took it from Weems, a biographer he never even knew, or from Weems' biography written after Washington's own death is an absurdity.

Lincoln could easily have found Washington's orders containing "under God" when he did his painstaking research for the Cooper Union address. For that speech, said Herndon, "He searched through the dusty volumes of congressional proceedings in the State library, and dug deeply into political history. He was painstaking and thorough in the study of his subject."[44] Or he could have come across the orders and the phrase during his passionate research into military history during his presidential years when he was looking everywhere for a strategy capable of conquering the South—feeling so frustrated that he read every book on military history and strategy that he could lay hands on and even talked of taking over battlefield command of the Union forces himself.

Both Washington and Lincoln had access to an earlier source who had used the very same phrase at another dramatic moment in military history. This was Queen Elizabeth in her famous "Armada Speech" delivered to her troops at Tilbury in 1588, a speech delivered just before the most famous victory in English history—the defeat of the Spanish Armada—the overwhelming victory that would make England a world power for the first time. Lincoln's intense interest in history and his great love for Shakespeare's *Henry VIII* would have provided powerful motives for his reading of the queen's speech.

> Let tyrants fear; I have always behaved myself that, under God, I have placed my chiefest strength and safeguard in the loyal hearts and good will of my subjects. And therefore I am come among you at this time, not as for my recreation or sport, but being resolved, in the midst and heat of the battle, to live or die amongst you all; to lay down, for my God, and for my kingdom, and for my people, my honour and my blood, even in the dust.[45]

Note how many of Elizabeth's phrases are close to Lincoln's—"I am come," "being resolved," "live or die," and especially the tripartite "for my God, and for my kingdom, and for my people" that is essentially repeated at the very end of her great speech in "we shall shortly have a famous victory over the enemies of my God, of my kingdom, and of my people."[46] Assuming that Lincoln intended to echo Queen Elizabeth and General Washington in his "under God," would he have expected anyone in his audience to "hear" his echo? Certainly he could not have expected the kind of immediate and nearly universal recognition of a source that he would have expected for his biblical metaphors and allusions. But he himself would surely have found great satisfaction if indeed he intentionally echoed two of the greatest political and military leaders of all time—leaders as distinguished for their wisdom and prudence as for their courage and character, the very qualities he most valued and aspired to in his own life and career.

The word "government" makes its single appearance in the same closing sentence as "under God" and "increased devotion." And what a perfect place! Isaiah, the prophet echoed by the Gospel of Matthew in the story of the birth of Christ, as he would be echoed centuries later by the great composer Handel in his *Messiah* oratorio, associates the Messiah specifically with both "government" and "increase" in Isaiah 9:6-7: "and the government shall be upon his shoulder: and his name shall be called Wonderful, Counsellor, The mighty God, The everlasting Father, The Prince of Peace. Of the increase of his government and peace there shall be no end." This is the biblical language behind Lincoln's stirring conclusion that we take "increased devotion" to the causes for which the Union dead have died, the highest cause of all being "that government of the people, by the people, for the people, shall not perish from the earth." The word "perish" is specifically associated both with the Messiah and with "nation" in John 11:50: "it is expedient for us, that one man should die for the people, and that the whole nation perish not." From the beginning to the end of the Gettysburg Address, this nation and its free and representative form of government are presented as the messiah who is conceived, born, and dedicated in the opening sentence and rebaptized, rededicated, reborn, and resurrected—perhaps for all time—in the closing. As Lincoln's address begins with an echo of the Messiah born at Christmas, so it closes with an echo of the Easter-like resurrection or rebirth of the Messiah who has died that his believers "should not perish" (John 3:16) and who therefore is no more "dead in vain" (Gal. 2:21) than the honored dead at Gettysburg. Thus from the beginning to the end of his immortal speech, Lincoln uses the metaphor of the Union as the messiah in a beautiful and perfectly consistent way.

The phrase "under God" works perfectly well with Lincoln's underlying metaphor of the United States as the messiah. Christian theology insists that the three Persons of the Trinity—Father, Son, and Holy Ghost—are coeternal and coequal. But there is no doubt that the Bible presents Jesus in the *flesh* and in *this mortal world*—Jesus the Christ, the Messiah, the Son of God—as "under" God the Father. In the most philosophical of the four Gospels, John presents the idea that the Son is coequal with the Father only as a charge made by the enemies of Jesus: "Therefore the Jews sought the more to kill him, because he not only had broken the sabbath, but said also that God was his Father, making himself equal with God" (John 5:18). In the very next verse and throughout the Gospel of John, Jesus is at pains to refute this charge: "Then answered Jesus and said unto them, Verily, verily, I say unto you, The Son can do nothing of himself, but what he seeth the Father do: for what things soever he doeth, these also doeth the Son likewise" (John 5:19). Later in the same chapter, Jesus is even more explicit: "I can of mine own self do nothing: as I hear, I judge: and my judgment is just; because I seek not mine own will, but the will of the Father which hath sent me" (John 5:30). The identical thought is repeated in John 6:38, 7:16, and 8:28. Jesus declares again and again that he is on earth because of the will of God his Father: "I proceeded forth and came from God; neither came I of myself, but he sent me" (John 8:42). "My Father," he says later, "is greater than all" (John 10:29), even though, in the mystery of the Trinity, "I and my Father are one" (John 10:30). The most famous example in the Bible of Jesus deferring to the will of the Father occurs in the Garden of Gethsemane the night before his crucifixion. All four Gospels record his agony on that occasion, and three of them record his famous words: "Father, if thou be willing, remove this cup from me: nevertheless not my will, but thine, be done" (Luke 22:42; see also Matt. 26:39 and Mark 14:36). Lincoln himself recalled those famous words when soon after his election he told a friend, "I have read, upon my knees, the story of Gethsemane, where the Son of God prayed in vain that the cup of bitterness might pass from him. I am in the Garden of Gethsemane now, and my cup of bitterness is full and overflowing."[47]

Saint Paul confirms the idea that the Son of God remains under God the Father until this mortal world has passed away: "And when all things shall be subdued unto him, then shall the Son also himself be subject unto him that put all things under him, that God may be all in all." (1 Cor. 15:28). If Jesus the Son of God serves under the will of God the Father in this world, then even more clearly is the United States—the messiah of freedom and democracy upon this earth—serving "under God." Lincoln always resisted the idea that God favored one side or the other in the Civil War. But he never resisted the idea that God opposed slavery. "If slavery is not wrong," Lincoln wrote to a Kentucky editor on April 4, 1864, "nothing is wrong."[48] Throughout the Gettysburg Address, Lincoln portrays this new nation as the messiah who "under God" is destined to embody and advance two great principles so long as this mortal world shall endure—the principle that "all men are created equal" and the principle that the only proper government for this dedicated nation of equals is "government of the people, by the people, for the people."

Let us turn at last to a word in the Gettysburg Address that has no religious source at all and yet traces as clearly as any other single word to a particular writer and a particular work. It is the most controversial word in the entire address, and it traces to a source far less beautiful in every sense of the word than the King James Bible or the Book of Common Prayer. It is the word "proposition."

Controversial Proposition

Those who fail to appreciate the difference between allusion and plagiarism will wrongly devalue Lincoln for echoing so many words and phrases from the Bible and the Book of Common Prayer. But it bears repeating that great writers have always echoed other writers to enrich their own works. The greatest of all, Shakespeare, changed numerous facts from Plutarch's history so that, by substituting a set of fictions for historical fact, he could connect the events surrounding the death of Julius Caesar with those surrounding the death and passion of Jesus Christ. This is but one instance of a predecessor known to Lincoln who made an extended biblical allusion the enduring pattern in a great work. When great writers echo other great writers and works, they *want* their audience to know what they are doing and indeed *expect* the audience to know. The plagiarist, as noted early on, tries to hide whatever has been taken, while the allusionist proudly and publicly puts a new edge on the borrowed ax. T. S. Eliot uses a different metaphor for the same idea: "Immature poets imitate; mature poets steal; bad poets deface what they take, and good poets make into something better, or at least something different."[1] In literary allusion, one writer transforms a word or a phrase from another writer into something that becomes his or her own. He or she does so by providing a new meaning, a new use, or a new context. Often the final result is something better than whatever was borrowed or stolen in the first place—or at least something provocatively and interestingly different. As we have seen time and again in the case of Lincoln, literary originality consists far more often in refashioning old clothes than in fashioning something entirely new from whole cloth.

Nor does the presence of one fundamental, controlling metaphor mean that other metaphors cannot also be present as well. Lincoln's pattern of Biblical allusion defines his work without monopolizing it. No great work can ever be fully explained or accounted for by any one pattern of metaphor and allusion. Smaller patterns always play around the larger, like children playing at the feet of a parent. In the Gettysburg Address, one of these smaller patterns is built around formal logic. Lincoln loved logic and its showcase, debating, and gained

CONTROVERSIAL PROPOSITION

his first national fame outdebating Stephen A. Douglas in 1858. Regarding Lincoln's habit of reading and studying far into the night after other circuit lawyers had gone to bed, Herndon wrote, "On the circuit in this way he studied Euclid until he could with ease demonstrate all the propositions in the six books."[2] The word "proposition" in Lincoln's opening sentence is clearly a term drawn from mathematical logic—in fact, drawn straight from Euclid. Shakespeare's *Hamlet*, which according to the painter F. B. Carpenter "had at all times a peculiar charm for Mr. Lincoln's mind,"[3] uses the language of debate in "To be or not to be: that is the question"(3.1.56). Other words in the Gettysburg Address that may relate to logic and debate include "engaged," "testing," "proper," "larger sense," "poor power to add or detract," "advanced," "cause," and "resolve." By focusing only on these words, one may see the Gettysburg Address as very much like a syllogism or proof. Lincoln's friend and fellow lawyer from Springfield, James C. Conkling, described his friend's mind in a way that provides a perfect context for this view of the Gettysburg Address: "It seemed as if every proposition submitted to his mind was subjected to the regular process of a syllogism, with its major proposition and its minor proposition and its conclusion. Whatever could not stand the test of sound reasoning he rejected."[4] But any vision of the Gettysburg Address as syllogism, proof, or formal debate is one that no open mind can *exclusively* maintain for very long before reverting to, or at least adding back in, the more powerful and overarching metaphor of birth, death, and rebirth.

Lincoln even manages to connect the two metaphors. He does this in one of the most effective and unusual phrases in the entire address—"highly resolve." In many years of teaching either law or literature, I can recall no other writer who used this phrase before Lincoln. The usual expression is "firmly resolve" or, less often, "fully resolve," never "highly resolve." "Highly" is a warm, airy, emotional, and religious word, whereas "resolve" is cool, liquid, reflective, and secular. The root meaning of "high" is "hill" or "heights." Even those innocent of etymology cannot fail to associate "high" with "mountain" and "sky." The word "resolve," on the other hand, is a liquid word. Think of its sister-word "dissolve" or of Hamlet's "O, that this too too sullied flesh would melt, / Thaw and resolve itself into a dew!" (1.2.129–30). "Resolve" appears in the King James only in the "resolved" of Luke 16:4, which has no relevance for the Gettysburg Address. Any reader is more likely to associate Lincoln's "resolve" with the secular language of mathematics or debate, or with the language of formal declarations issued by deliberative bodies of government. During Lincoln's eight years in the Illinois legislature and two more in Congress, official positions on many issues were expressed through resolutions beginning "Resolved, That." Unlike "resolve," the word "highly" makes dramatic and unforgettable appearances in the King James Bible. The Virgin Mary is "highly favored" (Luke 1:28), and her son Jesus is "highly exalted" (Phil. 2:9). Lincoln may have been inspired to his exotic phrase by his constant reading of

Shakespeare. In *Henry VI, Part 1* appears "a lady of so high resolve" (5.5.75) and in *Titus Andronicus*, "a power / Of high-resolved men" (4.4.63–64). Shakespeare could have intended no connection with the biblical phrases "highly favored" and "highly exalted," however, because they originate in the King James, and both of his plays appeared before it. Lincoln, on the other hand, certainly could have. Now *this* is what makes Lincoln unique as a writer—his use of perfectly simple words in fascinating combinations and unexpectedly original ways. Even when following an inspiration in Shakespeare or some other source, he never hesitates to go beyond his source into new and untraveled territory.

One of the best and clearest explanations of the ultimate thrust and meaning of the Gettysburg Address appears in *Lincoln's Sword*, the recent book by Douglas L. Wilson which makes a whole series of excellent points about the word "proposition." Wilson introduces his points by providing this context, in which he emends "was" from the quoted material to the more likely "has":

> Lincoln had a theory about public opinion. He told a meeting of his fellow Republicans in 1856 that public opinion "always has a '*central idea*,' from which all its minor thoughts radiate. That 'central idea' in our political public opinion, at the beginning was, and until recently has continued to be, 'the equality of men.' And although it [h]as always submitted patiently to whatever of inequality there seemed to be as matter of actual necessity, its constant working has been a steady progress towards the practical equality of all men." What had changed by 1856 was that the defenders of slavery had begun either to deny that this assertion from the Declaration of Independence was meant to apply to blacks, as Stephen A. Douglas would do in his debates with Lincoln, or to disparage it as a "self-evident lie."[5]

Wilson makes clear that Lincoln himself had announced both the theory and the principle on which he worked throughout his career. In effect, it is Lincoln himself who provides the context for understanding his fundamental meaning in the Gettysburg Address. Wilson convincingly demonstrates that the Gettysburg Address was the capstone of Lincoln's determined efforts throughout his career to keep the idea of equality at the very center of the national consciousness. It was this very idea that the president wrote into the opening sentence of an address that he also shaped to fit the circumstances of a special occasion. Lincoln's central idea is the high point of that opening sentence—the idea quoted directly from the Declaration of Independence—the idea "that all men are created equal."

As Wilson also observes, Lincoln introduced this famous idea with a different prefatory phrase from the one Jefferson had used, calling it not a self-evident truth but a "proposition." This word proved to be the most controversial of all Lincoln's choices for a speech that would turn out to be better known and remembered than the Declaration of Independence itself. Wilson undertakes to account for Lincoln's choice of the word:

In many respects, the linchpin of that extraordinary first sentence is surely the word "proposition." To the discriminating eye, it seems at first to be a word out of place, which is why both Seward and Senator Charles Sumner were said to have objected to it. Matthew Arnold is supposed to have refused to read any further. But as Sumner eventually saw, there is no other word for what Lincoln wanted to say. It perfectly conveys the sense in which the most revolutionary of American ideals, however revered, was not a universally accepted principle, but was instead something that needed to be demonstrated. If Lincoln had already formulated this template by the time he heard about the national cemetery being established at Gettysburg, the word that would have helped to make the connection was "dedication." That the "new nation" in his Euclidean version of the founding is *dedicated* to the ideal of equality provides an opportunity to connect it linguistically with a ceremony to dedicate a national cemetery for fallen soldiers. How a talented writer might exploit such a connection is given a definitive illustration in the Gettysburg Address.[6]

This says it well—that "the most revolutionary of American ideals, however revered, was not a universally accepted principle, but was instead something that needed to be demonstrated"—but does not say it all. What it does not give is the *method* or *means* by which this demonstration is to be made. The enemies of the Declaration of Independence always required and indeed demanded that to be "self-evident," an idea such as "all men are created equal" must be *immediately* self-evident. Lincoln conceived the whole issue differently from the way his conservative enemies always chose to present it. Lincoln saw that the proposition he quoted from Jefferson and Jefferson in turn quoted from John Locke is in fact self-evident, just as Jefferson said it was, but that it is *ultimately* self-evident instead of *immediately* so. Futhermore this proposition is self-evident for a specific reason. It can be demonstrated to be self-evident by one specific method.

Before that demonstration, however, we must be sure that we have located the full source of this controversial and fascinating word, remembering that in choosing words Lincoln was always in the habit of putting old wine into new bottles. Was there more to his source than Euclid? Was there a more immediate source as well? The answer is yes, and that source was the South's most outspoken defender, John C. Calhoun. So far as I know, no historian has ever identified Calhoun as a source for this word. My own discovery came from reading books written by Calhoun himself—not books *about* Calhoun and certainly not books about Lincoln. Anyone trying to track down this second source for "proposition" by following the path that most historians follow for determining what Lincoln did or did not read could never have succeeded, for the simple reason that the latest historical effort to list all the books and writers that Lincoln knew omits Calhoun altogether. This is the 2007 list by Robert Bray in the *Journal of the Abraham Lincoln Association*. "This bibliography attempts to list, in alphabetical order by author," Bray announces in his opening sentence, "all the books or parts of books that any serious scholar, biographer, or bibliographer has asserted that Abraham Lincoln read."[7] We may be reasonably confident, then, that no "serious scholar, biographer, or bibliographer" writing before Bray's study in 2007 had ever cited Calhoun as a source for Lincoln's "proposition." And yet, there can be no real doubt among those willing to look *inside* texts that the South Carolina senator was in fact Lincoln's source for this word—or more accurately, *one* of his sources, the other being the great Euclid that Lincoln had already mastered.

In numerous speeches delivered throughout his career, Lincoln referred to Calhoun by name, manifesting a precise knowledge of Calhoun's position on every important issue, above all on the intertwined issues of slavery and the Declaration of Independence. According to Herndon, Lincoln

> was a great admirer of the style of John C. Calhoun. I remember reading to him one of Mr. Calhoun's speeches in reply to Mr. Clay in the Senate, in which Mr. Clay had quoted precedent. Mr. Calhoun replied (I quote from memory) that "to legislate upon precedent is but to make the error of yesterday the law of today." Lincoln thought that was a great truth and grandly uttered.[8]

At the same time, it is impossible to imagine any two men who ever served together in the same Congress—Lincoln in the House, Calhoun in the Senate—with philosophies more diametrically opposed than these two. Whenever Lincoln echoed Calhoun, he was fully conscious that he was using the language of the enemy. After Calhoun's death, Lincoln adopted "John Calhoun" for the name of his archetypal antagonist in an editorial composed for the *Illinois Journal* of September 11, 1854—an anonymous composition but so clearly bearing the marks of Lincoln that it appears in the *Collected Works* as his own. There, in a little parable, Lincoln laid out everything he found wrong with the Kansas-Nebraska Act. On one level, he was almost certainly writing about his friend John Calhoun the Sangamon County surveyor, under whom Lincoln had served as deputy surveyor. According to Herndon, "*Speaking of John Calhoun, the Springfield Democrat who hired him as surveyor but opposed him on the stump, Lincoln said that*: Calhoun gave him more trouble in his debates than Douglas ever did, because he was more captivating in his manner and a more learned man than Douglas."[9] On the other hand, the droll Lincoln would have been the first to recognize the double meaning of the name, which inevitably recalls that Southern ghost of Caesar, John C. Calhoun. Calhoun, who stood for a right-wing view of government, was Caesar-like because he was the symbol and voice of Southern secession even after his death.

John C. Calhoun had died in 1850, but his theories of slavery, nullification, and secession kept appearing year after year in his *Collected Works* during the early 1850s, keeping alive and perhaps even expanding his appeal to those who passionately shared his views. Even in death, Calhoun still raised a powerful voice in favor of the unfettered extension of slavery and the dismemberment of the Missouri Compromise, which Lincoln feared in his newspaper piece was about to be abandoned forever:

> To illustrate the case—Abraham Lincoln has a fine meadow, containing beautiful springs of water, and well fenced, which John Calhoun had agreed with Abraham (originally owning the land in common) should be his, and the agreement had been consummated in the most solemn manner, regarded by both as sacred. John Calhoun, however, in the course of time, had become owner of an extensive herd of cattle—the prairie grass had become dried up and there was no convenient water to be had. John Calhoun then looks with a longing eye on Lincoln's meadow, and goes to it and throws down the fences, and exposes it to the ravages of his starving and famishing cattle. "You rascal," says Lincoln, "what have you done? what did you do this for?" "Oh," replies Calhoun, "everything is right. I have taken down your fence; but nothing more. It is my true intent and meaning not to drive my cattle into your meadow, nor to exclude them therefrom, but to leave them perfectly free to form their own notions of the feed, and to direct their own movements in their own way!"
>
> Now would the man who committed this outrage be deemed both a knave and a fool,—a knave in removing the restrictive fence, which he had solemnly pledged himself to sustain;—and a fool in supposing that there could be one man found in the country to believe that he had not pulled down the fence for the purpose of opening the meadow for his cattle?[10]

The almost comical overlap of the two names provided Lincoln a perfect opportunity to pour cold water, not so much on his old friend the Sangamon County surveyor as on the old firebrand John C. Calhoun of South Carolina, whose words, even after his death, still inflamed a nation.

Lincoln's most memorable contribution to the Thirtieth Congress had occurred in January 1849 when he introduced a House resolution with the aim of ending slavery in the District of Columbia. "Not deigning to mention Lincoln by name," biographer David Herbert Donald points out, "John C. Calhoun, the great Southern spokesman, used this proposal of 'a member from Illinois' as one of the reasons why Southerners must band together to protect their rights; only thus could the North be 'brought to a pause, and to a calculation of consequences.'"[11] Calhoun and his entourage quickly killed Lincoln's resolution by silencing the man who was both the mayor of Washington City and the influential editor of its leading newspaper, *The National Intelligencer*, which enjoyed a national circulation. This man was Colonel William Seaton, who had at first supported Lincoln's bill and rounded up local leaders to join him. "Mr. Seaton's withdrawal from the support of the plan," wrote Lincoln biographer J. G. Holland in 1865, "is said to have been owing to the visits and expostulations of members of Congress from the slave states."[12] Seaton and Senator Calhoun were old friends. Their wives, Sarah Seaton and Floride Calhoun, were even closer. Seaton could not have put up much of a fight. Just as Calhoun's only public reference to Lincoln never even named his enemy, so Lincoln's most famous allusion to the archangel of inequality, nullification, and secession would identify his foe only by a verbal fingerprint in the Gettysburg Address.

Historians have long condescended to Lincoln's one term in Congress. Edward Alfred Pollard wrote in 1866, "Mr. Lincoln had formerly served, without distinction, in Congress."[13] J. G. Randall wrote in 1945 that Lincoln's term in Congress had "little distinction."[14] No historian since seems to have taken serious issue with either view. But it was Calhoun who measured the true significance of efforts like Lincoln's to end slavery. In the last speech he ever made on the floor of the Senate in 1850, when he was so close to death that a colleague, James Mason of Virginia, had to read for him, Calhoun dated the beginning of organized resistance to slavery to petitions in 1835 to abolish slavery in the District of Columbia: "At the meeting of Congress, petitions poured in from the North, calling upon Congress to abolish slavery in the District of Columbia, and to prohibit, what they called, the internal slave trade between the States—announcing at the same time, that their ultimate object was to abolish slavery, not only in the District, but in the States and throughout the Union."[15] Although ineffectual at the time, Calhoun said, "This was the commencement of the agitation, which has ever since continued, and which, as is now acknowledged, has endangered the Union itself."[16] In addition to the swords he crossed with Calhoun over slavery, Lincoln took dead aim at the other great moral issue of the day, the Mexican War. On the floor of the House, he insisted that the war was immoral and unconstitutional and the result of a series of presidential lies. No Congressman opposing any American war at any time in history has ever been braver or more outspoken than Lincoln, whose opposition would later cost the Whigs his seat. Of President James Knox Polk's message justifying the Mexican War, Lincoln ruminated, "How like the half insane mumbling of a fever-dream, is the whole war part of his late message." In the same speech, he accused the president again and again of "the sheerest deception." He condemned President Polk for twisting "every silent vote given for supplies, into an endorsement of the wisdom and justice of his conduct." Lincoln voted for the supplies but in every other way voted against the war. He condemned Polk's message because it "no where intimates *when* the President expects the war to terminate." He referred to the president as "a bewildered, confounded, and miserably perplexed man."[17] To Herndon, who had argued for the expansive war powers of the presidency that unfortunately have remained in vogue to our own day, Lincoln bluntly replied, "The provision of the Constitution giving the war-making power to Congress, was dictated, as I understand it, . . . that *no one man* should hold the power of bringing this oppression upon us.

But your view destroys the whole matter, and places our President where kings have always stood."[18] If only all our members of Congress served their terms with such "little distinction"!

The Calhoun speech that would most influence the Gettysburg Address was the speech on the Oregon bill of June 17, 1848. This famous address was delivered during the Thirtieth Congress at which both Calhoun and Lincoln served. Almost certainly, Lincoln read Calhoun's speech in the Congressional records or the newspapers at the time it was delivered or in pamphlet form soon after. Just after it was made, the Senator wrote to his son James Edward, "My speech will be printed in pamphlet form in a few days when I will send you one. My friends think it the best I ever made, and if I may judge from the number of applications I have received for copies from the North [it] will be in great demand there."[19] Furthermore, Calhoun's collected works began to appear posthumously in 1851. In 1853, the first five volumes of an eventual six were published all together. In his caustic, dry-ice 1848 Oregon bill speech, the senator from South Carolina applied the word "proposition" to the very quotation, "all men are created equal," to which Lincoln would apply it fifteen years later at Gettysburg, when he echoed Calhoun's bitterly sarcastic choice of words for a very different purpose.

"Now, let me say, Senators," Calhoun harangued his colleagues in the Oregon bill speech, "if our Union and system of government are doomed to perish"—here the Senator invoked the biblical word "perish" that would form the last phrase of Lincoln's address—then its doom will trace finally, Calhoun continued, to "a proposition which originated in a hypothetical truism, but which, as now expressed and now understood, is the most false and dangerous of all political errors."[20] Even more than Lincoln in the Gettysburg Address, Calhoun relied on the language of mathematical logic by using words such as "proposition" and "axiom":

> The proposition to which I allude, has become an axiom in the minds of a vast majority on both sides of the Atlantic, and is repeated daily from tongue to tongue, as an established and incontrovertible truth; it is,—that "all men are born free and equal."[21]

Here Calhoun was citing not the Declaration of Independence but its literary and political godfather, John Locke. Locke had written in the second of his *Two Treatises of Government*, "Men being, as has been said, by Nature, all free, equal and independent, no one can be put out of this Estate, and subjected to the Political Power of another, without his own *Consent*."[22] Calhoun rejects what he called Locke's "proposition" out of hand: "Taking the proposition literally (it is in that sense it is understood), there is not a word of truth in it."[23] In his later *Disquisition on Government*, Calhoun would underscore the same point that "great and dangerous errors have their origin in the prevalent opinion that all men are born free and equal;—than which nothing can be more unfounded and false."[24]

To prove there is no truth in this ridiculous "proposition," Calhoun becomes quite literal in his Oregon bill rebuttal, arguing, "Men are not born. Infants are born." Even infants "are not born free"[25] but are subject to both parents and country. As his *Disquisition* later phrased it, "instead of being born free and equal, [they] are born subject, not only to parental authority but to the laws and institutions of the country where born, and under whose protection they draw their first breath."[26] In both these passages, Calhoun was being disingenuous. He knew perfectly well that Locke had taken great pains to show in the *First Treatise* that Adam had no absolute power over his children of the kind presupposed by the monarchist Sir Robert Filmer and that all children grow up into free and equal human beings. In his *Second Treatise*, Locke was even clearer:

> Thus we are *born Free*, as we are born Rational; not that we have actually the Exercise of either: Age that brings one, brings with it the other too. And thus we see how *natural Freedom and Subjection to Parents* may consist together, and are both founded on the same Principle. A *Child* is *Free* by his Father's Title, by his Father's Understanding, which is to govern him, till he hath it of his own.[27]

The disingenuous Calhoun continued in his Oregon bill speech:

> Nor is it less false that they are born "equal." They are not so in any sense in which it can be regarded; and thus, as I have asserted, there is not a word of truth in the whole proposition.[28]

Again Calhoun is being intellectually dishonest, for Locke had also made clear that the equality of men consists not in human abilities but in fundamental rights that Locke had summed up as "Life, Liberty and Estate,"[29] the rights that Jefferson had transformed into "Life, Liberty, and the pursuit of Happiness." Calhoun likewise completely disregards the point Henry Clay had made that the principle of "all men are created equal" remains true *as a principle* even when it cannot be *practically* applied. Lincoln himself would lay out Clay's position very clearly in his final debate with Douglas:

> Mr. Clay says *it is true as an abstract principle* that all men are created equal, but that we cannot practically apply it in all cases. He illustrates this by bringing forward the cases of females, minors and insane persons with whom it cannot be enforced; but he says it is true as an abstract principle in the organization of society as well as in organized society, and it should be kept in mind as a fundamental principle.[30]

This was just before Lincoln quoted Clay's declaration that slavery is "a great evil"[31] in a nation that had not yet figured out a practical way to end it.

There is clear and abundant evidence that Lincoln knew all about Calhoun's contempt for the proposition of "free and equal." In his eulogy for Clay delivered on July 6, 1852, Lincoln specifically called Calhoun the first public figure to repudiate the very idea. In his eulogy for the great Whig leader, Lincoln decried "an increasing number of men, who, for the sake of perpetuating slavery, are beginning to assail and to ridicule the white-man's charter of freedom—the declaration that 'all men are created free and equal.' So far as I have learned, the first American, of any note, to do or attempt this, was the late John C. Calhoun."[32] Calhoun, who had died during the four years between his Oregon bill speech and the time when Lincoln uttered these words, had made his most explicit attack upon Locke's free-and-equal doctrine in the Oregon speech and then repeated it almost verbatim in his posthumously published *Disquisition on Government*.

The point can hardly be overemphasized. Lincoln was saying that the first notable American to assail and ridicule the idea that all men are created equal was none other than John C. Calhoun. And nowhere did Calhoun assail and ridicule the idea more loudly and clearly than in this 1848 speech where he skewered the "free and equal" argument of Locke and the "all men are created" phrase of Jefferson in the Declaration of Independence. In Lincoln's mind, Calhoun was the public figure who had originated the most dangerous and pernicious doctrine in the history of this nation. On October 15, 1858, during the last debate with Douglas, Lincoln again decried Calhoun: "I know that Mr. Calhoun and all the politicians of his school denied the truth of the Declaration"[33]—Lincoln was referring here specifically to the declaration that all men are created equal. In invoking Calhoun, Lincoln was making a point that would remain at the heart of all his major speeches for the rest of his life. Our nation's long-revered declaration that "all men are created equal," said Lincoln, is now under siege from two schools of thought within the Democratic Party—or the Democracy, as it was commonly called in his day.

The first school, headed by Calhoun, bluntly insisted that this "proposition," as Calhoun called it, is not the "self-evident truth" Jefferson believed it to be but instead "a self-evident lie." Lincoln took the latter phrase straight from a man whom he placed in "the school of Calhoun," Representative John Pettit of Indiana.

> I know that Mr. Calhoun and all the politicians of his school denied the truth of the Declaration [that all men are created equal]. I know that it ran along in the mouths of some Southern men for a period of years, ending at last in that shameful though rather forcible declaration of Pettit of Indiana, upon the floor of the United States Senate, that the Declaration of Independence was in that respect a "self-evident lie," rather than a self-evident truth.[34]

The second school, headed by Douglas, has "the sneaking way of pretending to believe it and then asserting it did not include the negro." In the very same final debate with Douglas where all these statements appear, Lincoln called Douglas's position "this new proposition that no human being ever thought of three years ago." According to Lincoln, "I believe the first man who ever said it was Chief

Justice Taney in the Dred Scott case, and the next to him was our friend Stephen A. Douglas."[35] Dismantling Douglas's "new proposition" was the central purpose of Lincoln's Cooper Union address in 1860 that was such a critical step on his way to winning his party's nomination for President of the United States. At Cooper Union, Lincoln would demonstrate conclusively that a majority of the founding fathers not only believed that "all men are created equal" but had never restricted "men" to "white men" and instead, through both words and deeds, had actively opposed the spread of slavery in the United States and had looked forward to the end of that evil institution at the earliest possible time. Dismantling the school of Calhoun's "proposition" of a "self-evident lie" by reaffirming Locke's and Jefferson's original proposition of a "self-evident truth" was the central purpose of his later Gettysburg Address.

There comes a point in his Oregon bill speech where Calhoun applies the word "proposition" precisely to the phrase from the Declaration of Independence that "all men are created equal."

> If we trace it back, we shall find the proposition differently expressed in the Declaration of Independence. That asserts that "all men are created equal."[36]

According to Lincoln, Calhoun's assault on this "proposition" was the first in history from a public figure, but it was certainly not the last. Calhoun was the fountainhead for that dark stream of the denial of equality that would trap and drown the slaveholding South in the backwaters of secession. In its founding documents and the speeches of its major leaders, the Confederacy would explicitly commit to the right-wing, ultraconservative principle of *inequality*.

After becoming, in Lincoln's view, the first American public leader to deny that all men are created equal, Calhoun resorted to the reductive and literalistic in his Oregon bill speech: "All men are not created. According to the Bible, only two—a man and a woman—ever were—and of these one was pronounced subordinate to the other."[37] Calhoun then proclaims that it was totally unnecessary to insert the proposition that all men are created equal into the Declaration of Independence in the first place:

> It was inserted in our Declaration of Independence without any necessity. It made no necessary part of our justification in separating from the parent country, and declaring ourselves independent.[38]

Almost a decade after Calhoun's Oregon speech, in a June 16, 1857, speech on the Dred Scott decision, Lincoln made the same argument that the language of equality in the Declaration of Independence was, in practical terms, quite unnecessary to effect our nation's separation. However, unlike Calhoun, he found what was unnecessary to be at the same time quite useful and, over the long run, highly desirable:

The assertion that "all men are created equal" was of no practical use in effecting our separation from Great Britain; and it was placed in the Declaration of Independence, not for that, but for future use. Its authors meant it to be, thank God, it is now proving itself, a stumbling block to those who in after times might seek to turn a free people back into the hateful paths of despotism.[39]

In his next paragraph, Calhoun uses the word "proposition" for the fifth and final time in just two pages:

> If the proposition be traced still further back, it will be found to have been adopted from certain writers on government who had attained much celebrity in the early settlement of these States, and with those writings all the prominent actors in our revolution were familiar. Among these, Locke and Sidney were prominent.[40]

In this sentence, Calhoun explicitly reveals his own major source for his endlessly repeated choice of the word "proposition"—John Locke. Although Locke never applies "proposition" to any of his declarations of human equality, it is clearly one of his favorite words throughout the conclusionary chapters of his *Essay concerning Human Understanding*. In fact, one of those chapters is entitled "Trifling Propositions."

Calhoun's knowledge of Locke was impressive in its detail, and of long standing. He was only thirteen years old when he began the study of Locke's *Essay concerning Human Understanding* under the tutorship of his brother-in-law Moses Waddel. Then he took up Locke again at Yale, under a professor named Timothy David, who regarded Calhoun as the best student he ever had on this important subject: "No one, he thought, could explicate the language of John Locke with such clarity."[41] Calhoun would go on to become an honor graduate of Yale, graduating with membership in Phi Beta Kappa, at the time a social fraternity but with elements of the academic honorary it would later become. One of the reasons that Locke himself found "proposition" such a useful word was, of course, that it traces straight to Euclid, whom Locke had certainly read, as his own words tell us:

> So GOD might, by Revelation, discover the Truth of any Proposition in *Euclid*; as well as Men, by the natural use of their Faculties, come to make the discovery themselves. In all Things of this Kind, there is little need or use of *Revelation*, GOD having furnished us with natural, and surer means to arrive at the Knowledge of them.[42]

It bears repeating that Locke himself never applied "proposition" to his belief that all men are created free and equal. Nor did he often use the word in a disparaging sense, as Calhoun did in his speech on the Oregon Bill. Instead, Locke almost always used the word to mean a statement already perceived as true, either because it is self-evident on its face or because it derives logically from some other self-evident proposition:

In Propositions then, whose Certainty is built upon the clear Perception of the Agreement, or Disagreement of our *Ideas* attained either by immediate intuition, as in self-evident Propositions, or by evident deductions of Reason, in demonstrations, we need not the assistance of *Revelation*, as necessary to gain our Assent, and introduce them into our Minds.[43]

In the briefest of all his books, *The Reasonableness of Christianity*, written during the same period when he wrote his final version of *An Essay concerning Human Understanding*, Locke used the word only three times but always in the most honorific of ways. Thus, he called the doctrine that Jesus of Nazareth was the Messiah a "great proposition" and an "intelligible proposition," given by God to the common people of the world who can "comprehend plain propositions."[44] Only occasionally did Locke ever use the term to mean a statement whose truth or falsity is undetermined or in dispute. Even in his chapter in *Essay concerning Human Understanding* on "Trifling Propositions," Locke was referring to propositions that are true but are so obvious that he saw little or no reason for repeating them, his favorite example being "What is, is."[45] I can find only one instance when Locke ever uses "proposition" to mean a statement that he believes to be *un*true, which is exactly how Calhoun uses the word when referring to the proposition that all men are created equal. Locke's one highly uncharacteristic use of the word appears in his Preface to the first of his *Two Treatises of Government*. There he says he will reduce the arguments of Sir Robert Filmer, a passionate advocate for the divine right of kings, to "direct, positive, intelligible Propositions" that will immediately prove them to be "glib Nonsense."[46] How ironical and revealing that Calhoun used Locke's "proposition" to ridicule an idea that Locke himself passionately believed in, the idea of universal equality that Locke was in fact championing when he attacked Filmer's divine right of kings!

It is also ironical that Calhoun once had to defend himself on the floor of the United States Senate against the very charge that he was a follower of Filmer. On February 6, 1837, Senator William C. Rives of Virginia differed with Calhoun on Filmer *and* slavery. This is from the report of the committee on which both senators sat:

> Mr. Rives said that he had no desire to get into a family quarrel with Mr. Calhoun on this matter. He, for one, however, did not believe slavery was a good—morally, politically, or economically. And while he would defend the constitutional rights of the South to the end, that commitment would not cause him to return to the explo[d]ed dogmas of Sir Robert Filmer to vindicate the institution of slavery in the abstract.[47]

Calhoun was, as always, lightning-quick to defend himself:

> Mr. C. again adverted to the successful results of the experiment [slavery] thus far, and insisted that the slaveholders of the South had nothing in the case to lament

or to lay to their conscience. He utterly denied that his doctrines had anything to do with the tenets of Sir Robert Filmer, which he abhorred.[48]

Whether Calhoun was a follower of Filmer or merely sounded like one, he was most certainly an enemy to Locke, attacking every one of Locke's major principles. In the *Disquisition on Government*, Calhoun claimed that Locke's theories applied only to man in a state of nature, a purely hypothetical state for Calhoun that was therefore irrelevant for modern man:

> I refer to the assertion, that all men are equal in the state of nature; meaning, by a state of nature, a state of individuality, supposed to have existed prior to the social and political state; and in which men lived apart and independent of each other. If such a state ever did exist, all men would have been, indeed, free and equal in it; that is, free to do as they pleased, and exempt from the authority or control of others—as, by supposition, it existed anterior to society and government. But such a state is purely hypothetical. It never did, nor can exist; as it is inconsistent with the preservation and perpetuation of the race. It is, therefore, a great misnomer to call it *the state of nature*. Instead of being the natural state of man, it is, of all conceivable states, the most opposed to his nature—most repugnant to his feelings, and most incompatible with his wants. His natural state is, the social and political—the one for which his Creator made him, and the only one in which he can preserve and perfect his race.[49]

Again Calhoun intentionally ignores what Locke actually said, for Locke gave clear examples of where the state of nature had continued even into his own day: "'tis not every Compact that puts an end to the State of Nature between Men," which still exists, for example, "between a Swiss and an Indian, in the woods of America."[50] This was a situation actually occurring in the days of Locke, who saw clearly that the Swiss and the Indian do not know each other's laws and in any case have no agreement as to whose law will apply and are therefore in a state of nature where only natural law can apply.

Calhoun closed his Oregon Bill speech with the question that has always provided the clearest distinction between conservatives and liberals: Which is more important and more fundamental—security or liberty? Patrick Henry had declared for all liberals when he proclaimed, "Give me liberty, or give me death!" Henry was supported by Benjamin Franklin, who wrote, "Those, who can give up essential Liberty to obtain a little temporary Safety, deserve neither Liberty nor Safety."[51] Calhoun now declares for all conservatives with his unequivocal statement that "the power necessary for the safety of society is paramount to individual liberty."[52] He repeats the same point in his *Disquisition on Government*: "Liberty, indeed, though among the greatest of blessings, is not so great as that of protection. . . . And hence, when the two come into conflict, liberty must, and ever ought, to yield to protection, as the existence of the race is of greater moment than its improvement."[53] Another man of the same political persuasion as Calhoun, John Wilkes Booth, misspelled his way into a similar statement in December of 1860:

> I tell you that liberty of speech can be abused and should not be tollerated to the abuse thereof. Men have no right to entertain opinions which endanger the safety of the country. Such men I call trators and treason should be stamped to death and not alowed to stalk abroad in any land. So deep is my hatred for such men that I could wish I had them in my grasp And I the power to crush. I'd grind them into dust! . . . Then what are they who preach the Abolition doctrine who have in doing so nigh destroyed our country. I call them trators.[54]

Booth lacked Calhoun's cool head, but his position was far less extreme in the context of his own period than it sounds today. After all, he was writing at a time when in the state of Virginia, it was a crime punishable by imprisonment to advocate the abolition of slavery or even to question the right of a slavemaster to own his slaves.[55]

Safety or security being paramount to individual liberty in the eye of the conservative, it follows to Calhoun and his intellectual kinsmen and heirs that society can afford only a limited amount of liberty. From this almost economic doctrine of scarcity flows the classic conservative conclusion:

> It follows from this that the quantum of power on the part of the government, and of liberty on that of individuals, instead of being equal in all cases, must necessarily be very unequal among different people, according to their different conditions. For just in proportion as people are ignorant, stupid, debased, corrupt, exposed to violence within, and danger from without, the power necessary for government to possess, in order to preserve society against anarchy and destruction, becomes greater and greater, and individual liberty less and less, until the lowest condition is reached,—when absolute and despotic power becomes necessary on the part of the government, and individual liberty extinct. So, on the contrary, just as a people rise in the scale of intelligence, virtue, and patriotism, and the more perfectly they become acquainted with the nature of government, the ends for which it was ordered, and how it ought to be administered, and the less the tendency to violence and disorder within, and danger from abroad,—the power necessary for government becomes less and less, and individual liberty greater and greater. Instead, then, of all men having the same right to liberty and equality, as is claimed by those who hold that they are all born free and equal, liberty is the noble and highest reward bestowed on mental and moral development, combined with favorable circumstances. Instead, then, of liberty and equality being born with man,—instead of all men and all classes and descriptions being equally entitled to them, they are high

prizes to be won, and are in their most perfect state, not only the highest reward that can be bestowed on our race, but the most difficult to be won,—and when won, the most difficult to be preserved.[56]

Calhoun is even more explicit in the *Disquisition on Government*: "it is a great and dangerous error to suppose that all people are equally entitled to liberty. It is a reward to be earned, not a blessing to be gratuitously lavished on all alike;—a reward reserved for the intelligent, the patriotic, the virtuous and deserving;—and not a boon to be bestowed on a people too ignorant, degraded and vicious, to be capable either of appreciating or of enjoying it."[57] Here, stripped of all pretense, is the traditionally conservative or right-wing position that neither freedom nor equality comes to man as a birthright but must be "earned" in obscure and undefined ways. Calhoun's position would later be used to justify the systematic denial to most blacks of the right to vote in the former slaveholding states of the South between the end of Reconstruction and the passage of the Voting Rights Act in 1965.

What would have been greater poetic justice than for Lincoln to have echoed this right-wing prophet in reaffirming on the battlefield at Gettysburg the fundamental principle on which this nation was founded, that all men are created equal? In his cold-bloodedly aristocratical Oregon Bill speech—the most explicit and emphatic of all Calhoun's denunciations of Locke and Jefferson—the South Carolina prophet of nullification and secession had contemptuously dismissed the greatest principle of the Declaration of Independence as a ridiculous "proposition." In adopting Calhoun's word as his own, Lincoln voluntarily embraced the poison of it, transforming it in one magical moment of inspiration into something powerful, evocative, homeopathic, and healing.

Clearly, then, Calhoun applied the word "proposition" to the very idea—the absurd idea to him—that all men are created equal. He was the first political theorist, according to Lincoln, ever to apply "proposition" to Jefferson's "self-evident truth" from the Declaration of Independence. But by no means would he be the last. At least two of Calhoun's admirers used the word in exactly the way he did, no doubt in conscious emulation, in a tribute to the greatest prophet ever of white supremacy and everlasting inequality. The first to use it was a Presbyterian minister from Huntsville, Alabama, named Frederick Ross, author of the 1857 *Slavery Ordained of God* that provoked Lincoln into a rebuttal. It is worth remembering that Presbyterians were outranked only by Episcopalians in representing the slave-owning socially elite of the South. The second to use it was the Episcopal Bishop of Vermont, John Henry Hopkins, author of the 1863 tract called *Bible View of Slavery* that was the subject of that big, splashy, page-one story in John Forney's *Washington Chronicle* on November 7, 1863, less than two weeks before the Gettysburg Address. Bishop Hopkins had many friends among the Southern bishops, none better or closer than Bishop Leonidas Polk of Louisiana, who by the time Hopkins published his tract in 1863 was fighting as a general in the Confederate Army. As recently as the Christmas season of 1860, Hopkins had served as the first architect and campus designer for Bishop Polk's new University of the South, with its announced purpose of providing an education free of the taint of Northern influence for white Southern males. Because all the apologists for slavery read and repeated one another's arguments, it would be no surprise to find later that Hopkins and Ross were not alone as disciples who had read and consciously repeated Calhoun's chosen word, "proposition," as a substitute for Locke and Jefferson's "self-evident truth" that "all men are created equal."

Like Calhoun, whom he echoes at every turn, the Reverend Dr. Ross attacks the idea that all men are created equal, decrying what he saw as "the infidel theory of human government foisted into the Declaration of Independence." Responding to an antislavery clergyman from the North, Dr. Albert Barnes, author of *The Church and Slavery*, Dr. Ross quotes the entire opening paragraph of the Declaration and then attacks its opening assertion: "The *first* and controlling assertion is, 'that ALL MEN ARE CREATED EQUAL;' which proposition, as I understand it, is, that *every man and woman on earth is created with equal attributes of body and mind*." Here Ross directly echoes Calhoun by calling the assertion that all men are created equal a "proposition." Then he mimics the strategy of Calhoun by willfully distorting the meaning of both Jefferson and Jefferson's source, Locke. Neither Jefferson nor Locke ever once asserted that all human beings are created with equal attributes of body and mind. Ross surely knew this. He was a well-read man whose book invokes Socrates, Plato, Euclid, Copernicus, Voltaire, Agassiz, Thomas Paine, and Harriet Beecher Stowe. Yet he never stops repeating the same nonsense. At one point, he even asserts that no other meaning is *possible* for Jefferson's phrase: "All men—man and woman—are created equal,—equal in *attributes of body and mind*; (for *that* is the only sense in which they could be *created* equal;)." Exactly like Calhoun, he cavils at Jefferson's choice of "created" instead of "born," saying, "for '*all* men' have been 'created,' or, more correctly, *born*, (since the race was created only at the first)."[58]

But Ross keeps his heaviest artillery trained on what he has just called the "proposition" that "all men are created equal." He clearly means to call it a "proposition" a second time, because the word "position" below is an obvious misprint for the longer term that he has just introduced and will use yet again in his very next sentence.

> It is not a truth, *self-evident*, that all men are created equal. Webster, in his dictionary, defines "Self-evident—Evident without proof or reason: clear conviction upon a bare presentation to the mind, as that two and three make five."

Now, I affirm, and you, I think, will not contradict me, that the position, *"all men are created equal,"* is *not* self-evident; that the nature of the case makes it impossible to be self-evident. For the created nature of man is not in the class of things of which such self-evident propositions can by possibility be predicated.[59]

In a rebuttal to Ross that Lincoln began but never finished or published, Lincoln answers with a point he was fond of making on other occasions, that those who object to "self-evident truths" merely substitute their own logically unsupported personal assertions, which seem just as self-evident to themselves. Ross, for example, claims to know that slavery is moral because it is God's will, but because scripture is open to different interpretations of God's will on this matter and because God has not directly revealed his will on the matter to Ross, the minister is in truth, says Lincoln, giving the reader nothing more than his own opinion and a highly self-interested opinion at that:

> Certainly there is no contending against the Will of God; but still there is some difficulty in ascertaining, and applying it, to particular cases. For instance we will suppose the Rev. Dr. Ross has a slave named Sambo, and the question is "Is it the Will of God that Sambo shall remain a slave, or be set free?" The Almighty gives no audable answer to the question, and his revelation—the Bible—gives none, or, at most, none but such as admits of a squabble, as to it's meaning. . . . So, at last, it comes to this, that *Dr. Ross* is to decide the question. . . . If he decides . . . that God will's Sambo to be free, he thereby has to walk out of the shade, throw off his gloves, and delve for his own bread. Will Dr. Ross be actuated by that perfect impartiality, which has ever has ever been considered most favorable to correct decisions?
>
> But, slavery is good for some people!!! As a *good* thing, slavery is strikingly peculiar, in this, that it is the only good thing which no man ever seeks the good of, *for himself.*[60]

In Lincoln's response, as in so many of his writings, one can hear a fundamental principle from Locke's *Two Treatises of Government* echoing in the background, "That it is unreasonable for Men to be Judges in their own Cases, that Self-love will make Men partial to themselves and their Friends."[61]

Bishop Hopkins' attack on the Declaration of Independence in his *Bible View of Slavery* is couched in the very same language of John C. Calhoun, whose works published in the 1850s the bishop had obviously been devouring:

> First on this list stand the propositions of the far famed Declaration of Independence, "that all men are created equal; that they are endowed by their Creator with certain unalienable rights; that among these are life, liberty, and the pursuit of happiness." These statements are here called "self-evident truths." But with due respect to the celebrated names which are appended to this document, I have never been able to comprehend that they are "truths" at all.[62]

Hopkins goes on: "It was probably judicious to call their propositions 'self-evident truths' because it seems manifest that no man can prove them."[63] Before his argument ends, he has used the term a third time in exactly the same way:

> I have been, I fear, unreasonably tedious in thus endeavoring to show why I utterly discard these famous propositions of the Declaration of Independence. It is because I am aware of the strong hold which they have gained over the ordinary mind of the nation. They are assumed by thousands upon thousands, as if they were the very doctrines of divine truth. And they are made the basis of the hostile feeling against the slavery of the South, notwithstanding their total want of rationality.[64]

One can clearly see evidence of Calhoun in Hopkins's repeated use of the word "proposition" for the idea that all men are created equal, the very word that Calhoun had first applied to it and the very word that Ross had afterward applied to it in his *Slavery Ordained of God* in 1857.

Thus, at the very time Lincoln was considering what to say at Gettysburg, Forney's *Chronicle* shined its front-page light on a swirling controversy surrounding Hopkins' proslavery, prosecession tract in Forney's home state of Pennsylvania, where the Gettysburg consecration was soon to occur. Although Hopkins' tract had first been published in 1861, its reissue for distribution in Pennsylvania in 1863 was the source of all this controversy. If Lincoln had not already read Hopkins' pamphlet when it first appeared in Secretary of State Seward's home state of New York in 1861, then he surely would have read it when it reappeared in Secretary of the Senate Forney's home state of Pennsylvania during a crucial election in 1863. Forney published attacks on it in both his Philadelphia and Washington papers and no doubt had a copy of the pamphlet available for Lincoln to peruse in Washington. Because of Forney's huge front-page story on Hopkins in the *Chronicle*, Lincoln had a fresh reminder in the very month he wrote and delivered the Gettysburg Address that Calhoun's view of "all men are created equal" as an absurd "proposition" was still spreading its poison.

The enemies of the Declaration of Independence always claimed that a self-evident truth is something like "parallel lines never meet" or, to cite the example that the *Webster's* dictionary of Lincoln's day used in defining "self-evident," that "two and three make five," for these are ideas that are immediately assented to by any person of normal mind without any demand for demonstration or proof. But the only real difference between these statements and most of the propositions of Euclid is that Euclid's typically *do* require some demonstration. Typically this demonstration takes only a logical step or two and a few moments of reflection before a person of normal mind says, "Yes, I see; I agree." Once Euclid's propositions are worked through and understood in this way, the person of normal mind is perfectly willing to drop any further demand for demonstration or proof. The proposition becomes undeniable—to use a term Jefferson originally applied to these truths he would later describe as "self-evident" in his final draft of the Declaration of Independence. Locke himself had recognized this very same distinction between ideas to which the normal mind immediately assents and those arrived at through reasoning and deduction. He called the first category of ideas "intuitive" and the second category "demonstrative." He also referred to intuitive ideas as "self-evident Propositions" and to demonstrative ideas as *Knowledge by intervening Proofs.*"[65] The very fact that Locke joins the word "self-evident" to the word "proposition" illustrates that there can be no absolutely fixed line between the two categories. After all, "proposition" is a term that Locke himself specifically associated with Euclid, most of whose propositions are of the demonstrative and *not* the immediately intuitive kind. Furthermore, an idea or proposition that appears immediately self-evident to one person may, to another, require some degree of proof before it appears self-evident to the second person. Thus, what Jefferson ultimately preferred to regard as an intuitive or self-evident truth—"that all men are created equal"—seemed to others, especially to Jefferson's enemies but even to some of his supporters, to be instead a proposition requiring some proof or at least some pointed reflection. If only to answer the objectors, whether friends or enemies, Lincoln chose to regard Jefferson's "self-evident truth" as a demonstrative proposition like one of those 172 mathematical propositions he had mastered in the six books of Euclid. Reasonable human beings may, after all, have reasonable differences about how to designate or classify an idea even when they fully agree that the idea itself is true.

The thinking of Locke on this critical point is nowhere better stated than in *The Reasonableness of Christianity*, where he reflects upon the origins of morals and rules:

> Whatsoever should thus be universally useful, as a standard to which men should conform their manners, must have as its authority either from reason or revelation. 'Tis not every writer of morals, or compiler of it from others, that can thereby be erected into a law-giver to mankind; and a dictator of rules, which are therefore valid, because they are to be found in his books, under the authority of this or that philosopher. He that any one will pretend to set up in this kind, and have his rules pass for authentic directions, must shew, that either he builds his doctrine upon principles of reason, self-evident in themselves, and that he deduces all the parts of it from thence, by clear and evident demonstration; or, must shew his commission from heaven, that he comes with authority from God, to deliver his will and commands to the world.[66]

Thus, says Locke, reason provides us not only with self-evident principles but with deductions that flow demonstrably from them. Both kinds of truth may be called "self-evident," and both rank in authenticity with doctrines that come directly from God.

One of the difficulties in fully understanding and identifying Lincoln's thought on any subject is that his reading knowledge is so routinely underestimated, even by his supporters. This is true because of the simplistic way that many historians approach the whole problem, by accepting only one kind of evidence. Like old-fashioned law judges who value only "direct" evidence—confessions and eyewitness identifications—while dismissing fingerprints and DNA as "merely circumstantial," many historians accept as evidence of what a public figure has read only that person's own testimony or that of either an eyewitness or a written record that can place the book in his hand. Their approach may be illustrated by the same Robert Bray who omits Calhoun completely from his list of the books and authors that Lincoln read in his lifetime. Bray also dismisses Lincoln's reading of Locke as "Very unlikely."[67] This is because Bray cannot find either Lincoln's own record of reading Locke or an eyewitness who saw him reading Locke or a library card on which he had checked out a work by Locke. Nevertheless, the overwhelming circumstantial evidence proves Bray not only wrong but wrong beyond a reasonable doubt.

Consider first of all the outrageous implausibility that Lincoln, who loved both books and political ideas, never once bothered to read what he *knew* was the intellectual source of his all-time favorite legal document, the Declaration of Independence, the document that always formed the centerpiece of his entire political philosophy. Why would he *not* have read Locke once he read Jefferson? Certainly the issue of difficulty would not provide the answer, because Euclid is a far harder nut to crack than John Locke. Consider as well that Locke has always been remembered chiefly for just two famous books—*Two Treatises* and *Human Understanding*—that were no harder to obtain in Lincoln's day than in our own. Consider above all that there are powerful internal and verbal links between Lincoln and the source in question. Just as any open-minded reader can hear the unmistakable voice of John C. Calhoun in that most controversial word in the Gettysburg Address, "proposition," so any such reader can see unmistakable evidence of John Locke in Lincoln's only reference in a public speech to the Euclid he had so thoroughly mastered. Lincoln's reference occurs at the very end of his fourth debate with Douglas:

> If you have ever studied geometry, you remember that by a course of reasoning, Euclid proves that all the angles in a triangle are equal to two right angles. Euclid has shown you how to work it out. Now, if you undertake to disprove that proposition, and to show that it is erroneous, would you prove it to be false by calling Euclid a liar?[68]

Of all the 172 propositions Lincoln could have chosen from the six books of Euclid he had so thoroughly mastered, why in the world would he have chosen this one? It is by no means the simplest or the clearest. Furthermore, what Lincoln quotes is only one half—the second half at that—of Euclid's Proposition 32 from book 1:

In any triangle, if one of the sides be produced, the exterior angle is equal to the two interior and opposite angles, and the sum of the three interior angles of the triangle are equal to two right angles.[69]

Any reader who has worked his way though the conclusion of Locke's *Essay concerning Human Understanding* will immediately suspect the answer to this question, because there Locke uses the same second half of the very same Euclidean proposition as the standard against which he will measure all other demonstrative ideas that he says are built up, step by step, from intuitive or self-evident knowledge. The use by both Locke and Lincoln of the same half of a single proposition is all the more remarkable because Locke probably knew all thirteen books of Euclid, which contain a total of 464 propositions! About the idea of a Supreme Being, Locke declares, "I can as certainly know this Proposition to be true, as that a Triangle has three Angles equal to two right ones."[70] A few pages further on, he declares in another connection, "Thus the *Idea* of a right-lined Triangle necessarily carries with it an equality of its Angles to two right ones."[71] And after still another jump in pages, he declares, "It being as impossible, that Things wholly void of Knowledge, and operating blindly, and without any Perception, should produce a knowing Being, as it is impossible, that a Triangle should make it self three Angles bigger than two right ones."[72] In a book that is over seven hundred pages long, Locke singles out *no other proposition* from Euclid for this kind of extended application. To my knowledge, Lincoln never singled out any other proposition from Euclid in any public speech except the proposition quoted above, the same one that Locke singles out. Both men single out only the second half of that proposition. That, ladies and gentlemen of the jury, is not a colossal coincidence but a *fingerprint*—Lincoln's, keying in on a Locke he had clearly mastered.

Nor is this the only time that Lincoln refers to the same source. At the first debate with Douglas, Lincoln made another stirring point that seems specifically indebted to Locke, because nothing of the kind appears in Lincoln's usual political sources such as the Declaration of Independence. Defending himself against Douglas's most successful kind of attack, which was to brand Lincoln an "abolitionist" and "Black Republican" who always favored the black man over the white, Lincoln responded:

I hold that . . . there is no reason in the world why the negro is not entitled to all the natural rights enumerated in the Declaration of Independence, the right to life, liberty and the pursuit of happiness. I hold that he is as much entitled to these as the white man. I agree with Judge Douglas he is not my equal in many respects—certainly not in color, perhaps not in moral or intellectual endowment. But in the right to eat the bread, without the leave of anybody else, which his own hand earns, *he is my equal and the equal of Judge Douglas, and the equal of every living man.*[73]

This is an idea that comes very clearly from the *Second Treatise* of Locke:

> Though the Earth, and all inferior Creatures be common to all Men, yet every Man has a *Property* in his own *Person*. This no Body has any Right to but himself. The *Labour* of his Body, and the *Work* of his Hands, we may say, are properly his.[74]

Here is a natural right that is not mentioned in the Declaration of Independence at all and yet is treated as absolutely fundamental by Lincoln, exactly the way Locke treats it. Lincoln clearly and passionately believed in Locke's contention that "*Bread* is worth more than Acorns" because "*labour makes the far greatest part of the value* of things."[75] These are not the only instances where Lincoln betrays a specific knowledge of the godfather of the Declaration of Independence, but perhaps these two may be sufficient to prove the point. Those who would object that Lincoln never mentioned Locke in his speeches or letters should remember that he never mentioned Cowper either in any preserved writing and hardly ever mentioned the name of Euclid. But does anyone seriously doubt that he had read *those* authors?

Note that in his one lonely reference to Euclid during the first debate with Douglas, Lincoln is saying that one tests a proposition not by libeling its author but by *undertaking to prove it false*. Now how does one undertake to prove that something is false? The most obvious way to do so is to assume for a moment that the proposition *is* false—that all angles in a triangle are *not* equal to two right angles. Try to produce such a triangle with angles not equal to right angles, and the effort will forever fail. Of course, it will not take forever because one's mind will very soon experience the "Eureka" moment after two or three failures. This is so obvious to anyone who gives it a thought, and especially to anyone who has mastered Euclid, that Lincoln could easily have grasped it *without* reading Locke. He could easily have perceived, on his own, the difference between an intuitive or immediately self-evident idea on the one hand and a demonstrative idea on the other that requires one or two steps of proof built on simpler, self-evident ideas. Nevertheless, the internal evidence that he *did* read Locke is so strong that it only adds to our understanding of why Lincoln chose the word "proposition." The proposition that both Locke and Lincoln quote about the angles of a triangle is *ultimately* just as self-evident or undeniable as the principles that parallel lines never meet or that two and three makes five. The only difference is that this Euclidean proposition is not, at least to most minds, *immediately* self-evident. It takes more time and thought than the proposition about parallel lines before revealing itself as irrefutable to any open and diligent mind.

In this second and slower way, Jefferson's proposition that all men are created equal also turns out to be self-evident. That is, as soon as one tries to imagine the *opposite* or *negative* of the proposition, one is faced with either an indefensible position or a flat-out contradiction. By definition, parallel lines never met. By definition, two and three are five. These ideas are immediately self-evident. But the proposition about the angles of a triangle is not *immediately* self-evident to most minds. We need to test it or at least think about it, to see it and believe it. And we typically do this by trying to prove it *wrong*. We try to create a triangle with three interior angles that add up to more or less than two right angles. It is when we *fail* that we concede the proposition to be true. And because our reason alone has led us to the solution, we say that this idea is self-evident as well—but not *immediately* so. What has convinced us is that we have failed to create a triangle with angles that do *not* equal two right angles, no matter how long we may have labored in our effort to do so.

Clearly, then, Lincoln recognizes that one tests a Euclidean proposition by *undertaking to disprove it*. In practical terms, Locke and Jefferson arrived at the proposition that all men are created equal in exactly this way. Both men began with the fundamental point that a king has no natural, inborn right to rule others. Jefferson's practical application was that the King of England had no right to rule the colonists of America. To both men, there is neither a natural nor a divine right for a king to rule other human beings. If *no one*—no king, no slavemaster, no head of church or state—has an inherent, self-evident right to rule another person, then, politically speaking, men are indeed created equal and born equal. Jefferson made a positive statement of what may be more clearly conceived as an inference from a negative statement. It is really more a demonstrative than an intuitive statement. If no one is born with the right to permanently rule another, then in fact people are created as political equals, and it follows from this that we all have equal rights to life, liberty, and the pursuit of happiness. As for the practical question of *who* will rule, the equality of all implies the right of all to choose from among themselves, with an equal right to vote and to run as a candidate, and Locke goes on to make these corollaries of the original axiom perfectly clear. As Lincoln kept saying—and Wilson wisely reminds the reader that he never stopped saying this throughout his career and throughout his life—the fact that our nation has yet to achieve equality on the practical level (with every adult, for example, actually having the right to vote) is no proof that we should not dedicate ourselves to achieving actual political equality *as soon as we possibly can.*

Surely this was part of what Lincoln intended to convey by using the word "proposition." He was suggesting that the "proposition" that "all men are created equal" will prove, *upon reflection*, to be just as self-evident as any of the propositions of Euclid. This is exactly how Locke distinguishes between intuitive knowledge, which is self-evident, and demonstrative knowledge, which comes from proofs built step by step upon self-evident propositions. Thus we use the intuitive kind of knowledge in order to gain the demonstrative. "Certainty depends so wholly on this Intuition, that in the next degree of *Knowledge*, which I call *Demonstrative*," said Locke, "this intuition is necessary in all the Connexions of the intermediate *Ideas*, without which we cannot attain Knowledge and Certainty."[76] Here "connections" is simply another word for "proofs." "The next degree of Knowledge," Locke continues, "is, where the Mind perceives the Agreement or Disagreement of any *Ideas*, but not immediately."[77] In short, intuitive knowledge comes in the twinkling of an eye, whereas demonstrative knowledge comes more slowly because it comes in steps or proofs until the mind arrives at its "Eureka" moment. Again, the simplest step from intuitive to demonstrative knowledge is what happens when we test a proposition by assuming its opposite or negative to be true. If the opposite or negative turns out to be self-evidently false, then the original proposition is rightly considered true.

This is how exactly how Locke proceeded when he undertook to demonstrate, in his *Two Treatises of Government*, that all men are created politically equal, with equal rights at birth. Instead of beginning the *First Treatise* with a positive *assertion* of the principle of universal equality, Locke undertook a long, highly detailed *rejection* of Filmer's theory that kings are born with "a Divine Right to absolute Power" and that other men are "all born Slaves, and by Divine Right, are Subjects."[78] Locke's entire first treatise is not a positive proof but a *disproof*. And this makes perfectly good sense, because if kings claim a natural, inborn right to make others their subjects, then the burden of proof is on *them* and their advocates. Locke convincingly demonstrates that the advocates of divine right cannot meet their burden of proof, either through logic or through scripture. It is important to understand that a great deal of Locke's argument in the *First Treatise* consists of biblical explication. His demonstration or disproof in the *First Treatise* makes his *Second Treatise* infinitely easier, because if no one has a natural right from birth to rule over another, then it follows that all are indeed born politically equal.

I am well aware that Peter Laslett in his Cambridge edition of Locke's *Two Treatises of Government* contends that Locke wrote, or largely wrote, the *Second Treatise* before the *First*.[79] Even if Laslett's claim proves true, however, it will not change the fact that Locke chose which treatise he would call *First* and which he would call *Second*. It will not change Locke's obvious intention that all readers should read the *First Treatise* first and the *Second Treatise* second. Today the *First Treatise of Government* is almost never taught in our schools. Most university reading lists that include Locke cite only his *Second Treatise*. Even in most bookstores, academic or otherwise, one finds only the *Second* for sale. It is hard to resist the conclusion that here is yet another sign of the times, another implicit admission of biblical ignorance, another manifest reluctance to give equal status to a work so unabashedly built on biblical analysis. But the price of our prejudice is to make the "proposition that all men are created equal" more vulnerable to the attacks of the political and intellectual heirs of John C. Calhoun.

Calhoun himself recognized that great political issues, like law cases, often turn on the question of which side bears the burden of proof. As a young warhorse whooping it up in the House of Representatives in late 1811 for America to go to war with England, Calhoun turned to face a challenge from John Randolph, a "gentleman from Virginia":

> He said he found himself reduced to the necessity of supporting the negative side
> of the question, before the affirmative was established. Let me tell the gentleman,
> that there is no hardship in his case. It is not every affirmative that ought to proved.
> Were I to affirm, that the House is now in session, would it be reasonable to ask
> for proof? He who would deny its truth, on him would be the proof of so extraor-
> dinary a negative. How then could the gentleman, after his admission, with the
> facts before him and the country, complain? The causes are such as to warrant, or
> rather make it indispensable, in any nation not absolutely dependent, to defend
> its rights by force. Let him, then, show the reasons why we ought not so to defend
> ourselves. On him lies the burden of proof.[80]

Calhoun later acknowledged in his *Discourse on Government*, "Now it is a clear and well established principle, that the party who claims the right to exercise a power, is bound to make it good, against the party denying the right."[81] Exactly so! By Calhoun's own reasoning, this must put the burden of proof squarely on the king or slaveholder who claims to have been created with a right to rule others throughout their lives and *not* on the objector such as Locke, Jefferson, or Lincoln who *denies* that right and maintains that in terms of who is to rule whom, we are all born equal!

It is not just the order of the *Two Treatises* that supports Locke's argument in favor of no inborn right to rule. In both of his treatises, Locke connects the natural freedom and equality of man specifically with freedom from the claims of authority or superiority from other persons. Thus he rejects "a Divine Natural Right"[82] of one person to rule another and instead declares, "The *Natural Liberty* of Man is to be free from any Superior Power on Earth, and not to be under the Will or Legislative Authority of Man, but to have only the Law of Nature for his Rule."[83] He then goes on to show that man's natural liberty yields to majority rule when individuals leave the state of nature and unite in communities: "Whosoever therefore out of a state of Nature unite into a *Community*, must be understood to give up all the power, necessary to the ends for which they unite into Society, to the *majority* of the Community."[84] Locke bases the surrendering of this power upon the idea of the consent of the governed: "*Every Man* being, as has been shewed, *naturally free*, and nothing being able to put him into subjection to any Earthly Power, but only his own Consent; it is to be considered, what shall be understood to be a *sufficient Declaration of* a Mans Consent, *to make him subject* to the Laws of any Government."[85] One of the most moving passages in the first real biography of Lincoln, Holland's in 1865, is this account of an 1854 speech in which Lincoln brilliantly attacked Stephen A. Douglas for supporting the Kansas-Nebraska bill. Holland reports the account of one newspaper: "At the conclusion of the speech, every man felt that it was unanswerable—that no human power could overthrow it or trample it under foot. The long and repeated applause evinced the feelings of the crowd, and gave token of the universal assent to Lincoln's whole argument." Holland relates the highlight of Lincoln's argument: "My distinguished friend [Douglas] says it is an insult to the emigrants of Kansas and Nebraska to suppose they are not able to govern themselves. We must not slur over an argument of this kind because it happens to tickle the ear. It must be met and answered. I admit that the emigrant to Kansas and Nebraska is competent to govern himself, but (the speaker rising to his full height,) *I deny his right to govern any other person without that person's consent.*[86] Once again, Lincoln is echoing Locke directly. In short, from the beginning to the end of his career, Lincoln preached the principles and propositions of John Locke while resisting those of the anti-Lockean John C. Calhoun, often citing the words of both men.

Jefferson Davis, a colleague and disciple of Calhoun's in the Senate who differed from his leader only in the way they viewed "all men are created equal"—Calhoun denying it out of hand while the future President of the Confederacy joined Stephen A. Douglas in limiting its application to free white males—provides the best possible evidence that Lincoln was far from alone in seeing the political equality described in the Declaration of Independence as a direct consequence of John Locke's rejection of the theory of any divine or inborn rights of kings and nobles. In his farewell speech to the United States Senate on January 21, 1861, Davis explained his home state of Mississippi's secession from the Union by laying out his own interpretation of the Declaration of Independence that perfectly squares with Lincoln's position *on this one crucial point*:

> It has been a conviction of pressing necessity, it has been a belief that we are to be deprived in the Union of the rights which our fathers bequeathed to us, which has brought Mississippi into her present decision. She has heard proclaimed the theory that all men are created free and equal, and this made the basis of an attack upon her social institutions; and the sacred Declaration of Independence has been invoked to maintain the position of the equality of the races. That Declaration of Independence is to be construed by the circumstances and purposes for which it was made. The communities were declaring their independence; the people of those communities were asserting that no man was born—to use the language of Mr. Jefferson—booted and spurred to ride over the rest of mankind; that men were created equal—meaning the men of the political community; that there was no divine right to rule; that no man inherited the right to govern; that there were no classes by which power and place descended to families; but that all stations

were equally within the grasp of each member of the body-politic. These were the great principles they announced; these were the purposes for which they made their declaration; these were the ends to which their enunciation was directed. They have no reference to the slave; else, how happened it that among the items of arraignment against George III was that he endeavored to do just what the North has been endeavoring of late to do—to stir up insurrection among our slaves? Had the Declaration announced that the negroes were free and equal, how was the Prince to be arraigned for stirring up insurrection among them? And how was this to be enumerated among the high crimes which caused the colonies to sever their connection with the mother country? When our Constitution was formed, the same idea was rendered more palpable, for there we find provision made for that very class of persons as property; they were not put upon the footing of equality with white men—not even upon that of paupers and convicts; but, so far as representation was concerned, were discriminated against as a lower caste, only to be represented in the numerical proportion of three fifths.[87]

In this remarkable speech, Davis specifically connects the idea that "all men are created free and equal" with "no divine right to rule" and "no . . . inherited right to govern." At the same time, his speech overflows with contradictions, blithely assuming the inborn right of one human being to rule another in that most extreme dictatorship of all, which is human slavery.

In our own day, the proposition that all men are created equal is by no means fully accepted. It is most unlikely that a majority of the American people would now vote to put that idea again into any of our public laws or declarations. One has only to recall the recent fate of the Equal Rights Amendment, which was killed because conservatives claimed it was "unnecessary" to protect the rights of women—as unnecessary as Calhoun said "all men are created equal" was to the Declaration of Independence—and might be used instead to protect some other unfortunate group who were *in fact* being treated unequally before the law! But at least, thanks to Lincoln, it is no longer as fashionable as it was before his immortal Gettysburg Address for public figures to ridicule the whole idea of universal equality. Calhoun publicly reviled the idea that all men are created equal, but governors Ross Barnett and George Wallace did not, even though Wallace named the largest community college in Alabama, which serves my own district of the state, the John C. Calhoun Community College. Both these deep-Southern governors chose silence in the face of a "proposition" that so many schoolchildren, including perhaps themselves and their own children, had learned by heart at an early age.

The Jefferson-Lincoln proposition has prevailed where it counts the most and does the most good over the longest time—in the extension of the right to vote as our nation moves steadily toward the ideal goal of universal suffrage. Both liberals and conservatives recognize the fundamental importance of the right to vote, for this right is what ultimately determines which of the two will prevail in political contests. In his *Disquisition on Government*, Calhoun said, "I call the right of suffrage the indispensable and primary principle."[88] It goes without saying that he favored severe restrictions upon that right. Those who follow the thinking of Calhoun have always favored such restrictions, requiring property, poll taxes, education, and any other barriers they could throw up that did not block their own kind from voting. They have also voted to limit immigration—and thus future voters—to foreigners of their own racial, ethnic, religious, or economic class. What may well be the three most important legislative acts in America in the twentieth century—certainly the most enduring in their influence—were the Nineteenth Amendment guaranteeing the vote to women in 1920, the Civil Rights Act of 1965 guaranteeing the vote to blacks (which was opposed by the heirs of Calhoun's conservatism), and the Twenty-sixth Amendment in 1971 guaranteeing the vote to the age group that has shed more blood and given more lives fighting for this nation and her principles than any other. Someday, because of this ever-expanding suffrage, it may even be possible to affirm once again, in a document of law, the proposition that all men—all human beings—are created equal.

Kings who could not persuade those whom they wished to rule—or continue to rule—that monarchs enjoyed a natural or self-evident right to rule other men would invariably invoke a right from God or scripture. But the translated Bible had already persuaded most Englishmen and American colonists of the utter unsoundness of this doctrine, which is why the Bible-reading Presbyterians took the head off the Stuart monarchy with the sword of scripture before they took it off with the sword of steel. This is precisely the dilemma that defenders of slavery faced. They could and did ridicule the notion that all men are created equal by citing examples that Jefferson and the signers of the Declaration of Independence never intended in the first place—that some men are born bigger, smarter, wealthier, or whatever than other men. As Lincoln clearly saw, this was nothing but intentional reductionism designed to obscure the real issue. Unable to offer proof positive for their own position, namely, that slave-owners enjoy some natural or inherent right to rule other human beings, these owners were forced into asserting something very like the divine right of kings. For instance, they typically argued that the slave-owner has a right to own African slaves because Africans are the direct descendants of Noah's son Ham, who had been cursed by God in the Bible and forced to serve his brothers. This is exactly what the Southern Presbyterian minister Dr. Ross argued in his *Slavery Ordained of God*:

> When Ham, in his antediluvian recklessness, laughed at his father, God took occasion to give to the world the rule of the superior over the inferior. *He cursed him.*[89]

But as Lincoln pointed out in one of his writings, such arguments about scripture all come down to a "squabble."[90] Locke as a constitutional monarchist and the founding fathers as antimonarchists had found arguments from the Bible that directly challenged and undermined the divine right of kings. In the same manner, opponents of slavery who read the Bible closely saw that Ham was cursed not by God but by his drunken and dissolute father, Noah. (In our own day, Billy Graham pointed this out as part of his own efforts to end racial segregation.) This is one of the points that Theodore Parker made in his 1848 "Letter to a Southern Slaveholder." After demonstrating that the children of Canaan were not in fact negroes, Parker continued:

> But even if the negroes were the children of Canaan, as it is plain they are not, what title could you make out to hold them by? It would be this:—4000 years ago Noah cursed Canaan and, therefore, you hold one of Canaan's children as a slave. Now, do you think a *man* has the power to curse so far as that? But you will say, God gave the curse; well the Bible does not say so.[91]

Parker found a whole set of problems with this biblical argument for slavery:

> Before you can hold a single negro under that clause in Genesis ix:25, you must make out—1. That the negro is descended from Canaan; 2. That the curse was actually uttered as related; 3. That it announces personal slavery for more than 4000 years; 4. That the curse was authorized by God Himself. Now, there is not one of these four propositions which ever has been made out or ever can be.[92]

This was written the very same year that John C. Calhoun delivered his speech on the Oregon Bill, which had attacked the "proposition" that "all men are created equal"! It is fascinating to see that the arguments in Lincoln's day over slavery versus equality turned just as much on the interpretation of scripture as on the interpretation of the Declaration of Independence or the Constitution and that the two kinds of interpretation were conjoined and intertwined by everyone on every side of every issue.

In summary, then, neither unaided human reason nor any undisputed interpretation of the Bible ever supported any "inherent" or "undeniable" or "self-evident" right by one person to rule another. Jefferson's proposition having proved to be self-evident for essentially the same reason that the earlier mathematical propositions are self-evident—that to assume the opposite is to be inevitably involved in contradictory or indefensible positions—then, to use a modern metaphor, equality is the default position. Created equal, we all have equal rights to life, liberty, and the pursuit of happiness just by being born. That is why such rights are inalienable, because they are not given by some other human being or some group of human beings and therefore cannot be taken away by someone else. Lincoln's Euclidean "proposition" may thus be seen as a more cautious and studied version of Jefferson's "self-evident truth" and consequently less open to simplification and immediate dismissal. At the same time, and with equal justice, it may be seen as the quietly perfect answer to the doctrine of inherent inequality preached by John C. Calhoun and all of his political and spiritual allies and eternal heirs.

The Essence of Lincoln's Style

Now that all the key words in all the ten sentences of the Gettysburg Address have been examined, what may be said, in summary, about Lincoln's style in that great work? First, it is a style that values clarity above everything else. Not one word that Lincoln used in the Gettysburg Address would have given a moment's pause to his audience, either the live audience to whom he spoke or the much larger reading audience that soon followed. The one word in the entire speech that was becoming archaic in spoken and written English, as opposed to what was being *read*, was "score." Yet virtually everyone in Lincoln's day had a reading knowledge of the word because the King James Bible was so well and so widely known. The second outstanding feature of Lincoln's style is that it has a rhythm and musicality far more characteristic of poetry than of prose. It falls beautifully upon the ear. The third is that it joins words in unexpected ways such as "fathers brought forth" or "larger sense" or "highly resolve." Because of this, many phrases that at first sound perfectly simple and straightforward turn out to have hidden surprises and unexpected depths. Fourth, it is saturated in allusion, lovingly echoing the words and works of earlier writers, typically with great precision. Most of Lincoln's allusions are to works highly familiar in his own day, such as the King James Bible and the plays of Shakespeare. His allusions to the less-known Book of Common Prayer often implicated the Bible as well, since the Bible was the Prayer Book's own major source. His allusions to Shakespeare's plays came at a time when they and the King James Bible were easily the most beloved and familiar literary sources in the English language. Even the president's echoes of other works and writers he could hardly have expected most of his living audience to recognize, such as his "under God" that seems to flow from high-water moments in the careers of Queen Elizabeth and General Washington, enrich our *later* appreciation of a work that is so rich and resonant we may never bring up all its treasures from the ocean floor. Lincoln was never just a politician writing speeches. He was also a wise man and a very great writer, writing not only for his own age but for all to come. F. Scott Fitzgerald once said, "The wise writer, I think, writes for . . . his own generation, the critic of the next and the schoolmasters of ever afterward."[1] Fifth and finally, Lincoln's style is highly metaphorical. His central and sustained metaphor is the birth, death, and rebirth of the United States in terms of the birth, death, and rebirth of the Messiah as recorded in the familiar and inspired words of the King James Bible. Other metaphors come and go throughout the speech like the featured instruments of an orchestra, often reinforcing the central metaphor but never, in any case, drowning it out.

An easy way to measure the metaphorical character of Lincoln's style is to compare it with Jefferson's, the political fountain from which Lincoln drank so often and so deeply. For all their fundamental agreements about political questions, Jefferson and Lincoln are profoundly different as writers. Both men relied heavily on literary allusion. Everyone knows that Jefferson echoed the words of John Locke in the Declaration of Independence. But Jefferson's allusions are far more programmatic and far less subtle than Lincoln's. Both men write with admirable clarity. But it is hard for someone who has just read any work by Jefferson to walk away with anything more than mere *ideas* in mind. Except for eloquent rephrasings of Locke in phrases such as "all men are created equal," Jefferson's actual words typically have no staying power. On the other hand, most readers are drawn to remember the actual words of Lincoln instead of merely "translating" them into their own, but it is very hard to do this when reading Jefferson. The best that most readers can do with Jefferson is to remember his meaning—or the gist of it. He uses words like numbers or counters, denotatively and logically, with virtually no pictures or metaphors of any kind. One thinks of a mathematics teacher writing a formula on the board with one hand while erasing it with the other. Most of Jefferson's words seem to vanish almost as soon as they are read. Even when remembered, they rarely form a clear and lingering picture in the mind.

Take for example his "course of human events" in the Declaration of Independence. Is this a river course? Is it a roadway? Or is it neither, since the abstract idea is all that seems to matter to the author? It is the very abstractness of Jefferson's prose that makes it sound so much like a geometric proof or a syllogism worked out in a study or a lab. We have seen that whenever he refers to any idea from religion or the Bible, Jefferson uses the most neutral and antiseptic words available, words such as "nature's God," "Creator," "Providence," and "Being," to cite only the Declaration of Independence. Jefferson's occasional use of metaphor is memorable precisely because it is so rare, as when he writes of slavery, "But as it is, we have the wolf by the ears, and we can neither hold him, nor safely let him go."[2] (Lincoln liked this so well he often repeated it.) But no sooner does Jefferson give us this rare and arresting metaphor than he undercuts its power by switching to explanation: "Justice is in one scale, and self-preservation in the other." The trouble is, with our hands already holding a wolf by the ears, how can we add a scale? Or did Jefferson even think of "scale" as a metaphor? With Lincoln, we never have to ask such questions. He always works in the open air with familiar, pictorial, earthy, biblical, and allusive words that fly like sparks in many fascinating directions but always coalesce in the end into one flame, one star, one overarching metaphor shining above all the rest. This is why far more people today are able to recognize the Gettysburg Address than the Declaration of Independence, and why Lincoln far more than Jefferson has made "all men are created equal" an enduring touchstone of American political faith.

One way to measure Lincoln's use of literary allusion is to look at a little speech that he gave on July 7, 1863. This little speech came just after the great victories at Vicksburg and Gettysburg. It was delivered from the White House to a group of serenaders who had gathered on the street outside. In *The Eloquent President*, Ronald C. White Jr. calls this speech an "impromptu response."[3] But was it? To answer this, consider that whenever President Lincoln gave a truly impromptu speech, essentially all he ever said was that he had nothing to say. Before demonstrating this, it is important to distinguish between Lincoln's speeches delivered *before* he was president and those delivered *after*. As a lawyer in Illinois, Lincoln had often delivered impressive closing speeches without a text. By universal agreement among those who heard it, he had delivered one of the greatest speeches of his life without text or notes at the Illinois State Republican Convention on May 29, 1856. He had delivered one of the most beautiful speeches of his life in his spontaneous, nonpolitical farewell address to friends in Springfield as he was departing for Washington. But as president he was rightfully fearful that one unguarded remark had the power to create havoc in a deeply divided nation. Therefore he tried very hard to say nothing of substance when called upon to speak spontaneously as president. A perfect example of such spontaneity is another little speech he delivered almost exactly one year before this speech to the serenaders. The earlier, undeniably impromptu speech was given on the Fourth of July 1862 to a group of men led by William Seaton, friend of John C. Calhoun, publisher of the *National Intelligencer*, and president of the Association of the Surviving Soldiers of the War of 1812. Here is how the speech was reported in the *New York Tribune* on July 7, 1862, and later reprinted in Lincoln's *Collected Works*:

MR. PRESIDENT AND GENTLEMEN: I am indeed very grateful for this courtesy which you have thought fit to extend me (for the time being), the head of the Government. I am exceedingly sorry that the continual and intense engrossment of my attention by other matters has not permitted me to devote a moment's thought to the manner in which I should receive you. I have no pretty speech, or any other sort of speech, prepared, with which to entertain you for a single moment. I am indeed surrounded, as is the whole country, by very trying circumstances. I am grateful to you for the approbation which you give me of what I have done, and grateful for the support which the whole country seems to give me. I hope that, although far advanced in life as many of you are, you will, gentlemen, yet live to see better days than those which it is now our misfortune to behold. Thanking you for the support which you in this manner give me, unprepared as I am, I could not with any degree of entertainment detain you longer.[4]

Here are seven sentences that say almost nothing except that Lincoln has nothing to say. The speaker's lack of preparation is clear from the fact that all seven sentences use "I" for their subject, six of them opening with this personal pronoun. This speech is very much like the one Lincoln delivered the night before the Gettysburg Address, which also offers virtually nothing except an apology for the president's having nothing to say. It also contains seven sentences, each using "I" for its subject. In short, we see in these two speeches a model for a truly impromptu speech by Lincoln. It is always brief, apologetic, self-consciously loaded with the first-person-singular pronoun, and lacking in substance.

The speech given to serenaders on July 7, 1863, is very different, even though it starts out like an impromptu speech, with the three opening sentences sounding highly self-conscious:

Fellow-Citizens: I am very glad indeed to see you to-night. But yet I will not say I thank you for this call. But I do most sincerely thank Almighty God for the occasion on which you call.

Note, however, that the third of these sentences suggests that Lincoln might have given some prior thought to what he would say, for it displays some of the same iambic rhythm that the sentences of the Gettysburg Address would later exhibit. The fourth through the tenth sentences of the speech delivered to the serenaders sound even more planned and premeditated. They strongly support a claim made by Martin P. Johnson in an excellent Fall 2004 article of the *Lincoln Herald*—that this speech is not only longer than the truly impromptu speeches Lincoln delivered after other serenades but far more "coherent" and "highly structured."

Lincoln's predicament may have been somewhat easier in this instance, because sometime in the early evening he had received word of the coming serenade, and he had returned to the White House from the Soldier's Home, a few miles away, specially for the occasion. Lincoln was at the War Department when the first revelers arrived, but hurried to the White House to receive his jovial guests. Despite his tardiness, it is likely that he had some time to compose his thoughts before speaking, perhaps while traveling back to town from the Soldier's Home, because on this night Lincoln gave the longest extemporaneous speech to a serenading party of his presidency, well over twice as long as the average of his fourteen other serenade speeches for which there was no written draft.[5]

One might add to Johnson's point that this serenaders' speech was given only three days after the Fourth of July, for which Lincoln may very well have planned a speech never delivered because both he and the nation were caught up throughout that momentous weekend—the Fourth fell on a Saturday in 1863—in the tidal wave of news from the battles of Vicksburg and Gettysburg. Thus we may look into this speech as a kind of halfway house between a truly impromptu speech and a fully prepared one. Such a look will demonstrate just how powerful Lincoln's attraction to literary allusion really was.

Let us look particularly at those fourth through tenth sentences that bear evidence of advance composition. Although not as finished and polished as the sentences in most of Lincoln's prepared speeches, neither are they as simple and self-conscious as those in Lincoln's typical impromptu speech. The sentences below are quoted from the *Washington Daily Chronicle* instead of the *New York Tribune*, which is the basis for the text in Lincoln's *Collected Works*. Johnson makes a convincing case that the account in Forney's *Chronicle* is fuller and more reliable. Note that in these seven sentences, the personal pronoun "I" appears a mere three times, and two of these appearances are in a digressive "I have mentioned" and a parenthetical "I believe."

How long ago is it? Eighty-odd years, since upon the Fourth day of July, for the first time in the world, a union body of representatives was assembled to declare as a self-evident truth that all men were created equal. [Cheers.]

That was the birthday of the United States of America. Since then the fourth day of July has had several peculiar recognitions. The two most distinguished men who framed and supported that paper, including the particular declaration I have mentioned, Thomas Jefferson and John Adams—the one having framed it, and the other sustained it the most ably in debate, the only two of the fifty-five or fifty-six who signed it, I believe, who were ever President of the United States, precisely fifty years after they put their hands to that paper it pleased the Almighty God to take away from this stage of action on the Fourth of July. This extraordinary coincidence we can understand to be a dispensation of the Almighty Ruler of Events.

Another of our Presidents, five years afterwards, was called from this stage of existence on the same day of the month, and now on this Fourth of July just past, when a gigantic rebellion has risen in the land, precisely at the bottom of which is an effort to overthrow the principle that all men were created equal, we have a surrender of one of their most powerful positions and powerful armies forced upon them on that very day. [Cheers.] And I see in a succession of battles in Pennsylvania, which continued three days, so rapidly following each other as to be justly called one great battle, fought on the first, second, and third of July; and on the *fourth* the enemies of the declaration that all men are created equal had to turn tail and run. [Cheers.][6]

The usual assumption by historians is that Lincoln, speaking off the cuff, used "eighty-odd years" simply because he could not remember how many years had elapsed since July 4, 1776. Professor Barton may have been the first to make this assumption in his 1925 *Life of Lincoln*: "It will be noted that he recurred to this same thought in the following November when he delivered the address at Gettysburg, but that in the meantime he had looked up the exact number of years between 1776 and 1863, and found it 'four score and seven years.'"[7] This is so overwhelmingly improbable that even a little reflection will render it absurd. Would a man with a photographic memory, a man who loved the Declaration of Independence so much that he used it as a dating system for his endlessly issued proclamations, suddenly forget the date of this document that he himself declared was the source for all his political thoughts and feelings?

In his First Inaugural Address, Lincoln had recalled the exact number of years since the first inaugural of the first president: "It is seventy-two years since the first inauguration of a President under our national Constitution."[8] The very next month, on April 15, 1861, he had issued his first presidential proclamation, the Proclamation Calling Militia and Convening Congress. At the end of it, Lincoln first adopted the dating system that would become a routine, ritualized closing for all his proclamations: "Done at the city of Washington this fifteenth day of April in the year of our Lord One thousand, Eight hundred and Sixty-one, and of the Independence of the United States the Eighty-fifth."[9] Lincoln understood perfectly well that a child lives its first year of life *before* it turns one year old, and is living its second year *while* it is one. For the same reason, the 1800s are known as the nineteenth century, the 1900s as the twentieth, and the 2000s as the twenty-first. Lincoln dated his proclamations accordingly. Thus the Fourth of July in 1861 was the eighty-fifth birthday of the nation's independence, and the year leading up *to* that Fourth of July was its eighty-fifth year. On an eighty-fifth birthday, a person or a nation is *completing* the eighty-fifth year, not beginning it, so that when one turns eighty-five, one is beginning one's eighty-sixth year. The first proclamation Lincoln executed and signed after July 4, 1861, the Proclamation of a National Feast Day on August 12, 1861, is correctly dated: "In testimony whereof, I have hereunto set my hand, and caused the Seal of the United States to be affixed, this 12th. day of August A.D. 1861, and of the Independence of the United States of America the 86th."[10] We know, too, that when Lincoln spoke to the serenaders on July 7, 1863, he had just been reminded of the age of American independence.

On June 15, 1863, just three weeks before his serenader speech, the president had issued his Proclamation Calling for One Hundred Thousand Militia. It had ended with Lincoln's characteristic dating system: "Done at the City of Washington this fifteenth day of June, in the year of our Lord one thousand eight hundred and sixty-three, and of the Independence of the United States the eighty seventh."[11] The eighty-seventh year had been particularly drummed into Lincoln's head because 1863 was a year of one proclamation after another, beginning in January with the most famous, most reprinted, and most quoted of all his proclamations, the Emancipation Proclamation. That famous document closed with that invariable ritual ending, "Done at the City of Washington, this first day of January, in the year of our Lord one thousand eight hundred and sixty three, and of the Independence of the United States of America the eighty-seventh."[12] Other proclamations in February, March, April, and May of 1863 had all closed with the same ritual. There is no way that a man of Lincoln's prodigious memory could have had the least uncertainty that this nation had turned eighty-seven years old on July 4, 1863, thus ending its eighty-seventh year and beginning its eighty-eighth. Never had there been a Fourth of July so memorable as this one, which marked the two greatest victories of the Civil War at Vicksburg and Gettysburg, victories that Lincoln and everyone else already regarded as turning points in the war. His very next proclamation issued just eight days later on July 15, 1863, the Proclamation of Thanksgiving, got the new year exactly right: "Done at the city of Washington, this fifteenth day of July, in the year of our Lord one thousand eight hundred and sixty-three, and of the Independence of the United States of America the eighty-eighth."[13] But since it is perfectly clear that the president had no real uncertainty, why did he ask the serenades how long it had been and follow this question with the vague phrase "eighty-odd years"?

Note that Lincoln never said he did not *know* or could not *remember* how many years it had been. He said nothing of the sort. He merely asked the question how long it had been. Such a question is clearly rhetorical. Lincoln was very good at asking rhetorical questions. Consider his highly effective use of a rhetorical "Why?" in his Message to Congress in Special Session on July 4, 1861:

> Our adversaries have adopted some Declarations of Independence; in which, unlike the good old one, penned by Jefferson, they omit the words "all men are created equal." Why? They have adopted a temporary national constitution, in the preamble of which, unlike our good old one, signed by Washington, they omit "We, the People," and substitute "We, the deputies of the sovereign and independent states." Why ?[14]

Lincoln knew very well why, and he knew that his listeners knew why. In asking the serenaders the rhetorical question, "How long has it been?" Lincoln was setting the stage for "eighty-odd years." But in this choice of a number, he was *not* extemporizing. He was trying out a phrase for a troublesome number that was, by any standard, unimposing and unattractive. The death of Jefferson and Adams had occurred on a round number, the fiftieth birthday of this nation. The death of Monroe had occurred a memorable five years later. But what can one do with the *eighty-seventh* birthday of these United States? White finds "eighty-odd years" an "awkward antecedent"[15] for "four score and seven years." No one would disagree that the phrase Lincoln used before the serenaders is less effective, less musical, less evocative than "four score and seven" and that Lincoln was right to keep looking until he came up with the later and better phrase. But "eighty-odd" did *not* come off the top of his tall head. It came, as almost all his words and phrases came, from a previous work he had read again and again until even a person with a less-impressive memory than Lincoln's would have remembered it. It is an unusual but highly revealing example of Lincoln's natural and habitual use of allusion.

Johnson finds in Lincoln's phrase, "stage of action," a "nod toward Shakespeare,"[16] and indeed it is, reinforced elsewhere in the speech by "stage of existence." But there is more than a nod toward Shakespeare in "eighty-odd years." There is a direct allusion to one of the plays that ranked among Lincoln's favorites, *Richard III*. The very next month after Lincoln's July 7 speech—in August of 1863—John Hay records in his diary that at the Soldiers Home, Lincoln "read Shakespeare to me, the end of Henry VI and the beginning of Richard III."[17] This suggests that the president was particularly preoccupied with *Richard III* around the time of the great battles of Vicksburg and Gettysburg and for some time after.

In act 4 of this memorable play focused on the longest and bloodiest of England's own civil wars, the Wars of the Roses, the Duchess of York laments the death of her son Edward IV, the murder of her two grandsons by the diabolical Richard III, and many other calamities of a terrible time in the nation's history. In her numbing grief, she cries out to first to a daughter and then to Edward's widow in a moving, mournful speech:

> Go thou to Richard, and good angels guard thee!
> Go thou to sanctuary, and good thoughts possess thee!
> I to my grave, where peace and rest lie with me!
> Eighty odd years of sorrow have I seen,
> And each hour's joy wreck'd with a week of teen. (4.1.94–97)

Shakespeare's "years of sorrow" clearly recalls the same Psalm 90:10 from which Lincoln would later take his "fourscore." Writing before the King James Bible was even translated, Shakespeare was echoing either the Geneva Bible or the Cranmer translation from the Prayer Book. The Geneva reads, "The time of our life is threescore yeeres and ten, and if they be of strength, fourscore yeeres: yet their strength is but labour and sorow." The Cranmer reads, "The days of our age are threescore years and ten; and though men be so strong that they come fourscore years, yet is their strength then but labour and sorrow." Both Bibles, then, contain the key word "sorrow" after a term meaning eighty—"fourscore." This sorrow is predicted for anyone who is *eighty or older*. Is the Duchess of York so old and dotty that she cannot even remember her own age? Nothing in the entire play portrays her in such a light. She is a vigorous, outspoken old woman. She is speaking here in the grip of a great passion. Shakespeare is using her vagueness as a literary device. Children's stories, which are often told by old people, typically begin with an intentional vagueness about time, as in "long, long ago." Such beginnings suggest a ruminative, mysterious, evocative quality. That is what Shakespeare achieved, and it is what Lincoln was almost certainly *trying* to achieve. It was a desire for a literary effect, not any uncertainty at all, that produced Lincoln's phrase. He clearly knew how many years had elapsed since 1776, just as the old lady knew her own age. By the time he sat down later to write the Gettysburg Address, he had decided that he could do better than "eighty-odd." In a moment of inspiration that reflected his whole lifetime of reading and memorizing, he remembered the Bible's "four score and seven," satisfying with this brilliant choice every standard that makes up the essence of his style. But like any good writer, he got there by digging here and digging there, borrowing this and trying out that, and learning as much or more from what had *failed* to work as from what had worked reasonably well on his first, second, or third try.

In the opening sentence of the Gettysburg Address, Lincoln would focus on the nation's birth date instead of its birth year. After July 4, 1863, the nation was in its eighty-eighth year of the Declaration of Independence. But the Fourth of July of 1863 was the birth*day* on which, in an almost miraculous coincidence, the great victory of Gettysburg had occurred. And it is this eighty-seventh birth*day* that Lincoln invokes in his great speech.

The last six sentences of the July 7, 1863, speech to the serenaders return to the more impromptu tone of the first three. All of them have "I" as their only subject or as the subject of one or more independent clauses in a compound sentence. No fewer than twelve *I*'s appear in the last six sentences. And yet even these closing sentences display a balance and musicality untypical of Lincoln's truly impromptu speeches. They display such qualities even when Lincoln is doing little more than apologizing for his lack of a speech, as, for example, in this nicely balanced sentence: "Gentlemen, this is a glorious theme and a glorious occasion for a speech, but I am not prepared to make one worthy of the theme and worthy of the occasion."[18]

Johnson makes the additional point that in composing this speech, Lincoln was almost certainly responding to an former colleague, Alexander Stephens, now vice-president of the Confederacy. As we saw earlier with regard to Calhoun, Lincoln's speeches very often took their shapes and even specific words from a political enemy whom he respected but disagreed with. All of Lincoln's greatest speeches are as much rebuttal as they are assertion. When a rebuttal never cites the words of the enemy but causes those words to be remembered, this is not, strictly speaking, literary allusion. But it is remarkably similar. Lincoln's words sometimes cause one to hear in the background words that the apologists for slavery and inequality have uttered in the past and that Lincoln is now, in the present, refuting. As in courtroom trials, one is always conscious that there are two sides to the question before the bar and that Lincoln is arguing *for* one side and *against* the other. This is a powerful and consistent part of his speechmaking. In his July 4, 1861, speech quoted earlier, Lincoln's rebuttal of Southern positions on human rights and equality and on representative government is explicit. The same rebuttal of the same positions is implicit in the Gettysburg Address. In the days immediately following the Battle of Gettysburg, says Johnson,

> Lincoln and his entire cabinet had been deeply enmeshed in considering how to respond to a recent overture from the Confederate government. On July 4, 1863, the same day that Lee's army began its retreat from Gettysburg, Alexander Stephens, Vice President of the Confederate States of America, had presented himself under a flag of truce to Union forces on the James River in Virginia, asking to cross the naval blockade to deliver an unspecified message from Jefferson Davis to Lincoln. The exchange of prisoners of war was the pretext for this mission, but Stephens later admitted that the request had been in part designed to undermine Republican chances at the upcoming fall elections should Lincoln refuse the offer of high-level negotiations. Lincoln took the offer seriously enough to propose going to Virginia to meet Stephens personally, and he conferred with members of his cabinet for several days before rebuffing the overture by referring Stephens to lower-level military authorities for any "needful communication."[19]

Johnson thinks that the close encounter with Stephens sparked a memory in Lincoln of previous exchanges between the two men. In particular it brought to Lincoln's mind the provocative speech of Stephens when, accepting the vice-presidency of the Confederacy, his former colleague had flatly declared that the Confederacy was founded upon "the great truth that the negro is not equal to the white man; that slavery, subordination to the superior race, is his natural and moral condition."[20] Johnson argues persuasively that Lincoln's powerful emphasis on the Union army as fighting for the declaration that all men are created equal owes a debt to Stephens and the Southern commitment to slavery and white supremacy. I could not agree more. The next chapter turns from Lincoln's style to his content and examines the meanings and message that the Gettysburg Address conveyed to its audience and to the world on November 19, 1863, particularly the president's masterful response to Vice-President Stephens and to so many like-minded Southern defenders of slavery and secession. It focuses on the heart of Lincoln's message as a rebuttal of human inequality and undemocratic government and as the greatest restatement ever of those enduring principles of the "good old" Declaration of Independence—that "all men are created equal" and that a government for the equally created can only be "of the people, by the people, for the people."

The Heart of the Message

Lincoln's style is so beautiful that it alone makes the Gettysburg Address immortal. But the meaning of the work is just as beautiful in its own way. To hear that meaning in anything approaching its fullness requires us once again to cast off twenty-first-century preconceptions and take on the assumptions of the speaker and of the time in which he spoke. Lincoln always insisted that the founding fathers were right to declare "that all men are created equal" and that "all men" meant "the whole human family"[1]—men and women, black and white, rich and poor, people of all colors and conditions. He also insisted that the fathers were right when a majority of them voted to halt the spread of slavery and made known their hopes that one day the institution itself would be ended. The essence of Lincoln's message in the Gettysburg Address, and indeed throughout his entire political career, was that this nation can "long endure" only by pursuing and fulfilling the principles of those founding fathers—the principles of the Declaration of Independence, chief among them that all men are created equal and its logical corollary, that the only government appropriate for equal human beings is a government of the people, by the people, for the people.

It is crucial to remember today what Lincoln himself never forgot—that there was a great divide in the way that slavery was regarded by the founding fathers, even in the slaveholding South, and the way it was regarded in his own time. From the founding of this nation in 1776 until around the time of the War of 1812, national sentiment clearly favored the gradual emancipation of slaves and an end to this horrific institution. This was true in the South as well as the North. Jefferson's condemnation in the Declaration of both slavery and the king of England for supporting that slavery was struck in committee for fear that it would weaken support from delegates representing the slave states. But the fact is that every delegate from every slaveholding state signed this document holding as a self-evident truth that "all men are created equal." The large majority of the founding fathers, North and South, agreed that slavery was a violation of the great principles of the Declaration of Independence and ought to be ended as soon as practically possible. But the practical difficulties, as everyone also saw, seemed intractable to even the most dedicated emancipationist. Slavery had been interwoven for too long into the social and economic fabric of the continent. African slaves had been in the American colonies longer than any European settlers except those at Jamestown. The first slaves had arrived in 1619, the year before the Pilgrims landed at Plymouth Rock. Nobody knew how to displace so many millions of human beings. How would their former owners be compensated? Would the freed slaves all be sent back to Africa? Would sending them back mean liberation—or death and disaster? Would keeping them here mean liberation—or death and disaster? There was even a legitimate question in the minds of many slaveholders who *wanted* to emancipate their own slaves: would freedom, instead of improving, only *worsen* the plight of the freed? After all, many free blacks in America lived a miserable existence, with precious few rights even in the nonslave states and in constant peril of being returned to slavery by harsh laws and unscrupulous traders. If all the slaves were emancipated and *not* returned to Africa, could the social and economic fabric of the new nation absorb them? Would the freed blacks compete with white labor and spark uncontrollable civil strife? These were issues for which there were no good answers and no good prospects of finding any. In short, there was a twofold consensus at the birth of this nation—first, that slavery was wrong and, second, that no one could think of any practical way to end it. It is nonsense to look back from our vantage today and see any one of these issues as a bright line dividing good people from bad, racist from nonracist. The most dedicated and passionate of abolitionists, including free blacks such as Martin Delany, sometimes urged colonization—a return to the African homeland—as the best hope of resolving the riddle and horror of slavery while numerous defenders of slavery who saw slavery as a blessing and a mandate from God strongly *opposed* it. Yet today the reflex among many individuals representing a whole variety of political persuasions is to regard anyone who ever favored colonization back to Africa or to some other sanctuary in central or south America or the Caribbean as automatically a racist. This kind of historical provincialism is forever complicating the national dialogue about Lincoln.

The second half of this consensus survived even after the nation slowly hardened into proslavery and antislavery factions. The half of the consensus that survived was the conviction that ending slavery was a riddle without an answer. Because the institution of American slavery ended so suddenly during the Civil War, later generations who were not alive when it ended had a hard time understanding what a miracle its ending had seemed at the time—and indeed what a miracle it *was*. Clearly the political skill of Abraham Lincoln was the single greatest reason for this miracle. Hindsight should not blind us, however, to how utterly impossible, in practical terms, the abolition of slavery had seemed to most Americans *before* the war. It seemed this way to people on both sides of the question. Thus John C. Calhoun had declared in a speech from 1837:

The relation which now exists between the two races in the slave-holding States has existed for two centuries. It has grown with our growth, and strengthened with our strength. It has entered into and modified all our institutions, civil and political. None other can be substituted. We will not, cannot permit it to be destroyed.[2]

Calhoun said elsewhere that freeing the slaves would only "change the form of slavery."

It would make them the slaves of the community, instead of the slaves of individuals, with less responsibility and interest in their welfare on the part of the community than is felt by their present masters.[3]

We have seen that Theodore Parker was one of the most outspoken abolitionists of the prewar period. Yet here is what Parker told other abolitionists in 1856:

All kinds of schemes, too, have been proposed to end this wickedness of Slavery. There has been a most multifarious discussion of the idea; for, after we have the right sentiment, it is difficult to get the intellectual work done, done well, in the best way. It takes a large-minded man, with great experience, to cipher out all this intellectual work, and show how we can get rid of Slavery, and what is to take its place, and how the thing is to be done.[4]

That man turned out to be Lincoln, who would not become a national figure until the debates with Douglas two years later, in 1858. Parker saw perfectly well that none of the radical abolitionists such as William Lloyd Garrison and Wendell Phillips—or himself for that matter—had the strength, experience, or talent to end it. Recognizing the extraordinary difficulty of getting rid of the whole evil institution, Parker accurately predicted in January 1858:

Slavery is a moral wrong and an economical blunder; but it is also a great political institution. It cannot be put down by political economy, nor by ethical preaching; men have not only pecuniary interests and moral feelings, but also political passions. Slavery must be put down politically, or else militarily. If not peacefully ended soon, it must be ended wrathfully by the sword.[5]

It was ended finally by the sword of the Civil War and by the brilliantly shaped political plowshares of the Emancipation Proclamation and the Thirteenth Amendment, reinforced by Lincoln's brilliant speeches, among which the Gettysburg Address is the greatest.

Part of the reason that slavery proved so hard to end is that the young nation had its hands so full of many problems in the early years and did such a poor job of handling so many of them. The Revolutionary War lasted for seven agonizing years and was followed by internal economic turmoil and warfare under the ineffectual Articles of Confederation, when "not worth a Continental" dollar became an enduring part of the American language. All the while, an uneasy relationship with the Indian tribes periodically erupted into violence and war. In brief, the nation started out hoping to stop the spread of slavery until it could figure out a way to end it permanently. It took major steps in the right direction by ending the slave trade and by keeping slavery out of new territories such as the Northwest Territory donated to the Union by the state of Virginia and Governor Thomas Jefferson with the expectation that slavery would not be permitted there. America was taking the right steps, intermediate though they were, in the hope that someone, somehow would finally figure out how to end slavery where it already existed, a problem so vast that it typically met with little more than silence from a beleaguered nation and its leadership.

Most Americans in the early years saw slavery the way they saw the "Indian problem," as an enormous continental problem that defied even the best and brightest minds. Even when a clear majority supports a given proposition over a sustained period of time, this is no guarantee at all that the proposition will become reality. To do so, it must overcome the gravity of tradition, the huge weight and inertia of whatever the *present* reality is, and the unsettling effects of a hostile and vocal minority that may at any moment explode into a majority. Consider just one recent example—the Equal Rights Amendment. A clear majority of Americans favored it for a long time, and yet it died, like Moses, within sight of the Promised Land. As for slavery where it was already established in the early years of these United States, things *could* just go on as they were without inevitably disrupting the country. But the young nation's desire for westward expansion—"Go West, young man, go West"—assured that the Indian problem would *never* stop erupting. For this reason, all the early presidents except Washington spoke time and again of the Indian problem in their inaugural addresses. Washington chose to address *no* specific problems in his two inaugurals, but every one of his successors from John Adams through Andrew Jackson spoke of "Indian tribes" or "aboriginal neighbors" while saying nothing directly about blacks or slaves. It was not until the eighth president and the thirteenth administration that this long pattern was reversed. At his inauguration in 1837, Martin Van Buren said nothing about the Indian tribes but loudly declared that he would oppose all efforts to end slavery in the District of Columbia or in any of the slave states. Secretary William Seward enjoyed telling an amusing story about an old Episcopal priest who insisted that once his favorite, Andrew Jackson, left office, he would no longer say the Prayer Book's Prayer for the President because "I don't like Mr. Van Buren"[6]—perhaps because of this very issue. By 1837, the times had changed with regard to the old, intractable problem of slavery. The nation had entered upon its second period.

The change had begun as far back as the nation's second war in 1812 when the national antislavery consensus began to weaken, particularly in the South.

One reason was that over time, slavery became more profitable as Eli Whitney's cotton gin came to be adopted more and more widely. The gin was invented in 1793 and patented the following year. Over time, this ingenious contraption would transform the Southern economy. A new attitude toward slavery changed the Southern song-and-dance to a do-si-do. The South turned its back on the proposition that slavery was wrong. It began, slowly at first but with an increasing tempo, to dance to the lilting music that slavery was in fact a very good thing, ordained by God Himself. More and more Southerners responded to this new upbeat between the War of 1812 and the Civil War, with the do-si-do becoming all the rage throughout the South between Nat Turner's Rebellion in 1831 and the outbreak of the Civil War in 1861.

Lincoln was born in 1809, on the early cusp of this great continental shift in thought. Over the years of his political career, Lincoln devoted a great deal of passion and energy arguing in one speech after another that a clear majority of the founding fathers, including many Southerners, had *condemned* slavery and looked forward to its ultimate demise. Lincoln kept saying this to everyone in the nation who would listen, disputing at every turn those spurious claims to the contrary by Stephen A. Douglas. Douglas and many of his fellow Democrats had set out in the 1850s, particularly from 1854 onward, to undermine those compromises of the past that had managed, however precariously, to control the spread of slavery and to keep alive some hope—some reasonable hope—of its ultimate extinction.

Indeed, Lincoln had taken as his thesis for the Cooper Union address that would make him president an insistence by Senator Douglas that the national policy on slavery should follow the views of the founding fathers. At Cooper Union, Lincoln had brilliantly demonstrated that an overwhelming majority of the founding fathers had opposed slavery on both moral and political grounds. These men had not only expected but *welcomed* its ultimate demise and had done all they could to hasten that end by first stopping the *spread* of slavery. Arguments like those of Senator Calhoun, Dr. Frederick Ross, and Bishop John Henry Hopkins that slavery, far from being a great social evil, was in fact a very good thing attracted sizable numbers of followers only after the War of 1812 and became commonplace only in the thirty years immediately preceding the Civil War. Even Bishop Hopkins admitted in a tract written in 1851 that slavery was long disfavored by Southerners: "Their most eminent men were opposed to it, before, as well as after, the Revolution."[7] Setting aside the issue of how much the great change from slavery as evil to slavery as good was prompted by economics, it is sufficient for purposes of this study simply to observe the *fact* of it.

One of the best accounts of the changes between the views of the founding fathers and those of those advocates and apologists for slavery who emerged between the War of 1812 and the Civil War is William E. Dodd's in *The Cotton Kingdom*:

The discrediting of Jefferson did not begin to take effect in the lower South till such great Virginians as John Randolph and Chief Justice Marshall had successfully ridiculed his teachings as glittering fallacies. Four years after Jefferson's death [he died July 4, 1826], the Virginia constitutional convention openly disavowed the equalitarian teachings which had underlain the politics of the South since 1800; and two years later [1832], when the Nat Turner Insurrection was under discussion in the Virginia Legislature, a young teacher at William and Mary College appeared before the committee on abolition and presented a new system of social science. This man was Thomas R. Dew, a trained political scientist, recently returned from the German universities where he had been taught that the inequality of man was fundamental to all social organization.

According to Dodd, Dew demonstrated to legislators, as to his students, "that slavery had been the condition of all ancient culture, that Christianity approved servitude, and that the law of Moses had both assumed and positively established slavery." Dodd goes on:

How much easier to justify the idea of negro servitude to men who had inherited their slaves from honored ancestors, when it was made plain that the Bible taught that even white servitude was right and proper! It was a time when men, especially Southern men, were studying their classics afresh.

Dew's influence, buttressed by both the cutting-edge "science" of his day and the classics that included the Bible, only increased after he ascended to the presidency of William and Mary, from which platform he pontificated to the entire South:

The exclusive owners of property have ever been, ever will and perhaps ever ought to be the virtual rulers of mankind. . . . It is the order of nature and of God that those being of superior faculties and knowledge, and therefore of superior power, should control and dispose of those who are inferior.[8]

Thus did German "science" help to change the prevailing view in the South about what both nature and God had intended for man in terms of social hierarchy and slavery.

Chancellor William Harper of the Supreme Court of South Carolina built upon Dew's "scientific" foundation in *A Memoir on Slavery*, published in 1838: "Is it not palpably nearer the truth to say that no man was ever born free and that no two men were ever born equal, than to say that all men are born free and equal? . . . Man is born to subjection. . . . The proclivity of the natural man is to domineer or to be subservient." Furthermore, said Chancellor Harper without the least apology for viewing slaves as barely animals, "if there are sordid, servile, and laborious offices to be performed, is it not better that there should be sordid, servile, and laborious human beings to perform them?"[9]

Dodd places John C. Calhoun directly in this line of thought: "In 1837 Calhoun, the greatest and sincerest of all Southern leaders, openly announced that he held slavery to be a positive good and that Southerners should no longer apologize for it." Dodd quotes Calhoun himself: "I hold slavery to be a good; . . . moreover, there never has yet existed a wealthy and civilized society in which one portion of the community did not in point of fact live on the labor of the other." Calhoun, said Dodd, learning from men like Dew and Harper as well as from political events in which he was personally involved, "had changed his mind; he meant what he said; he believed in the caste system of which in the South slavery was the mainstay. In his view nothing could be more unfounded and false than the opinion that all men are born free and equal."[10]

In his *Church and State in the United States*, Anson Phelps Stokes underscores the same point about the great shift throughout the South on the question of the morality of slavery:

> During the Revolutionary period and in the early days of the republic much progress was made in almost all the states in ameliorating the lot of the slave; in freeing exceptional Negroes through manumission; and in developing a sentiment favorable to the gradual abolition of slavery. Thomas Jefferson was highly influential in advocating all these measures, and was representative of the best thought of the South in the matter. He included an antislavery plank in his suggestions to Virginia delegates to the Continental Congress. In his original draft of the Declaration slavery had been severely condemned as "cruel war against human nature itself, violating its most sacred rights of life and liberty." This was unfortunately deleted in committee, but the well-known phrases on human equality and the inborn rights of life and liberty were retained, and their implications gradually worked into the consciousness of the nation. He wrote much on the subject, but none of his statements is more impressive than the words incised on one of the four panels of the Jefferson Memorial at the nation's capital.

>> God who gave us life gave us liberty. Can the liberties of a nation be secure when we have removed a conviction that these liberties are the gift of God? Indeed I tremble for my country when I reflect that God is just, that His justice cannot sleep forever. Commerce between master and slave is despotism. Nothing is more certainly written in the book of fate than that these people are to be free.

Stokes goes on to show that Jefferson's views were shared by fellow Virginians George Wythe, Patrick Henry, and numerous other Southerners. Washington, for example, not only praised the hundreds of free black soldiers who had fought bravely and well under him in the Revolutionary War but freed his own slaves in his will. Indeed, for forty years after the establishment of the government, "All thoughtful groups, North and South, at least considered slavery inadvisable, and most believed that it should ultimately be done away with." Stokes concludes, "This general attitude, which resulted in the freeing of slaves by Washington and many of his representative contemporaries, lasted for about a generation. We find it even after the War of 1812 and until the early 'thirties."[11]

Calhoun, who was Stephen A. Douglas' fellow Democrat in the United States Senate and the Southern political leader who more than any other turned the antislavery tide into a proslavery tide throughout the slaveholding states, even attracting supporters in the free states, fully acknowledged that many early Southerners held to a different view of slavery from his own. He said this of slavery in a Senate speech of January 10, 1838:

> Many in the South once believed that it was a moral and political evil. That folly and delusion are gone. We see it now in its true light, and regard it as the most safe and stable basis for free institutions in the world.[12]

Calhoun's position favoring slavery was adamant and bordered on the evangelical. He had seen the light, and now he must enlighten others. The gauntlet he threw down was taken up by a number of equally passionate voices in the Southern clergy who quickly found justification for slavery in holy scripture. Stokes observes that *The Christian Doctrine of Slavery*, a book published in 1857 by the Reverend George D. Armstrong, D.D. (1813–99), pastor of the Presbyterian Church in Norfolk, Virginia, considered slavery "God's appointment" for certain people, and found it justified in the Bible.[13] We have already looked at the 1857 *Slavery Ordained of God* from Ross of the same denomination. Mary Todd had grown up in Kentucky in the same Presbyterian church, a denomination second only to the Episcopal in representing the slave-owning socially elite of the South. Like Calhoun and like Bishop Hopkins, Ross in 1857 acknowledged a great shift in the thinking of Southerners on the whole issue of slavery:

> Twenty-five years ago, and previously, the whole slave-holding South and West had a strong tendency to emancipation, in some form. But the abolition movement then began, and arrested the Southern and Western leaning to emancipation.[14]

This is the very opposite of what actually happened. Abolitionism in the North grew stronger precisely because the South grew more implacable in its defense of slavery and not the other way around. The South came to insist, for example, that the federal government could not prevent slavery even in the territories. But it is typical of all who are defending any behavior they know is considered immoral by others to blame their critics, especially when their own consciences are not as settled and at ease as they may wish to believe. This reflex has been so powerful in the South for so long that it helps to account for the dark history of violence in my own native region against "uppity blacks" and "carpetbaggers" and "outside agitators" and all other "trouble-makers." The same specious argument was resurrected against the civil-rights movement in the 1950s and 1960s, when Southern apologists insisted that the South had been moving steadily toward equal rights for blacks *until* the civil-rights movement killed all the white folks' good will! It is fascinating to hear what otherwise intelligent people will solemnly swear is the truth under the influence of threats to their own piety and self-esteem.

Ross also attributed the South's previous weakness for emancipation to "Northern training."

> Twenty-five years ago the religious mind of the South was leavened by wrong Northern training, on the great point of the right and wrong of slavery. Meanwhile, powerful intellects in the South, following the mere sight of a healthy good sense, guided by the common grace of God, reached the very truth of this great matter,—namely, that the relation of the master and slave is not sin; and that, notwithstanding its admitted evils, it is a connection between the highest and the lowest races of man, revealing influences which may be, and will be, most benevolent for the ultimate good of the master and the slave,—conservative on the Union, by preserving the South from all forms of Northern fanaticism, and thereby being a great balance-wheel in the working of the tremendous machinery of our experiment of self-government. This seen result of slavery was found to be in absolute harmony with the word of God.[15]

John Wilkes Booth proclaimed the same gospel when he wrote of slavery and slaves in December of 1860: "And instead of looking upon slavery as a sin . . . I hold it to be a happiness for themselves and a social & political blessing for us."[16] Ross's abomination of "Northern training" in regard to slavery was echoed by Bishop/General Leonidas Polk in his dream for a University of the South where young minds would be entirely liberated from that unholy influence. Stokes' *Church and State in the United States* points out the role of Polk in the Southern glorification of slavery that closed its ears to Northern opposition and formed the dominant policy of the region from 1835 to 1861:

> But free discussion of the tabooed subject virtually disappeared. "From 1835 to 1861 the South pursued a policy of silence in regard to the removal of slavery" [Clement Eaton]. When it discussed the question in public at all it generally tried to defend the institution, or to revile the abolitionist leaders, many of whose utterances and methods were recognized by earnest friends of Negro emancipation in the North, including Abraham Lincoln, to be extreme and provocative. Even the Christian point of view, formerly so favorable to the gradual emancipation of the slave, had so changed that Bishop Leonidas Polk (1806–64), later famous as a general of the Confederacy, carried out in 1860 his plan for a University of the South at Sewanee, Tennessee, in which along with the Christian religion, and a curriculum emphasizing the classics and other cultural subjects, "sound" doctrines on slavery could be taught instead of having students "polluted" by attending Northern colleges.[17]

Yet, as a young man at West Point and for some time after, Polk had *opposed* slavery. *Jefferson Davis and His Generals* points out that Polk's religious conversion had occurred at West Point. "As a young convert," says the author, Stephen Woodworth, "he had considered slavery an evil that ought to be slowly phased out."[18]

According to Ross in his 1857 defense, Northern abolitionists such as Dr. Albert Barnes, who once had public sentiment on their side throughout the whole nation, have now lost public approbation, especially in the South:

> The time was when *you* had the very *public sentiment* you are now trying to form. From Maine to Louisiana, the American mind was softly yielding to the impress of emancipation, in some hope, however vague and imaginary. Southern as well as Northern men, in the church and out of it, not having sufficiently studied the word of God, and, under our own and French revolutionary excitement, looking only at the evils of slavery, wished it away from the land. It was a *mistaken* public sentiment.

In short, says Ross, the South was wrong to question and oppose slavery but did so only because misled and "leavened" by absurd Northern ideas, one of which was that "the negro . . . might reach, in a day, the liberty and equality which the Anglo-Saxon had attained after the struggle of his ancestors during a thousand years!" Now, having seen the light with the help of the South's most enlightened native sons such as Calhoun, the whole region has come to regard slavery as nothing less than the very will and blessing of God. Ross never explains why he had himself "emancipated slaves whose money-value would now be $40,000"[19]—a fortune at the time. Did this happen because he himself had been influenced by those Northern teachings he now deplored? Or did he only mean to show that, like the narrator of Jonathan Swift's *Modest Proposal*, he had nothing pecuniary to gain from his own preachings?

Unlike most other Southern apologists, Ross never claimed that the abolition movement rested on a factual misunderstanding of how terrible slavery was at its worst. He fully acknowledged that the picture *Uncle Tom's Cabin* gave of slaveholders at their worst was in fact true. "That book of genius,—over which I and hundreds in the world have freely wept,—true in all its facts, false in all its impressions,—yea, as false in the prejudice it creates to Southern social life as if Webster, the murderer of Parkman, may be believed to be a personification of the *elite* of honor in Cambridge, Boston, and New England." A few pages later, he repeats the same point with no qualification: "Sir, I have admitted, and do again admit, without qualification, that every fact in Uncle Tom's Cabin has occurred in the South." But, says Ross, the bad behavior portrayed in that "book of genius" was not *typical* behavior. What mattered far more to the tough-minded Presbyterian was his conviction that *all* unequal relationships may be abused without undermining their biblical sanction at all. Biblical teachings, according to Ross, show, unanswerably, that "God as really sanctioned the relation of master and slave as those of husband and wife, and parent and child; and that all the obligations of the moral law, and Christ's law of love, might and must be as truly fulfilled in the one relation as in the other." As for slavery in particular, God has "sanctioned it under the Old Testament and the New, and ordains it now while he sees it best to continue it."[20]

What Lincoln took above all from Ross is the minister's repeated conviction that a single proposition—the proposition that all men are created equal—is the absolute key to the differences between those who favor slavery and those who oppose it. Ross views the arguments of Barnes and other abolitionists as an edifice built upon five affirmations from the Declaration of Independence that have been wrongly asserted to be self-evident truths. He makes perfectly clear his belief that these affirmations are not only wrong but ungodly. Overflowing with biblical allusions, Ross insists that "God gives no sanction to the affirmation that he has created all men equal."[21] God has in fact cursed all of the "self-evident truths" of the Declaration of Independence:

> All this—every word of it, every jot and tittle—is the liberty and equality claimed by infidelity. God has cursed it seven times seven in France since 1793; and he will curse it there seventy times seven, if Frenchmen prefer to be pestled so often in Solomon's mortar. He has cursed it in Prussia, Austria, Germany, Italy, Spain. He will curse it as long as time, whether it is affirmed by Jefferson, Paine, Robespierre, Ledru Rollin, Kossuth, Greeley, Garrison, or Barnes.[22]

Later Ross makes perfectly clear that a single one of Jefferson's five affirmations— the very first one of the five—is the key to the whole edifice:

> The whole battle-ground, as to the truth of this series of averments, is on the first affirmation, "that all men are created equal." Or, to keep up my first figure, the strength of the chain of asserted truths depend on *that* first link.[23]

Thus, when Lincoln singled out "all men are created equal" as the "proposition" to which this nation was dedicated at its birth, he knew perfectly well that to Calhoun, Ross, Hopkins, and all their compeers who so passionately opposed the Declaration of Independence, the whole battleground over slavery versus emancipation, over inequality versus equality, centered on this very proposition and no other. In short, the Civil War was being fought, according to the South's own leading spokesmen, over the issue of Bible-sanctioned African slavery as a disproof—a long-standing, living, breathing rebuke—of a claim they insisted was wrong from the start, this foolishly mistaken "proposition" from the Declaration of Independence that all men are created equal.

Then, on November 7, 1863, less than two weeks before Lincoln would deliver his Gettysburg Address, the same virulent arguments of Dew, Harper, Calhoun, Armstrong, and Ross—the latter two representing those "eminent Divines, Doc-

tors of Divinity, and Bishops"[24] whom Frederick Douglass had identified as leading the apologists for slavery—were implicitly repeated yet again by the Episcopal
Bishop of Vermont in a huge page-one article in the Washington newspaper
that was closer to Lincoln, both personally and politically, than any other. This
article was a long letter by a group of Episcopal priests in Pennsylvania defending
their own bishop, who opposed slavery, and attacking Bishop Hopkins, whose
recent tract repeated once again his long-standing contention that the Bible fully
approves slavery. It was his exasperation with men like Ross and Hopkins that
would lead the president to declare, in the Second Inaugural Address, "It may
seem strange that any men should dare to ask a just God's assistance in wring-
ing their bread from the sweat of other men's faces; but let us judge not, that
we be not judged," and then to say about the Civil War, "yet, if God wills that
it continue, until all the wealth piled by the bond-man's two hundred and fifty
years of unrequited toil shall be sunk, and until every drop of blood drawn
with the lash, shall be paid by another drawn with the sword, as was said three
thousand years ago, so still it must be said 'the judgments of the Lord are true
and righteous altogether.'"[25]

Lincoln must have wondered, as he read in Forney's *Daily Chronicle* about
Bishop Hopkins' cold-blooded defense of slavery—the same defense Hopkins
had laid out in a series in a series of books and pamphlets between 1851 and
1863—how the same church where Salmon Chase, John Hay, William Seward,
and Gideon Welles worshipped, four men from his inner circle who were rock-
solid in their commitment to ending the tyranny of slavery, could at the same
time be represented by men like John Henry Hopkins, Kensey Johns Stewart,
and Robert Gatewood (the Episcopal priest who became head of the Confederate
secret service), not to mention John C. Calhoun, Jefferson Davis, Robert E. Lee,
and Leonidas Polk. The Southern leadership was overwhelmingly Episcopalian
and formed an extended family, with all sorts of brotherly and cousinly, father-
and-son interconnections. Davis, Lee, and Polk had all been in attendance at West
Point at the very time that institution was under the department of Secretary of
War Calhoun. Frederick Douglass understood very well the Southern domination
of West Point in the years between the War of 1812 and the Civil War, as when
he wrote in his autobiography about General Ulysses S. Grant:

> My confidence in Gen. Grant was not entirely due to his brilliant military suc-
> cesses, but there was a moral as well as military basis for my faith in him. He had
> shown his single-mindedness and superiority to popular prejudice by his prompt
> cooperation with President Lincoln in his policy of employing colored troops and
> by his order commanding his soldiers to treat such troops with due respect. In this
> way he proved himself to be not only a wise general, but a great man—one who
> could adjust himself to new conditions, and adopt the lessons taught by the hour.
> This quality in General Grant was and is made all the more conspicuous with his

West Point education and his former political associations, for neither West Point nor the Democratic Party have been good schools in which to learn justice and fair play to the Negro.[26]

For years, it was the Democratic Secretary of War Calhoun who had personally interviewed and approved or rejected all candidates for West Point.[27] It was Calhoun who selected and appointed as the academy chaplain the Episcopal clergyman Dr. Charles McIlvaine, afterwards Bishop of Ohio. McIlvaine's preaching would stir a religious awakening at West Point. Polk was the first and most passionate of all the student converts, causing the young cadet to switch careers from the military to the ecclesiastical, at least until the outbreak of the Civil War.[28]

Polk was far from alone among Episcopalians who accepted Jefferson Davis's offer of a Confederate generalship. According to Glenn Robins' biography of Polk:

Of the major Protestant denominations, the Old South's planter elite were most comfortable with the Episcopal tradition. By virtue of their elevated socioeconomic and political status, they played an especially prominent role in the development of the various strands of Southern nationalism. Of the known religious affiliations of the participants in Southern secession conventions, Episcopalians comprised 32 percent of delegates and represented the largest single religious group. Likewise, when the Confederate government began to take shape, Episcopalians occupied many of the most prominent positions. President Jefferson Davis, Secretary of the Treasury Christopher Memminger, and Secretary of the Navy Stephen Mallory were Episcopalian. Within the military, seven of the Confederacy's eight full generals were Episcopalian. The denomination also provided an inordinate number of chaplains in comparison to the number of churchmen serving in the ranks. In summary, Southern Episcopalians expressed the values of the Southern slave society, and through their positions of leadership quite literally guided the Confederate quest for an independent republic.[29]

Typical of this Southern leadership were the more than sixty Confederate generals of all three grades who belonged to the Episcopal Church: the two Andersons, Armistead, Beale, Bee, Boggs, Bragg, Bratton, Cabell, Cantey, Carter, Clayton, Cleburne, Conner, Cooper (his wife the granddaughter of George Mason), Cox, Cumming, William Davis, Duke, Echols, Early, Forney, Fry, Gordon, Gorgas, Govan (his wife the daughter of Bishop Otey of Tennessee), Gracie, Hampton, Hardee, Hawes, Helm, Heth, Hoke, Hume, Jenkins, "Allegheny" Johnson, Albert Sidney Johnston, Joseph E. Johnston, Lane, Fitzhugh Lee, George Washington Custis Lee, Robert E. Lee, William Henry Fitzhugh Lee, Longstreet, Loring, Mahone, Manigault, Martin, Morgan, Page, Pegram, Pemberton, Pendleton, Pettigrew, Pickett, Leonidas Polk and his nephew Lucius Eugene Polk, Shoup, Edmund Kirby Smith, J. E. B. Stuart, Taliaferro, Walthall, Wheeler, and Wickham (his father an Episcopal clergyman). The list is not exhaustive. In addition to all of these, Stonewall Jackson, who had married the daughter of a Presbyterian minister and joined her church, was born and christened in the Episcopal Church. At least two Confederate generals were Episcopal priests. Polk served simultaneously as Bishop of Louisiana and as a Confederate major general, saying just after he received his commission from Jefferson Davis at the Capitol in Richmond, "I buckle the sword over the gown."[30] He died wearing that sword on Pine Mountain, Georgia, in 1863, taking a direct hit from one of William Tecumseh Sherman's artillery shells and instantly dying as the final act of a military career remembered more for the general's personal courage than for his achievements as a commander. William Nelson Pendleton was a brigadier general who served as chief of artillery for Lee's Army of Northern Virginia at Gettysburg and later, after the war, as General Lee's priest in Lexington, Virginia, when Lee was president of Washington College.

Gone with the Wind is giddy with fantastic lotus dreams about the beauty of race relations during slavery and the glories of the Ku Klux Klan during Reconstruction—dreams fueled by Margaret Mitchell's enraptured viewings of D. W. Griffiths' *Birth of a Nation* when she was a young girl. But it gets the church part absolutely right when Rhett Butler, trying to advance the social future of his and Scarlett's daughter, determines to win over the aristocrats of Atlanta: "And the congregation of the Episcopal Church almost fell out of their pews when he tiptoed in, late for services, with Wade's hand held in his." Captain Butler has brought along Scarlett's son, Wade, from her first marriage in order to increase the psychological effect even though "the little boy was supposed to be a Catholic" like his socially compromised mother whose unconventional behavior has earned her the censure of polite society. Later, the dashing Butler "subscribed handsomely to the fund for the repairs of the Episcopal Church."[31]

Calhoun's religious affiliation is described by Pulitzer Prize–winning biographer Margaret L. Coit as the old South Carolina firebrand approached his death in 1850:

> Proud, solitary, independent of any intellect but his own, Calhoun refused even spiritual assistance in these last days. His religious pilgrimage had been a strange one. Always devout, yet never "professing" Christianity, his life had been a search for the faith which would fill the needs of his soul and yet satisfy the demands of his reason. Reacting against the stern Presbyterianism of his youth, caught midway between the Calvinism of the up-country and the deism of the intellectual Jeffersonian groups, he had drifted into attendance at his wife's Episcopal church, of which it was said in Carolina that this was "the only way to heaven for a gentleman."[32]

It was Calhoun who had led the fight among both friends and enemies for the new Southern doctrine that the Declaration of Independence was wrong and that slavery was right. We have already examined his fierce attack in the Oregon bill speech of 1848 on the egalitarian doctrines of the Declaration of Independence. Calhoun went on to say in the same speech that the idea that all men are born free and equal

> had strong hold on the mind of Mr. Jefferson, the author of that document, which caused him to take an utterly false view of the subordinate relation of the black to the white race in the South; and to hold, in consequence, that the former, though utterly unqualified to possess liberty, were as fully entitled to both liberty and equality as the latter; and that to deprive them of it was unjust and immoral. To this error, his proposition to exclude slavery from the territory northwest of the Ohio may be traced,—and to that the ordinance of 1787,—and through it the deep and dangerous agitation which now threatens to ingulf, and will certainly ingulf, if not speedily settled, our political institutions, and involve the country in countless woes.[33]

In his *Disquisition on Government*, which both Hopkins and Lincoln almost certainly read, Calhoun countered with equal vehemence the idea of equality, asserting that "individuals differ greatly from each other, in intelligence, sagacity, energy, perseverance, skill, habits of industry and economy, physical power, position and opportunity."[34] Willfully distorting Locke's position again and again, as we have seen, Calhoun went to his death insisting that an eternal inequality was the natural state of man. Death, that great and final equalizer of all humankind, came like an uninvited guest only days after Calhoun had announced his expectation of "a full restoration of my strength."[35]

During his long career in Washington, the nationally known Calhoun, undoubtedly influenced by proslavery arguments from academics like Dew and Harper, became the greatest spokesman for this cause. In his halcyon days, it was his formulations—his words and arguments—that set not just the tone but also the language for everyone who wrote after him. In time, the arguments of Calhoun, Armstrong, Ross, Hopkins, and all the other proslavery advocates sounded so much alike that to read any one of them was to read them all. Thus Bishop Hopkins sounded very much like Calhoun as he attacked all the usual objections to slavery and especially as he attacked the egalitarian doctrines of the Declaration of Independence in his *Bible View of Slavery*:

> In what respect are men "created equal," when every thoughtful person must be sensible that they are brought into the world with all imaginable differences in body, in mind, and in every characteristic of their social position? Notwithstanding mankind have all descended from one common parent, yet we see them divided into distinct races, so strongly marked, that infidel philosophers insist on the impossibility of their having the same ancestry. . . . Where is the equality *in mind* between one who is endowed with talent and genius, and another whose

intellect borders on idiocy? Where is the equality in *social position* between the son of the Esquimaux or Hottentot, and the heir of the American statesman or British peer?[36]

How revealing that Hopkins, himself an Irish immigrant, should cite "the heir of the American statesman or British peer," blithely ignoring the fact that American statesmen had outlawed the peerage and all titles of nobility in the very same United States Constitution that Hopkins had so long and piously defended! James Madison, the Father of the Constitution, wrote in the *Federalist Papers*, "Could any further proof be required of the republican complexion of this system, the most decisive one might be found in its absolute prohibition of titles of nobility."[37] But for Hopkins, who descended in his paternal line from an English family that had lived for centuries in Ireland and had intermarried with the Irish long before emigrating to America—just as for John C. Calhoun before him, whose ancestry also traced to Ireland—inequality is a gift from God, whose glorious creations reflect that great chain of being so beloved by all conservatives:

> The Deity seems to take pleasure in exhibiting a marvelous wealth of power through the rich variety of all his works, so that no two individuals of any species can be found in all respects alike. And hence we behold a grand system of ORDER and GRADATION, from the thrones, dominions, principalities, and powers in heavenly places, rank below rank, to man. And then we see the same system throughout our earth displayed in the races—some higher, some lower in the scale.[38]

It presented no problem at all to the heart or head of Bishop Hopkins that the "lower" races have been put on earth by God himself in order to serve the "higher" ones.

Lincoln had heard the very same argument in his debates with Stephen Douglas, during one of which the Little Giant had roared:

> I am aware that all the Abolition lecturers that you will find traveling about through the country are in the habit of proclaiming and reading the Declaration of Independence, to prove that all men were created equal, and endowed by their Creator with certain inalienable rights, among which are life, liberty and the pursuit of happiness. Mr. Lincoln is much in the habit of following in the track of Lovejoy in this particular, by reading that portion of the Declaration of Independence to prove that the negro was endowed by the Almighty with the inalienable right of equality with white men. Now, I state to you, my fellow-citizens, in my opinion, the Signers of the Declaration had no reference whatever to the negro, when they declared all men to have been created equal. The Signers of the Declaration were white men, of European birth and European descent, and had no reference either to the negro or to savage Indians, or the Fejee, or the Malay, or any other inferior or degraded race, when they spoke of the equality of men.[39]

This was from the last debate, but Douglas had repeated some variation on this same theme in all seven. The senator was to be thoroughly repudiated by the slaveholding South in 1860, however, after Lincoln got him to admit that squatter sovereignty could be used to keep slavery out of a territory and not just to bring it in. By 1863, defeated in his run against Lincoln for the presidency because he could not hold the South that had turned on him, Douglas lay a-moldering in his grave like Calhoun, the torch of their doctrines on race and aristocracy passed on to intellectual heirs such as Bishop John Henry Hopkins of Vermont, the birth state of Senator Douglas.

Behind Lincoln's immortal reaffirmation of "all men are created equal" in the opening sentence of his Gettysburg Address are all the great speeches he had given earlier in defense of the same principle. On February 22, 1861, on his way to the White House for his inauguration, Lincoln had offered an eloquent defense in Independence Hall of the Declaration of Independence and its central doctrine of equality:

> I have often pondered over the dangers which were incurred by the men who assembled here and adopted that Declaration of Independence—I have pondered over the toils that were endured by the officers and soldiers of the army, who achieved that Independence. I have often inquired of myself, what great principle or idea it was that kept this Confederacy [the original United States] so long together. It was not the mere matter of the separation of the colonies from the mother land; but something in that Declaration giving liberty, not alone to the people of this country, but hope to the world for all future time. It was that which gave promise that in due time the weights should be lifted from the shoulders of all men, and that *all* should have an equal chance.[40]

Lincoln's finest and fullest explanation of the principle that all men are created equal appeared in his speech in Springfield, Illinois, on June 26, 1857, a sliver of which was quoted earlier:

> Chief Justice Taney, in his opinion in the Dred Scott case, admits that the language of the Declaration is broad enough to include the whole human family, but he and Judge Douglas argue that the authors of that instrument did not intend to include negroes, by the fact that they did not at once, actually place them on an equality with the whites. Now this grave argument comes to just nothing at all, by the other fact, that they did not at once, *or ever afterwards*, actually place all white people on an equality with one or another. And this is the staple argument of both the Chief Justice and the Senator, for doing this obvious violence to the plain unmistakable language of the Declaration. I think the authors of that notable instrument intended to include *all* men, but they did not intend to declare all men equal *in all respects*. They did not mean to say all were equal in color, size, intellect,

moral developments, or social capacity. They defined with tolerable distinctness, in what respects they did consider all men created equal—equal in "certain inalienable rights, among which are life, liberty, and the pursuit of happiness." This they said, and this they meant. They did not mean to assert the obvious untruth, that all were then actually enjoying that equality, nor yet, that they were about to confer it immediately upon them. In fact they had no power to confer such a boon. They meant simply to declare the *right*, so that the *enforcement* of it might follow as fast as circumstances should permit. They meant to set up a standard maxim for free society, which should be familiar to all, and revered by all; constantly looked to, constantly labored for, and even though never perfectly attained, constantly approximated, and thereby constantly spreading and deepening its influence, and augmenting the happiness and value of life to all people of all colors everywhere. The assertion that "all men are created equal" was of no practical use in effecting our separation from Great Britain; and it was placed in the Declaration of Independence, not for that, but for future use. Its authors meant it to be, thank God, it is now proving itself, a stumbling block to those who in after times might seek to turn a free people back into the hateful paths of despotism. They knew the proneness of prosperity to breed tyrants, and they meant when such should re-appear in this fair land and commence their vocation they should find left for them at least one hard nut to crack.[41]

Lincoln thought so well of this, his greatest defense ever of "all men are created equal," that in his final debate with Douglas, he repeated verbatim its last eleven sentences. Yet today all these great speeches are remembered mainly by scholars, while the Gettysburg Address is remembered by everyone. The famous assertion that "all men are created equal" is indeed revered today—if not by all Americans, at least by too many for the heirs of Calhoun in our own day to attack it with impunity. And it is revered because Lincoln in the Gettysburg Address transformed Jefferson's political doctrine into something as familiar and sacred as holy scripture.

Among the leaders of the Confederacy, the one most squarely in the intellectual tradition of Calhoun was Lincoln's former colleague from the U.S. House of Representatives, Alexander H. Stephens of Georgia. Shortly after the election of 1860, the president-elect had an exchange of letters with Stephens, in which he invoked a friendship that he hoped was not dead despite their political differences and despite the cataclysmic events swirling around both men.

Do the people of the South really entertain fears that a Republican administration would, *directly*, or *indirectly*, interfere with their slaves, or with them, about their slaves? If they do, I wish you to assure you, as once a friend, and still, I hope, not an enemy, that there is no cause for such fears.[42]

As always, Lincoln put the truth clearly and honestly to a man who had been a friend and who, Lincoln hoped, would never be an enemy. Without minimizing or overstating the one fundamental difference between the two old friends, he simply stated what it was:

> You think slavery is *right* and ought to be extended; while we think it is *wrong* and ought to be restricted. That I suppose is the rub. It certainly is the only substantial difference between us.[43]

To Lincoln, Stephens and Calhoun were the voices of an enemy he never chose to have and certainly never chose to hate. Nowhere in any of its founding documents did the Confederacy include the doctrine that all men are created equal. Instead, after being elected vice president of the Confederacy, Stephens, sounding exactly like the godfather of all the fire-eaters, Calhoun, announced that the cornerstone of the Confederacy was instead a commitment to *inequality*—a racial inequality that specifically repudiated the teachings of Jefferson. The repudiation was so thorough and so sweeping as to make Lincoln's simple statement of the difference between Stephens and himself sound more generous than the reality. It was "slavery," said Stephens, that formed "the immediate cause of the late rupture and present revolution." But it was not just slavery that Stephens was defending. It was slavery based foursquare on the fundamental principle of racial inequality instituted and perpetuated by God Himself. All those Jeffersonian teachings about equality that were explicit in the Declaration of Independence, Stephens roared, had remained in the minds even of those who made the Constitution, until finally the Constitution and the Union had to be rejected as well. Stephens blamed Jefferson and the other founding fathers:

> The prevailing ideas entertained by [him] and most of the leading statesmen at the time of the formation of the old Constitution were, that the enslavement of the African was in violation of the laws of nature; that it was wrong in principle, socially, morally, and politically. It was an evil they knew not well how to deal with; but the general opinion of the men of that day was, that, somehow or other, in the order of Providence, the institution would be evanescent and pass away. This idea, though not incorporated in the Constitution, was the prevailing idea at the time. The Constitution, it is true, secured every essential guarantee to the institution while it should last, and hence no argument can be justly used against the constitutional guarantees thus secured, because of the common sentiment of the day. Those ideas, however, were fundamentally wrong. They rested upon the assumption of the equality of races. This was an error. It was a sandy foundation, and the idea of a Government built upon it—when the "storm came and the wind blew, it *fell.*"[44]

Like Calhoun, Stephens was raised a Presbyterian, but in Stephens' case, the stern hair-shirt of Dr. Ross's Calvinism was the right fit and fabric for a man who took his daily dose of the Bible straight and stayed a true believer his whole life. In the last sentence above, the Confederate leader echoes one of the parables of Jesus, about the man who built his house on sand, a parable Lincoln had echoed in his "House Divided" speech.

Stephens was much blunter in his advocacy of the principle of inequality than his gentlemanly Episcopal friend Jefferson Davis of Mississippi. In his inaugural address the month before, President Davis, making no mention of slavery or inequality, had anointed the heads of his listeners with a cup overflowing with the blessings of "consent of the governed," "right of the people," "the blessings of liberty," inalienable" rights, "rights of person and property," "courage and patriotism," and even "honor, right, liberty and equality."[45] No such Episcopal oil and honey would flow from the pen of Bible-quoting, inequality-loving Presbyterian Vice President Alexander Stephens of Georgia!

> Our new Government is founded upon exactly the opposite ideas; its foundations are laid, its cornerstone rests, upon the great truth that the negro is not equal to the white man; that slavery, subordination to the superior race, is his natural and moral condition. [Applause.] This, our new Government, is the first, in the history of the world, based upon this great physical, philosophical, and moral truth.[46]

Calhoun himself had never been more explicit about white supremacy as the basis of Southern society than Stephens was in this fiery speech that Lincoln most certainly read. The *anti-slavery* fanatics," Stephens went on, " . . . were attempting to make things equal which the Creator had made unequal." For these reasons, the Confederacy "is the first Government ever instituted upon principles in strict conformity to nature, and the ordination of Providence." Said the stern Calvinist, in explanation of Old Testament condemnation of slavery, "the classes thus enslaved, were of the same race, and in violation of the laws of nature." By contrast, "the negro by nature, or by the curse against Canaan, is fitted for that condition." All of this is "in conformity with the Creator."[47]

One of the strangest twists of history, which continues to twist history even to this day, is that *before* and *during* the Civil War, all the leaders of Southern public opinion insisted that the chief cause of the war was *slavery*. There was no apology for this position, because slavery was regarded as nothing less than God's plan for all mankind. But no sooner did the war end, by which time the institution of slavery had been repudiated by the Emancipation Proclamation, the Thirteenth Amendment, and the public opinion of a majority of the nation, than Southern apologists immediately insisted that slavery had *never* been the cause of either secession or the Civil War. Suddenly, the *true* cause became "states' rights" and all the bunting associated with that doctrine. This shift allowed the postwar Southern apologists to invoke even the formerly detested Jefferson as an ally. To this day, one hears from proponents of a whole range of political persuasions that the Civil War was about states' rights and not about slavery at all except in the most incidental of ways, whereas Lincoln's Second Inaugural clearly stated the conflict as it was perceived by both sides *at the time*:

> One eighth of the whole population were colored slaves, not distributed gener-
> ally over the Union, but localized in the Southern part of it. These slaves constituted
> a peculiar and powerful interest. All knew that this interest was, somehow, the
> cause of the war. To strengthen, perpetuate, and extend this interest was the object
> for which the insurgents would rend the Union, even by war; while the govern-
> ment claimed no right to do more than to restrict the territorial enlargement of it.
> Neither party expected for the war, the magnitude, or the duration, which it has
> already attained. Neither anticipated that the *cause* of the conflict might cease with,
> or even before, the conflict itself should cease. Each looked for an easier triumph,
> and a result less fundamental and astounding.[48]

Lincoln goes on in the Second Inaugural to an uncharacteristic use of the word "just" when he refers to a "just God." In this, he was surely echoing Jefferson's famous statement about slavery, "I tremble for my country when I reflect that God is just."[49] Jefferson and Lincoln saw slavery as the cause of a virtually inevitable war, and so, too, did their political opposites Calhoun and Stephens.

The truth is that during the war, the Presbyterian basso profundo song of inequality was perfectly in harmony with the Episcopal tenor. The *Southern Presbyterian* on December 15, 1860, highlighted the key word in its unequivo-cal declaration: "The real contest now in hand between the North and South, is for the preservation or destruction of *slavery*."[50] Presbyterian minister Thomas Smyth wrote an article in April 1863 that went even further: "The war now carried on by the North is a war against slavery, and is, therefore, treasonable rebellion against the Constitution of the United States, and against the word, providence, and government of God."[51] Immediately after quoting Smyth, Stokes writes in his *Church and State*, "The Right Reverend Leonidas Polk, D.D., Bishop of the Episcopal Church in Louisiana . . . and several other representative Episcopal bishops took nearly the same position. They were supported by virtually every newspaper in the Southern states and by many in the border states."[52]

President Davis had politely avoided the subject of slavery in his inaugural address. But he addressed it unflinchingly in his opening message to the Pro-visional Congress of the Confederate States of America on April 29, 1861. There he trumpeted that slavery was "indispensable" to the economic welfare of the "superior race" in the South.[53] The last and greatest victim of the Civil War was Lincoln himself, assassinated by a Southern spy and passionate lover of the insti-tution of slavery named John Wilkes Booth. Asia Booth Clarke, who was closer to her brother Wilkes than any other person in his life, recalled the moment when Booth's trips to Confederate cities and his mysterious late-night absences finally made the truth clear to her: "I knew now that my hero was a spy, a blockade-runner, a rebel!"[54] Just four months before his assassination of Lincoln, Booth proclaimed that slavery was God's blessing to a favored nation:

> This country was formed for the *white* not for the black man. And looking upon *African slavery* from the same stand-point, held by those noble framers of our Constitution I for one, have ever considered *it*, one of the greatest blessings (both for themselves and us,) that God eve[r] bestowed upon a favored nation.[55]

Clearly it is not just the Bible that has been forgotten today. It is our own national history in the words of those who made it and recorded it *at the time*.

One of the clearest contemporary statements of the root cause of the Civil War came from Frederick Perry Stanton. He and his brother Thomas Henry Stanton of Kentucky both supported slavery when they served together in the U.S. House of Representatives, and both supported their Democratic Party's nominee for president in 1856, James Buchanan. For five consecutive terms, from 1845 to 1855, Stanton represented the Memphis district, which had more slaves than any other in the state, after which he retired undefeated. According to the *Dictionary of American Biography*, "at the height of his congressional career, Buchanan characterized him as persevering, industrious, faithful, and able, credited him with 'practical sense and sound judgment,' and designated him as 'the most promising' young man in the lower house."[56] During his congressional years Stanton voted against freeing slaves in the District of Columbia and against the admission of California as a free state. He even threatened secession unless a compromise satisfactory to the South could be reached—as it was reached—in 1850. It was his experience as acting governor of Kansas, where Stanton came to see that Buchanan was using every device, legal, moral, and otherwise to force slavery onto an unwilling majority, which caused Stanton to question what had always been the orthodoxy of his life and to cast his lot with the Union when the Civil War broke out. In 1861, Stanton moved to Washington to practice law before the Supreme Court. There he became coeditor of the *Continental Monthly* in which Nicolay's poem and "Oh! Let My People Go" were both published in 1862. F. N. Stanton, as he called himself in the eloquent essays he wrote for the *Continental Monthly*, declared in November 1862 that "slavery alone had the power to produce the civil war":

> Slavery alone, with the vast material prosperity apparently created by it, with the debatable and exciting questions, moral, political, and social, which arise out of it, and with the palpable dangers, which, in spite of every effort to deny it, plainly brood over the system—slavery alone had the power to produce the civil war, and to shake the continent to its foundations. In the present crisis of the struggle, it would be a waste of time and of thought to attempt to trace back to its origin the long current of excitement on the slavery question, beginning in 1834, and swell-

ing in magnitude until the present day; or to seek to fix the responsibility for the various events which marked its progress, from the earliest agitation down to the great rebellion, which is evidently the consummation and the end of it all. The only lesson important to be learned, and that which is the sum of all these great events, plainly taught by the history of this generation, and destined to characterize it in all future time, is, that slavery had in itself the germs of this profound agitation, and that, for thirty years, it stirred the moral and political elements of this nation as no other cause had power to do.[57]

Stanton focused on the events of the preceding thirty years for the same reason that Calhoun and so many others focused on them—because those years represented a seismic change in the way the South regarded the institution of slavery. Stanton recalled President Andrew Jackson's suppression of an earlier attempt at the nullification of a tariff law and the secession of Southern states that had been led by Calhoun: "Gen. Jackson, after having crushed the incipient rebellion of 1832, wrote, in a private letter, recently published, that the next attempt to overthrow the Union would be instigated by the same party, but based upon the question of slavery." Stanton contrasted heroic Old Hickory with that "pliant instrument of treason," President Buchanan. Although he himself was a lifelong Southerner except for his brief stay in Kansas, Stanton saw from his own experience that Jackson's prophecy had been correct: "The idea of an independent Southern confederacy, to be constituted of a fragment of the Union, survived the contest of 1832, and has been cherished with zeal and enthusiasm, by a small party of malcontents, from that day to this." How did these malcontents finally succeed by the early 1860s in persuading other Southerners to support secession? They succeeded, said Stanton, by playing upon "State pride," "a strict construction of the Constitution," the tariff issue, and "the doctrine of secession," recognizing all the while that no one of these had the emotional power to create a separate Southern confederacy but that all would be useful supplements when the time came and the flashpan issue of slavery finally drove the South from the Union. For the issue to serve its purpose, "the theory of slavery was carried to an extreme never before known in the history of mankind." To the revolting South in the thirty years before secession,

> Slavery, therefore, was not only justifiable; it was the only possible condition on which free society could be organized, and liberal institutions maintained. This was "the cornerstone" of the new confederacy. The opposite system in the free States, at the first touch of internal trouble and civil war, would prove the truth of the new theory by bread riots and agrarian overthrow of property and of all other institutions held sacred in the true conditions of social order.

This writer who knew the South and its leaders so well, who had himself been one of them for so long, saw that Lincoln's election was but an excuse for the Southern malcontents to do what they had wanted to do for three decades, which was "the reopening of the slave trade" or, failing that, a remarriage with the North on more-favorable terms than before, including a demand "that slavery should be recognized everywhere within the national domain; and that the Federal power should be pledged for its protection, even against the votes of the majority of the people."[58]

But it was not just slavery—it was outright racism, according to Stanton, that made the majority of the South who were *not* slaveholders not only willing but positively and even passionately eager to accept secession, once the election of Lincoln had ignited fears that the slaves would soon be emancipated:

> One of the most effective appeals made to the nonslaveholders of the South, in order to start the revolution, was to their fears and prejudices against the threatened equality and competition of the emancipated negro. The immense influence of this appeal can scarcely be estimated by those not intimately acquainted with the social condition of the great mass of the Southern people.
>
> Among them, the distinction of color is maintained with the utmost rigor, and the barrier between the two races, social and political, is held to be impassable and eternal. The smallest taint of African blood in the veins of any person is esteemed a degradation from which he can never recover. [Stanton might have added that this was why both Lincoln and his vice-presidential running mate Hannibal Hamlin were often accused during the campaign of 1860 of being racially mixed.] Toward the negro, as an inferior, the white man is often affable and kind, cruelty being the exception, universally condemned and often punished; but toward the black man as an equal, an implacable hostility is instantly arrayed. This intense and unconquerable prejudice, it is well known, is not confined to the South; but it prevails there without dissent, and is, in fact, one of the fundamental principles of social organization.[59]

Nor were Stanton's views confined to those Southerners who remained loyal to the Union. Perhaps the clearest statement ever made about the role of race in appealing to the whites of the South who never owned a slave was made by Jefferson Davis in a speech in Aberdeen, Mississippi, on May 26, 1851, as reported in the indirect quotations of the journalistic style of the day. Davis is called "Col. Davis" not as a vague honorific title but because that was his rank when he commanded troops during the Mexican War.

> Col. Davis said that he had heard it said that the poor men, who own no negroes themselves, would all be against the institution, and would, consequently, array themselves on the side of the so called Union men—that the submissionists claimed them. But that he could not believe, that the poor men of the country, were so blind to their own interests, as to be thus cheated out of their privileges, which they now enjoy. That *now they stand upon the broad level of equality with*

the rich man. Equal to him in every thing, save that they did not own as much property; and that, even in this particular, the road to wealth was open to them, and the poor man might attain it; and even if he did not succeed, the failure did not degrade him. That no white man, in a slaveholding community, was the menial servant of anyone. That whenever the poor white man labored for the rich, he did so upon terms of distinction between him and the negro. It was to the interest of the master to keep up a distinction between the white man in his employment, and his negroes. And that this very distinction elevated, and kept the white laborer on a level with the employer; because the distinction between the classes throughout the slaveholding states, is a distinction of color. Between the classes there is no such thing, here, as a distinction of property; and he who thinks there is, and prides himself upon it, is grossly mistaken. Free the negroes, however, and it would soon be here, as it is in the countries of Europe, and in the North, and every where else, where negro slavery does not exist. The poor white man would become a menial for the rich, and be, by him, reduced to an equality with the free blacks, into a degraded position.[60]

In short, the whites who owned no slaves had a powerful motive, said Davis, for resisting the Unionists and the "submissionists" because the presence of blacks lower than themselves in the social scale made them feel equal to the whites above them who employed them. Stanton and Davis agreed that this was the most powerful motive of all among the less-privileged whites. It would continue to be the most powerful motive among this class in the South for a very long time afterward and remains so to this day in certain places.

The claim that the Civil War had never truly been about slavery became part of the Lost Cause narrative that began to sanitize the slaveholding South and demonize the North even before the war was over. Perhaps the earliest version of this claim appeared in the *Richmond Examiner* on August 2, 1864, when the handwriting of Southern defeat—the "Mene, Mene, Tekel"—was already scrolling on the wall. Less than a month later, Sherman would capture Atlanta, ensuring with one great victory the reelection of Abraham Lincoln and the ultimate triumph of the Union army. One of the editors of the *Examiner*, Edward A. Pollard, who had been studying to be an Episcopal priest when the war first broke out, was evidently the first Southerner to use "the Lost Cause" as a phrase, publishing a book with that very title in 1866. This 1864 editorial in the *Richmond Examiner* declared that slavery had been but "one of the minor issues" of the Civil War, while the "whole cause" was instead state sovereignty, or "sovereign independence." Pollard could not have written this editorial because he was captured earlier in 1864 while trying to run a blockade, but the writing clearly reflects his way of thinking. The *Examiner* was angry with Jefferson Davis for having come to this awareness too late:

Mr. Davis, in conversation with a Yankee spy, named Edward Kirk, is reported by said spy to have said, "We are not fighting for slavery; we are fighting for independence." This is true; and it is a truth that has not sufficiently been dwelt upon. It would have been very much to be desired that this functionary had developed the idea in some message, or other State paper . . . instead of having it to be promulgated through the doubtful report of an impudent blockade-runner. . . . The sentiment is true, and should be publicly uttered and kept conspicuously in view; because our enemies have diligently labored to make all mankind believe that the people of these States have set up a pretended State sovereignty and based themselves upon that ostensibly, while their real object has been only to preserve to themselves the property in so many negroes, worth so many millions of dollars. The reverse is the truth. The question of slavery is only one of the minor issues; and the cause of the war, the whole cause, on our part, is the maintenance of the sovereign independence of these States.[61]

Clearly, state sovereignty or "sovereign independence" was the code phrase for a white supremacy expressed through slavery, just as the same white supremacy would later be expressed through state-mandated racial segregation that would rack the South and make the lives of black Southerners miserable for a full century after the Civil War. This editorial fully acknowledges that the view of the war it presents has *not* been the announced public position of the Confederate leadership. It was this new and sanitized version of a Lost Cause—replacing the proud public statements in support of slavery from John C. Calhoun, President Davis, Vice President Stephens, Dr. Ross, and countless other preachers and leaders before and during the war—that would become the official "truth" in the textbooks adopted by most Southern schools for a hundred years or more after the war. Pollard followed *The Lost Cause* with *The Lost Cause Regained* in 1868, in which he championed the necessity for continuing the rule of white supremacy in the postwar South.

The Lost Cause theory of the Civil War consists of two points: first, that the Civil War was not caused by slavery and, second, that Southern slavery was nevertheless a beautiful thing. The Calhoun school had of course taken the opposite position on the first point but completely agreed on the second. The Lost Cause was propagated not just in textbooks but in enormously popular novels and films. The most popular of these were D. W. Griffith's *Birth of a Nation* (1915), the film version of Thomas Dixon's *The Clansman* (1904), and Margaret Mitchell's *Gone with the Wind* (1936 novel, 1939 film release). Pollard wrote in 1865:

The slavery question is not to be taken as an independent controversy in American politics. It was not a moral dispute. It was the mere incident of a sectional animosity, the causes of which furnished a convenient line of battle between the disputants; it was the most prominent ground of distinction between the two sections. it was, therefore, naturally seized upon as a subject of controversy, became the dominant theatre of hostilities, and was at last so conspicuous and violent that occasion was mistaken for cause, and what was merely an incident came to be regarded as the main cause of the conflict.[62]

"For, we repeat," Pollard continued at a later point in the same book, "the slavery question was not a moral one in the North, unless, perhaps, with a few thousand persons of disordered conscience." Pollard even doubted whether the term "slavery" could be "properly applied to that system of servitude in the South which was really the mildest in the world." Insisting that slavery was not the cause of the war, Pollard nevertheless felt compelled to defend it: "Slavery established in the South a peculiar and noble type of civilization," producing "notions of chivalry," "many noble and generous virtues," "extraordinary culture," and "elevated . . . standards of scholarship." Nowhere is Pollard's ambivalence clearer than in his account of "the tragical death of President Lincoln, in a public theatre, at the hands of one of the most indefensible but courageous assassins that history has ever produced." Pollard's sympathy clearly does not lie with Lincoln, a man he has already described as having brought to the White House "the buffoonery and habits of a demagogue of the back-woods," a man "destitute of the higher order of sensibilities."[63] Lincoln's assassination was "tragical," but at the same time, his "indefensible" assassin was "courageous." It is impossible to resist seeing Booth here as the surrogate of the courageous South, indefensible in certain ways but unfailingly courageous during the Reconstruction when Pollard was writing his passionate and polemical account. Only later would the Lost Cause as represented in Griffith's *Birth of a Nation* substitute for Pollard's antipathy and ambivalence a President Lincoln who is so dear a friend to the seceded Southern states that he is made to say about their return to the Union, "I shall deal with them as though they had never been away." The true cause of the Civil War, Pollard insisted, was sectionalism and the trampling by the North on the South's states' rights. Thus, in the Lost Cause narrative, the South becomes the victim, never the aggressor or provocateur. Pollard's mantra that slavery did *not* cause the war is now repeated by people across the political spectrum. Thus a war that both sides insisted *at the time* was fought over slavery has become, to many in our own day, a war caused only by politely differing philosophies of government.

Note that Confederate Vice President Stephens's Presbyterianism, which had stood for the *equality* of man during the English Civil War, stood for the *inequality* of man during the American Civil War. It was black slavery that led the Old South's Calvinists to join the Episcopal Cavaliers. Even so, many of the old distinctions between Episcopalians and Presbyterians still survived. There were differences of class between President Davis and Presbyterian Vice President Stephens, just as there were between General-in-Chief Robert E. Lee and Presbyterian Lieutenant General Nathan Bedford Forrest. One of the things that made Calhoun such a powerful force was that he combined within one voice the essence of those two powerful religious groups and what they stood for. The fact that Calhoun had grown up in the Presbyterian Church but never joined it and then attended the Episcopal Church but never joined it either seems a perfect reflection of the ambivalent nature of the man who provided the gospel that justified nullification and secession while insisting that he himself was a unionist. Pollard in *The Lost Cause* has a hard time giving full faith and credit to Calhoun's insistence: "Mr. Calhoun professed, and perhaps not insincerely, an ardent love for the Union."[64] Calhoun had professed his union credentials as early as 1831:

> Nearly half my life has been passed in the service of the Union, and whatever public reputation I have acquired is indissolubly identified with it. To be too national has, indeed, been considered by many, even of my friends, to be my greatest political fault.[65]

Yet one of Calhoun's last letters to his beloved daughter Anna Maria, written on December 31, 1849, declared:

> The South is more roused and united than I ever knew it to be; and I trust that we shall persist in our resistance until the restoration of all our rights, or disunion, one or the other, is the consequence. We have borne the wrongs and the insults of the North long enough. It is time they should cease.[66]

No matter what his true feelings about the Union may have been, Calhoun certainly helped to induce men representing all the religious faiths of the South to forsake their country and set up a new one based proudly and unflinchingly on the idea of inequality.

By reminding all Americans with his Gettysburg Address—including those Rebels and Copperheads who were listening—that this nation was founded on and "dedicated to" the "proposition that all men are created equal," Lincoln accurately identified the core issue that separated North and South. Those Southern spokesmen who learned of his speech might have been reminded of their own admissions that at the time of the Declaration of Independence and for many years after it, most Southerners had been as morally opposed to slavery as most Northerners had been. There had been in this nation a consensus that all men were created equal and that slavery was wrong. Lincoln was once again reminding everyone who would listen of this historical reality. With his allusions to the Bible, Lincoln was using a language shared with the enemy to refute the enemy. Jesus often told his audiences, "He that hath ears to hear, let him hear" (Mark 4:9, Luke 8:8). In Lincoln's audience at Gettysburg and in the larger audience that included the Confederate leadership, virtually everyone had ears for the King James Bible. But the president's echoes of the Prayer Book would have been heard

by a much smaller group of ears that would have included the top Episcopal leaders in the South and their aiders and abettors in the North, particularly Bishop
Hopkins. Lincoln used the language of the Bible to out-herod Herod, to answer
the Bible-quoting preachers like Dr. Ross and the Bible-quoting politicians like
Vice President Stephens. In a far more subtle way, Lincoln used the language of
the Prayer Book to answer John C. Calhoun, Leonidas Polk, and John Henry
Hopkins. Lincoln could not help knowing that he was echoing a Prayer Book
better known and more beloved by his enemies than his friends, especially when
the line was drawn in the overheated sand of the proposition that "all men are
created equal." But Lincoln also recognized that even though Northerners and
Southerners squabbled about the meanings of both the Bible and the Prayer
Book, he could use these ancient and revered works to bring people together in
support of principles of freedom and equality and perhaps, over time, to turn
enemies into friends again—perhaps even to return the South to where it had
first stood on slavery before turning its back on the sacred principles of the
Declaration of Independence and dancing straight into that national disaster
called the Civil War.

Epilogue: Catechism and Conclusion

The justification of slavery as God's glorious plan for an inherently unequal mankind spoke with both a Presbyterian and an Episcopal voice. Its Presbyterian champions included the Reverend Dr. Ross of Alabama and the Honorable Alexander Stephens of Georgia, vice president of the Confederacy. But because the Confederate leadership was so overwhelmingly Episcopalian from President Davis to commanding General Lee to Bishop/General Polk and on down the hierarchy and because this leadership had powerful colleagues in the North such as Bishop John Henry Hopkins, its language in defense of slavery and other Southern positions typically reflected the Book of Common Prayer. One hears that language in a satirical article entitled "The Lincoln Catechism," which appeared on May 22, 1863, in the *Southern Illustrated News* of Richmond, a weekly journal modeled after *Harper's* magazine. This article appeared just six weeks before the Fourth of July that was to prove so disastrous a day for Confederate arms at the battles of Vicksburg and Gettysburg. According to Herbert Mitgang in *Lincoln as They Saw Him*, a book about newspaper coverage of Lincoln, "This 'Lincoln Catechism' was widely reprinted throughout the South."[1] We may be sure that all this reprinting happened because Southern editors were confident that their readers—certainly their richest and most influential readers—would understand the metaphor of the catechism. Catholic catechisms date back to Saint Augustine, and Luther and Calvin had composed catechisms for their followers. But in the South, "catechism" in a major newspaper or magazine clearly meant what it meant to Shakespeare when he has Falstaff parody it in *Henry IV—the* catechism from the Book of Common Prayer.

"The Lincoln Catechism" is too polemical to be humorous and too bitter to be persuasive. It was obviously designed to elicit a hard grin or a grimace, depending on whether the reader's visceral response was approval or antipathy. We do not know whether Lincoln ever saw it at all. All we know is that the president, according to John Hay's diary, liked to read the "Rebel papers."[2] In any event, this article is a perfect illustration of two things about the South that he always understood. First, the Southern leadership was dominated by Episcopalians who venerated the words of the Prayer Book. Second, the basic political assumptions of the South derived from the United States Constitution and not from the Declaration of Independence. Indeed, the differences between the two political documents formed a kind of litmus test that always separated Lincoln from his political enemies everywhere who called themselves conservatives—the word was as popular then as now—and called him every name but. In both North and South, conservatives either rejected out of hand (as in the case of Calhoun) or severely limited (as in the case of Douglas) the liberal Jeffersonian principles of the Declaration of Independence and focused instead and exclusively on the Constitution. Before the Civil War and before the Thirteenth and Fourteenth amendments, the Constitution had been used in the Dred Scott decision to declare that slaves, far from being created equal, had no rights as human beings at all and were, legally speaking, mere property or chattel. Because of its implicit approval of slavery, the Constitution was as despised by many of the abolitionists as it was revered by the slaveholders. Thus Frederick Douglass wrote of William Lloyd Garrison's American Anti-Slavery Society, "They affirm the Constitution of the United States to be pro-Slavery in its character, and therefore denounce it."[3]

Bishop Hopkins forms a perfect example of the conservative position once he had abandoned his early admiration for the Declaration of Independence and had published in 1857 a book called *The American Citizen: His Rights and Duties, According to the Spirit of the Constitution of the United States*. In this, the bishop argues that religion—the Christian religion, of course—is required by the Constitution, that men are inherently superior to women in intellect and thus in civil rights and duties, and that slavery, approved by the Constitution and a blessing to the slaves, has nevertheless become so contentious that gradual, voluntary, compensated emancipation and colonization may now be the most practical answer.[4] Only four years later, in 1861, he would change gears once again in his *Bible View of Slavery*, arguing that both the immediate and the ultimate fate of Bible-approved, Constitution-approved slavery should be left entirely to the discretion of the Southern states and their slave owners. Bishop Polk had followed a similar path in his increasingly conservative views. Between the War of 1812 and the end of the Civil War, Southern politicians and newspapers, as well as their Northern supporters, referred to the Declaration of Independence only to revile or refute it. For them the key document—the *only* document from the formative years of this nation that mattered in the least—was the slave-condoning Constitution.

"The Lincoln Catechism," reprinted below, defines "traitor" satirically as "One who is a stickler for the Constitution and laws," while saying nothing anywhere, not a single word, about the Declaration of Independence. In short, this article glorifies the two documents most venerated by Southern slaveholders and their sympathizers North and South—the Prayer Book and the Constitution—while ignoring those most venerated by liberals North and South—the King James Bible and the Declaration of Independence. Those today who call Lincoln a racist would do well to read the documents of his day written by his political enemies and polar opposites, men like Calhoun, Ross, Hopkins, Polk, and the authors of this piece of political sarcasm that is so defiantly and unapologetically grounded in *real* racism, the kind that glorified slavery and despised every man who opposed it.

THE LINCOLN CATECHISM

Question. What is the Constitution?

Answer. A league with hell—now obsolete.

Q. What is the Government?

A. Abraham Lincoln, Charles Sumner and Owen Lovejoy.

Q. What is the President?

A. A general agent for negroes.

Q. What is Congress?

A. A body organized for the purpose of appropriating funds to buy Africans, and to make laws to protect the President from being punished for any violations of law he may be guilty of.

Q. What is an army?

A. A provost guard to arrest white men and set negroes free.

Q. Whom are members of Congress supposed to represent?

A. The President and his Cabinet.

Q. What is understood by coining money?

A. Printing green paper.

Q. What does the Constitution mean by "freedom of the press?"

A. The suppression of Conservative newspapers.

Q. What is the meaning of the word "liberty?"

A. Incarceration in a bastile.

Q. What is a Secretary of War?

A. A man who arrests people by telegraph.

Q. What are the duties of a Secretary of the Navy?

A. To build and sink gunboats.

Q. What is the business of a Secretary of the Treasury?

A. To destroy State Banks, and fill the pockets of the people with irredeemable U.S. shinplasters.

Q. What is the meaning of the word "patriot?"

A. A man who loves his country less and the negro more.

Q. What is the meaning of the word "traitor?"

A. One who is a stickler for the Constitution and laws.

Q. What are the particular duties of a Commander-in-Chief?

A. To disgrace any General who does not believe that the negro is better than a white man.

Q. What is the meaning of the word "law?"
A. The will of the President.
Q. How were the States formed?
A. By the United States.
Q. Is the United States Government older than the States which made it?
A. It is.
Q. Have the States any rights?
A. None whatever, except what the General Government bestows.
Q. Have the people any rights?
A. None, except what the President gives.
Q. What is the *habeas corpus*?
A. It is the power of the President to imprison whom he pleases.
Q. Who is the greatest martyr of history?
A. John Brown.
Q. Who is the wisest man?
A. Abraham Lincoln.
Q. Who is Jeff Davis?
A. The Devil.[5]

This article takes for granted all of the Confederate dogmas dating back to Calhoun—in particular, that the United States was formed by the Constitution instead of the Declaration of Independence, that the sovereignty of the individual states is anterior to and superior to the sovereignty of the United States, and that there is absolutely nothing wrong with slavery and white supremacy except what might have been inflicted by attacks from abolitionists and egalitarians such as Lincoln, Charles Sumner, Elijah Lovejoy, and John Brown.

If Lincoln saw this piece, he was probably more amused than offended. Lincoln often found humor where others, including his own cabinet on many occasions, found none. To his mind, the conflict was never between North and South but between those who believed in human equality and those who did not. He refused to say, even when specifically asked, that God was on the Northern side and not the Southern. He was born in the South, and he was married to a Southern woman. At the price of much criticism, he gave safe passage and comfort to his wife's Southern sister Emilie and niece Katherine in the White House after they had lost husband and father fighting for the Confederacy at Chickamauga. This was General (and Episcopalian) Ben Hardin Helm—a young man Lincoln had loved like a son and to whom he had offered a high-ranking commission in the Union army at the outbreak of the war. Lincoln's three greatest political heroes were all Southerners—George Washington, Thomas Jefferson, and Henry Clay. He had a genuine respect for many of his political enemies from the South, including Calhoun and Stephens. It was principle that mattered to Lincoln, not partisanship or sectionalism of any kind.

Mark Twain, who like Lincoln was born in a border state—Missouri—and from early years held untypically progressive views on race, wrote late in his own life that it was Lincoln's Kentucky roots that prepared the president for his greatest achievements. Walt Whitman had already emphasized Lincoln's Southernness in an introduction written in 1890 to a lecture he had delivered for many years on the anniversary of Lincoln's death: "Have you ever realized it, my friends, that Lincoln, though grafted on the West, is essentially in . . . character a Southern contribution?"[6] But it was Twain who focused on the significance of Lincoln's birth and upbringing in the *border* South.

> [I]t was no accident that planted Lincoln on a Kentucky farm, half way between the lakes and the Gulf. The association there had substance in it. Lincoln belonged just where he was put. If the Union was to be saved, it had to be a man of such an origin that should save it. No wintry New England Brahmin could have done it, or any torrid cotton planter, regarding the distant Yankee as a species of obnoxious foreigner. It needed a man of the border, where civil war meant the grapple of brother and brother and disunion a raw and gaping wound. It needed one who knew slavery not from books only, but as a living thing, knew the good that was mixed with its evil, and knew the evil not merely as it affected the negroes, but in its hardly less baneful influence upon the poor whites. It needed one who knew how human all the parties to the quarrel were, how much alike they were at bottom, who saw them all reflected in himself, and felt their dissensions like the tearing apart of his own soul. When the war came Georgia sent an army in gray and Massachusetts an army in blue, but Kentucky raised armies for both sides. And this man, sprung from Southern poor whites, born on a Kentucky farm and transplanted to an Illinois village, this man, in whose heart knowledge and charity had left no room for malice, was marked by Providence as the one to "bind up the Nation's wounds."[7]

If ever there was a man who had malice toward none, it was Abraham Lincoln. Was it not the subtlest form of irony for Lincoln to have echoed in the Gettysburg Address not just Locke and Jefferson and Theodore Parker with whom he agreed but also the Honorable John Caldwell Calhoun, Dr. Frederick Ross, and the Very Reverend John Henry Hopkins with whom he disagreed? No man ever lived who was better at offering peace to his enemies by embracing their words. Had he lived longer, his genius and his mercy would surely have reconstructed his country as brilliantly as he had held it together during the darkest hours of its civil war, ending with what surely would have been a more perfect union. He would have "won" reconstruction as brilliantly as he won the war, by producing the greatest and most enduring good for all. With the most audible and accessible part of his voice in the Gettysburg Address, Lincoln reminded everyone of our common heritage, as in his crystal-clear allusions to the Declaration of

Independence and the King James Bible. But more softly, more subtly, and in the same breath, he was quietly addressing those who, favoring the Prayer Book and the Constitution, had wandered from the fold.

And for this, he was rewarded with unrelenting hatred from both Confederates and Copperheads. It was the conservative preference for the Constitution over the Declaration of Independence that lay at the very heart of the objections to Lincoln's Gettysburg Address by the Copperhead *Chicago Times* on November 23, 1863. Piously pretending to speak for the Union soldiers, the *Times* accused the president of "a misstatement of the cause for which they died" and "a perversion of history." After quoting Lincoln's opening lines and then certain clauses from the Constitution that implicitly recognized slavery by distinguishing "free" from "other" persons and by providing for the return of any "other" who shall escape from the slavery that is never called by its own name, the *Times* triumphantly raised the rhetorical question, "Do these provisions in the constitution dedicate the nation to 'the proposition that all men are created equal'?"

> Mr. Lincoln occupies his present position by virtue of this constitution, and is sworn to the maintenance and enforcement of these provisions. It was to uphold this constitution, and the Union created by it, that our officers and soldiers gave their lives at Gettysburg. How dared he, then, standing on their graves, misstate the cause for which they died, and libel the statesmen who founded the government? They were men possessing too much self-respect to declare that negroes were their equals, or were entitled to equal privileges.[8]

Lincoln held that our fundamental and formative document was the Declaration of Independence and that it makes all of us—men and women, what Lincoln himself called "people of all colors"—equal, one and all. We celebrate its adoption on Independence Day, not the adoption of the Constitution, and we would still be the United States of America if we repealed the entire United States Constitution tomorrow. The Declaration of Independence was written to create a nation and to state eternal principles that would never be repealed. The Constitution was created from the first only to "form a more perfect union." It was designed to be capable of everlasting change by amendment. It was in fact amended under Lincoln's leadership to outlaw slavery by means of the Thirteenth Amendment. During what would have been his second term had an assassin not vetoed by violence and murder the will of the American people, the Fourteenth Amendment was added. This became the greatest protector of individual liberty in the nation precisely because it extended as against the state governments the protections of "due process" and "equal protection" that individuals already enjoyed as against the federal government. Jefferson had advocated states' rights as a check on the federal government, that element of the government he believed most likely to abuse individual rights and liberties. But it was the states who had turned out to be the great thieves and abusers of freedom and equality while the federal government had proven in most cases the protector of both as against the states, a situation that would continue for a hundred years after the Civil War. Because of Lincoln and the reverence that most Americans hold for the Gettysburg Address, the proposition that "all men are created equal" is at least no longer despised and rejected and is now seen by most Americans as in no way inconsistent with the federal Constitution. More than any other document, including the Declaration of Independence itself, Lincoln's immortal address has persuaded millions of Americans that indeed "all men are created equal."

Lincoln changed our national dialogue by defending and reaffirming original principles that have led to astonishing changes over time. Today, at the same University of the South first conceived by Bishop Leonidas Polk as a university where white Episcopal Southern males would be freed from the taint of a liberal Northern education, a university brought forth in the form of spectacular mountaintop views and magnificent Gothic buildings laid out by his dear friend the amateur architect Bishop Hopkins, young men and women of all colors, from all corners of the earth, learn together and worship together, free and equal in exactly the sense that Jefferson and Lincoln always intended, in their inalienable right to life, liberty, and the pursuit of happiness. The Prayer Book is recited in All Saints' Chapel every day of the week, beneath stained-glass windows that honor not only Jesus Christ but also Bishop Polk and Bishop Hopkins. It is most unlikely that anyone praying in that serene chapel today would find any reason to remember that this Prayer Book once stood as a mighty and terrible sword brazenly defending what Bishop Stephen Elliot of Georgia, also honored in one of Sewanee's stained-glass windows, described at Polk's funeral in Augusta as the "sacred trust" of Southern slavery.[9]

Men are never so violent as when defending a cause they know in their hearts is wrong. The difference between the anger, contempt, and condescension of the slavery-defenders Calhoun, Hopkins, Polk, and Elliot and the toleration and forgiveness of Lincoln appears time and again in the president's never-failing predisposition not just to *forgive* his enemies but to give *to* them. This is perfectly illustrated by Lincoln's last public reference to John C. Calhoun in a letter to Secretary of War Edwin M. Stanton of October 9, 1863, just over a month before he delivered the Gettysburg Address:

> Sir—Mrs. Thomas G. Clemsin is a daughter of the late Hon. John C. Calhoun, and is now residing near Bladensburg in Maryland.
>
> She understands that her son, Calhoun Clemsin, is now a prisoner of War to us at "Johnson's Island["]; and she asks the previlege merely of visiting him. With your approbation, I consent for her to go.
> Yours truly   A. Lincoln[10]

Anna Maria Clemson was the brightest of Calhoun's children and the one to whom he was closest. Indeed, he was closer to her than to anyone else in his whole life, often sharing with her his latest political thoughts and inspirations. Calhoun biographer John Niven writes, "Of all his children, she remained his favorite and in later years became his confidante." She was just fifteen when he wrote to her in 1832: "I am not one of those, who think your sex ought to have nothing to do with politicks."[11] Yet his reactionary bias immediately reined in his liberal impulse: "[Your sex] have as much interest in the good condition of their country, as the other sex, and tho' it would be unbecoming them to take an active part in political struggles, their opinion, when enlightened, cannot fail to have a great and salutary effect."[12] "Unbecoming" flows straight from Calhoun's right-wing belief that women have their place—a protected place on a moral pedestal but, in terms of all political rights and privileges, a place eternally subordinate to males. It is part of his larger right-wing philosophy that society must remain hierarchical throughout. Unlike Lincoln, Calhoun in all of his voluminous writings never once suggested that the suffrage should ever be extended to women. It boded ill for Calhoun's daughter that Secretary of War Stanton breathed as much fire for his causes as former Secretary of War Calhoun ever breathed for his, and it was no surprise that she approached Lincoln instead of Stanton. There can be little doubt that without the president's help, Mrs. Clemson would never have visited her son in prison. Thus did Lincoln repay with kindness the greatest intellectual enemy of his entire political career. Does anyone doubt that Lincoln would have done the same thing for the families of Bishop Polk or Bishop Hopkins or Vice President of the Confederacy Alexander Stephens or any other political enemy? In every imaginable way, Lincoln treated his enemies as friends. In doing so, he turned again and again the swords of the past into the plowshares of the future.

Not one person in a thousand today knows the words of John C. Calhoun and not one in ten thousand the words of Dr. Ross or Bishop Hopkins. When Polk is remembered at all, it is usually in connection with the University of the South that has turned out to be the very opposite of what he intended once it opened the doors of its classrooms to the very ideas and the very students he most desired to keep out. When the name of John Henry Hopkins is remembered, it is most often in connection with the Christmas carol for which his son and namesake wrote the words and the music, called "We Three Kings of Orient Are," first performed at Union Theological Seminary in 1857 and first published in 1863. This carol is often credited simply to John Henry Hopkins, with no "Jr." after the name, no doubt making others believe, as I did for a time, that the Bishop was its author. The son who in fact wrote the carol also wrote the biography of his father that was quoted earlier. This biography reveals countless ways in which the son was a direct heir to the strengths and sins of his father. Hopkins Jr., also an Episcopal priest, could just as easily have opened his carol with "We Wise Men of Orient are," since the Bible account of Matthew 2:1 mentions neither number nor kingship and refers only to "wise men from the east" who are bringing gifts to the baby Jesus and worshipping him as if *he* were a king, not they. Like his father, the younger Hopkins chose instead to affirm hierarchy and aristocracy by accepting a nonbiblical tradition of three kings. Once again, we find an Episcopal priest from the Hopkins family favoring the proposition, not that all men are created equal but that *some* men are created with the God-given right to rule others, whether as kings or as slaveholders. Ironically, whether the father or the son knew it or not, it is an old tradition dating to Saint Bede the Venerable, who lived in the late 600s and early 700s that the three Magi "represented the continents of Europe, Asia, and Africa."[13] If so, then one of the wise men was black. Indeed, in Jan Gossart's sixteenth-century painting *Adoration of the Magi*, one of them *is* black. Just when this third king became known as King Balthazar of Ethiopia remains uncertain.

What an odd and revealing fact that one of Calhoun's words echoed by Ross and Hopkins and later by Lincoln himself—the "proposition" that all men are created equal—lives on in the most famous speech ever written by anyone! It is a quiet immortality, to be sure, and perhaps not what Calhoun imagined when he first substituted his own word for that "self-evident truth" of Thomas Jefferson that Calhoun so despised. But there it is, and there it will remain for all time. Also there in the same quiet way are so many of the words from the Book of Common Prayer that Senator Calhoun and Bishop Hopkins and Bishop Polk recited in the churches of their day—a Prayer Book that had unabashedly served the principle of inequality but at Gettysburg was transformed into the sacred service of "the proposition that all men are created equal."

The principles immortalized in the Declaration of Independence were openly reviled by defenders of slavery between the War of 1812 and the end of the Civil War. The Gettysburg Address reaffirmed the great principles of the American Revolution that were, as Lincoln always hoped they would be, revitalized and reborn in the American Civil War—especially at Gettysburg, where the tide of the war turned and where the most famous and enduring words in American history were imprinted forever on the consciousness of America. At Gettysburg, Abraham Lincoln framed the sacred principles of the Declaration of Independence in the immortal words of the King James Bible. But Lincoln also invoked the ritualized beauty of the Book of Common Prayer. On November 19, 1863, the Prayer Book that is even older than the King James Bible ended its long reign as the queen of inequality and became instead part of the self-evident truth—the Euclidean proposition—that all men are created equal, with no one born to rule, no one born to serve, all born the children of God, all endowed by their Creator with certain inalienable rights. Can anyone imagine now, with the immortal words of Abraham Lincoln ringing forever in our ears, that this nation will ever question or abandon those sacred principles again?

APPENDIX
NOTES
WORKS CITED
INDEX

Appendix: Four Versions of the Gettysburg Address

On the following two facing pages and two to a page, four versions of Abraham Lincoln's Gettysburg Address are given for comparison. The so-called Final Text or Bliss Copy that is almost always used today whenever the Gettysburg Address is printed or spoken is identical with the text sent to George Bancroft except for one change. The Bancroft text had been handwritten on the two sides of the same sheet of paper. When Lincoln was asked on March 4, 1864, to recopy the text onto two separate sheets, he omitted the "here" that appears before "gave" in the final sentence.

LINCOLN'S DELIVERY TEXT

(as written down by Joseph Ignatius Gilbert of the Associated Press
from the written speech and just after the president had read it)

Four score and seven years ago our fathers brought forth upon this continent a new nation, conceived in liberty and dedicated to the proposition that all men are created equal. Now we are engaged in a great civil war, testing whether that nation, or any nation so conceived and so dedicated, can long endure. We are met on a great battle-field of that war. We are met to dedicate a portion of it as the final resting-place of those who here gave their lives that that nation might live. It is altogether fitting and proper that we should do this. But, in a larger sense, we cannot dedicate, we cannot consecrate, we cannot hallow this ground. The brave men, living and dead, who struggled here have consecrated it far above our poor power to add or detract. The world will little note nor long remember what we say here; but it can never forget what they did here. It is for us, the living, rather to be dedicated here to the unfinished work that they have thus far so nobly carried on. It is rather for us to be here dedicated to the great task remaining before us; that from these honored dead we take increased devotion to that cause for which they here gave the last full measure of devotion; that we here highly resolve that these dead shall not have died in vain; that the nation shall, under God, have a new birth of freedom; and that Governments of the people, by the people, and for the people, shall not perish from the earth.

LINCOLN'S SPOKEN ADDRESS

(as taken down in shorthand and transcribed by Charles Everett Hale)

Fourscore and seven years ago, our fathers brought forth upon this continent a new nation, conceived in liberty and dedicated to the proposition that all men are created equal.

Now we are engaged in a great civil war, testing whether that nation—or any nation, so conceived and so dedicated—can long endure.

We are met on a great battle-field of that war. We are met to dedicate a portion of it as the final resting-place of those who have given their lives that that nation might live.

It is altogether fitting and proper that we should do this.

But, in a larger sense, we cannot dedicate, we cannot consecrate, we cannot hallow, this ground. The brave men, living and dead, who struggled here, have consecrated it, far above our power to add or to detract.

The world will very little note nor long remember what we say here; but it can never forget what they did here.

It is for us, the living, rather, to be *dedicated*, here, to the unfinished work that they have thus far so nobly carried on. It is rather for us to be here dedicated to the great task remaining before us; that from these honored dead we take increased devotion to that cause for which they here gave the last full measure of devotion; that we here highly resolve that these dead shall not have died in vain; that the nation shall, under God, have a new birth of freedom, and that government of the people, by the people, for the people, shall not perish from the earth.

LINCOLN'S TEXT REVISED AND SENT TO
EDWARD EVERETT ON FEBRUARY 4, 1864

Four score and seven years ago our fathers brought forth upon this continent, a new nation, conceived in Liberty, and dedicated to the proposition that all men are created equal.

Now we are engaged in a great civil war, testing whether that nation, or any nation so conceived, and so dedicated, can long endure. We are met on a great battle-field of that war. We have come to dedicate a portion of that field, as a final resting place for those who here gave their lives, that that nation might live. It is altogether fitting and proper that we should do this.

But, in a larger sense, we can not dedicate—we can not consecrate—we can not hallow—this ground. The brave men, living and dead, who struggled here, have consecrated it, far above our poor power to add or detract. The world will little note, nor long remember, what we say here, but it can never forget what they did here. It is for us, the living, rather, to be dedicated here to the unfinished work which they who fought here, have, thus far, so nobly advanced. It is rather for us to be here dedicated to the great task remaining before us—that from these honored dead we take increased devotion to that cause for which they here gave the last full measure of devotion—that we were highly resolve that these dead shall not have died in vain—that this nation, under God, shall have a new birth of freedom—and that, government of the people, by the people, for the people, shall not perish from the earth.

LINCOLN'S TEXT REVISED AND SENT TO GEORGE
BANCROFT ON FEBRUARY 29, 1864

Four score and seven years ago our fathers brought forth, on this continent, a new nation, conceived in Liberty, and dedicated to the proposition that all men are created equal.

Now we are engaged in a great civil war, testing whether that nation, or any nation so conceived, and so dedicated, can long endure. We are met on a great battle-field of that war. We have come to dedicate a portion of that field, as a final resting-place for those who here gave their lives, that that nation might live. It is altogether fitting and proper that we should do this.

But, in a larger sense, we can not dedicate—we can not consecrate—we can not hallow—this ground. The brave men, living and dead, who struggled here, have consecrated it far above our poor power to add or detract. The world will little note, nor long remember what we say here, but it can never forget what they did here. It is for us the living, rather, to be dedicated here to the unfinished work which they who fought here have thus far so nobly advanced. It is rather for us to be here dedicated to the great task remaining before us—that from these honored dead we take increased devotion to that cause for which they here gave the last full measure of devotion—that we here highly resolve that these dead shall not have died in vain—that this nation, under God, shall have a new birth of freedom—and that government of the people, by the people, for the people, shall not perish from the earth.

Notes

ABBREVIATIONS

CW *The Collected Works of Abraham Lincoln*. Edited by Roy P. Basler. 9 vols. New Brunswick, NJ: Rutgers University Press, 1953–55.

RW *Recollected Words of Abraham Lincoln*. Compiled and edited by Don E. Fehrenbacher and Virginia Fehrenbacher. Stanford, CA: Stanford University Press, 1996.

PROLOGUE: ANOTHER TIME, ANOTHER PLACE

1. Daniel Webster, *The Great Orations and Senatorial Speech of Daniel Webster* (Rochester, NY: Hayward, 1853), 11.

2. Hardin Craig, ed., introduction, *The Complete Works of Shakespeare* (Glenview, IL: Scott, Foresman, 1961), 43.

3. Kenyon Cox, *The Classic Point of View: Six Lectures on Painting* (1911; Freeport, NY: Books for Libraries Press, 1968), 3–4.

4. William Herndon, *Herndon's Life of Lincoln*, ed. Paul M. Angle (New York: Da Capo, 1942, 1983), 292–93.

5. Theodore Parker, "A Sermon of the Dangers Which Threaten the Rights of Man in America," *The Collected Works of Theodore Parker*, ed. Frances Power Cobbe (London: Trubner, 1864), 6:132.

6. Ibid., 6:133, 6:132–33 (the same phrase appears in almost identical words on 6:117); 6:132, 6:154, 6:134.

7. Abraham Lincoln, *The Collected Works of Abraham Lincoln*, ed. Roy P. Basler, 9 vols. (New Brunswick, NJ: Rutgers University Press, 1953), 2:465–66. Hereafter cited as "*CW*."

8. *CW*, 4:464.

9. Ibid.

10. Parker, *Collected Works of Theodore Parker*, 6:156.

11. Ibid., 6:138.

12. Ibid.

13. *CW*, 2:461.

14. Mark M. Smith, "The Touch of an Uncommon Man," *Chronicle Review* 54:24, February 22, 2008, B8.

15. Jefferson Davis, *Jefferson Davis: The Essential Writings*, edited by William J. Cooper Jr. (New York: Modern Library by Random House, 2003), 69; "sacred," 197, 209, 218, 364; "just," 315, 348; "holy," 229, 323, 348; Savannah speech, 348, 346.

1. THE FORGOTTEN BIBLE

1. John Russell Young, *Men and Memories: Personal Reminiscences* (New York: Neely, 1901), xiii.

2. George M. Marsden, "Everyone One's Own Interpreter? The Bible, Science, and Authority in Mid-Nineteenth-Century America," in Nathan O. Hatch and Mark A. Noll,

NOTES TO PAGES 11–16

eds., *Bible in America: Essays in Cultural History* (New York: Oxford University Press, 1982), 79.

3. Thomas Babington Macaulay, "John Dryden," *Edinburgh Review* 47 (January 1828): 250.

4. *CW*, 7:542.

5. Gabor Boritt, *The Gettysburg Gospel: The Lincoln Speech That Nobody Knows* (New York: Simon & Schuster, 2006), 138, 139.

6. Ralph Waldo Emerson, "Abraham Lincoln: Remarks at the Funeral Services Held at Concord, April 19, 1863," in *Miscellanies* (Boston: Houghton Mifflin, 1884), 311.

7. Boritt, *Gettysburg Gospel* 138.

8. William E. Barton, *Lincoln at Gettysburg: What He Intended to Say; What He Said; What He Was Reported to Have Said; What He Wished He Had Said* (Indianapolis, IN: Bobbs-Merrill, 1930), 141.

9. Bruce Barton, introduction, in William E. Barton, *The Autobiography of William E. Barton* (Indianapolis, IN: Bobbs-Merrill, 1932), xv.

10. Ibid., xiv.

11. W. E. Barton, *Autobiography*, 230, 270.

12. Ibid., 273.

13. William E. Barton, *The Soul of Abraham Lincoln* (New York: Doran, ca. 1920), 47.

14. Even in a book he published in 1928 called *Abraham Lincoln and Walt Whitman* (Indianapolis, IN: Bobbs-Merrill, 1928) in which he quotes poems, letters, diary entries, and essays by the poet, Barton never once undertakes the slightest literary analysis of any of them. His entire focus is on historical issues, as when he carefully dissects and eventually debunks a letter written to Whitman purporting to show that the writer had identified Whitman to Lincoln and that Lincoln had answered with a favorable comment. 96–105.

15. Grant Wacker, "The Demise of Biblical Civilization," in Hatch and Noll, *Bible in America*, 122–23.

16. Gustav Niebuhr, "When Words Get in the Way of the Word: Language of the Venerable King James Bible Is Hardly English to Young Readers," *Washington Post*, June 12, 1993, B6.

17. Karen R. Long, "Biblical Illiteracy Rampant among Christians," *Huntsville (Alabama) Times*, July 2, 1994, B4.

18. Carl Sandburg, introduction, *Lincoln's Devotional* (Great Neck, NY: Channel Press, 1957), viii.

19. William J. Wolf, *The Almost Chosen People* (Garden City, NY: Doubleday, 1959), 169.

20. Garry Wills, *Lincoln at Gettysburg* (New York: Simon & Schuster, 1992), 88.

21. Edward Everett to Abraham Lincoln, November 20, 1863, Abraham Lincoln Papers, Library of Congress, Washington, DC.

22. Glenn LaFantasie, "Lincoln and the Gettysburg Awakening," *Journal of the Abraham Lincoln Society* 16, no. 1 (1995): 74.

23. Allen Guelzo, *Abraham Lincoln: Redeemer President* (Grand Rapids, MI: Eerdmans, 1999), 373–74.

24. Lucas Morel, *Lincoln's Sacred Effort: Defining Religion's Role in American Self-Government* (Lanham, MD: Lexington Books, 2000), 44–45.

25. Ibid., 56.

26. Joseph Fornieri, *Abraham Lincoln's Political Faith* (DeKalb: Northern Illinois University Press, 2003), 46, 46–47.

27. Boritt, *Gettysburg Gospel*, 120.

28. Harold Holzer, *Lincoln at Cooper Union: The Speech That Made Abraham Lincoln President* (New York: Simon & Schuster, 2004). See esp. 221–24.

29. William Herndon, *Herndon's Life of Lincoln*, ed. Paul M. Angle (New York: Da Capo Press, 1983), 324–25, 326.

30. Ronald C. White Jr., *The Eloquent President: A Portrait of Lincoln through his Words* (New York: Random House, 2005), 243.

31. Philip L. Ostergard, *The Inspired Wisdom of Abraham Lincoln* (Carol Stream, IL: Tyndale House, 2008), 246.

2. LINCOLN'S KNOWLEDGE OF BIBLE AND PRAYER BOOK

1. This inscription was read aloud to me via telephone by the reference librarian, who indicated the capital letters and all punctuation marks. See also *CW*, 7:542–43.

2. *CW*, 7:542.

3. *CW*, 4:546.

4. Sandburg, introduction, xi.

5. Frederick Iglehart, "Lincoln as Pastor," in *Lincoln Talks: An Oral Biography*, ed. Emanuel Hertz (New York: Bramhall House, 1986), 101, 102.

6. Henry Champion Deming, *Eulogy of Abraham Lincoln* (Hartford, CT: Clark, 1865), 42–43. Available online at books.google.com.

7. Guelzo, *Abraham Lincoln*, 151–52.

8. Don E. Fehrenbacher and Virginia Fehrenbacher, comps. and eds., *Recollected Words of Abraham Lincoln* (Stanford, Calif.: Stanford University Press, 1996), 151. Hereafter cited as "*RW*."

9. *RW*, 54.

10. Noah Brooks, *Washington in Lincoln's Time*, ed. Herbert Mitgang (1895; New York: Rinehart, 1958), 75–76. Brooks is but one of many witnesses to attest to Lincoln's phenomenal memory. One of Lincoln's best friends from the New Salem days, James Short, recalled, "He read very thoroughly, and had a most wonderful memory. Would distinctly remember almost everything he read." Nathaniel W. Branson to William Herndon, in William Herndon, *Herndon's Informants: Letters, Interviews, and Statements about Abraham Lincoln*, ed. Douglas L. Wilson and Rodney O. Davis (Urbana: University of Illinois Press, 1998), 90.

11. Ibid., 76, 76–77.

12. *RW*, 413.

13. The Book of Common Prayer according to the Protestant Episcopal Church in the United States of America (New York: Gray, 1828). All citations to the prayer book are to this text. No page numbers are supplied for prayer-book citations.

14. Marion J. Hatchett, *The Making of the First American Book of Common Prayer* (New York: Seabury, 1982), 136.

15. Herndon, *Herndon's Life of Lincoln*, 180–81.

16. Wolf, *Almost Chosen People*, 67.

17. Allen Guelzo, "Did the Lincoln Family Employ a Slave in 1849–50?" *For the People: A Newsletter of the Abraham Lincoln Association* 3 (Autumn 2001): 1, 1, 6.

18. Emilie Todd Helm, quoted in Katherine Helm, *The True Story of Mary, Wife of Lincoln* (New York: Harper & Brothers, 1928), 116–17.

19. Wolf, *Almost Chosen People*, 80.

20. Keith Jennison, *The Humorous Mr. Lincoln* (New York: Bonanza, 1965), 41.

21. Herndon, *Herndon's Life*, 213.

22. John Hanks, "Lincoln's Boyhood Days in Indiana," in *Lincoln among His Friends*, ed. Rufus Rockwell Wilson (Caldwell, ID: Caxton, 1942), 35.

23. William E. Dodd, *The Cotton Kingdom* (1919; New Haven, CT: Yale University Press, 1920), 99.

24. *New York Herald*, February 25, 1861, 1, col. 4, cited in Wayne C. Temple, *Abraham Lincoln: From Skeptic to Prophet* (Mahomet, IL: Mayhaven, 1995), 133.

25. Deacon Martha Bradley and Archdeacon Shawn Denney, e-mail message to author and telephone interview with author, records of baptism, confirmation, and marriage records, Saint Paul's Episcopal Church, Springfield, Illinois, September 22, 2007.

26. Temple, *Abraham Lincoln*, 86.

27. Frederick W. Seward, *Reminiscences of a War-time Statesman and Diplomat* (New York: Putnam's Sons, 1916), 147.

28. John Hay, *Inside Lincoln's White House: The Complete Civil War Diary of John Hay*, ed. Michael Burlingame and John R. Turner Ettlinger (Carbondale: Southern Illinois University Press, 1997), 90, 118.

29. Temple, *Abraham Lincoln*, 154, 169.

30. Ibid., 153–54.

31. Edward Steers Jr., *Blood on the Moon: The Assassination of Abraham Lincoln* (Lexington: University of Kentucky Press, 2001), 52.

32. William E. Tidwell, *Come Retribution: The Confederate Secret Service and the Assassination of Abraham Lincoln* (Jackson: University Press of Mississippi, 1988), 274.

33. Mary Todd Lincoln, *Mary Todd Lincoln: Her Life and Letters*, ed. Justin G. Turner and Linda Levitt Turner (New York: Fromm International, 1987), 125.

34. Henry Drisler, *A Reply to the "Bible View of Slavery, by J. H. Hopkins, D.D., Bishop of the Diocese of Vermont"* (New York: Westcott, 1863), 1. On its cover, however, the title of the book is *"Bible View of Slavery, by John H. Hopkins, D.D., Bishop of the Diocese of Vermont," Examined*.

35. John Henry Hopkins, *Episcopal Government. A Sermon Preached at the Consecration of the Rev. Alonzo Potter, D.D., as Bishop of the Diocese of Pennsylvania* (Philadelphia, PA: King and Baird, 1845), 8, 12.

36. John Henry Hopkins Jr., *The Life of the Late Reverend John Henry Hopkins* (New York: Huntington, 1873), 331–32.

37. John Henry Hopkins, *Bible View of Slavery* (New York: Society for the Diffusion of Political Knowledge, 1863), 123. This 1863 publication is a reprint of original 1861 Kost publication, except that the argument justifying secession is omitted.

38. Daniel Kilham Dodge, *Abraham Lincoln: Master of Words* (New York: Appleton, 1924), 136, 137–38, 138.

39. Philip B. Kunhardt Jr., *A New Birth of Freedom: Lincoln at Gettysburg* (Boston, MA: Little, Brown, 1983), 209.

40. Rita Felski, "Remember the Reader," *Chronicle Review*, December 19, 2008, B8.

41. *CW*, 1:382.

42. *CW*, 7:542.

43. *RW*, 137.

3. BIRTH AND REBIRTH

1. Three other versions of the address appear in the appendix to the current volume.

2. *CW*, 4:332.

3. *CW*, 6:239–40. A footnote reads, "Numerous original signed copies of this printed order are extant. Each of these documents has the blanks properly filled in by a War Department clerk and bears Lincoln's full signature, 'Abraham Lincoln.'" This fact only increases the number of times that Lincoln signed under his own double-dating system.

4. William Shakespeare, *The Complete Works of Shakespeare*, ed. Hardin Craig (Glenview, IL: Scott Foresman, 1961).

5. David Herbert Donald, *Lincoln* (New York: Simon & Schuster, 1995), 462.

6. *Oxford English Dictionary*, 2nd. ed., s.v. "testing."

7. *CW*, 6:392.

8. Herndon, *Herndon's Informants*, 64, 21.

9. *OED*, s.v. "dedicate."

10. John C. Calhoun, *The Collected Works of John C. Calhoun*, ed. Richard K. Cralle, 6 vols. (New York: Appleton, 1854), 1:115–16. The *Collected Works* were published over several years and then in their entirety in 1854.

11. *CW*, 4:190.

12. *RW*, 189.

13. *CW*, 4:191.

14. Theodore Parker, *The Collected Works of Theodore Parker*, ed. Frances Power Cobbe, 13 vols. (London: Trubner, 1864), 8:132.

15. Jefferson Davis, *Jefferson Davis: The Essential Writings*, ed. William J. Cooper Jr. (New York: Modern Library by Random House, 2003), 194, 202. In the first of these speeches, he also invoked "our trust in God." 194.

16. *CW*, 4:240.

17. *OED*, s.v. "liberty."

18. John Bunyan, *The Pilgrim's Progress*, vol. 15, *Harvard Classics* (New York: Collier, 1909), 27. *The Pilgrim's Progress* was first published in 1678.

19. Benson Bobrick, *Wide as the Waters: The Story of the English Bible and the Revolution It Inspired* (New York: Simon & Schuster, 2001), 295–96.

20. *CW*, 4:265.

21. Mason L. Weems, *The Life of Washington*, ed. Marcus Cunliffe (1800; Cambridge, MA: Harvard University Press, 1962), 6.

22. *CW*, 7:23.

23. *CW*, 7:167–68.

24. *CW*, 7:21.

25. *CW*, 4:269.

26. Deming, *Eulogy of Abraham Lincoln*, 42.

27. John Henry Hopkins, *A Lecture Delivered before the Young Men's Associations of the City of Buffalo and Lockport on Friday, January 10, and Monday, January 13, 1851* (Buffalo, NY: Phinney, 1851), 5.

28. Ibid., 18–19.

29. Carl Sandburg, *Lincoln's Devotional* (Great Neck, NY: Channel Press, 1957), 77.

30. *CW*, 1:279.

31. Parker, *Collected Works of Theodore Parker*, 6:156.

32. *OED*, s.v. "survive." This word entered the English language as a legal term from the Rolls of Parliament at the very beginning of the Renaissance and of Modern English at a time when lawyers, scientists, and other scholars were borrowing or creating new words from Greek, Latin, and other languages in an explosion of vocabulary ignited by the printing press and the new learning.

33. Ronald Mansbridge, "The Percentage of Words in the Geneva and King James Versions Taken from Tyndale's Translation," Tyndale Society, www.tyndale.org/TSJ/3/mansbridge.html.

34. Edward Everett, *Address of Hon. Edward Everett, at the Consecration of the National Cemetery at Gettysburg, 19th November, 1863, with the Dedicatory Speech of President Lincoln* (Boston: Little, Brown, 1864), 32.

35. Webster, *Great Orations and Senatorial Speeches*, 15.

36. Robert McCrum, William Cran, and Robert MacNeil, *The Story of English*, 1st American ed. (New York: Viking, 1986), 113, 102.

37. G. Wills, *Lincoln at Gettysburg*, 174.

38. McCrum, Cran, and MacNeil, *Story of English*, 58. Other counts of the one hundred most common words have yielded slightly different results, but Anglo-Saxon always accounts for the overwhelming majority.

39. Everett, *Address of Hon. Edward Everett*, 64.

4. FITTING AND PROPER

1. *CW*, 6:332.
2. *CW*, 4:332.
3. *CW*, 6:496–97.
4. John G. Nicolay, *With Lincoln in the White House: Letters, Memoranda, and Other Writings of John G. Nicolay, 1860–1865*, ed. Michael Burlingame (Carbondale: Southern Illinois University Press, 2000), 134.
5. Gideon Welles, *Lincoln and Seward: Remarks upon the Memorial Address of Chas. Francis Adams, on the Late Wm. H. Seward* (1869; repr., Freeport, NY: Books for Libraries Press, 1969), 47.
6. *OED*, s.v. "helpmeet."
7. *RW*, 189–90.
8. Holzer, *Lincoln at Cooper Union*, 201.
9. *CW*, 4:205.
10. *CW*, 4:220.
11. *CW*, 4:225.
12. *CW*, 4:226.
13. *CW*, 4: 231.
14. *CW*, 4:230.
15. *CW*, 4:230–31.
16. *CW*, 4:239.
17. *CW*, 4:169.
18. John M. Taylor, *William Seward: Lincoln's Right Hand* (Washington, DC: Potomac Books, 1991), 224.
19. Ibid., 140–41.
20. *CW*, 4:271.
21. James Madison, "The Federalist No. 14: An Objection Drawn from the Extent of Country Answered," in *The Federalist Papers*, ca. 1787, ed. Clinton Rossiter (New York: New American Library, 1961), 104.
22. Everett, *Address of Hon. Edward Everett*, 61–62.
23. *CW*, 7:17–18.
24. *CW*, 8:332.
25. *CW*, 8:333.

5. CONSECRATE—DEDICATE—HALLOW

1. *OED*, s.vv. "consecrate," "dedicate."

2. *The English Hexapla* (London: Bagster, 1841), Acts 17:23.

3. David Wills to Abraham Lincoln, 2 November 1863, American Treasures of the Library of Congress, Library of Congress, 5 December 2002, http://www.loc.gov/exhibits/treasures/images/vc009210.jpg. This Web page is a holograph of Wills' invitation.

4. Everett, *Address of Hon. Edward Everett*, 16.

5. Quoted in David Herbert Donald and Harold Holzer, eds., *Lincoln in The Times* (New York: St. Martin's, 2005), 187.

6. Ibid., 190.

7. *OED*, s.v. "dedication."

8. *RW*, 395–96.

9. Thomas Gray, "Elegy Written in a Country Churchyard," in *The Complete Poetical Works of William Collins, Thomas Gray, and Oliver Goldsmith*, ed. Epes Sargent (Boston: Crosby, Nichols, Lee, 1860), 62, 61, 60.

10. F. B. Carpenter, *The Inner Life of Abraham Lincoln: Six Months at the White House*, ed. Mark E. Neely Jr. (1880; repr., Lincoln: University of Nebraska Press, 1995), 51.

11. Ibid., 51, 51, 52.

12. Ibid., 52.

13. Robert Louis Stevenson, "Style in Literature: Its Technical Elements," *Contemporary Review* 47 (April 1885): 555.

14. David Irving, *Elements of English Composition* (Philadelphia, PA: Plowman, 1803), 71.

15. Ibid., 69.

16. Alexander Jamieson, *Grammar of Rhetoric and Polite Literature, Comprehending the Principles of Language and Style, the Elements of Taste and Criticism; with Rules for the Study of Composition and Eloquence* (New Haven, CT: Maltby, 1826), 92–93.

17. W. F. Barton, *Lincoln at Gettysburg*, 147.

18. Brooks, *Washington in Lincoln's Time*, 267.

19. *CW*, 2:126.

20. Francis B. Vinton, "Universality and Primitive Authority of a Liturgy," *Liturgic Worship: Sermons on the Book of Common Prayer, by Bishops and Clergy of the Protestant Episcopal Church* (New York: Pott, 1864), 99.

21. Harriet Beecher Stowe, *Men of Our Times; or Leading Patriots of the Day* (Hartford, CT: Hartford, 1868), 59–60.

6. O BRAVE NEW WORDS

1. James McNeill Whistler, *The Gentle Art of Making Enemies* (London: Heinemann, 1890), 45. For Hamerton's comment, see 44.

2. *OED*, s.v. "brave."

3. Roger Taney, introduction, *Poems of the Late Francis S. Key, Esq.* (New York: Carter & Brothers, 1857; Whitefish, MT: Kessinger, 2007), vii–viii. Citations are to the Kessinger edition.

4. Williams Collins, "Ode, Written in the Beginning of the Year 1746," quoted in Carpenter, *Inner Life of Abraham Lincoln*, 224. The stanza quoted is from Collins' brief, twelve-line poem.

5. Winfred Scott, quoted in Everett, *Address of Hon. Edward Everett*, 19.

6. Helm, *True Story of Mary, Wife of Lincoln*, 101.

7. John Locke, *Two Treatises of Government*, ed. Peter Laslett (1689; Cambridge: Cambridge University Press, 1960), 224ff.

8. *CW*, 4:245.

9. *OED*, s.vv. "detract," "detraction,":"subtract," "subtraction."

10. Robert Bray, "What Abraham Lincoln Read—an Evaluative and Annotated List," *Journal of the Abraham Lincoln Association* 28 (Summer 2007): 58.

11. Thomas Jefferson to John Adams, September 4, 1785, *The Papers of Thomas Jefferson*, ed. Julian P. Boyd, 34 vols. (Princeton, NJ: Princeton University Press, 1950–2005), 8:473.

12. *CW*, 3:315.

13. Sandburg, *Lincoln's Devotional*, 8, 13, 17, 27, 31, 46, 50, 170. Lincoln owned the fourth edition, published in 1852, of *The Believer's Daily Treasure*, originally published by the Religious Tract Society of London, England; Sandburg reprinted this edition.

14. Thomas Paine, *Dissertation on First Principles of Government*, in *The Life and Works of Thomas Paine* (1795; New Rochelle, NY: Thomas Paine National Historical Association, 1925), 216, 241, 241–42. Bray assigns a strong probability to Lincoln's having read Paine's complete political works.

15. Parker, *Collected Works of Theodore Parker*, 6:145.

16. *OED*, s.v. "measure."

17. Julia Ward Howe, "The Battle Hymn of the Republic," *Atlantic Monthly* 9, February 1862, 10.

18. Boritt, *Gettysburg Gospel*, 119.

19. Herndon, *Herndon's Life of Lincoln*, 323.

20. Parker, "Some Account of My Ministry," in *Additional Speeches*, in *Collected Works of Theodore Parker*, 2:365.

21. Parker, "Slave Power in America," in *Collected Works of Theodore Parker*, 5:105.

22. Parker, "Some Thoughts on the Progress of America," in *Collected Works of Theodore Parker*, 6:14–15.

23. Guelzo, *Abraham Lincoln*, 372.

24. W. E. Barton, *Lincoln at Gettysburg*, 136.

25. Andrew Jackson to Martin Van Buren, August 30, 1832, *Correspondence of Andrew Jackson*, ed. John S. Bassett, 7 vols. (Washington, DC: Carnegie Institution, 1926–35), 4:470, quoted in Margaret L. Coit, *John C. Calhoun: American Portrait* (Boston: Houghton Mifflin, 1950), 239.

26. Daniel Webster, *The Great Debate: Webster's Reply*, ed. Lindsay Swift (Boston: Houghton Mifflin, 1898), 186–87. Webster delivered his reply on January 26, 1830.

27. Herndon, *Herndon's Life of Lincoln*, 386.

28. Calhoun, *Collected Works of John C. Calhoun*, 1:128.

29. Mark Twain to George Bainton, October 15, 1888, in *Bartlett's Familiar Quotations*, 17th ed. (New York: Little, Brown, 2002), 561.

7. "UNDER GOD"—AFORETHOUGHT OR AFTERTHOUGHT?

1. Wolf, *Almost Chosen People*, 169.

2. Boritt, *Gettysburg Gospel*, 272ff.

3. W. E. Barton, *Lincoln at Gettysburg*, 81.

4. Julius Ignatius Gilbert, "Lincoln in 1861; Lincoln in 1863; Lincoln at Washington; the Assassination," *Nineteenth Annual Convention, National Shorthand Reporters' Association, Proceedings of the Annual Meeting* (La Porte, IN: Chase & Shepherd, 1917), 134.

5. Ibid., 137. Barton reprints a portion of what Gilbert said at the Shorthand Reporters' Convention, including, with a few errors, the sentences cited in this footnote and in footnote 4 above.

6. W. E. Barton, *Lincoln at Gettysburg*, 83.

7. Associated Press, "AP History," *Associated Press*, 2009, www.ap.org/pages/about/history_first.html.

8. Douglas L. Wilson, *Lincoln's Sword: The Presidency and the Power of Words* (New York: Vintage Books, 2006), 224.

9. Young, *Men and Memories*, 2.

10. Ibid., 4.

11. Ibid., 48.

12. Gilbert, "Lincoln in 1861," 137.

13. W. E. Barton, *Lincoln at Gettysburg*, 63.

14. Young, *Men and Memories*, 59, 69, 70.

15. W. E. Barton, *Lincoln at Gettysburg*, 85.

16. D. L. Wilson, *Lincoln's Sword*, 225.

17. Young, *Men and Memories*, 69.

18. John Nicolay, "Lincoln's Gettysburg Address," *Century Magazine* 47, February 1894, 604–5.

19. Ibid., 605.

20. Ibid., 604.

21. D. L. Wilson, *Lincoln's Sword.*, 222.

22. *CW*, 7:16–17.

23. William E. Barton, *The Life of Abraham Lincoln* (Indianapolis, IN: Bobbs Merrill, 1925), 2:210–11.

24. J. G. Randall, *Lincoln the President*, 2 vols. (1945; London: Eyre & Spottiswoode, 1952), 2:312. Citations are to the 1952 edition.

25. Ibid., 2:314.

26. Benjamin P. Thomas, *Abraham Lincoln: A Biography* (New York: Barnes & Noble, 1952), 402.

27. White, *Eloquent President*, 250.

28. Boritt, *Gettysburg Gospel*, 120.

29. Nicolay, "Lincoln's Gettysburg Address," 604.

30. *New York Times*, November 20, 1863, in Donald and Holzer, *Lincoln in The Times*, 187.

31. W. E. Barton, *Lincoln at Gettysburg*, 75.

32. Ibid., 203.

33. Harold Holzer, *Lincoln President Elect: Abraham Lincoln and the Great Secession Winter, 1860–1861* (New York: Simon & Schuster, 2008), 255, 256.

34. James Buchanan, fourth annual message to Congress on the State of the Union, December 3, 1860, in John T. Woolley and Gerhard Peters, "The American Presidency Project," University of California, Santa Barbara, 1999–2009, *University of California*, http://www.presidency.ucsb.edu/ws/?pid=29501. All of the inaugural addresses are available online at http://www.presidency.ucsb.edu/inaugurals.php, and all of the State of the Union addresses are available at http://www.presidency.ucsb.edu/sou.php.

35. George Washington, fourth annual message, November 6, 1792, in John T. Woolley and Gerhard Peters, "The American Presidency Project," University of California, Santa Barbara, 1999–2009, *University of California*, http://www.presidency.ucsb.edu/ws/index.php?pid=29434.

36. *CW*, 4:271.

37. Salmon Chase to Charles D. Cleveland, October 22, 1841, micro 5:0485, Chase Papers, Library of Congress, Washington, DC. This is an autograph letter.

38. *CW*, 4.339.

39. George Washington, *The Writings of George Washington*, ed. John C. Fitzpatrick, 39 vols. (Washington, DC: GPO, 1931–44), 30:247.

40. Ibid., 5:246.

41. Ibid., 5:245.

42. Weems, *Life of Washington*, 166.

43. W. E. Barton, *Lincoln at Gettysburg*, 143.

44. Herndon, *Herndon's Life of Lincoln*, 367.

45. Elizabeth I, Queen of England, "The Armada Speech," *Speeches That Changed the World*, ed. Cathy Lowne (London: Bounty Books, 2005), 86–87.

46. Ibid., 87.

47. Rufus Rockwell Wilson, ed., *Intimate Memories of Lincoln* (Elmira, NY: Primavera, 1945), 333.

48. *CW*, 7:281.

8. CONTROVERSIAL PROPOSITION

1. T. S. Eliot, "Philip Massinger," *The Sacred Wood: Essays on Poetry and Criticism* (1920; London: Methuen, 1950), 125. The citation is to the 1950 edition.

2. Herndon, *Herndon's Life of Lincoln*, 248.

3. Carpenter, *Inner Life of Abraham Lincoln*, 49.

4. James B. Conkling, "Some of Lincoln's Associates at the Bar," *Lincoln among His Friends*, ed. Rufus Rockwell Wilson (Caldwell, ID: Caxton, 1942), 107.

5. D. L. Wilson, *Lincoln's Sword*, 202. Wilson cites *CW* 2:385. The editorial brackets are his.

6. Ibid., 234.

7. Bray, "What Abraham Lincoln Read," 28.

8. Herndon, *Herndon's Life of Lincoln*, 421.

9. *RW*, 244.

10. *CW*, 2:230.

11. Donald, *Lincoln*, 137.

12. J. G. Holland, *J. G. Holland's Life of Abraham Lincoln* (1865; New York: Paperback Library, 1961), 103.

13. [Edward] Alfred Pollard, *The Lost Cause* (1866; New York: Treat, 1867), 101.

14. Randall, *Lincoln the President*, 1:18.

15. Calhoun, *Collected Works of John. C Calhoun*, 4:553.

16. Ibid, 4:554.

17. *CW*, 1:440, 433, 432, 441, and 441–42.

18. *CW*, 1:451–52.

19. John C. Calhoun, *Correspondence of John C. Calhoun*, ed. J. Franklin Jameson (Washington, DC: GPO, 1900), 759.

20. Calhoun, *Collected Works of John. C Calhoun*, 4:507.

21. Ibid.

22. Locke, *Two Treatises*, 330.

23. Calhoun, *Collected Works of John. C Calhoun*, 4:507.

24. Ibid., 1:57.

25. Ibid., 4:507.

26. Ibid., 1:58–59.

27. Locke, *Two Treatises*, 308.

28. Calhoun, *Collected Works of John. C Calhoun*, 4:508.

29. Locke, *Two Treatises*, 323.

30. *CW*, 3:303.

31. *CW*, 3:304.

32. *CW*, 2:130.

33. *CW*, 3:301.

34. *CW*, 3:301–2.

35. *CW*, 3:302, 3:304, 3:302.

36. Calhoun, *Collected Works of John C. Calhoun*, 4:508.

37. Ibid.

38. Ibid.

39. *CW*, 2:406.

40. Calhoun, *Collected Works of John C. Calhoun*, 4:509.

41. Timothy David, qtd. in John Niven, *John C. Calhoun and the Price of Union: A Biography* (Baton Rouge: Louisiana State University Press, 1988), 18.

42. John Locke, *An Essay concerning Human Understanding*, ed. Peter H. Nidditch (1689; Oxford, UK: Oxford University Press, 1975), 690.

43. Ibid., 691.

44. John Locke, *The Reasonableness of Christianity* (1695; Stanford, CA: Stanford University Press, 1958), 32, 76.

45. Locke, *Essay*, 609.

46. Locke, *Two Treatises*, 137.

47. William C. Rives, quoted in John C. Calhoun, *Union and Liberty*, ed. Ross M. Lence (Indianapolis, IN: Liberty Fund, 1992), 468. The word "exploded" is misprinted in this source as "explored."

48. Calhoun, *Union and Liberty*, 468–69.

49. Calhoun, *Collected Works of John C. Calhoun*, 1:58.

50. Locke, *Two Treatises*, 276–77.

51. Benjamin Franklin, *The Writings of Benjamin Franklin*, ed. Albert Henry Smyth (New York: Macmillan, 1906), 6:382.

52. Calhoun, *Collected Works of John C. Calhoun*, 4:510.

53. Ibid., 1:55.

54. John Wilkes Booth, *"Right or Wrong, God Judge Me": The Writings of John Wilkes Booth* (Urbana: University of Illinois Press, 2001), 56.

55. Parker, *Collected Works of Theodore Parker*, 5:303.

56. Calhoun, *Collected Work of John C. Calhoun*, 4:510–11.

57. Ibid., 1:55.

58. Frederick Ross, *Slavery Ordained of God* (Philadelphia, PA: Lippincott, 1857), 116, 122, 127–28, 126.

59. Ibid., 123–24.

60. *CW*, 3:204–5.

61. Locke, *Two Treatises*, 275.

62. J. H. Hopkins, *Bible View of Slavery*, 7.

63. Ibid., 8.

64. Ibid., 9.

65. Locke, *Essay*, 531, 532, 597, 532.

66. Locke, *Reasonableness of Christianity*, 63.

67. Bray, "What Abraham Lincoln Read," 62.

68. *CW*, 3:168.

69. Euclid, *The Elements Books I–XIII Complete and Unabridged*, trans. Thomas L. Heath (1908; New York: Barnes and Noble, 2006), 164.

70. Locke, *Essay*, 549–50.

71. Ibid., 559.

72. Ibid., 620.

73. *CW*, 3:16.

74. Locke, *Two Treatises*, 287–88.

75. Ibid., 297.

76. Locke, *Essay*, 531.

77. Ibid., 531.

78. Locke, *Two Treatises*, 142.

79. Peter Laslett, ed., introduction, *Two Treatises of Government*, by John Locke, 1689 (Cambridge, UK: Cambridge University Press, 1960), 65.

80. Calhoun, *Collected Works of John C. Calhoun*, 2:4–5.

81. Ibid. 1:297.

82. Locke, *Two Treatises*, 233.

83. Ibid., 283.

84. Ibid., 333.

85. Ibid., 347.

86. Holland, *Life of Abraham Lincoln*, 116.

87. Jefferson Davis, farewell address, to the U.S. Senate, U.S. Capitol, January 21, 1861, in *Jefferson Davis*, 193.

88. Calhoun, *Collected Works of John C. Calhoun*, 1:13.

89. Ross, *Slavery Ordained of God*, 22.

90. *CW*, 3:204.

91. Theodore Parker to a Southern slaveholder, February 2, 1848, in John Weiss, *Life and Correspondence of Theodore Parker*, 2 vols. (New York: Appleton, 1864), 1:82. The letter also appears at www.geocities.com/capitolhill/1764/slavery.html.

92. Ibid, 1:81–83.

9. THE ESSENCE OF LINCOLN'S STYLE

1. F. Scott Fitzgerald, "Self-Interview," *F. Scott Fitzgerald in His Own Time: A Miscellany* (n.p.: Kent State University Press, 1971), 162.

2. Thomas Jefferson to John Holmes, 22 April 1820, *Writings of Thomas Jefferson*, ed. Andrew A. Lipscomb, 20 vols. (Washington, DC: Thomas Jefferson Memorial Association, 1903–4), 15:249.

3. White, *Eloquent President*, 236.

4. *CW*, 5:306.

5. Martin P. Johnson, "Lincoln Greets the Turning Point of the Civil War, July 7, 1863," *Lincoln Herald* 106, no. 3 (2004): 104.

6. Ibid., 104–5.

7. W. E. Barton, *Life of Lincoln*, 2:186.

8. *CW*, 4:264.

9. *CW*, 4:332.

10. *CW*, 4:483.

11. *CW*, 6:278.

12. *CW*, 6:30.

13. *CW*, 6:333.

14. *CW*, 4:438.

15. White, *Eloquent President*, 236.

16. Johnson, "Lincoln Greets the Turning Point," 109.

17. John Hay, *Inside Lincoln's White House*, 76.

18. Johnson, "Lincoln Greets the Turning Point," 104.

19. Ibid., 111.

20. Ibid., 112.

10. THE HEART OF THE MESSAGE

1. *CW*, 2:405.

2. Calhoun, *Collected Works of John C. Calhoun*, 2:488.

3. Ibid., 5:205.

4. Parker, *Collected Works of Theodore Parker*, 6:219–20.

5. Ibid., 6:320–21.

6. William H. Seward, *The Autobiography of William H. Seward* (New York: Appleton, 1877), 329.

7. Hopkins, *Lecture Delivered*, 19.

8. Dodd, *Cotton Kingdom*, 48–49, 49-50, 50, 53.

9. Ibid., 56–57, 57.

10. Ibid., 58–59, 59, 59.

11. Anson Phelps Stokes, *Church and State in the United States*, 2 vols. (New York: Harper & Brothers, 1950), 2:127–28, 2:133, 2:132.

12. John C. Calhoun, *Papers of John C. Calhoun*, ed. Clyde N. Wilson (Columbia: University of South Carolina Press, 1981), 14:84. The speech was first printed in the *Congressional Globe* for the 25th Congress, 2nd Session, appendix, 60–65.

13. Stokes, *Church and State*, 2:193.

14. Ross, *Slavery Ordained of God*, 31.

15. Ibid., 15–16.

16. Booth, *"Right or Wrong, God Judge Me,"* 62.

17. Stokes, *Church and State*, 2:196.

18. Stephen Woodworth, *Jefferson Davis and His Generals* (Lawrence: University Press of Kansas, 1990), 28.

19. Ross, *Slavery Ordained of God*, 41–42, 15, 42, 14.

20. Ibid., 16, 23, 16, 28.

21. Ibid., 46.

22. Ibid.

23. Ibid., 55.

24. Frederick Douglass, *Love of God, Love of Man, Love of Country*, address delivered in Syracuse, New York, September 24, 1847, *Infoplease.com*, http://www.infoplease.com/t/hist/love-of-god-man-country/.

25. *CW*, 8:333.

26. Frederick Douglass, *Life and Times of Frederick Douglass* (rev. ed. 1892; New York: Collier Books, 1962), 357.

27. Coit, *John C. Calhoun*, 130.

28. Glenn Robins, *The Bishop of the Old South: The Ministry and Civil War Legacy of Leonidas Polk* (Macon, GA: Mercer University Press, 2006), 25 ff. for Polk's conversion and 31 for Calhoun's role in appointing McIlvaine.

29. Ibid., xi.

30. William M. Polk, *Leonidas Polk: Bishop and General* (New York: Longmans, Green, 1915), 1:362.

31. Margaret Mitchell, *Gone with the Wind* (1936; Macmillan; New York: Scribner, 1996), 840, 841. The 1996 edition is the sixtieth-anniversary edition.

32. Coit, *John C. Calhoun*, 508.

33. Calhoun, *Collected Works of John C. Calhoun*, 4:512.

34. Ibid., 1:56–57.

35. John C. Calhoun to Thomas G. Clemson, March 1850, in Calhoun, *Correspondence of John C. Calhoun*, 784.

36. J. H. Hopkins, *Bible View of Slavery* (1861), 19.

37. James Madison, "Federalist No. 39: The Conformity of the Plan to Republican Principles," in *The Federalist Papers*, ed. Clinton Rossiter (New York: New American, 1961), 242.

38. Hopkins, *Bible View of Slavery* (1861), 21.

39. Stephen Douglas, qtd. in Harold Holzer, ed., *Lincoln-Douglas Debates* (New York: HarperCollins, 1993), 151.

40. *CW*, 4:240.

41. *CW*, 2:405–6.

42. *CW*, 4:160.

43. Ibid.

44. Alexander H. Stephens, "Cornerstone Address, March 21, 1861," in *The Rebellion Record: A Diary of American Events with Documents, Narratives, Illustrative Incidents, Poetry, etc.*, vol. 1, ed. Frank Moore (New York: Putnam, 1862), 44–46. *Modern History Sourcebook*, www.fordham.edu/halsall/mod/1861stephens.html.

45. Jefferson Davis, inaugural address as president of the Confederate States of America, February 1861, Montgomery, Alabama, *Southern Historical Society Papers* 1 (January 1876), in *Jefferson Davis*, 198–203; *Civil War Home*, http://www.civilwarhome.com/davisinauguraladdress.htm.

46. Stephens, "Cornerstone Address."

47. Ibid.

48. *CW*, 8:332–33.

49. Thomas Jefferson, *Notes on Virginia. Query XVIII*, in Jefferson, *Writings of Thomas Jefferson*, 2:227.

50. *Southern Presbyterian*, qtd. in Stokes, *Church and State*, 2:237.

51. Ibid., 2:236.

52. Ibid.

53. Jefferson Davis, "Confederate States of America—Message to Congress, April 29, 1861 (Ratification of the Constitution)," Avalon Project, Lillian Goldman Law Library, Yale University Law School, New Haven, CT, *Yale University. Yale University*, http://avalon.law.yale.edu/19th_century/csa_m042961.asp.

54. Asia Booth Clarke, *The Unlocked Book: A Memoir of John Wilkes Booth* (London: Faber, 1888), 115.

55. Booth, *"Right or Wrong, God Judge Me,"* 125.

56. *Dictionary of American Biography*, s.v. "Stanton, Frederick Perry" (1943 edition).

57. F. P. Stanton, "The Causes of the Rebellion," *Continental Monthly*, November 1862, 518.

58. Ibid., 513–14, 514, 515, 516, 517, 518, 519, 520, 520.

59. Ibid., 522–23.

60. Davis, *Jefferson Davis*, 94.

61. Edward A. Pollard, "We Are Fighting for Independence, Not Slavery," *Richmond Examiner*, August 2, 1864, *TeachingAmericanHistory.org*, http://teachingamericanhistory.org/library/index.asp?document=1483.

62. Pollard, *Lost Cause*, 47.

63. Ibid., 49, 50–51, 102, 101.

64. Ibid., 42.

65. John C. Calhoun, *Union and Liberty*, 371.

66. Calhoun, *Correspondence*, 778.

EPILOGUE: CATECHISM AND CONCLUSION

1. Herbert Mitgang, ed., *Lincoln as They Saw Him* (New York: Rinehart, 1956), 342.

2. Hay, *Inside Lincoln's White House*, 85.

3. Frederick Douglas, "*Frederick Douglass' Paper*, 16 November 1855," in *Frederick Douglass: The Narrative and Selected Writings*, ed. Michael Myer (New York: Modern Library, 1984), 356.

4. John Henry Hopkins, *The American Citizen: His Rights and Duties, According to the Spirit of the Constitution of the United States* (New York: Pudney & Russell, 1857), chap. 1, 356, and chap. 9.

5. Mitgang, *Lincoln as They Saw Him*, 342–43.

6. Walt Whitman, "The Death of Lincoln, a Lecture by Walt Whitman," *Boston Transcript*, April 15, 1890, repr. in W. E. Barton, *Abraham Lincoln and Walt Whitman*, 267.

7. Mark Twain, "A Lincoln Memorial: A Plea by Mark Twain for the Setting Apart of His Birthplace," *New York Times*, January 13, 1907; *www.twainquotes.com*, www.twainquotes.com/nytindex.html.

8. Mitgang, *Lincoln as They Saw Him*, 360, 361, 361.

9. Stephen Elliot, *Funeral Service at the Burial of the Right Rev. Leonidas Polk, D.D. Together with the Sermon Delivered in St. Paul's Church, Augusta, Ga., on June 29, 1864: Being the Feast of St. Peter the Apostle* (Columbia, SC: Evans & Cogswell, 1864), 16.

10. *CW*, 6:507–8. Lincoln misspelled "privilege" as "previlege."

11. Niven, *John C. Calhoun and the Price of Union*, 157.

12. John C. Calhoun to Anna Maria Calhoun, March 10, 1832, in Calhoun, *Correspondence of John C. Calhoun*, 316.

13. Jacques Duchesne-Guillemin, Edward John Joyce, and Margaret Stevenson, "Magi." *New Catholic Encyclopedia*, 2nd ed., vol. 9 (Detroit, MI: Thomson/Gale, 2003), 34.

Works Cited

Associated Press. "AP History." *Associated Press*, 2009. www.ap.org/pages/about/history/history_first.html.

Barton, Bruce. Introduction. In W. E. Barton, *Autobiography*, vii–xx.

Barton, William E. *Abraham Lincoln and Walt Whitman*. Indianapolis, IN: Bobbs-Merrill, 1928.

———. *The Autobiography of William E. Barton*. Indianapolis, IN: Bobbs-Merrill, 1932.

———. *The Life of Abraham Lincoln*. 2 vols. Indianapolis, IN: Bobbs-Merrill, 1925.

———. *Lincoln at Gettysburg: What He Intended to Say; What He Said; What He Was Reported to Have Said; What He Wished He Had Said*. Indianapolis, IN: Bobbs-Merrill, 1930.

———. *The Soul of Abraham Lincoln*. New York: Doran, ca. 1920.

Bible, Holy. Authorized or King James Version. London, 1611; New York: Oxford University Press, n.d.

Bobrick, Benson. *Wide as the Waters: The Story of the English Bible and the Revolution It Inspired*. New York: Simon & Schuster, 2001.

Book of Common Prayer According to the Protestant Episcopal Church, The. New York: James A. Gray, 1828.

Booth, John Wilkes. *"Right or Wrong, God Judge Me": The Writings of John Wilkes Booth*. Urbana: University of Illinois Press, 2001.

Boritt, Gabor. *The Gettysburg Gospel: The Lincoln Speech That Nobody Knows*. New York: Simon & Schuster, 2006.

Bray, Robert. "What Abraham Lincoln Read—an Evaluative and Annotated List." *Journal of the Abraham Lincoln Association* 28 (Summer 2007): 28–81.

Brooks, Noah. *Washington in Lincoln's Time*. 1895. Edited by Herbert Mitgang. New York: Rinehart, 1958.

Buchanan, James. Fourth annual message to Congress on the State of the Union, December 3, 1860. In John T. Woolley and Gerhard Peters, "The American Presidency Project," University of California, Santa Barbara, 1999–2009." http://www.presidency.ucsb.edu/ws/?pid=29501.

Bunyan, John. *The Pilgrim's Progress*. Vol. 15. *Harvard Classics*. New York: Collier, 1909.

Calhoun, John C. *The Collected Works of John C. Calhoun*. Edited by Richard K. Cralle. 6 vols. New York: Appleton, 1854.

———. *Correspondence of John C. Calhoun*. Edited by J. Franklin Jameson. Washington, DC: GPO, 1900.

———. *Papers of John C. Calhoun*. Edited by Clyde N. Wilson. Columbia: University of South Carolina Press, 1981.

———. *Union and Liberty*. Edited by Ross M. Lence. Indianapolis, IN: Liberty Fund, 1992.

Carpenter, F. B. *The Inner Life of Abraham Lincoln: Six Months at the White House*. 1880. Edited by Mark E. Neely Jr. Reprint, Lincoln: University of Nebraska Press, 1995.

Chase, Salmon. To Charles D. Cleveland, October 22, 1841. Autograph, micro 5:0485, Chase Papers, Library of Congress, Washington, DC.

Clarke, Asia Booth. *The Unlocked Book: A Memoir of John Wilkes Booth.* London: Faber, 1888.

Coit, Margaret L. *John C. Calhoun: American Portrait.* Boston: Houghton Mifflin, 1950.

Collins, William. *The Complete Poetical Works of Williams Collins, Thomas Gray, and Oliver Goldsmith.* Edited by Epes Sargent. Boston: Crosby, Nichols, Lee, 1860.

Conkling, James C. "Some of Lincoln's Associates at the Bar." In *Lincoln among His Friends,* edited by Rufus Rockwell Wilson, 105–12. Caldwell, ID: Caxton, 1942.

Cowper, William. *Cowper's Poetical Works.* New York: Crowell, n.d. (ca. previous to 1881).

Cox, Kenyon. *The Classic Point of View: Six Lectures on Painting.* 1911. Freeport, NY: Books for Libraries Press, 1968.

Craig, Hardin, ed. Introduction. In *The Complete Works of Shakespeare,* by William Shakespeare, 1–79. Glenview, IL: Scott Foresman, 1961.

Davis, Jefferson. "Confederate States of America—Message to Congress, April 29, 1861 (Ratification of the Constitution)." Avalon Project, Lillian Goldman Law Library, Yale University Law School, New Haven, CT. *Yale University,* http://avalon.law.yale.edu/19th_century/csa_m042961.asp.

———. Farewell address to the United States Senate, January 21, 1861, U.S. Capitol. In Davis, *Jefferson Davis,* 190–94.

———. Inaugural address as president of the Confederate States of America, February 1861, Montgomery, Alabama. *Southern Historical Society Papers* 1 (January 1876): 198–203. In *Jefferson Davis,* 198–203. Available at *Civil War Home,* http://www.civilwarhome.com/davisinauguraladdress.htm.

———. *Jefferson Davis: The Essential Writings.* Edited by William J. Cooper Jr. New York: Modern Library by Random House, 2003.

Deming, Henry Champion. *Eulogy of Abraham Lincoln.* Hartford, CT: Clark, 1865. Available at books.google.com.

Dodd, William E. *The Cotton Kingdom.* 1919. New Haven, CT: Yale University Press, 1920.

Dodge, Daniel Kilham. *Abraham Lincoln: Master of Words.* New York: Appleton, 1924.

Donald, David Herbert. *Lincoln.* New York: Simon & Schuster, 1995.

Donald, David Herbert, and Harold Holzer, eds. *Lincoln in* The Times. New York: St. Martin's, 2005.

Douglass, Frederick. "*Frederick Douglass' Paper,* 16 November 1855." In *Frederick Douglass: The Narrative and Selected Writings.* Edited by Michael Myer. New York: Modern Library, 1984.

———. *Life and Times of Frederick Douglass.* 2 vols. Reprint, revised edition 1892; New York: Collier Books, 1962.

———. *Love of God, Love of Man, Love of Country.* Address delivered in Syracuse, New York, September 24, 1847. *Infoplease.com.* http://www.infoplease.com/t/hist/love-of-god-man-country/.

Drisler, Henry. *A Reply to the "Bible View of Slavery, by J. H. Hopkins, D.D., Bishop of the Diocese of Vermont."* New York: Westcott, 1863. The pamphlet also has the title "*Bible View of Slavery, by John H. Hopkins, D.D., Bishop of the Diocese of Vermont," Examined.*

Duchesne-Guillemin, Jacques, Edward John Joyce, and Margaret Stevenson. "Magi." *New Catholic Encyclopedia.* 2nd ed. Vol. 9. Detroit, MI: Thomson/Gale, 2003.

Eliot, T. S. "Philip Massinger." *The Sacred Wood: Essays on Poetry and Criticism.* 1920. London: Methuen, 1950.

Elizabeth I, Queen of England. "The Armada Speech." In *Speeches That Changed the World*, edited by Cathy Lowne. London: Bounty Books, 2005.

Elliot, Stephen. *Funeral Service at the Burial of the Right Rev. Leonidas Polk, D.D. Together with the Sermon Delivered in St. Paul's Church, Augusta, Ga., on June 29, 1864: Being the Feast of St. Peter the Apostle.* Columbia, SC: Evans & Cogswell, 1864.

Emerson, Ralph Waldo. "Abraham Lincoln: Remarks at the Funeral Services Held at Concord, April 19, 1863." In *Miscellanies*, 305–16. Boston: Houghton Mifflin, 1884.

English Hexapla, The. London: Bagster, 1841.

Euclid. *The Elements Books I–XIII Complete and Unabridged.* Translated by Thomas L. Heath. 1908. Reprint, New York: Barnes and Noble, 2006.

Everett, Edward. *Address of Hon. Edward Everett, at the Consecration of the National Cemetery at Gettysburg, 19th November, 1863, with the Dedicatory Speech of President Lincoln.* Boston: Little, Brown, 1864.

———. To Abraham Lincoln, November 20, 1863. Abraham Lincoln Papers. Library of Congress, Washington, DC.

Fehrenbacher, Don E., and Virginia Fehrenbacher, comps. and eds. *Recollected Words of Abraham Lincoln.* Stanford, CA: Stanford University Press, 1996.

Felski, Rita. "Remember the Reader." *Chronicle Review. Chronicle of Higher Education*, December 19, 2008, B8.

Fitzgerald, F. Scott. "Self-Interview." *F. Scott Fitzgerald in His Own Time: A Miscellany.* N.p.: Kent State University Press, 1971.

Fornieri, Joseph. *Abraham Lincoln's Political Faith.* DeKalb: Northern Illinois University Press, 2003.

Franklin, Benjamin. *The Writings of Benjamin Franklin.* Edited by Albert Henry Smyth. Vol. 6. New York: Macmillan, 1906.

Gilbert, Joseph Ignatius. "Lincoln in 1861: Lincoln in 1863; Lincoln at Washington; the Assassination." *Nineteenth Annual Convention, National Shorthand Reporters' Association, Proceedings of the Annual Meeting*, 131–40. La Porte, IN: Chase & Shepherd, 1917.

Gray, Thomas. "Elegy Written in a Country Churchyard." In *The Complete Poetical Works of William Collins, Thomas Gray, and Oliver Goldsmith*, edited by Epes Sargent, 59–62. Boston: Crosby, Nichols, Lee, 1860.

Greene, William H. William H. Greene to William H. Herndon. Interview. May 30, 1865. In Herndon, *Herndon's Informants*, 17–21.

Guelzo, Allen. *Abraham Lincoln: Redeemer President.* Grand Rapids, MI: Eerdmans, 1999.

———. "Did the Lincoln Family Employ a Slave in 1849–50?" *For the People: A Newsletter of the Abraham Lincoln Association* 3 (Autumn 2001): 1, 6–7.

Hanks, John. "Lincoln's Boyhood Days in Indiana." *Lincoln among His Friends*, edited by Rufus Rockwell Wilson, 33–39. Caldwell, ID: Caxton, 1942.

Hatch, Nathan O., and Mark A. Noll, eds. *The Bible in America: Essays in Cultural History.* New York: Oxford University Press, 1982.

Hatchett, Marion J. *The Making of the First American Book of Common Prayer.* New York: Seabury, 1982.

Hay, John. *Inside Lincoln's White House: The Complete Civil War Diary of John Hay.* Edited by Michael Burlingame and John R. Turner Ettlinger. Carbondale: Southern Illinois University Press, 1997.

Helm, Katherine. *The True Story of Mary, Wife of Lincoln.* New York: Harper & Brothers, 1928.

Herndon, William. *Herndon's Informants: Letters, Interviews, and Statements about Abraham Lincoln*. Edited by Douglas L. Wilson and Rodney O. Davis. Urbana: University of Illinois Press, 1998.

———. *Herndon's Life of Lincoln*. Edited by Paul M. Angle. New York: Da Capo Press, 1983.

Holland, J. G. *J. G. Holland's Life of Abraham Lincoln*. 1865. New York: Paperback Library, 1961.

Holzer, Harold. *Lincoln at Cooper Union: The Speech That Made Abraham Lincoln President*. New York: Simon & Schuster, 2004.

———, ed. *Lincoln-Douglas Debates*. New York: HarperCollins, 1993.

———. *Lincoln President Elect: Abraham Lincoln and the Great Secession Winter, 1860–1861*. New York: Simon & Schuster, 2008.

Hopkins, John Henry. *The American Citizen: His Rights and Duties, According to the Spirit of the Constitution of the United States*. New York: Pudney & Russell, 1857.

———. *Bible View of Slavery*. New York: Kost, 1861.

———. *Bible View of Slavery*. New York: Society for the Diffusion of Political Knowledge, 1863. (Reprint of original 1861 Kost publication, except that the argument justifying secession is omitted).

———. *Episcopal Government. A Sermon Preached at the Consecration of the Rev. Alonzo Potter, D.D., as Bishop of the Diocese of Pennsylvania*. Philadelphia, PA: King and Baird, 1845.

———. *A Lecture Delivered before the Young Men's Associations of the City of Buffalo and Lockport on Friday, January 10, and Monday, January 13, 1851*. Buffalo, NY: Phinney, 1851.

Hopkins, John Henry, Jr. *The Life of the Late Reverend John Henry Hopkins*. New York: Huntington, 1873.

Howe, Julia Ward. "The Battle Hymn of the Republic." *Atlantic Monthly* 9, February 1862, 10.

Iglehart, Frederick. "Lincoln as Pastor." *Lincoln Talks: An Oral Biography*. Edited by Emanuel Hertz. New York: Bramhall House, 1986.

Irving, David. *Elements of English Composition*. Philadelphia, PA: Plowman, 1803.

Jamieson, Alexander. *Grammar of Rhetoric and Polite Literature, Comprehending the Principles of Language and Style, the Elements of Taste and Criticism; with Rules for the Study of Composition and Eloquence*. New Haven, CT: Maltby, 1826.

Jefferson, Thomas. *Jefferson's Works*. Edited by Andrew A. Lipscomb. Vol. 2. Washington, DC: Thomas Jefferson Memorial of the United States, 1903.

———. *The Papers of Thomas Jefferson*. Edited by Julian P. Boyd. 34 vols. Princeton, NJ: Princeton University Press, 1950–2005.

———. *The Writings of Thomas Jefferson*. Edited by Andrew A. Lipscomb. 20 vols. Washington, DC: Thomas Jefferson Memorial Association, 1903–4.

Jennison, Keith. *The Humorous Mr. Lincoln*. New York: Bonanza, 1965.

Johnson, Martin P. "Lincoln Greets the Turning Point of the Civil War, July 7, 1863." *Lincoln Herald* 106, no. 3 (2004): 102–15.

Kunhardt, Philip B., Jr. *A New Birth of Freedom: Lincoln at Gettysburg*. Boston, MA: Little, Brown, 1983.

LaFantasie, Glenn. "Lincoln and the Gettysburg Awakening." *Journal of the Abraham Lincoln Society* 16, no. 1 (1995): 73–89.

Laslett, Peter, ed. Introduction. *Two Treatises of Government*. By John Locke. 1689. Cambridge: Cambridge University Press, 1960.

Lincoln, Abraham. *The Collected Works of Abraham Lincoln*. Edited by Roy P. Basler. 9 vols. New Brunswick, NJ: Rutgers University Press, 1953–55.

———. Papers. Library of Congress, Washington, DC.

Lincoln, Mary Todd. *Mary Todd Lincoln: Her Life and Letters*. Edited by Justin G. Turner and Linda Levitt Turner. 1972. New York: Fromm International, 1987.

Locke, John. *An Essay concerning Human Understanding*. 1689. Edited by Peter H. Nidditch. Oxford, UK: Oxford University Press, 1975.

———. *The Reasonableness of Christianity*. 1695. Stanford, CA: Stanford University Press, 1958.

———. *Two Treatises of Government*. 1689. Edited and with an introduction by Peter Laslett. Cambridge, UK: Cambridge University Press, 1960.

Long, Karen R. "Biblical Illiteracy Rampant among Christians." *Huntsville (Alabama) Times*, July 2, 1984, B4.

Macaulay, Thomas Babington. "John Dryden." *Edinburgh Review* 47 (January 1828).

Madison, James. "The Federalist No. 14: An Objection Drawn from the Extent of Country Answered." In *The Federalist Papers*, ca. 1787, edited by Clinton Rossiter, 99–105. New York: New American Library, 1961.

———. "Federalist No. 39: The Conformity of the Plan to Republican Principles." In *The Federalist Papers*, ca 1787, edited by Clinton Rossiter, 240–46. New York: New American Library, 1961.

Mansbridge, Ronald. "The Percentage of Words in the Geneva and King James Versions Taken from Tyndale's Translation." Tyndale Society. www.tyndale.org/TSJ/3/mansbridge.html.

Marsden, George M. "Everyone's Own Interpreter? The Bible, Science, and Authority in Mid-nineteenth-century America." In Hatch and Noll, *Bible in America*, 79–100.

McCrum, Robert, William Cran, and Robert MacNeil. *The Story of English*. 1st American ed. New York: Viking, 1986.

Mitchell, Margaret. *Gone with the Wind*. 1936. Reprint, New York: Scribner, 1996.

Mitgang, Herbert, ed. *Lincoln as They Saw Him*. New York: Rinehart, 1956.

Morel, Lucas. *Lincoln's Sacred Effort: Defining Religion's Role in American Self-Government*. Lanham, MD: Lexington Books, 2000.

Nicolay, John G. "Lincoln's Gettysburg Address." *Century Magazine* 47, February 1894, 596–608.

———. *With Lincoln in the White House: Letters, Memoranda, and Other Writings of John G. Nicolay, 1860–1865*. Edited by Michael Burlingame. Carbondale: Southern Illinois University Press, 2000.

Niebuhr, Gustav. "When Words Get in the Way of the Word; Language of the Venerable King James Bible Is Hardly English to Young Readers." *Washington Post*, June 12, 1993, B6.

Niven, John. *John C. Calhoun and the Price of Union: A Biography*. Baton Rouge: Louisiana State University Press, 1988.

Ostergard, Philip L. *The Inspired Wisdom of Abraham Lincoln*. Carol Stream, IL: Tyndale House, 2008.

Paine, Thomas. *The Life and Works of Thomas Paine*. New Rochelle, NY: Thomas Paine National Historical Association, 1925.

Parker, Theodore. *The Collected Works of Theodore Parker*. Edited by Frances Power Cobbe. 13 vols. London: Trubner, 1864.

———. "To a Southern Slaveholder." February 2, 1848." In Weiss, *Life and Correspondence of Theodore Parker*, 81–83.

Polk, William M. *Leonidas Polk: Bishop and General*. New York: Longmans, Green, 1915.

Pollard, Edward Alfred. *The Lost Cause*. 1866. New York: Treat, 1867.

——. *The Lost Cause Regained*. New York: Carleton, 1868.

——. "We Are Fighting for Independence, Not Slavery." *Richmond Examiner*, August 2, 1864. *TeachingAmericanHistory.org*. http://teachingamericanhistory.org/library/index.asp?document=1483.

Randall, J. G. *Lincoln the President*. 2 vols. 1945. London: Eyre & Spottiswoode, 1952.

Richmond Examiner, August 2, 1864. teachingamericanhistory.org./library/index.asp/document=1483.

Robins, Glenn. *The Bishop of the Old South: The Ministry and Civil War Legacy of Leonidas Polk*. Macon, GA: Mercer University Press, 2006.

Ross, Frederick. *Slavery Ordained of God*. Philadelphia, PA: Lippincott, 1857.

Sandburg, Carl. Introduction. Sandburg, *Lincoln's Devotional*, v–xv.

——, ed. *Lincoln's Devotional*. Great Neck, NY: Channel Press, 1957.

Seward, Frederick W. *Reminiscences of a War-time Statesman and Diplomat*. New York: Putnam's Sons, 1916.

Seward, William H. *The Autobiography of William H. Seward*. New York: Appleton, 1877.

Shakespeare, William. *The Complete Works of Shakespeare*. Edited by Hardin Craig. Glenview, IL: Scott Foresman, 1961.

Smith, Mark M. "The Touch of an Uncommon Man." *Chronicle Review. Chronicle of Higher Education*, February 22, 2008, B8.

Stanton, F. P. "The Causes of the Rebellion." *Continental Monthly*, November 1862, 513–24.

Steers, Edward, Jr. *Blood on the Moon: The Assassination of Abraham Lincoln*. Lexington: University of Kentucky Press, 2001.

Stephens, Alexander H. "Cornerstone Address, March 21, 1861." In *The Rebellion Record: A Diary of American Events with Documents, Narratives, Illustrative Incidents, Poetry, etc.*, edited by Frank Moore, vol. 1, 44–46. New York: Putnam, 1862. *Modern History Sourcebook*. www.fordham.edu/halsall/mod/1861stephens.html.

Stevenson, Robert Louis. "Style in Literature: Its Technical Elements." *Contemporary Review* 47 (April 1885): 548–61.

Stokes, Anson Phelps. *Church and State in the United States*. 2 vols. New York: Harper & Brothers, 1950.

Stowe, Harriet Beecher. *Men of Our Times; or Leading Patriots of the Day*. Hartford, CT: Hartford, 1868.

Stuart, John T. "John T. Stuart (WHH interview)." June 1865. In Herndon, *Herndon's Informant*, 63–65.

Taney, Roger. Introduction. *Poems of the Late Francis S. Key, Esq*. New York: Carter, 1857. Photostat. Whitefish, MT: Kessinger, 2007. Citations are to the 2007 facsimile.

Taylor, John M. *William Seward: Lincoln's Right Hand*. Washington, DC: Potomac Books, 1991.

Temple, Wayne C. *Abraham Lincoln: From Skeptic to Prophet*. Mahomet, IL: Mayhaven, 1995.

Thomas, Benjamin P. *Abraham Lincoln: A Biography*. New York: Barnes & Noble, 1952.

Tidwell, William E. *Come Retribution: The Confederate Secret Service and the Assassination of Abraham Lincoln*. Jackson: University Press of Mississippi, 1988.

Twain, Mark. "A Lincoln Memorial." *New York Times*, January 13, 1907. www.twainquotes.com/nytindex.html.

———. To George Bainton, October 15, 1888. In *Bartlett's Familiar Quotations*. 17th ed. New York: Little, Brown, 2002.

Vinton, Francis B. "Universality and Primitive Authority of a Liturgy." *Liturgic Worship: Sermons on the Book of Common Prayer, by Bishops and Clergy of the Protestant Episcopal Church*, 7–20. New York: Pott, 1864.

Wacker, Grant. "The Demise of Biblical Civilization." In Hatch and Noll, *Bible in America*, 121–38.

Washington, Booker T. *The Booker T. Washington Papers, Open Book Edition. University of Illinois*. http://www.historycooperative.org/btw/.

Washington, George. Fourth annual message, November 6, 1792. In John T. Woolley and Gerhard Peters, "The American Presidency Project," University of California, Santa Barbara, 1999–2009. http://www.presidency.ucsb.edu/ws/index.php?pid=29434.

———. *The Writings of George Washington*. Edited by John C. Fitzpatrick. 39 vols. Washington, DC: GPO, 1931–44.

Webster, Daniel. *The Great Debate: Webster's Reply*. Edited by Lindsay Swift. Boston: Houghton Mifflin, 1898.

———. *Great Orations and Senatorial Speeches of Daniel Webster*. Rochester, NY: Hayward, 1853.

Weems, Mason L. *The Life of Washington*. 1800. Edited by Marcus Cunliffe. Cambridge, MA: Harvard University Press, 1962.

Weiss, John. *Life and Correspondence of Theodore Parker*. 2 vols. New York: Appleton, 1864.

Welles, Gideon. *Lincoln and Seward: Remarks upon the Memorial Address of Chas. Francis Adams, on the Late Wm. H. Seward*. 1869. Reprint, Freeport, NY: Books for Libraries Press, 1969.

Whistler, James McNeill. *The Gentle Art of Making Enemies*. London: Heinemann, 1890.

White, Ronald C., J. *The Eloquent President: A Portrait of Lincoln through His Words*. New York: Random, 2005.

Whitman, Walt. "The Death of Lincoln, a Lecture by Walt Whitman," *Boston Transcript*, April 15, 1890. Reprinted in W. E. Barton, *Abraham Lincoln and Walt Whitman*, 254–67.

Wills, David. To Abraham Lincoln. 2 November 1863. American Treasures of the Library of Congress, *Library of Congress*. http://www.loc.gov/exhibits/treasures/images/vc009210.jpg. 5 December 2002.

Wills, Garry. *Lincoln at Gettysburg*. New York: Simon & Schuster, 1992.

Wilson, Douglas L. *Lincoln's Sword: The Presidency and the Power of Words*. New York: Vintage Books, 2006.

Wilson, Rufus Rockwell, ed. *Intimate Memories of Lincoln*. Elmira, NY: Primavera, 1945.

———. *Lincoln among His Friends*. Caldwell, ID: Caxton, 1942.

Wolf, William J. *The Almost Chosen People*. Garden City, NY: Doubleday, 1959.

Woodworth, Steven E. *Jefferson Davis and His Generals*. Lawrence: University Press of Kansas, 1990.

Young, John Russell. *Men and Memories: Personal Reminiscences*. New York: Neely, 1901.

Index

abolitionism in the North, 197

Abraham Lincoln's Political Faith (Fornieri), 16

Adams, John, 1–2, 72–73, 184

Adoration of the Magi (Gossart), 227

African slaves, arrival in North America, 191

alliteration, Lincoln's use of, 97

allusions: in Jefferson's work, 181–82; in Lincoln's work, 3–5, 100–101, 102, 111–12, 149, 180, 182–84 (*see also* Gettysburg Address, analysis of words and phrases contained in); role in classical art forms, 1

antislavery consensus, weakening of, 193–94

"Armada Speech" (Queen Elizabeth), 146

Armstrong, George D., 197

Arnold, Matthew, 152

Arnold, Newton, 28

assonance, Lincoln's use of, 56, 75, 96

Baker, Edward D., 26–27

baptisms: in Book of Common Prayer, 47, 49–50, 61, 85, 92, 97, 114; in Edwards family, 28; in Episcopal Church, 24; by fire, 54–55, 76; by immersion, 22–23; of Jesus, 47, 51; references to, in Gettysburg Address, 51, 55; as sign of new birth, 49; by water, 54, 76

Barna Research Group, survey on King James Bible (1993), 13–14

Barnett, Ross, 176

Barton, William E.: analysis of Gettysburg Address by, 11; criticism of Lincoln's writing style by, 96; on delivery text of Gettysburg Address, 132–33; lack of literary analysis in works by, 236n. 14; *Lincoln at Gettysburg*, 129–30; on Lincoln's use of "eight-odd years," 185; on Lincoln's use of "under God," 136–37; silence of, on Lincoln's biblical allusions, 12–13; on sources of Lincoln's echoes, 123; on Washington's use of "under God," 145

Bible, Holy: basis of old testament *vs.* new testament, 57–58; differing interpretations of, and Civil War, 8; Lincoln on the truth of, 38–39; Lincoln's, 21; role in Western thought and literature, 1, 58. *See also* King James Bible

Bible View of Slavery (Hopkins), 32–34, 166–67, 204–5, 220

biblical language, in mid-19th century, 57

Bill of Rights, as source for Gettysburg Address, 126

birth-baptism-rebirth metaphor, 51, 76

birth-death-rebirth metaphor, 38, 49, 71, 97, 114

Birth of a Nation (Griffiths), 203, 215–16

birth-rebirth-baptism metaphor, 98

Bobrick Benson, 58

Book of Common Prayer: 1828 edition, 35; "Almighty God" in, 141; appearances of "last" *vs.* "final/finally," 53; Articles of Religion, 48–49, 98–99; author's knowledge of, 19; Burial of the Dead, 55, 69, 106, 116; Catechism, 48–49, 85, 98–99; closing blessings in, 52; Consecration of a Church or Chapel, 49–50, 82, 88–90, 93, 97; Everett's reference to, in address at Gettysburg, 74; familiar rites in, 24; Forms of Prayer to Be Used at Sea, 78; Holy Baptism, 47, 50, 61, 85, 92, 97, 114; Holy Communion, 65, 83–85, 114; language of ritual in, 101; Lincoln's echoes of, 29, 217–18; Lincoln's familiarity with, 27–28; Litany, 75; "meet and right" in, 77–78, 79; Prayer for the President of the United States, 30–31, 143, 193; preface of, 142–43; reconfigured or repeated scriptural passages in, 101; ritualized beauty of, 227; Shakespeare and, 187; Solemnization of Marriage, 64–65, 67, 69; text of, 53–54; use in present day, 225; "we-us-our" in, 75–76; Whitsuntide prayer, 55, 144

Booth, John Wilkes, 163, 198, 210–11

Boritt, Gabor, 16–17, 121, 129, 137

Bradford, John, 25

Bray, Robert, 111, 152–53, 169

Brooks, Noah, 23–24, 237n. 10

Buchanan, James, 63, 140, 141, 211–12

A former prosecutor in Jackson, Mississippi, public defender in Las Vegas, Nevada, and staff attorney for Legal Services of Alabama in Tuscaloosa, where he also taught criminal law at the University of Alabama Law School, **A. E. Elmore** is now a professor of literature and law at Athens State University. He has published essays in books and journals on various legal issues and on Henry David Thoreau, William Faulkner, F. Scott Fitzgerald, and the poet Robert Herrick. While a student at Millsaps College in Jackson, Mississippi, he worked with Medgar Evers in the civil rights movement, graduating the year before Evers' assassination. Elmore holds a PhD in English and American literature from Vanderbilt University and has won grants from the National Endowment for the Humanities for postdoctoral study at the University of California–Berkeley, City University of New York, and the University of Chicago.